Orientalism Revisited

The publication of Edward Said's *Orientalism* in 1978 marks the inception of Orientalism as a discourse. Since then, Orientalism has remained highly polemical and has become a widely employed epistemological tool. Three decades on, this volume sets out to survey, analyse and revisit the state of the Orientalist debate, both past and present.

The *leitmotiv* of this book is its emphasis on an intimate connection between art, land and voyage. Orientalist art of all kinds frequently derives from a consideration of the land which is encountered on a voyage or pilgrimage, a relationship which, until now, has received little attention.

Through adopting a thematic and prosopographical approach, and attempting to locate the fundamentals of the debate in the historical and cultural contexts in which they arose, this book brings together a diversity of opinions, analyses and arguments.

Ian Richard Netton is Sharjah Professor of Islamic Studies, University of Exeter. His primary research interests are Islamic theology and philosophy, Sufism, medieval Arab travellers, anthropology of religion, Arabic and Islamic bibliography, comparative textuality and semiotics, and comparative religion. He is the author or editor of twenty books of which the most recent is *Islam, Christianity and the Mystic Journey: A Comparative Exploration* (2011).

Culture and Civilization in the Middle East
General Editor: Ian Richard Netton
Professor of Islamic Studies, University of Exeter

This series studies the Middle East through the twin foci of its diverse cultures and civilisations. Comprising original monographs as well as scholarly surveys, it covers topics in the fields of Middle Eastern literature, archaeology, law, history, philosophy, science, folklore, art, architecture and language. While there is a plurality of views, the series presents serious scholarship in a lucid and stimulating fashion.

Previously published by Curzon

1 **The Origins of Islamic Law**
The Qur'an, the Muwatta' and Madinan Amal
Yasin Dutton

2 **A Jewish Archive from Old Cairo**
The history of Cambridge University's Genizah Collection
Stefan Reif

3 **The Formative Period of Twelver Shi'ism**
Hadith as discourse between Qum and Baghdad
Andrew J. Newman

4 **Qur'an Translation**
Discourse, texture and exegesis
Hussein Abdul-Raof

5 **Christians in Al-Andalus 711–1000**
Ann Rosemary Christys

6 **Folklore and Folklife in the United Arab Emirates**
Sayyid Hamid Hurriez

7 **The Formation of Hanbalism**
Piety into power
Nimrod Hurvitz

8 **Arabic Literature**
An overview
Pierre Cachia

9 **Structure and Meaning in Medieval Arabic and Persian Lyric Poetry**
Orient pearls
Julie Scott Meisami

10 **Muslims and Christians in Norman Sicily**
Arabic-speakers and the end of Islam
Alexander Metcalfe

11 **Modern Arab Historiography**
Historical discourse and the Nation-State
Youssef Choueiri

12 **The Philosophical Poetics of Alfarabi, Avicenna and Averroes**
The Aristotelian reception
Salim Kemal

Published by Routledge

1 **The Epistemology of Ibn Khaldun**
Zaid Ahmad

2 **The Hanbali School of Law and Ibn Taymiyyah**
Conflict or conciliation
Abdul Hakim I. Al-Matroudi

3 **Arabic Rhetoric**
A pragmatic analysis
Hussein Abdul-Raof

4 **Arab Representations of the Occident**
East–West encounters in Arabic fiction
Rasheed El-Enany

5 **God and Humans in Islamic Thought**
Abd al-Jabbār, Ibn Sīnā and al-Ghazālī
Maha Elkaisy-Friemuth

6 **Original Islam**
Malik and the madhhab of Madina
Yasin Dutton

7 **Al-Ghazali and the Qur'an**
One book, many meanings
Martin Whittingham

8 **Birth of The Prophet Muhammad**
Devotional piety in Sunni Islam
Marion Holmes Katz

9 **Space and Muslim Urban Life**
At the limits of the labyrinth of Fez
Simon O'Meara

10 **Islam and Science**
The intellectual career of Nizam al-Din al-Nisaburi
Robert G. Morrison

11 **Ibn 'Arabî – Time and Cosmology**
Mohamed Haj Yousef

12 **The Status of Women in Islamic Law and Society**
Annotated translation of *al-Ṭāhir al-Ḥaddād's Imra'tunā fi 'l-sharīʿa wa 'l-mujtamaʿ*, with an introduction
Ronak Husni and Daniel L. Newman

13 **Islam and the Baha'i Faith**
A comparative study of Muhammad 'Abduh and 'Abdul-Baha 'Abbas
Oliver Scharbrodt

14 **Comte de Gobineau and Orientalism**
Selected Eastern writings
Translated by Daniel O'Donoghue
Edited by Geoffrey Nash

15 **Early Islamic Spain**
The history of Ibn *al-Qūṭīya*
David James

16 **German Orientalism**
The study of the Middle East and Islam from 1800 to 1945
Ursula Wokoeck

17 **Mullā Ṣadrā and Metaphysics**
Modulation of being
Sajjad H. Rizvi

18 **Schools of Qur'anic Exegesis**
Genesis and development
Hussein Abdul-Raof

19 **Al-Ghazali, Averroes and the Interpretation of the Qur'an**
Common sense and philosophy in Islam
Avital Wohlman, translated by David Burrell

20 **Eastern Christianity in the Modern Middle East**
Edited by Anthony O'Mahony and Emma Loosley

21 **Islamic Reform and Arab Nationalism**
Expanding the crescent from the Mediterranean to the Indian Ocean (1880s–1930s)
Amal N. Ghazal

22 **Islamic Ethics**
Divine command theory in Arabo-Islamic thought
Mariam al-Attar

23 **Muslim Fortresses in the Levant**
Between Crusaders and Mongols
Kate Raphael

24 **Being Human in Islam**
The impact of the evolutionary worldview
Damian Howard

25 **The UAE and Foreign Policy**
Foreign aid, identities and interests
Khalid S. Almezaini

26 **A History of Early al-Andalus**
The Akhbar Majmu'a
David James

27 **Inspired Knowledge in Islamic Thought**
Al-Ghazali's theory of mystical cognition and its Avicennian foundation
Alexander Treiger

28 **Shi'i Theology in Iran**
The challenge of religious experience
Ori Goldberg

29 **Founding Figures and Commentators in Arabic Mathematics**
A History of Arabic sciences and mathematics, volume 1
Roshdi Rashed, translated and edited by Nader El-Bizri

30 **The Muslim Conquest of Iberia**
Medieval Arabic narratives
Nicola Clarke

31 **Angels in Islam**
Jalal al-Din al-Suyuti's al-Haba'ik fi akhbar al-mala'ik
Stephen Burge

32 **Theological Approaches to Qur'anic Exegesis**
A practical comparative-contrastive analysis
Hussein Abdul-Raof

33 **Ibn al-Haytham and Analytical Mathematics**
A history of Arabic sciences and mathematics, volume 2
Roshdi Rashed, translated and edited by Nader El-Bizri

34 **Ghazali's Politics in Context**
Yazeed Said

35 **Orientalism Revisited**
Art, land and voyage
Edited by Ian Richard Netton

Orientalism Revisited

Art, land and voyage

Edited by
Ian Richard Netton

Routledge
Taylor & Francis Group
LONDON AND NEW YORK

First published 2013
by Routledge
2 Park Square, Milton Park, Abingdon, Oxon OX14 4RN

Simultaneously published in the USA and Canada
by Routledge
711 Third Avenue, New York, NY 10017

Routledge is an imprint of the Taylor & Francis Group, an informa business

British Library Cataloguing in Publication Data
A catalogue record for this book is available from the British Library

Library of Congress Cataloging in Publication Data
Orientalism revisited : art, land and voyage / edited by Ian Richard Netton.
p. cm.—(Culture and civilization in the Middle East: 35)
Includes bibliographical references and index.
1. Orientalism. 2. Middle East—Civilization. 3. Said, Edward W.—Influence. Netton, Ian Richard.
DS61.85.O7554 2012 956—dc23
2012021442

ISBN: 978-0-415-53854-1 (hbk)
ISBN: 978-0-415-53856-5 (pbk)
ISBN: 978-0-203-07941-6 (ebk)

Typeset in Times New Roman
by Bookcraft Ltd, Stroud, Gloucestershire

MIX
Paper from responsible sources
FSC www.fsc.org FSC® C004839

Printed and bound in Great Britain by the MPG Books Group

For Sue with much love and gratitude.

Contents

List of illustrations xii
Notes on contributors xiii
Other books by Ian Richard Netton xvii
Acknowledgements xviii
Introduction xix
Note on the text xxv

PART I
Imagining the Orient 1

1 The Muslim world in British historical imaginations: 're-thinking *Orientalism*'? 3
K. HUMAYUN ANSARI

2 Can the (sub)altern resist? A dialogue between Foucault and Said 33
ARSHIN ADIB-MOGHADDAM

3 Edward Said and the political present 55
NADIA ABU EL-HAJ

4 New Orientalisms for old: articulations of the East in Raymond Schwab, Edward Said and two nineteenth-century French orientalists 87
GEOFFREY NASH

5 Orientalism and Sufism: an overview 98
LINDA SIJBRAND

PART II
Art **115**

6 Orientalism in arts and crafts revisited: the modern and the anti-modern: the lessons from the Orient 117
JOHN M. MACKENZIE

7 Visual ethnography, stereotypes and photographing Algeria 128
SUSAN SLYOMOVICS

PART III
Land **151**

8 Revisiting Edward W. Said's Palestine: between Nationalism and post-Zionism 153
ILAN PAPPÉ

9 Studies and souvenirs of Palestine and Transjordan: the revival of the Latin Patriarchate of Jerusalem and the rediscovery of the Holy Land during the nineteenth century 165
PAOLO MAGGIOLINI

10 Arabizing the Bible: racial supersessionism in nineteenth-century Christian art and biblical scholarship 176
IVAN DAVIDSON KALMAR

11 Orientalism and bibliolatry: framing the Holy Land in nineteenth-century Protestant Bible customs texts 187
DANIEL MARTIN VARISCO

PART IV
Voyage **205**

12 The Orient's medieval 'Orient(alism)': the *Riḥla* of Sulaymān al-Tājir 207
NIZAR F. HERMES

13 Ibn Baṭṭūṭa in wanderland: voyage as text: was Ibn Baṭṭūṭa an orientalist? 223
IAN RICHARD NETTON

Illustrations

7.1 "Algerian Photography," Alary and Geiser Advertising Sheet 130
7.2 "Types Algériens. Famille d'une femme des Ouled Nails" 130
7.3 Duhousset drawing of a Berber type in Paul Topinard, *Anthropology* 133
7.4 Portrait of Amine Amrouche, brought to the table of his mother, Nacéra Dutour 137
7.5 Yamina Ben Yelles, Berber family photographs, Tlemcen 139
7.6 Dennis Adams, "Recovered 10 on 10 (Adams on Garanger)" 142
10.1 Gustave Doré, *The Ascension*, woodblock engraving (Figure 223, *Doré Bible Illustrations*, ed. by Millicent Rose, New York, Dover, 1974) 181
10.2 Gustave Doré, *The Descent of the Spirit*, woodblock engraving (Figure 224, *Doré Bible Illustrations*, ed. by Millicent Rose, New York, Dover, 1974) 181
11.1 "Fords of the Jordan" (frontispiece in William H. Thomson, *The Land and the Book* (1901)) 195
11.2 Women grinding at a mill (Thomson, *The Land and the Book*, p. 527) 196
11.3a Syrian gentlemen in full dress and dress (Thomson, *The Land and the Book*, pp. 116) 197
11.3b Syrian or Egyptian lady (Thomson, *The Land and the Book*, pp. 119) 197
11.4 Dancing Girls (Thomson, *The Land and the Book*, p. 555) 199
11.5 "The mihrab, pulpit, and candlestick in the mosk" (Henry J. Van-Lennep, *Bible Lands: Their Modern Customs and Manners Illustrative of Scripture* (1875), p. 719) 201

Contributors

Nadia Abu El-Haj is a professor in the Departments of Anthropology at Barnard College and Columbia University, and at the Center for the Study of Race and Ethnicity at Columbia. She is also the Co-Director of the Center for Palestine Studies, which was founded at Columbia in the fall of 2010. She has held fellowships at Harvard University's Academy for International and Area Studies, the University of Pennsylvania Mellon Program, and the Institute for Advanced Study at Princeton and is a former Fulbright Fellow. Her research and scholarship have been supported by the Wenner-Gren Foundation for Anthropological Research and the National Endowment for the Humanities. In addition to numerous articles, Professor Abu El-Haj is the author of two books: *Facts on the Ground: Archaeological Practice and Territorial Self-Fashioning in Israeli Society* (2001), which was awarded the Middle East Studies Association's Albert Hourani Annual Book Award in 2002, and *The Genealogical Science: The Search for Jewish Origins and the Politics of Epistemology* (2012).

Arshin Adib-Moghaddam is Reader in Comparative Politics and International Relations and Chair of the Centre for Iranian Studies at SOAS, University of London. He is the author of *The International Politics of the Persian Gulf: A Cultural Genealogy* (2006, 2009), *Iran in World Politics: The Question of the Islamic Republic* (2008, 2010), and *A Metahistory of the Clash of Civilisations: Us and Them Beyond Orientalism* (2011). Educated at the University of Hamburg, American University (Washington DC) and University of Cambridge, where he received his MPhil and PhD, he was the first Jarvis Doctorow Fellow in International Relations and Peace Studies at St Edmund Hall and the Department of Politics and International Relations, University of Oxford. Since 2007, Adib-Moghaddam has been based in the Department of Politics and International Studies at SOAS.

K. Humayun Ansari is Professor of Islam and Cultural Diversity and Director of the Centre for Minority Studies, Department of History, at Royal Holloway College, University of London. His research interests include radical Islamic thought, ethnicity, identity, migration and multiculturalism. He has written extensively on the subject of Muslims in Western society, South Asia, ethnic diversity and cross-cultural issues. His publications include: *The Emergence* *of Socialist Thought among North Indian Muslims* (1990), *Managing Cultural Diversity at Work* (1995), *'The Infidel Within', Muslims in Britain since 1800* (2004), *Attitudes to Jihad, Martyrdom and Terrorism among British Muslims* (2005), *Islam in the West* (2008), *The Making of the East London Mosque, 1910–1951* (2011) and *From the Far Right to the Mainstream: Islamophobia in Party Politics and the Media* (2012). In his role as a public historian, he has advised and addressed a wide spectrum of institutions and provided consultancy in the field of ethnicity and equal opportunities for organisations in the public, private and voluntary sectors, including government departments and agencies, further and higher education, and within industry and commerce. Professor Ansari has provided briefings to senior policy makers and contributed extensively to local, national and international print and broadcast media. He was awarded an OBE in 2002 for his services to higher education and race relations in the community.

Nizar F. Hermes received his PhD in Comparative Literature from the University of Toronto, where he had served as a Lecturer in Arabic Studies. Currently, he serves as a Lecturer in Near Eastern Studies at Princeton University. His main research centres on the premodern and modern cross-cultural encounter between Arabs and their 'others'. He has published journal articles, book chapters and creative pieces in English and Arabic and presented papers at several international conferences. His monograph, *The [European] Other in Medieval Arabic Literature and Culture, Ninth–Twelfth Century AD*, was published in April 2012.

Ivan Davidson Kalmar is a Professor of Anthropology at the University of Toronto. He has published widely on various topics of anthropological linguistics and cultural history. His recent writing and lecturing have been on the joint construction of Jew and Muslim in Western Christian cultural history. He was a contributor to *Orientalism and the Jews* (2005), which he co-edited with Derek J. Penslar. His latest book is *Imagined Islam and the Notion of Sublime Power* (2012). His survey of the nineteenth-century notion of 'the Semite' is due to appear soon in the *Cambridge History of Judaism*. Currently Kalmar is working on an annotated translation of elements of Ernest Renan's *General History and Comparative System of the Semitic Languages*.

John M. MacKenzie is Emeritus Professor of Imperial History at Lancaster University. He also holds honorary professorships at Aberdeen, Stirling, St Andrews and Edinburgh universities and is a Fellow of the Royal Society of Edinburgh (FRSE). He has been editing the Manchester University Press 'Studies in Imperialism' series since 1984 and it has now very nearly reached its 100th volume. He published his (respectful) critique of Edward Said in his *Orientalism: History, Theory and the Arts* in 1995. His essay in this book is based on a paper given at Tate Britain in association with its *Lure of the East* exhibition. More recently, he has published *Peoples, Nations and Cultures: An A–Z of the Peoples of the World Past and Present* (2005), *The Scots in South Africa* (2007) and *Museums and Empire* (2009), while two edited volumes entitled *European Empires and the People* and *Scotland and the British Empire* came out in 2011.

Paolo Maria Leo Cesare Maggiolini is a Teaching Assistant in the Faculty of Political Science of the Catholic University of the Sacred Heart, Milan, from which he received his PhD in Politics. He published *Arabi Cristiani di Transgiordania. Spazi politici e cultera tribal (1841–1922)* in 2011 and is currently engaged in research and writing in the field of the history and institutions of the Middle East with special reference to Arab Christianity in the Near East. He has conducted research into the relationship between tribe and state in the Arab world, focusing on the Arab Christian minority in Jordan and its connection to the Jordanian political field, and on the role of religion in formulating politics in the Balkans and in the Near East.

Geoffrey Nash graduated from Oxford with a BA in English and holds a PhD in English Literature from the University of London. His research specialisms are nineteenth-century British and French orientalists, travel writing on the Middle East, Arab Anglophone fiction and autobiography and Islamic themes in contemporary English fiction. Recent publications include the monographs *Writing Muslim Identity* (2012), *The Anglo-Arab Encounter: Fiction and Autobiography by Arab Writers in English* (2007), *From Empire to Orient: Travellers to the Middle East, 1830–1926* (2005). He has edited (translator Daniel O'Donoghue) *Comte de Gobineau and Orientalism: Selected Eastern Writings* (2008) and *Travellers to the Middle East: From Burckhardt to Thesiger: An Anthology* (2009). He is at present researching a study of Ernest Renan's writings on Judaism, Christianity and Islam.

Ian Richard Netton graduated with a BA in Arabic from SOAS, University of London and a PhD in Arabic and Islamic Studies from the University of Exeter, specialising in medieval Islamic Philosophy. From 1977 to 1995 he taught at Exeter University, where he was latterly Reader in Arab and Islamic Civilization and Thought. In September 1995 he became the University of Leeds' first Professor of Arabic Studies and he remained in Leeds until 2007, serving four terms as Head of that University's Department of Arabic and Middle Eastern Studies. He also served as Director of Leeds University's Centre for Medieval Studies from 1997 to 2002. In 2007 he was appointed to his present post as Sharjah Professor of Islamic Studies in the University of Exeter. Professor Netton's primary research interests are Islamic theology and philosophy, Sufism, medieval Arab travellers, anthropology of religion, Arabic and Islamic bibliography, comparative textuality and semiotics, and comparative religion. He is the author or editor of twenty books, of which the most recent is *Islam, Christianity and the Mystic Journey: A Comparative Exploration* (2011).

Ilan Pappé is a Professor and Director of the European Centre for Palestine Studies in the Institute for Arab and Islamic Studies of the University of Exeter. He is also the Co-Director of the Exeter Centre for Ethno-Political Studies at Exeter. He was awarded a DPhil from the University of Oxford in 1984 and his recent books include *The Ethnic Cleansing of Palestine* (2006), *The Modern Middle East* (2009), *The Husaynis: The Rise and Fall of a Palestinian Dynasty* (2010), *The Forgotten Palestinians* (2010) and *The War of Gaza* (2010), co-authored with Noam Chomsky.

Zahia Smail Salhi is Professor of Modern Arabic Studies in the School of Arts, Languages and Cultures, University of Manchester. She is the author of *Politics, Poetics and the Algerian Novel* (1999) and editor of *The Arab Diaspora: Voices of an Anguished Scream* (with Ian Netton) (2006, 2011), and *Gender and Diversity in the Middle East and North Africa* (2008, 2010). Forthcoming volumes will include *Gender and Violence in Islamic Societies: Patriarchy, Islamism and Politics in the Middle East and North Africa* (2013) and *Occidentalism, Maghrebi Literature and the East–West Encounter* (2013).

Linda Sijbrand holds a *doctoraal* (equivalent to an MA) in History and a BA in Religious Studies from the University of Leiden in the Netherlands. She is now working for her PhD in Islamic Studies at the University of Exeter. She specialises in the Middle East and Islam and her main research interests include Sufism, nationalism and historiography. Her current research focuses on the Yashrutiyya, a contemporary Sufi brotherhood with Palestinian roots. She is a co-founder of the Palestine Studies Group, a postgraduate research group associated with the European Centre for Palestine Studies in the University of Exeter.

Susan Slyomovics is Professor of Anthropology and Near Eastern Languages and Cultures at the University of California, Los Angeles (UCLA). Among her publications as editor are *Clifford Geertz in Morocco* (2010) and *Waging War, Making Peace: Reparations and Human Rights* (2008); and, as author, *The Performance of Human Rights in Morocco* (2005) and *The Object of Memory: Arab and Jew Narrate the Palestinian Village* (1998).

Daniel Martin Varisco is an anthropologist and historian who has conducted ethnographic and historical research in the Middle East since 1978, including ethnographic fieldwork in Yemen, Egypt and Qatar. He is Professor of Anthropology and Director of Middle Eastern and Central Asian Studies at Hofstra University. His most recent book is *Reading Orientalism: Said and the Unsaid* (2007). He is editor of *Contemporary Islam* and Editor-in-Chief of *CyberOrient*.

Other books by Ian Richard Netton

Across the Mediterranean Frontiers (ed. with D.A. Agius)
The Alexander Romance in Persia and the East (ed. with Richard Stoneman and Kyle Erickson)
Allāh Transcendent: Studies in the Structure and Semiotics of Islamic Philosophy, Theology and Cosmology
The Arab Diaspora: Voices of an Anguished Scream (ed. with Z.S. Salhi)
Arabia and the Gulf: From Traditional Society to Modern States (ed.)
Encyclopedia of Islamic Civilisation and Religion (ed.)
Al-Fārābī and his School
Golden Roads: Migration, Pilgrimage and Travel in Mediaeval and Modern Islam (ed.)
Islam, Christianity and the Mystic Journey: A Comparative Exploration
Islam, Christianity and Tradition: A Comparative Exploration
Islamic and Middle Eastern Geographers and Travellers (4 vols) (ed.)
Islamic Philosophy and Theology (4 vols) (ed.)
Middle East Materials in United Kingdom and Irish Libraries: A Directory (ed.)
Middle East Sources (ed.)
Muslim Neoplatonists: An Introduction to the Thought of the Brethren of Purity (Ikhwān al-Ṣafāʾ)
A Popular Dictionary of Islam
Seek Knowledge: Thought and Travel in the House of Islam
Studies in Honour of Clifford Edmund Bosworth, volume 1: Hunter of the East: Arabic and Semitic Studies (ed.)
Sufi Ritual: The Parallel Universe
Text and Trauma: An East-West Primer

Acknowledgements

I am deeply grateful to my editors, Joe Whiting and Kathryn Rylance, at Routledge, Taylor and Francis, for their commitment to this volume; their help and enthusiasm have been invaluable.

I am also grateful to the following publishers:

- K. Humayun Ansari, "The Muslim World in British Historical Imaginations: Re-thinking *Orientalism*", *British Journal of Middle Eastern Studies,* Vol. 38:1 (2011), pp. 73–93 is reprinted by permission of Taylor & Francis Ltd, www.tandfonline.com.
- Nizar F. Hermes, *The [European] Other in Medieval Arabic Literature and Culture*, (2012), pp. 22–35 are reprinted by permission of Palgrave Macmillan.
- Nadia Abu El-Haj, "Edward Said and the Political Present", is reproduced by permission of the American Anthropological Association from *American Ethnologist*, Volume 32, Issue 4, pages 538–555, November 2005. Not for sale or further reproduction.
- In the essay by Susan Slyomovics, we are grateful to the Getty Research Institute, Autograph Publications and copyright Dennis Adams, 1993 (produced by MFC-Michèle Didier, Brussels) for permission to reproduce images. Fuller credits appear beneath each image in her essay in this volume.

My final, and deepest, thanks must go to my wife, Sue, whose tolerance, support and affection are beyond price!

Introduction

The Encyclopedia of Islamic Civilisation and Religion (ed. Ian Richard Netton, London and New York: Routledge, 2008, p. 496) defines Orientalism, broadly, as "the study of the culture, languages and peoples east of the Mediterranean ..." The article notes that "Orientalists claimed to be working in an 'objective' and 'unbiased' fashion, but this claim, [Edward] Said argued, was itself part of the rhetoric of Empire, an attempt to objectify the 'Orient'". Since Edward Said's (1935–2003) seminal work, *Orientalism* (London: Routledge & Kegan Paul, 1978), there are few scholars working in the Middle Eastern or Asian fields who feel comfortable adopting the designation of 'Orientalist'. Yet several, most notably Robert Irwin (*For Lust of Knowing: The Orientalists and Their Enemies*, London: Penguin Books, Allen Lane, 2006), have pointed out the flaws in many of Said's polemical arguments.

This volume sets out to survey, analyse and *revisit* the state of the Orientalist debate, past and present. It adopts both a thematic and a prosopographical approach and attempts to locate the fundamentals of the debate in the historical and cultural contexts in which they arose. It presents a diversity of views which are often passionate and dynamic but also scholarly. One of its chief merits is to bring together 'under one roof' a variety of opinions, analyses and arguments.

Its most important feature, and that which provides an internal coherence to the whole volume, as well as its originality, is the stress on an intimate connection between art, land and voyage: *Orientalist ART of all kinds frequently derives from a consideration of the LAND which is encountered on a VOYAGE or pilgrimage.* This is the key *leitmotiv* of this book. There have been many books, articles and essays over the years on Orientalism and Edward Said; the man bequeathed a potential industry! None, however, to the best of my knowledge, has attempted to bring together, link and contextualise, in the context of the Orientalist debate, the triple themes of Art, Land and Voyage *in the manner of this volume.*

After this Introduction the volume is divided into five parts as follows:

I Imagining the Orient
II Art
III Land
IV Voyage
V The Occidental Mirror

Part I is much concerned with the Orientalist imagination, theories of Orientalism, its impact on a country like the UK or a group like the Sufis, together with a re-evaluation of Edward Said. Part II re-evaluates the role of Orientalism in art, ethnography and photography. Part III looks both at Said's Palestine and the European and Orientalist images of 'the Holy Land'. Part IV concentrates on the voyage and focuses in particular on the travels of two famous medieval Muslim travellers. Finally, Part V provides a striking and dynamic 'reverse-mirror' for Orientalism in its examination of a theory of Occidentalism.

As I have observed, the primary theme and emphasis in this volume is the perceived link between art, land and voyage. Firstly, however, the whole *idea* of Orientalism requires its context. Thus Humayun Ansari presents *The Muslim world in British historical imaginations: 'Re-thinking* Orientalism*'* (Chapter 1), in which he notes that world-renowned scholars of Arabic and Islamic Studies like "A.J. Arberry (1905–1969) … while denying that he himself had any political agendas, accepted that politics, nonetheless, intruded upon academic scholarship." Ansari holds that "absolute claims such as these, however, demand closer inspection" and he lays out his position as follows: "What I want to explore in this essay is how far there were scholars who were genuinely 'purely' interested in Islam and Muslim societies and so studied them for their own sake. I will do this by looking at the places that Islam and Muslims have occupied in British historical imaginations from the outset of the early modern period to the present."

Of course, the 'Orientalist' thesis has frequently been wrapped up in, or at least, involved in, debates about knowledge, power and world politics. In his essay entitled *Can the (sub)altern resist? A dialogue between Foucault and Said* (Chapter 2), Arshin Adib-Moghaddam cites Michel Foucault's arch-dialectical phrase that "where there is power, there is resistance". Adib-Moghaddam goes on to note that "in *Orientalism*, Edward Said took seriously Foucault's ideas about the way knowledge is implicated in power". But he believes that, in the last analysis, Said "did not fully appreciate that for Foucault power cannot be total". These and related themes are developed in a striking "dialogue between Foucault and Said" which is highlighted with particular reference to the Iranian Revolution of 1979.

The general theme of Orientalism and politics is pursued in our third essay, by Nadia Abu El-Haj, entitled *Edward Said and the political present* (Chapter 3). Here the author "offers a reading of Edward Said's legacy. [The essay] engages Said's scholarly and political insights, on the one hand, and his vision of, and life as, an intellectual on the other hand. [The essay] focuses on his broader conceptual and methodological interventions, his analysis of the politics of empire (in the Middle East) and his passionate attachment to the question of Palestine. It also contextualizes Said's work in light of the contemporary political moment, arguing that he, and that for which he is seen to stand, have emerged as key flash points in the latest U.S. culture wars". And, neatly linking to the previous essay, Abu El-Haj cites Stuart Hall's argument that "*Orientalism* was perhaps Foucauldian in inspiration more than in method."

Geoffrey Nash, in an essay entitled *New Orientalisms for old: articulations of the East in Raymond Schwab, Edward Said and two nineteenth-century French orientalists* (Chapter 4), goes behind Said's seminal text, *Orientalism*, and examines how that text treats two French Orientalists, Renan and Gobineau, as well as "presenting a comparative analysis of Said's *Orientalism* and Raymond Schwab's *Oriental Renaissance*". Nash contends that "in linking Gobineau with what he also termed 'scholarly' Orientalism, Said crucially mistook the orientation of Gobineau's relations with the East".

Of course, the perceived exoticism identified in the Orientalist debate often focused on the more exotic aspects of Islam itself, in particular Sufism (Islamic mysticism). In a wide-ranging and insightful article entitled *Orientalism and Sufism: an overview* (Chapter 5), Linda Sijbrand explores the link between these two *topoi* and reveals the perennial fascination of Western scholars, whatever their intentions and motivations, for this most irenical branch of the Islamic faith. Sijbrand makes several references to Carl W. Ernst's *The Shambhala Guide to Sufism* (1997), which discusses Orientalist scholars and their influence on Sufi studies. She draws attention to the point which he makes that the Orientalists have had a major influence on how Sufism is seen today and also on how Muslims – non-Sufis and Sufis alike – have viewed Sufism, as well as the distinction which some made between philosophical and practical Sufism. While accepting that this is an interesting stance, Sijbrand believes that it needs to be nuanced, since these Orientalists often based their work on sources written by Muslims and on discussions with Muslims, and thus followed ideas that were already current in the Muslim world, to which they added their own interpretation. Sijbrand therefore chooses to combine the discussion of Orientalism with the discussion of 'anti-Sufism' in the Muslim world.

General works about the East, whether Orientalist in the Saidean sense or not, could also metamorphose into artistic representations of that same area of enchantment. Regarding his essay entitled *Orientalism in arts and crafts revisited: the modern and the anti-modern: the lessons from the Orient* (Chapter 6), John M. MacKenzie believes that Edward Said's *Orientalism* viewed all representation as actually mis-representation, such that Western writers and, by implication, politicians and administrators, created a fabricated East in order the better to control and dominate it. When Said came to apply this concept to the arts, its weakness became exposed – for example, in his passage on Verdi's opera *Aida* in his later book *Culture and Imperialism* (1993). For MacKenzie, Verdi's predilections and the import of that opera were gravely misunderstood in Said's interpretation. Similarly, when these ideas are applied to the extensive production of Orientalist art in the nineteenth century, the Saidean paradigm becomes particularly threadbare. MacKenzie's essay analyses a number of paintings to reveal the manner in which a fascination with the crafts of the Middle East and elsewhere in Asia is repeatedly expressed by many of the painters in the period. And he shows a strong awareness that the interest in 'Middle Eastern' crafts, including carpet making, ceramics, metal work, wood carving and textiles, in fact fed into the aesthetic concerns represented by William Morris and the Arts and Crafts movement.

Art as expressed in painting is complemented in our own age by photography, and that area of creativity can also fall into what Said might have termed an

Orientalist 'trap'! In her essay entitled *Visual ethnography, stereotypes and photographing Algeria* (Chapter 7), Susan Slyomovics articulates the problem: "'The imperial conquest', Edward Said writes, 'was not a one-time tearing of the veil, but a continually repeated institutionalized presence in French life, where the response to the silent and incorporated disparity between French and subjugated cultures took on a variety of forms'" (*Culture and Imperialism*, p. 35). In Algeria, Slyomovics tells us, the camera and French conquest "overlapped chronologically". By exploring "visual cultural forms of biometric technologies that marked the French colonial bureaucratic presence", this essay first considers tourist postcards of Algeria (*Scènes et Types*) alongside "French-imposed identity photographs and anthropometric classification systems". What is the legacy of the 'Orientalist' image in Algeria?

Algeria, of course, was by no means the only, or even the main, land of the East which infatuated and enchanted Orientalist and other scholars, writers, linguists, artists and photographers. Perhaps because of its role as the birthplace of two of the three great monotheistic world religions, Judaism and Christianity, and the reverence accorded by the third, Islam, to that area – not to mention the overriding significance of Jerusalem – Palestine, or the Holy Land as it became known colloquially, figures largely in any debate about Orientalism and re-evaluation of that *topos*. In his essay entitled *Revisiting Edward W. Said's Palestine: between Nationalism and post-Zionism* (Chapter 8), Ilan Pappé revisits Said's Palestine by noting that it is possible "to trace a dialectical relationship" between "Edward Said's theoretical work on literature and culture" and "his writings on Palestine". In the light of this, his essay examines "Said's relationship with Israeli scholarship and academics". For Pappé, "the crystallization of Said's universal humanism provided a common basis between him and post-Zionists in Israel". His conclusion is thought provoking: "Said … 'the exile intellectual' was attractive to Jewish intellectuals far more than Said 'the Palestinian'. The picture, however, was more complicated as this exilic, almost Jewish intellectual, was still the voice of Palestine in the West. He was still in those days, and until his death, the sharpest critic of Oslo and its follies."

It is a truism that Palestine is a land which has been visited, revisited, discovered and rediscovered, conquered and reconquered by countless generations of visitors, pilgrims, warriors, merchants and many others down the ages. In his essay *Studies and souvenirs of Palestine and Transjordan: the revival of the Latin Patriarchate of Jerusalem and the rediscovery of the Holy Land during the nineteenth century* (Chapter 9), Paolo Maggiolini stresses that the revival of the Latin Patriarchate of Jerusalem in 1847, under the auspices of Uniatism, represented another dimension of the meeting between the West and the East. He analyses the socio-political and cultural implications of this revival which aimed at permanently reunifying the East and the West, and investigates the interactions between memory, historical past and imagined future. The essay reconsiders the consequences of creating a specific image of the Holy Land, deeply rooted in its biblical and pre-modern past, a land to be saved and revived. All these factors give rise to a single question: was this an Orientalist project in the Saidean sense?

In another, complementary, essay, entitled *Arabizing the Bible: racial supersessionism in nineteenth-century Christian art and biblical scholarship* (Chapter 10), Ivan Kalmar argues that "the relationship imagined to hold between the 'Aryan' races of Europe and the 'Semitic' races of Asia was the latest manifestation of a long, theological tradition of Christian supersessionism. Christian supersessionists believe that the Christian gospels announced the replacement of Judaism and the Old Testament as the vanguard of sacred history, with the place of Israel taken by the Christian Church." Kalmar stresses that "inherited Christian notions were developed into newer ideas about the Orient. These ideas were expressed in the ostensibly secular, pseudo-scientific vocabulary of 'race'". His conclusion is that "the Aryanization of Jesus played an important role in establishing, during the long nineteenth century, the extra-European character of the imagined Semitic 'race'".

Parallel to this, Daniel Martin Varisco, in an essay entitled *Orientalism and bibliolatry: framing the Holy Land in nineteenth-century Protestant Bible customs texts* (Chapter 11), detects and analyses "a secret sharer of Said's Orientalism, the bibliolatry of nineteenth-century Protestant Holy Land and Bible customs texts". He goes on: "More than three decades after Said's important, but flawed, intellectual reconstruction of Orientalism" as a hegemonic discourse, there is a need to shift from continued debate over the merits of Said's argument to one "fleshing out the nuances of an admittedly imagined East versus West dichotomy". Varisco notes that "absent from Said's text is the genre that was most widely read in nineteenth-century Europe and America, specifically Holy Land travel texts that cited contemporary customs and manners of Arabs and other groups encountered as illustrations of Bible characters for popular consumption, especially among Protestants". Varisco's essay examines two major nineteenth-century texts by William Thompson and Henry Van-Lennep, both for their depiction of contemporary peoples in Bible lands and for the visual illustrations that frame the narrative.

And the land, whether Algeria or Palestine or, as was often the case, Mecca and Medina, as exposed and articulated in text, painting and photograph, necessarily involved and invoked the concept of voyage and travel. Both Eastern and Western writers travelled to explore, to wander, to wonder, to trade or to undertake a pilgrimage among a whole host of diverse objectives. *The land, then, together with its textual or artistic representation, is usually bound up with the voyage.* This *topos* is explored in two major essays in Part IV of our volume.

It is also important to note that we may identify a species of Eastern "Orientalism" at work, where Eastern Islamic travellers exhibited a fascination for the exotic which paralleled that of the Western European traveller. In his essay *The Orient's medieval "Orient(alism)": The Riḥla of Sulaymān al-Tājir* (Chapter 12), Nizar F. Hermes argues that "Al-Tajir's account is a mine of socio-cultural, religious, political and economic information about India and China in the ninth century. In fact, from the beginning of his journey, the merchant seems to abandon his initial trade and become a keen observer and a preoccupied explorer who finds himself captivated not only by the spectacle of the Oriental Other he will soon meet, but also by the authentic *'ajā'ib/gharā'ib* (marvels/wonders) of the Indian ocean".

Complementing this account, Ian Richard Netton, in a provocative essay entitled *Ibn Baṭṭūṭa in Wanderland: Voyage as Text: was Ibn Baṭṭūṭa an Orientalist?* (Chapter 13), asks whether that most famous of medieval Arab travellers, Ibn Baṭṭūṭa (AD 1304–1368/69 or 1377), whose career matched that of Marco Polo, should be considered as an Orientalist in the Saidean sense. Certainly, in his love for the exotic Other, the answer seems to be a resounding "yes"! Indeed, in his probable invention of visits to places such as China, and his definite invention of a visit to Bulghar, Ibn Baṭṭūṭa exhibits an almost painful need to show himself as a connoisseur of exotic lands, people and The Other. Netton's essay makes comparisons with other writers who also travelled in search of the exotic, such as Marco Polo and Robert Louis Stevenson, as well as with the author of the purely fantastical tale of Baron Munchausen.

Our volume ends, fittingly, with an essay about the reverse side of the Orientalist coin: Occidentalism. Zahia Smail Salhi, in her essay *The Maghreb and the Occident: towards the construction of an Occidentalist discourse* (Chapter 14), has, as her starting-point, Said's *Orientalism*, in which Salhi perceives "the seeds of Occidentalism, both as a concept and as a natural reaction of the people of the Orient to the host of stereotypes and (mis) representations which were created and propagated by some Orientalists about an Orient they often did not know very well. It is the aim of this essay to ponder the concept of 'Occidentalism' and its multifarious meanings as defined by critics from both the Orient and the Occident with a special focus on the Maghrebi experience of the East–West encounter which ultimately resulted in the creation of an Occidentalist discourse in the Maghreb."

Orientalism and Occidentalism! Have we come full circle? The reader will decide. This volume is presented as an exciting and dynamic aid to that further scholarly and popular reflection.

Professor Ian Richard Netton
Sharjah Professor of Islamic Studies
University of Exeter
1 May 2012

Note on the text

The authors of the essays contained in this volume come from a diversity of backgrounds and degrees of linguistic experience. Consequently no attempt has been made to enforce a common system of transliteration from Arabic and other languages, nor to impose diacritics where none were preferred. American spellings have been retained in essays by American authors and, in one case where an essay is a reprint from an American journal, a mixture of textual and endnotes has been permitted. Finally, the views of the authors are their own and do not necessarily reflect those of the Editor nor of their co-authors.

Part I
Imagining the Orient

1 The Muslim world in British historical imaginations

'Re-thinking *Orientalism*'?

K. Humayun Ansari

Ever since the publication of *Orientalism* in 1978 there has been a great deal of debate about Edward Said's thesis and propositions. His study has provoked much controversy but it has also generated an immense amount of positive intellectual development across many humanities and social sciences disciplines. Said's objective was to explore the relationship between power and knowledge; between imperialism and scholarship. He thus viewed 'Orientalism' as a Western discourse that essentialises the Muslim world in pejorative ways, one intimately entwined with imposition of imperial power and offering ideological justifications for it.[1]

While a wide range of academics have subsequently developed or refined Said's framework, others have challenged and, indeed, denounced it, as Robert Irwin puts it, as a perverted muddle of 'malignant charlatanry'.[2] In terms of the production of historical knowledge about the peoples, politics and cultures of the Orient, the disagreements have been to do with approaches, sources, and interpretive paradigms. An increasing number of scholars more generally have come to accept that knowledge is socially constructed and that complex developments contribute towards shaping our understandings of the world.[3] Hence, social and political interests play a significant role in the adoption of one way of construing reality rather than another. Others claim that they tell it like it is; they allow facts to speak for themselves, and have no interest in the social utility of the historical knowledge that they produce. Intellectual curiosity, the lust for knowing, is their only drive.[4] Bernard Lewis, thus, defended Orientalism as 'pure scholarship', a discipline that strove towards objectivity.[5] On the other hand, A.J. Arberry (1905–1969) in his compilation, *Oriental Essays: Portraits of Seven Scholars* (1960), while denying that he himself had any political agendas, accepted that politics, nonetheless, intruded upon academic scholarship.[6] Indeed, it could be argued that politics is always present, but not necessarily where people claim to locate it, since politics has less to do with interactions than actions and results, which are always unpredictable. It is thus difficult to put intentions on trial.[7]

Absolute claims such as these, however, demand closer inspection, and so what I want to explore in this essay is how far there were scholars who were genuinely 'purely' interested in Islam and Muslim societies and so studied them for their own sake. I will do this by looking at the places that Islam and Muslims have occupied in British historical imaginations from the outset of the early modern period to the present.

One of the key reasons for examining the past is to uncover the shape of human experience: can we discern any patterns in it, and how can we make sense of it through time? For many centuries, in the context of Britain, 'the march of history' was understood in sacred terms. For Christian writers historical knowledge bore witness to the grand theme of Creation and the Last Judgement. But as Islam spread through the Mediterranean, posing a potentially lethal theological and political threat as it conquered the bastions of Eastern Christendom, the mysterious rise of this 'falsehood', against the truth of Christianity, compelled an explanation. How to stem its rising tide and protect Christians and Christendom [and convert Muslims] from this scourge?

The response of medieval and early modern Christian scholars was to create 'a body of literature concerning the faith, its Prophet, and his book, polemic in purpose and scurrilous in tone, designed to protect and discourage rather than to inform'.[8] Attacks on Islam were in part a way of propping up ideological conformity among various Christian denominations, in Britain as elsewhere.[9] With military power unable to withstand Islamic expansion, refutation through argument and missionary work was considered the best option for overcoming the challenge, for which knowledge of the Muslim adversaries, their beliefs and practices, was considered crucial. The lengthy title of William Bedwell's (1562–1632) best-known work – *Mahomet Unmasked. Or a Discoverie of the manifold Forgeries, Falsehoods, and horrible impieties of the blasphemous seducer Mahomet. With a demonstration of the Insufficienie of his Law, contained in the cursed Alcoran. Written long since in Arabicke and now done in English* – underlined its similar polemical rationale.[10] In much of this scholarship, therefore, a repertoire of Christian legends nourished by imaginative fantasies, rather than hard historical evidence about Islam and Muslims, served the purpose. While the explanations provided were never fully satisfying, writers such as Bedwell succeeded in creating a portrait of an exotic, and deluded, 'other' – and helped to embed a negative perception in the 'British' social imaginary, something that possesses considerable emotional resonance even to this day.

That said, when we look at the early modern period, we find that, in the British Isles at large, there was little popular awareness of, let alone curiosity about, Muslims – and even less so in serious literature. Most of those who had sufficient resources and interest to sponsor Arabic studies were either churchmen (as was the case with most forms of learning, not just this field) or closely aligned with their causes who, while acknowledging that acquisition and study of Arabic manuscripts was useful insofar as they contained much valuable scientific information,[11] primarily aimed at producing materials to achieve salvation of oneself and of wayward Middle Eastern Christians and Muslims.[12] Thomas Adams (1586–1668), a wealthy draper, created the Chair of Arabic at Cambridge in 1632 in the hope that he might, through his patronage, contribute to converting Muslims.[13] Four years later, William Laud (1573–1645), Archbishop of Canterbury and Chancellor of the University of Oxford, established its Professorship in Arabic, primarily as part of the struggle against Catholicism.

In the sixteenth to eighteenth centuries, those in Europe who studied Islam tended to do so not out of interest in that faith per se, but primarily to pursue intra-confessional polemic.[14] During the Reformation, Islam was frequently used by one group of Christians to criticise another. Protestants were likened to Muslims for deviating from and perverting the true faith. Such developments, of course, need to be located in the context of Ottoman expansion in competition with other European states. It is noticeable that, while there was considerable conflict between the states, it did not take the form of 'Islamdom' versus 'Christendom'.

The 1600s are credited with having marked the beginning of 'modern' British historical writing.[15] The confident authority of the Christian world-view began to crumble as secularised interpretations of history, centred on human rather than divine activity, gained ground. Reason combined with empirical evidence was coming to be accepted as the final authority for deciding what was historically credible. Scholars now increasingly possessed the resources and linguistic potential to investigate more rigorously than before the nature of Muslim beliefs, history, traditions and practices. Hence, writings on Islam became contradictory, reflecting the fragmented views held by Europeans on the subject, influenced by political thinkers such as Descartes and Spinoza.[16] The old stereotypes were repeated by most writers, but now alongside newer observations that found favourable things in Islam. For example, there was *The General Historie of the Turkes* (1603) by Richard Knolle (c. 1540–1610). A fear-inducing chronicle, it was filled with accounts of Ottoman atrocities, cruelties and torture. Knolle, like earlier English writers, called the Ottoman Empire the 'great terror of the world', Islam the work of Satan and Muhammad a false prophet. But – here is the difference – Knolle also acknowledged Turkish determination, courage and frugality, and the massive twelve hundred-page account contained much positive information about Muslims, until then considered mortal enemies.

Edward Pococke's *Specimen Historae Arabum* (1649), while casting Islam as the religion of the false prophet, likewise managed, by deploying Arabic sources and historians, to avoid the distortions of medieval polemic and presented what was, for its time, an arguably more balanced view of Muslim society.[17] A little later Paul Rycaut, in *The Present State of the Ottoman Empire* (1668), drew a picture of Ottoman despotism, unequivocally corrupt and backward, straight out of the old stock of ignorance and fear. But it also recounted accurate, knowledgeable and insightful details of Turkish life and history, of Ottoman political, military and religious organisation, of the diversity of Islamic beliefs and traditions. In it there was also acknowledgement of mutuality of commercial interests and benefits and admiration of many aspects of Islamic culture.[18] Most importantly, having been written by British men, these histories inevitably lacked the breadth of understanding of Muslim societies that women travellers such as Lady Mary Wortley Montagu (1689–1762) would contribute, thanks to their experiences of spheres of life to which they, as females, had exclusive access.

By the end of the seventeenth century, while the intellectual climate had changed significantly in favour of 'freethinking', both orthodox Christians and so-called 'deviants' continued to critique each other. Humphrey Prideaux's (1648–1724) *Life of Mahomet* (1697) aimed to uncover 'The true nature of imposture fully displa'd in the life of Mahomet, with a discourse annex'd for the vindication of

Christianity from this charge',[19] while Henry Stubbe's (1632–1676) anti-Trinitarian tract, *Account of the Rise and Progress of Mahometanism* (written in 1671 but not eventually published until nearly 250 years later),[20] trenchantly challenged 'the fabulous inventions of the Christians'[21] in the light of reason, contrasting this with his positive assessment of the life of Muhammad and Islam's rationality.[22] What is particularly interesting is that both these authors used Pococke's work and sources extensively but interpreted them in radically different ways to arrive at the opposite poles in their conclusions – one hostile (it should be added, largely in response to the challenge of Deism rather than Islam), the other sympathetic, to Islam and Muslims.[23]

What we see emerging out of these controversies by the eighteenth century are more sophisticated understandings of Islam, though, given the broader religious context in which they were operating, their authors could hardly be expected to write wholly positively of a religion that had proved 'the first ruin of the eastern church'.[24] So, while in Simon Ockley's (1678–1720) *The History of the Saracens* (2 volumes, 1708–1718) Mahomet, as for Prideaux, remained 'the great Imposter'[25] and the Arab conquests 'that grievous Calamity',[26] there is patent admiration for the martial and moral qualities and learning of the Arabs.[27] Similarly, while George Sale (1697–1736), in the *Preliminary Discourse* to his translation of the Qur'an (1734), again followed Prideaux by saying that the Arabs 'seem to have been raised up on purpose by GOD, to be the scourge to the Christian Church',[28] his use of Muslim sources of history marked an enormous advance.

The late eighteenth century was a period of transition in British imperial history, and, not surprisingly, this had an impact on how Islam and Muslims were viewed by contemporaries. The East India Company (EIC) from the mid-eighteenth century had been steadily establishing dominance in India, often taking power from Muslim rulers in the process, but it was still navigating its way towards finding the right strategies in order to establish firm control. Many who ran the EIC in India admired and appreciated indigenous cultures, saw merit in their history and assimilated.[29]

William Robertson (1721–1793) was one Enlightenment historian who expressed an early willingness to value Indian culture and society as the development of an equivalent and equally valid civilisation to that of Europe. However, whereas Europe was seen to have 'progressed', India was perceived to have 'stagnated' in relative terms. Hence, Robertson believed that India should be facilitated but not coerced in its socio-economic and cultural development by a form of imperial rule and commerce that demonstrated respect for India's cultural heritage.[30]

This development approach to history associated with the Scottish Enlightenment, in the works of Adam Smith (1723–1790), David Hume (1711–1776) and Robertson, from the 1750s to the 1790s, concluded that the human record was one of material and moral improvement, of cultural development from 'savagery' and 'barbarism' to 'civilisation', and that their society stood at the pinnacle of achievement.[31] Since Muslim societies were judged as, at best, semi-barbaric, colonialism – Empire – was justified. Alexander Dow (1735/6–1779), another secular enlightenment historian, accepted that the Mughal Empire, having achieved much, was declining as others had in the past, and the British should supplant it.[32]

As British imperial expansion progressed, there was a further shift in general attitudes to Islam. There was perhaps less prejudice and a greater sense of curiosity; while history continued to be written as a moral tale, critical enquiry gave birth to new historical values. The rejection of metaphysical authority became increasingly mainstream, opening the way for a more empirical approach to Islam, replacing distorted accounts constructed to an extent on flights of fancy and ignorance with more nuanced and balanced ones. Yet Orientalist stereotyping persisted. While Edward Gibbon (1737–1794), when exploring how Christianity ended European classical civilisation in his *History of the Decline of the Roman Empire* (1788),[33] imbued Islam with several positive attributes, his final moral judgement on Muhammad was that he ended up an ambitious impostor.[34] And whatever its virtues, Gibbon did not want Europe to be over-run by Islam.[35] While Gibbon and William Jones, two of Britain's most eminent Enlightenment scholars, were admirers of Muslim civilisations, they still firmly believed in the superiority of the European, because, for them, Europe had forged ahead in gathering useful knowledge, in its command of 'Reason' and in its application of the scientific method – in all these fields, they believed, Asians lagged far behind.[36]

Like Gibbon, Jones could attribute 'the decided inferiority' of Asian peoples to the prevalence of despotism in Asia.[37] Indeed, those who judge Jones's scholarly work as entirely motivated by aesthetic and academic interest really need to look at his life and career more closely; this would reveal him to be not only complex, inconsistent and contradictory but also one who undoubtedly possessed utilitarian propensities. For instance, he published his *A Grammar of the Persian Language* in 1771 to equip those who wished to serve the EIC more proficiently in a language in which commercial affairs in India were conducted.[38] He believed that 'laws are of no avail ... unless they are congenial to the disposition and habits, to the religious prejudices, and approved immemorial usages, of the people, for whom they are enacted',[39] and felt that the democratic system was 'wholly inapplicable' to India and Indians were 'incapable of civil liberty; few of them have any idea of it; and those, who have, do not wish it'. Jones also claimed that 'millions are so wedded to inveterate prejudices and habits, if liberty could be forced upon them by Britain, it would make them as miserable as the cruellest despotism':[40] consequently, they 'must and will be governed by absolute power', albeit taking an enlightened form.[41] Jones went to India to serve his country as a judge of the EIC's Bengal Supreme Court – the primary purpose for which he learnt Sanskrit was to prepare his digest of Indian laws that would break the monopoly of *pandits* (Hindu religious scholars) and *maulvis* (Muslim religious scholars) in the court, and which shaped and reflected the ethos of his employer, the Company, in the late eighteenth century. Indeed, he sought to develop a political strategy on 'how the British Possessions in the East Indies may be held and governed with the greatest security and advantage to this country, and by what means the happiness of the native inhabitants may best be promoted'.[42] In Mukherjee's assessment, far from being a disinterested Orientalist, Jones was a late eighteenth-century 'liberal imperialist' who had no doubt in his mind about 'the excellence of our constitution, and the character of a perfect king of England'.[43] Jones was of the view that British rule could be best legitimised in an Indian idiom. He had no doubt that 'a knowledge of *Mahomedan* jurisprudence, and consequently of the *languages* used by *Mahomedan* writers, are essential to a complete administration of justice in our *Asiatick* territories'.[44]

The ways in which British historians analysed, imagined and depicted the 'Orient' were, thus, often intertwined, in complex ways, with growing British power. The generation of certain images of the 'Orient' was linked with the parallel growth of European control over Muslim peoples. These realities began to shape historical accounts. The Romanticist influence on historical writing was also felt. The Orient attracted interest as it became less threatening while remaining exotic. One key (though not uncontested) element of nineteenth-century thought on the 'Orient' was a particular concentration on difference between East and West. Islam constituted a distinct type in terms of civilisation, cultural essence and core values – these, many Orientalists of the time believed, shaped a different Muslim consciousness, mind-set and behaviour.

Scottish Enlightenment thinking continued to be the leading intellectual influence. John Malcolm (1769–1833) and Mountstuart Elphinstone (1779–1859), both highly instrumental in relation to the extension of British power in India and West Asia,[45] would have seen themselves as no more than subscribing to the forces that drove societies from one stage to another. Both belonged to a broad band of historians comprising conservatives and many liberals and radicals, among whom imperial expansion, born out of human enlightenment and effort, and underpinned by utilitarian ideas, became a dominant vision.[46] They were supported by a growing evangelical public sentiment which viewed Empire as the work of Providence. Notwithstanding their kinship with different schools of thought, all British historians during this period assumed the intellectual and moral superiority of contemporary Great Britain over the Muslim world.

But the single most influential work in the early nineteenth century was perhaps James Mill's (1773–1836) *The History of British India* (1817). Mill's motivation was primarily to critique and challenge the existing political order in Britain. For Mill, knowledge was nothing if it was not a source of power – a tool of change. Understanding the past was good 'only for the improvement of the future'.[47] Since Indo-Muslim society, a product of despotism, superstition and poverty, given to insecurity and lacking in progress, measured 'lower' in his scale of civilisation, British authoritarian rule was justified. Similarly, Macaulay (1800–1859), a great admirer of Mill's *History*, also believed in the benevolent impact of British rule in India and elsewhere. Macaulay's[48] dismissal of, and contempt for, the natives could be said to have been the epitome of Saidian Orientalism.[49]

Now, while it might be argued that this 'Orientalist' history writing was hegemonic by the nineteenth century, Said's argument leaves little room for the kind of contestation and contrasting approaches to Islam that were evidently emerging in this period. Take, for instance, the works of Edward Lane (1801–1876), a scholar who was to have an enormous influence on Middle Eastern studies. From Lane's life, it is immediately clear that, in the context of the early nineteenth-century excitement about Egypt, while he remained committed to his own cultural heritage, he became genuinely interested in Egyptian society – its traditions, customs and people – to the point where he adopted the Egyptian lifestyle, dress and language. While many scholars have levelled charges of Orientalism against Lane – his awareness of his difference from an essentially alien culture, the coded sense of superiority in his major works, his views regarding the unchanging character of Middle Eastern societies, to mention just a few – Leila Ahmed, his biographer, has shown that Lane possessed a relatively accurate and sympathetic understanding of Islam.[50] It is true that he comes across, occasionally, as condescending, patronising, even admonishing, in his best-known *An Account of the Manners and Customs of the Modern Egyptians* (1836),[51] but, when read in the context of his personal interaction, it could be argued that for the most part he strove for and largely succeeded in presenting an account of Egyptian society and its people that was respectful, and one that a 'native' of that culture could broadly accept as authentic and accurate.[52] More usefully, it created a space for British scholars within which emotively charged and hostile traditions could be more effectively challenged.

Towards the middle of the century, new perceptions of Muhammad, accompanied by new attitudes to his religion, were also emerging. This period was particularly crucial in British historical understanding of Islam, for it was a time when the enduring images of Muhammad as a heretic were juxtaposed with new ones of him as a noble figure.[53] In contrast to Said's methodological emphasis on the unity of the Orientalist discourse, what we witness here is a considerable plurality of approaches to Islam. Thus, discourse about Islam became richer, more diverse and more complex than Said's arguments have demonstrated.

The reasons for this shift were many. Burgeoning knowledge about Islam and increased information made early stereotypes increasingly untenable. The demise of Christian apocalypticism and the rise of secular historical method created the Muhammad of history, relegating to the shadows the Muhammad of Christian legend. The Victorians' proclivity for great men, coupled with their fascination for an exotic East, created a sympathetic environment for the partial rehabilitation of Muhammad and Islam. And the rise of British power over Muslim lands made for a context in which the Prophet and his religion could be treated more benevolently, even while it continued to encourage and support criticism of its modern expressions.

This juxtaposition is clearly visible in Carlyle's (1795–1881) famous lecture on Muhammad. In 1840, after centuries during which Muhammad had been called an impostor, a seducer or worse, Carlyle made the 'first strong affirmation in the whole of European literature, medieval or modern of a belief in the sincerity of Muhammad'.[54] And yet, he too uncritically deployed Orientalist tropes and attitudes in his rhetoric: Islam for Carlyle was 'a confused form of Christianity', fit for semi-barbaric Arabs.[55]

What, then, were the main assumptions of historical writing at this time? Paternalism and utilitarianism. Both contributed to the British assumption of superiority over the East and to the justification of colonial rule. À la Whig interpretation of history, Victorians believed that they were positioned at the pinnacle of human development. Historians did not dispense knowledge of the past for its own sake, or simply to inculcate practical lessons – that is, to sustain British rule. Above all, they strove to preach a moral sermon, to hold up the virtues that they believed had won empire in the East and which alone could preserve it.

William Muir (1819–1905), scholar and colonial administrator at the time of the so-called Indian Mutiny of 1857–1858, in his historical works consistently denigrated Muhammad and the Qur'an, misrepresented Muslims and undervalued Islam, often through a conscious manipulation of, at times, questionable sources, in order to demonstrate the superiority of Christianity and British culture in justification of colonial dominance.[56] Similar motivations can be discerned in the writings of both H.M. Elliot and John Dowson, the latter's *The History of India as told by its own Historians* (1867–1877) receiving the explicit support of the Secretary of State for India. Both were deemed by critics to have disseminated 'not a few inexactitudes', as well as 'some false and distorted history'.[57]

By the late nineteenth century, biology, anthropology and other sciences had combined with Sir Henry Maine's (1822–1888) demonstration of the historicity of ideas and Darwin's law of natural selection to produce a relative ranking of world civilisations along racial lines. Muslim societies did not fare well. Britain, it would seem, had developed the highest ideal of social happiness and devised the scientific instrument of law to enforce it.[58] Writing at the zenith of the Imperialist phase in Britain, William Hunter (1840–1900) stressed the importance of the national character of the British race – 'adventurous, masterful, patient in defeat and persistent in executing its designs' – as the key to its imperial success.[59]

J.R. Seeley's (1834–1895) *Expansion of England*, published in 1883, stated that the study of history could offer lessons for those serving the Empire.[60] Lord Acton (1834–1902), Seeley's successor at Cambridge at the beginning of the twentieth century, likewise considered the making of moral judgements to be the mark of true historical writing. For him, the British Empire had an essentially noble purpose and was a benevolent and progressive force in human history. But while Seeley believed in the necessity and moral justification of the continuance of British rule, a question that troubled him was how the British could reconcile the despotism of the Indian Empire with the democracy enjoyed by the colonies of white settlers (and indeed, the British themselves): how Britain could 'be in the East at once the greatest Mussulman Power in the world … and at the same time in the West be the foremost champion of free thought and spiritual religions?'[61] For such historians, Indian society being un-progressive and perhaps decadent, the important thing was to do Indians good in spite of themselves; to lead India (and the rest of the Empire) with a paternal, authoritarian hand.[62] The histories of the period up to 1914 broadly reflected these assumptions.[63]

This was not, it is true, invariably the attitude in the late nineteenth and early twentieth centuries. Drawing inspiration from William Cobbett (1763–1835), John Bright (1811–1889) and Richard Cobden (1804–1865), scholars such as J.A. Hobson (1858–1940) challenged the justifications for imperial rule.[64] Nevertheless, this undoubtedly remained the hegemonic view. The majority of Orientalist historians agreed with Seeley's analysis. Re-evaluative trends in British Islamic scholarship were still at an embryonic stage, and thinly veiled disparagement of Islam and Muhammad such as that of David Margoliouth

(1858–1940), fervently Christian professor of Arabic at Oxford, continued to inform influential historical analysis.[65]

However, while Islamic history offered much scope to Orientalist scholars to draw favourable comparisons regarding the virtues and truth of Christianity, there had also emerged considerable questioning of the Christian faith and this led to the re-evaluation of both academic and popular attitudes towards other belief-systems. T.W. Arnold (1864–1930),[66] who spent much time in scholarly pursuits in northern India, was part of a small group of historians who presented interpretations of Christian and Muslim cultural history and interaction that challenged the arguments of the orthodox orientalist paradigm. Both in conception and in construction, his *The Preaching of Islam*, published in 1896, represented a radical departure in British Islamic scholarship. In contrast to reductionist constructions of Islam as monolithic, having only one authentic expression, Arnold affirmed the validity of all the varying and sometimes contradictory currents within it, and concluded in his *The Islamic Faith* (1928) that, since religion was defined by individual understanding and practice of faith, 'no single formula – beyond the brief simple words of the creed – can sum up [Islam's] many diversities'.[67] Arnold's historical analysis refuted the traditional assumptions of Orientalism and led him to conclude that European and Muslim cultures had interacted in the past in mutually influential and beneficial ways. He dismissed the distinction between East and West and argued that the Christian and Muslim worlds were both heirs of the same civilisation. Curiously, he remained a 'convinced believer in the great destiny of the British Empire',[68] but with Muslims as equals. In line with orientalist suspicion of pan-Islamism and religious nationalism, he viewed attempts to create a sense of global Islamic community as potentially destabilising.

E.G. Browne (1862–1926), too, exuded enthusiasm for and empathy with Arab, Persian and Turkish cultures and peoples. A scholar of enormous erudition, he travelled in Persia and his *A Year Among the Persians* (1893) represented a sympathetic portrayal of Persian society. His monumental *Literary History of Persia*, which was published in 1902, further valorised its refinements. An adherent of the liberal view of progress in historical development, he became passionately interested in the politics of contemporary Persia, and supported the Constitutional Movement and resistance to European imperialist encroachments. Browne's positive analysis in his *The Persian Revolution of 1905–1909*, published in 1910, not only countered the imperialist notions of Persian capriciousness and corruption as essential contributors of lack of progress; of their incapacity for democratic self-government, but also, by means of a 'nationalist [counter] Orientalism', announced the revival of an eastern people whose national character had empowered past historical achievements and might well do so again.[69]

The climate of opinion in early twentieth-century Britain was, thus, simultaneously sympathetic towards and highly suspicious of Muslims. Muslim political activism imposed new demands on British authority, and pan-Islamism became a cause of increasing political concern as conflict with the Ottoman Empire intensified. Muslim aspirations seemed in sharp conflict with British imperial ambitions and political strategic security. These priorities were reflected in literature of the period. Lord Cromer's (1841–1917) *Modern Egypt* (1908), for instance, effectively ignored Egypt's achievements, highlighted its deficiencies through selective use of empirical materials and offered an unbalanced rationalisation of British imperial rule. What was needed was a system that would 'enable the mass of the population to be governed according to the code of Christian morality'.[70] V.A. Smith's (1848–1920) *Oxford History of India: from the earliest times to 1911* (1919) similarly concluded that India would be plunged into political chaos, her normal condition, 'if the firm, although mild control exercised by the paramount power should be withdrawn'.[71]

The aftermath of the First World War witnessed the revival of the idea of British colonial mission and imperial obligation. The Empire's history as the unfolding of the story of liberty re-emerged as the dominant mode of interpretation. With the break-up of the Ottoman Empire, Britain became much more politically and strategically dominant in the Middle East, responsible for lands that were perceived to be inhabited by people not yet able to stand by themselves under the strenuous conditions of the modern world. Representing a main trend in British historical writing, historians such as Reginald Coupland (1884–1952) still believed in the moral qualities of the British to shape a better world and saw the history and purpose of the Empire as the gradual unfolding of liberty. While not an officer of the Empire, he spent much time in its service and he made influential, historically rigorous contributions to the debates on the direction of the Empire and imperial policy making.[72] But other historians rejected the benevolent purpose of the Empire and thought it exploitative and ruthless.[73] Edward Thompson and G.T. Garratt's *Rise and Fulfilment of the British Rule in India* offered a balanced assessment of the nationalist movement and criticised the racist behaviour of the British. George Antonius's *The Arab Awakening: The Story of the Arab Nationalist Movement* (London: H. Hamilton, 1938) sought to understand sympathetically the impulses behind Arab nationalism as well to challenge British rule in Palestine. But even these two studies accepted the idea of British trusteeship and, rather than abolish the Empire, suggested reform and greater accountability.

The post-Second World War years witnessed rapid change and much instability as the pace of decolonisation quickened and the Cold War began. In this context, Asia and Africa increasingly became the battlegrounds for geopolitical rivalries. Western governments felt the urgent need for reliable knowledge about critical areas so as to inform policy making. But, in the late 1950s and 1960s, scholars such as Richard Southern (1912–2001) and Norman Daniel (1919–1992) showed that it was not so much new positive knowledge that was being produced by disinterested scholars, but rather the diffusion in more refined and complex forms of greatly distorted *existing* elaborations, creating inaccurate images of Islam and Muhammad, based on dubious sources and distorted readings of texts and scriptures, leading to crude and derogatory assertions.[74]

Take Hamilton Gibb (1895–1971) and Bernard Lewis (1916–), two towering figures in the field in this period. Their interest in Islam and Muslim peoples' current affairs undoubtedly emanated from their desire to influence policy makers. Gibb, for instance, was concerned that Western governments were acting largely out of ignorance, and it was his belief that understanding of Muslim peoples' beliefs and cultures by careful study of their specific past was essential for effective policy making. However, the categories he used to organise the knowledge and to interpret Islam and the history of the Muslim peoples are illustrative of what many critics would eventually argue were the grave shortcomings of the Orientalist tradition. For instance, in *Modern Trends in Islam* (1947), Gibb started from the assumption that there was an unchanging and distinctive Arab or Muslim 'mind' whose nature he could infer from his knowledge of the traditional texts of Islam and which could be implicitly or explicitly contrasted with an equally singular and essentialised 'Western mind'.[75] On this basis Gibb was able to offer sweeping generalisations about the innate deficiencies of Muslims' thought processes, imagination and ethics that had caused them to stagnate and fail to modernise. Robert Irwin suggests that, '[a]s a Christian moralist, he was inclined to blame Islam's decline on carnality, greed and mysticism'.[76] In *Islamic Society and the West*, deploying Toynbee's category of distinct civilisations, he argued that Islam was a coherent civilisation whose historical dynamics, institutions, thought and way of life were expressions of a basically unitary and stable set of core values and beliefs. Based on these premises, Gibb explained Ottoman decline by locating it in its specifically Islamic despotic character.[77] Yet, as Roger Owen pointed out, Gibb's analysis was largely flawed, as his data in fact suggested that in the groups and activities of the Ottoman Empire there was little that could be considered as specifically 'Islamic' – indeed, developments under the Ottomans had close parallels in non-Muslim Europe and Asia.[78] More recently Caroline Finkel has challenged even more convincingly such 'myths' of Ottoman decay.[79]

Bernard Lewis was the other 'big gun' in the field of British scholarship on Islam, and, like Gibb, he believed that the Orientalists' deep understanding of Islamic civilisation rendered them uniquely capable of shedding light on policy matters. Lewis, in a 1953 Chatham House lecture on 'Communism and Islam'[80] that ignored local contexts and histories, elaborated his conception of Islam, similar to that of Gibb, as a civilisation with a distinct, unique and basically unchanging essence. For Lewis, among Islam's core features was an essentially autocratic and totalitarian political tradition that made Communism potentially appealing to Muslims. Lewis accepted that, while Muslims were obliged to resist impious government, their subservience to authority took precedence. This contrasted sharply with 'the spirit of resistance to tyranny and misrule ... inherent in the core values of Western civilisation'.[81] This line of argument ignored what Muslims had *actually* done over the centuries when confronted with impious or tyrannical rule. But such overarching, monolithic delineations of 'Islamic civilisation', underpinned by apparently timeless and uniform 'Islamic concepts', became very attractive towards the end of the twentieth century, with Lewis, for instance, pointing to 'a clash of civilisations', in his words 'the perhaps irrational but surely historic reaction of an ancient rival against *our* Judeo-Christian heritage, *our* secular present, and the worldwide expansion of both'.[82] In this, one can see many of the key features of Said's Orientalism.

The ideas of Gibb and Lewis, like Orientalism in the Saidian sense more generally, dovetailed 'Modernisation theory', the dominant paradigm from the

1950s to the 1970s.[83] A common set of assumptions about the character and trajectory of historical change, it denoted the process of transition from traditional to modern society as universal, linear and initiated by the West. Why Muslim societies had not modernised according to the Western model, it was argued, had little to do with practical social, political and economic forces – legacies of colonialism, continuing foreign domination or economic underdevelopment – rather, they had become disoriented because of their essentially static nature, psychological deficiencies and cultural pathologies.[84] Unlike the early modern Europe's insatiable thirst for discovering the 'secrets' of Muslim advances, Muslims seemed uninterested in learning about the sources of Europe's growing strength. Their societies were, therefore, unable to develop the institutions and internal dynamics that might lead to fundamental social transformation from within. Lewis, in his *From Babel to Dragomans* and *The Muslim Discovery of Europe*, had identified the failure of Muslim societies to modernise in their lack of the spirit of enquiry, their misplaced sense of superiority, insularity and hostility to the West. According to Lewis, 'Few Muslims travelled voluntarily to the land of the infidels ... The question of travel for study did not arise, since clearly there was nothing to be learned from the benighted infidels of the outer wilderness.' Consequently, just 'a few notes and fragments ... constitute almost the whole of Muslim travel literature of Europe'.[85] And so, Lewis argued, change had to come from outside. New historical findings, however, challenge his analysis and show that Indian and Iranian Muslims were, actually, intensely curious about and fascinated by European societies and peoples in the early modern period. Nabil Matar's work has underlined that Arabic-speaking Muslims were deeply inquisitive about scientific, literary and political developments in '*bilad al-nasara*' (the lands of the Christians) and, like their European counterparts, wrote 'detailed and empirically based' accounts of Europe in the seventeenth century.[86]

Already beginning to emerge in the 1960s and 1970s, this challenging of the framework of interpretation, which had hitherto shaped both historical analyses and conclusions, and their perceived complicity with Western power in the Muslim world brings me now to reflect on the current state of play. There still remains an influential strand in historical writing, buttressed by those who hold reins of power, which links in with Orientalist paradigms and rationalises Western superiority, tutelage and domination. It insists that the modern West remains at the pinnacle of a new hierarchy of human evolution; that Muslim lands need to follow suit through the enfeeblement of Islam.

Niall Ferguson, for one, offering refurbished Whiggish wisdom, has furnished a historical basis for the current Anglophone liberal imperial project. He has argued that the British Empire was a powerful force of order, justice and development for much of its existence and built much of the modern world; its paternalistic, authoritarian practice of government, through a properly trained and knowledgeable administrative corps competent to dispense fairness and justice, ushered in 'civilisation'/modernisation, setting the natives on the path to progress. Alternatives to empire would have involved despotism, endemic disorder and economic decay, and would have resulted in dangerous instability.[87]

In Ferguson's writing, therefore, we seem to have come full circle – he offers canards once championed by old nineteenth-century imperialists such as Mill and Macaulay. While he agrees with Marx's deterministic approach to the evolution of human history, he, unlike Marx, is much more positively disposed to British rule and argues that the Empire was forced to make painful decisions in pursuit of 'liberal' objectives. Systematically ignoring sources that analyse or present the perspectives of the colonised, there emerges, as Gopal puts it, a 'poisonous fairytale' of 'a benign developmental mission'[88] – a pattern that tends to reinforce the prejudices of those whom Ferguson seeks to influence. Highly provocative, Ferguson's re-telling of the history of the British Empire constructs the lessons that we are to learn from the rise and demise of the British world order. What are they? As part of the building of a similar empire, the invasion of Iraq in 2003 was the right thing to do. For him, ruthlessness in its prosecution was justified: 'what happened at Abu Ghraib prison was no worse than the initiatory "hazing" routine in many army camps and even student fraternities'.[89]

So what conclusions can we draw from all of these developments? Dichotomous notions of the 'clash of civilisations',[90] 'the end of history'[91] and 'liberal international interventionism',[92] while still popular and influential in policy-making circles, are now being challenged from both the contemporary and historical perspectives. On the theoretical level, the category of 'civilisation', while tangible in geopolitical, cultural and material terms, seems diffuse. In terms of cultures, values or systems of belief, civilisations can be shown to be ever changing and adaptable to new conditions. Hence, unlike conflicts between states, it is difficult to know in what ways they could be construed to 'clash'. Moreover, it is being increasingly argued that Islamic civilisation, with distinctly recognisable features, like its Roman and Greek counterparts, has disappeared.[93] Equally, with the globalisation of modernity, Western civilisation also appears to have lost its specifically European character. This line of argument makes the 'clash of civilisations' thesis seem untenable. Historically too, many scholars are coming to reject the portrayal of the relations and interaction between the so-called Muslim world and the West (both contentious terms because of their homogenising, reductionist and essentialist undertones) as simply a story of perpetual opposition and conflict. They have sought to show historically that civilisations have never been hermetically sealed, separate entities – the story of Asia and Europe is replete with uninterrupted mutual exchange.[94]

More specifically, Christian and Islamic 'civilisations' are being shown to have interacted fruitfully and to have borrowed from each other with mutually formative effects. The idea of 'multiple modernities' challenges the classical theory of modernisation as a uniquely and specifically European project. So-called 'oriental globalisation'[95] literature, with its longer time-frame, contests this thesis, demonstrating historically that many of the characteristics that have come to be associated with the eighteenth-century British industrial revolution had emerged earlier in China, and that the Middle East was ahead of Europe in this period. Thanks to Jardine and Brotton, among others, we are now much more aware of the highly symbiotic relationship between Muslim and other European cultures and the profound influence of developments in Muslim societies on the emergence of European Renaissance and Enlightenment thinking – especially the role of the Ottoman Empire in generating mechanisms that lay behind European 'modernisation'.[96] There was, in reality, no monolithic and unitary Europe confronting the Ottoman enemy. Nor was 'Islam' unremittingly ranged against the 'West'.[97] Yes, there were conflicts, but there was also trade and the exchange and mingling of ideas, technologies and institutions. An alternative view is now developing, thanks to modern historical research suggesting that those ideas that are associated with modernity – democracy, individualism, freedom – were found in West Asia too;[98] and that not all modernity must beat the European path nor follow the European model: Islamist forces, it might be argued, have had a significant modernising effect.[99] Equally, it is self-evident that Muslim societies are no less subject to processes of economic, social, ideological and political change than the other, non-Muslim states that have emerged from colonial and Cold War experiences in Latin America, Asia and Africa.

This brings us to the question about how this challenging of the Eurocentric paradigm has emerged. Surely much of the answer lies in the changed context and the changing relations and balance of power in today's world and the impact of this on the character of the historical knowledge being produced. Shifts in history writing reflect the shift in world politics, as the West is gradually de-centred by multi-centric global processes. Analysis of history writing about the Muslim world in Britain, as I have suggested here, reveals that it has always been produced in complex, diverse and non-monolithic ways. Nor, as Said contended more generally in *Orientalism*, has it been entirely systematically constructed; there has never been one totalising vision of the West's Islamic 'Other'. British historians could certainly write about the Muslim world 'as often consumed by admiration and reverence as by denigration and depreciation'.[100] But as British power expanded, some came to think of Islam and the Muslim world as ontologically different from, and inferior to, the 'West'; and many such scholars placed their knowledge at the disposal of the Empire. Others, albeit more commonly at the margins, opposed imperialism or wrote more sympathetically about Islamic cultures and societies, though not necessarily deploying a different interpretive frame from mainstream Orientalists.[101]

Said's proposition that all knowledge is the product of its age and necessarily contingent has become almost a truism. As such, it is now largely accepted that at least the knowledge that became linked with imperial authority was inevitably distorted by the relationship between the two. As I have tried to show, many of those who produced histories of the Orient did indeed legitimise political ideologies *of their time*, and some continue to do so now. On the other hand, we have to exercise care when making such judgements – much historical knowledge may not have been reconstructed with such specific purposes, at least consciously, in mind. Yet, individual historians are always products of their pasts as well as their presents. They cannot escape, to quote Bernard Lewis perhaps ironically (since he seems to have excluded himself from his own comment), 'the prejudices of their culture and age … Even when writing of the past historians are captive of their own times – in their materials and their methods, their concepts and their concerns.'[102] Furthermore, it is widely acknowledged that the construal of what facts should be deemed as significant and relevant for the specific purpose of producing historical knowledge is made on the basis of the judgement of their value, much of which is derived from an individual's political, social and cultural interests – and it is these that bring the relationship between power and knowledge into play. What historians choose to emphasise or to play down, and what determines the choice of these 'shades' in constructing their narratives, in their interpretations, involves, implicitly or explicitly, some sense of how they see the world.

Said claimed that all representations of one culture by another are inevitably distortions of the 'Other'. This is because, he argued, all selection in order to construct representations, in some measure, distorts – though some representations or images distort more or less than others.[103] But if Said's argument is valid, then, as Sadik al-'Azm put it, the Occident in producing representations of the Orient 'is behaving perfectly naturally and in accordance with the general rule – as stated by Said himself – governing the [inevitably distorting] dynamics of the reception of one culture by another'.[104] We seem to be irresolvably trapped in an epistemological dilemma. Presumably then, as British historians, less distortion and greater accuracy is all for which we can strive.

If we accept Said's point regarding the 'determining imprint of individual authors'[105] on their historical productions, then the influence of diverse attitudes, motives and purposes on different interpretation of historical material and reading of the texts cannot be excluded. That is why, as I have sought to demonstrate, history writing about Islam and the Muslim world was never a unified and universally accepted project among British administrators and scholars, though it would be hard to deny that the dominant discourse dovetailed the colonialist experience; perspectives have shifted in the post-colonial globalising context as relations of power have changed.

The limitations of British historical writing about the Muslim world having been acknowledged, are there any alternatives to the existing paradigms? We have become aware of the dangers and limitations in every approach that we can contemplate. Said's critique has undoubtedly helped us to become more acutely and self-critically aware of the existence of multiple perspectives and the need to consider them in any historical analysis. The empowered, and much more articulate and confidently vocal, Muslim subaltern has contributed to the shifts in historical thinking and approaches. Moving away from global generalities, due attention is now being given to local and regional social and political dynamics, hierarchies of power and historical contexts. But, all the same, it appears impossible to escape completely the essentialism that continues to inhere even in current historical epistemologies – a cultural essentialism that, for Said, was the hallmark of Orientalism. All, perhaps, that one can do is be aware of the limits of one's own essentialism and seek to minimise it.

Notes

1 '[B]y Orientalism I mean several things, all of them, in my opinion, interdependent. The most readily accepted designation for Orientalism is an academic one, and indeed the label still serves in a number of academic institutions. Anyone who teaches, writes about, or researches the Orient – and this applies whether the person is an

anthropologist, sociologist, historian, or philologist – either in its specific or its general aspects, is an Orientalist, and what he or she says or does is Orientalism … Orientalism is a style of thought based upon ontological and epistemological distinction made between "the Orient" and (most of the time) "the Occident". Thus a very large mass of writers, among whom are poets, novelists, philosophers, political theorists, economists, and imperial administrators, have accepted the basic distinction between East and West as the starting point for elaborate accounts concerning the Orient, its people, customs, "mind", destiny, and so on … the phenomenon of Orientalism as I study it here deals principally, not with a correspondence between Orientalism and Orient, but with the internal consistency of Orientalism and its ideas about the Orient … despite or beyond any correspondence, or lack thereof, with a "real" Oriental.' See Edward W. Said, *Orientalism: Western Conceptions of the Oriental* (Harmondsworth, Penguin Books, 1978: 1995 edition), pp. 2–3, 5.

2 Robert Irwin, *For Lust of Knowing: The Orientalists and their Enemies* (Harmondsworth: Penguin Books, 2007), p. 4.

3 See Peter L. Berger and Thomas Luckmann, *The Social Construction of Reality: A Treatise in the Sociology of Knowledge* (New York: Anchor, 1967); Michel Foucault, *The Order of Things: An Archaeology of Human Sciences* (London: Tavistock Publications, 1970); Michel Foucault, *The Archaeology of Knowledge* (London: Routledge, 1972).

4 As Irwin asserts in *For Lust of Knowing* (p. 302), 'there are such things as pure scholars. I have even had tea with a few of them.'

5 *Ibid.*, p. 301. See also Bernard Lewis, 'The Question of Orientalism', *The New York Review of Books*, 29, 11 (24 June 1982), pp. 49–56, and the subsequent exchange between Said, Lewis and Oleg Grabar in 'Orientalism: An Exchange', *The New York Review of Books*, 29, 13 (29 August 1982), https://www.nybooks.com/articles/6517 (accessed 8 April 2010).

6 A.J. Arberry, *Oriental Essays: Portraits of Seven Scholars* (London: George Allen & Unwin Ltd., 1960), pp. 239–242; Arberry's own career – as Assistant Librarian in the India Office, his work as 'a propagandist' during the Second World War, and his involvement in the Report of the Interdepartmental Commission of Inquiry on Oriental, Slavonic East European and African Studies in 1947 – somewhat contradicts his wider claims. Perhaps, it would be more accurate to argue that a dialectical relationship exists between politics and scholarship.

7 See Hannah Arendt, *On Revolution* (London: Faber & Faber, 1963).

8 Bernard Lewis, *Islam and the West* (Oxford: Oxford University Press, 1993), pp. 85–86.

9 For example, English and Scottish Protestants directed the Bible's prophetic verses against Muhammad as well as the Pope to validate their own beliefs. Many agreed with Martin Luther that 'Turks and the Pope do not differ in the form of their religion, unless it be in the rituals', and considered the latter to be the real Antichrist and hence a greater menace. Overcoming generations, they invoked Luther's prayer for Jesus Christ's return to 'smite both Turk and pope to the earth'. See Nabil Matar, *Islam in Britain 1558–1685* (Cambridge: Cambridge University Press, 1998), pp. 153–154. See also Thomas Burman, *Reading the Qur'an in Latin Christendom* (Philadelphia: University of Pennsylvania Press, 2009). Even when Islam was praised, its purpose was to make fellow Christians aware of their own shortcomings – the success of Islam as God's punishment for Christian failings.

10 For more details about the influence of 'the father of Arabic studies in England', see Alistair Hamilton, *William Bedwell, the Arabist 1563–1732* (Leiden: E.J. Brill, 1985), p. 1. For Bedwell's pioneering contribution to the study of Arabic and Islam, see, G.J. Toomer, *Eastern Wisedome and Learning: The Study of Arabic in Seventeenth-Century England* (Oxford: Clarendon Press, 1996), pp. 57–63.

11 See Toomer, *Eastern Wisedome and Learning.* This study offers a rigorous and persuasive analysis of the factors, including the influence of trade with the Ottoman

Empire and mistrust of Islam, that first resulted in the 'boom' in the study of Arabic during the sixteenth and seventeenth centuries and then in its rapid decline from the end of the seventeenth century. Bedwell too called attention to the prime importance of Arabic as 'a tonge which was the only language of religion and the chief language of diplomacy and business and from the Fortunate Islands to the China Seas'; see Arberry, *Oriental Essays*, p. 12. In the 1620s and 1630s there was a growing recognition that much useful scientific knowledge, contained in Arabic manuscripts, remained worthy of scrutiny. Laud was part of this thinking. He used his influence with King Charles I to advance the collection of such manuscripts. In 1634 he obtained a royal letter to the Levant Company requiring that each of its ships returning from the East should bring one Persian or Arabic manuscript back, see A.F.L. Beeston, *The Oriental Manuscript Collections of the Bodleian Library*, 1 (reprinted from the *Bodleian Library Record*, vol. 2, 1954).

12 Religion provided much of the impetus for the study of Arabic in England in this period, primarily as a tool for achieving a deeper understanding of the biblical text, as well as engaging in religious debates with the Muslims in the Middle East. There emerged a desperate desire among the English scholars to establish the Truth about the Bible. David A. Pailin's chapter, 'The treatment of Islam', in his *Attitudes to Other Religions: Comparative Religion in Seventeenth- and Eighteenth-Century Britain* (Manchester: Manchester University Press, 1984, p. 104), concludes, 'With a few exceptions, Islam is examined in order to show that it is inferior to Christianity and offers no plausible threat to the various proofs of the truth of the Christian revelation.' See also Shereen Khairallah, 'Arabic Studies in England in the Late Seventeenth and Early Eighteenth Centuries', unpublished PhD thesis, London, School of Oriental and African Studies, 1972.

13 Sir Thomas Adams became increasingly influential in public affairs and provided considerable patronage. He was elected the Lord Mayor of the City of London in 1643 and a Member of Parliament in the 1650s. He paid for the printing of the Gospels in Persian, and for sending them into the east. See Toomer, *Eastern Wisedome and Learning*, p. 91.

14 Protestants and Catholics likened each other to Muslims for deviating from and perverting the true faith and used Islam against Christian sects such as the Socinians, Unitarians and Deists. For example Henry Oldenburg (1619–1677), troubled by 'heretical' texts circulating in England, 'saw that it was essential to defend the divinity of Scripture' and 'to justify the New Testament ... as genuine, unaltered, and altogether free from additions and diminutions'. Oldenburg was deeply concerned to defend Scripture against his opponents in England who were deploying the charges of corruption and other Islamic objections in their polemics against Trinitarian Christianity. See Justin A.I. Champion, 'Legislators, Imposters and the Politic Origins of Religion: English Theories of "Imposture" from Stubbe to Toland', in Silvia Berti, Françoise Charles-Dubert and Richard H. Popkin (eds), *Heterodoxy, Spinozism and Free Thought in Early Eighteenth-Century Europe* (Dordrecht: Kluwer Academic Publishers, 1996), p. 14 (electronic copy also available at hhttp://digirep.rhul.ac.uk/file/3421c5d2-70b7-71fb-2ee3-9aff1d11494c/4/Champion_TRAITE2.pdf).

15 See J.R. Hale (ed.), *The Evolution of British Historiography: From Bacon to Namier* (Cleveland: The World Publishing Company, 1964), p. 9. '[N]ot only are events related, but their causes and effects explained; the characters of the actors are displayed; the manners of the age described ...', *ibid.*, p. 28.

16 See Jonathan I. Israel, *Radical Enlightenment: Philosophy and the Making of Modernity, 1650–1750* (Oxford: Oxford University Press, 2001).

17 Edward Pococke (1604–1691) was chaplain for the Levant Co. at Aleppo between 1630 and 1636, during which period he became interested in Arab society. His *Specimen Historae Arabum* offers a defence of kingly government. Through the study of Arabic authors themselves, he wanted to find out what Muslims really believed: a knowledge of Arabic, he thought, 'would enable Christians to refute genuine Muslim errors ...'

and, hopefully, bring about their conversion, see P.M. Holt, *Studies in the History of the Near East* (London: Frank Cass, 1973), pp. 17, 21. See also P.M. Holt, 'The Study of Arabic Historians in Seventeenth-Century England: The Background and Work of Edward Pococke', *Bulletin of the School of Oriental and African Studies*, 19, 3 (1957), pp. 444–455. According to Toomer, Pococke had indeed 'envisioned the possibility of converting Muslims' (*Eastern Wisedome and Learning*, pp. 216–217), but while 'his attitude towards Muhammad is clearly one of dislike – he regularly uses the title 'false prophet' and he charges him with 'libidousness' and of 'laying the bloody foundations of his religion and his empire at the same time' (*ibid.*, pp. 223–224) – Pococke refrains from hurling the usual abuses. Indeed, he is credited with having shown a high regard for Arabic as a language – its clarity, elegance and richness – and celebrating Arab contributions to philosophy and the sciences.

18 Paul Rycaut, *The Present State of the Ottoman Empire* (London: John Starkey and Henry Brome, 1668: reprint, Westmead: Gregg International Publishers, 1972).

19 This is the subtitle of Prideaux's *Life of Mahomet.* He intended his text not only as a polemic against Islam but also as a warning that the advance of the Socinian, the Deist and the Quaker 'may … raise up some *Mahomet* against us for our utter Confusion', see Holt, *Studies in the History of the Near East*, p. 51.

20 While, thanks to sponsorship by Muslim subscribers to the Islamic Society, including Hafiz Mahmud Khan Shairani, Stubbe's text, entitled *An Account of the Rise and Progress of Mahometanism – with the Life of Mahomet* (subtitled, 'And a vindication of him and his religion from the calumnies of the Christians') (London: Luzac & Co.), was eventually published in 1911; a number of copies of the manuscript had already been in circulation at the end of the 1670s.

21 Stubbe, *Mahometanism*, p. 141.

22 See, P.M. Holt, *A Seventeenth-Century Defender of Islam: Henry Stubbe (1632–76) and His Book* (London: Dr. Williams's Trust, 1972), p. 22.

23 Shairani 'recognized the work [*Mahometanism*] as constituting one of the earliest appreciations of Islam we have in English, remarkable for its lack of Christian bias and its intuitive and sympathetic grasp of Muslim faith and practice'. See James R. Jacob, *Henry Stubbe, Radical Protestantism and the Early Enlightenment* (Cambridge: Cambridge University Press, 2002), p. 64.

24 Simon Ockley, *The History of the Saracens*, 6th edn (London: Henry G. Bohn, 1857), p. xvi.

25 *Ibid.*, p. 79.

26 *Ibid.*, p. xvi.

27 Ockley writes, 'The Arabians … since the time of Mahomet have rendered themselves universally remarkable, both by arms and learning,' *ibid.* As a 'modern' historian, Ockley says: 'I have let them tell their own story: and I have abstained as much as possible from intermixing reflections of my own, unless where they have appeared a necessity of illustrating something that might not be obvious to persons unacquainted with oriental affairs.' See Arberry, *Oriental Essays*, p. 45. All the same, Ockley continued in the main to follow Prideaux's line and kept nonconformists and deviant Christians at arm's length. And, in his *History*, he clearly intended to expose and counter 'a great many Errors' – 'the Whimsies and Conceits of the Arab Enthusiasts … or even that plentiful crop which the Devil has sow'd of them in our times', *ibid.*, p. 24.

28 George Sale, *The Koran, commonly called the Alcoran of Mohammed*, vol. I (London: printed for L. Hawes, W. Clarke, and R. Collins; and T. Wilcox, 1764), p. 47. When Sale opined that the Qur'an was a forgery and that it was absolutely necessary to expose Muhammad's imposture, he, like Prideaux, was parroting the mediaeval church historians. However, Sale's position was a little more complex and nuanced. For instance, he disagreed with Prideaux's uncompromising position that Muhammad 'made that nation [the Arabs] exchange their idolatry for another religion altogether as bad', *ibid.*, p. 51.

29 Even in the late eighteenth century, by which time the EIC had become the dominant power in many parts of India, Dalrymple tells us that, in contrast to the later policy of social distance and separation from the so-called 'natives', the British in India, including the elite, such as Kirkpatrick, Palmer and Ochterlony, were happy to mingle with Indians – they delighted in Indian cultures and ways of living, loved and married Indian women, adopted modes of Indian dress and spoke Indian languages. See William Dalrymple, *White Mughals: Love and Betrayal in Eighteenth-Century India* (London: Harper Collins Publishers, 2003), pp. xlvi–xlix.

30 See W. Robertson, *An Historical Disquisition concerning the Knowledge which the Ancient had of India* (London: printed for A. Strahan [and 2 others], 1791).

31 The thinkers of the Scottish Enlightenment, while sharing the humanist and rationalist outlook of the European Enlightenment, asserted the ability of man to effect changes for the better in society and nature, guided only by reason. They were distinguishable in their emphasis on the empiricist approach. See Arthur Herman, *The Scottish Enlightenment: The Scots' Invention of the Modern World* (London: Fourth Estate Limited, 2003). The development approach to history, associated with the Scottish Enlightenment, offered a unique and profoundly influential eighteenth-century narrative known as the four-stage thesis. In the works of Smith, Hume and Robertson, from the 1750s to 1790s, it concluded that the human record was one of material and moral improvement, of cultural development from 'savagery' and 'barbarism' to 'civilisation', and that their society stood at the pinnacle of achievement. Savages did not have the capacity for self-government, while serfs, slaves and peasants, on the other hand, might be so schooled in obedience that their capacity for rationality would be stifled. Only in commercial society were the material and cultural conditions ideal for individuals to realise and exercise their potential. The consequence of this logic was that civilised societies like Britain were acting in the interest of less-developed peoples by governing them. Colonialism, from this perspective, was not primarily a form of political domination and economic exploitation but rather a paternalistic practice of government that exported 'civilisation' (later modernisation) in order to foster improvement in native peoples. Despotic government (James Mill does not hesitate to use this term) was a means to the end of improvement and, ultimately, self-government.

32 Alexander Dow, *History of Hindostan* (London: T. Becket and P.A. De Hondt, 1772), p. 382.

33 See, J.G.A. Pocock, *Barbarism and Religion, The Enlightenments of Edward Gibbon, 1737–1764*, vol. 1 (Cambridge: Cambridge University Press, 1999).

34 Assessing Muhammad, Gibbon asked whether he was an enthusiast or impostor; in Gibbon's view, Muhammad was 'compelled ... to comply in some measure with the prejudices and vices of his followers and employed even the vices of mankind as instruments of salvation'. While the 'use of fraud and perfidy were subservient to the propagation of faith ... the character of Mahomet must have gradually been stained ... and the influence of such pernicious habits [assassination] would be poorly compensated by the practice of personal and social virtues ... Of his last years, ambition was the ruling passion; and a politician will suspect, that he secretly smiled (a victorious imposter!)'. See Edward Gibbon, *The History of the Decline and Fall of the Roman Empire* (London: T. Cadell, 1837), p. 883.

35 'Perhaps the interpretation of the Koran would now be taught in the schools of Oxford, and her pulpits might demonstrate to a circumcised people the sanctity and truth of the revelation of Mahomet ... From such calamities was Christendom delivered by the genius and fortune of one man [Charles Martel, 732 A.D.]', see Edward Gibbon, *The History of the Decline and Fall of the Roman Empire*, vol. V, chapter 52 (London: Methuen & Co., 1896), p. 15.

36 Lord Teignmouth (ed.), *The Works of Sir William Jones*, vol. I (London: John Stockdale, 1807), p. 19.

37 Teignmouth (ed.), *The Works of Sir William Jones*, vol. III, p. 216. Montesquieu (1689–1755) developed the concept of despotism in his *The Spirit of the Law* (1748)

as the rule of a single person subject to no restraint, constitutional or moral. During the nineteenth century the concept of 'Oriental despotism' became a powerful idea for explaining the supposed backwardness of 'Oriental' societies and as a justification for colonial systems. According to this scheme, British rule was the agent of economic modernisation – and thus colonialism, unwittingly, became a progressive force. See Z. Lockman, *Contending Visions of the Middle East: The History and Politics of Orientalism* (Cambridge: Cambridge University Press, 2004), pp. 45–48, 83–85.

38 Teignmouth (ed.), *The Works of Sir William Jones*, vol. II, p. 133.

39 Cited in Javed Majeed, *Ungoverned Imaginings: James Mill's* The History of British India and Orientalism (Oxford: Clarendon Press, 1992), p. 19.

40 S.N. Mukherjee, *Sir William Jones: A Study in Eighteenth Century British Attitudes to India* (Cambridge: Cambridge University Press, 1968), p. 125.

41 Jones, 'To Arthur Lee', 1 October, 1786, letter 443 of William Jones, *The Letters of William Jones*, vol. II (Oxford: Clarendon, 1970), pp. 712–713. Also see John Shore Teignmouth (ed.), *Memoirs of the Life, Writings and Correspondence of Sir William Jones* (London: J. Hatchard, 1806), p. 236.

42 Majeed, *Ungoverned Imaginings*, p. 8.

43 *Ibid.*, p.22.

44 Arberry, *Oriental Essays*, p. 58.

45 John Malcolm, in his *The history of Persia, from the most early period to the present time* (London: John Murray, 1815), wrote: 'the prosecution of my public duties first led me to feel the want of a history of Persia'. See M.E. Yapp, 'Two British Historians of Persia', in Bernard Lewis and P.M. Holt (eds), *Historians of the Middle East* (Oxford: Oxford University Press, 1962), p. 343.

46 Malcolm's study of the Persians led him to conclude that they were a barbarian and uncivilised people who did not know the value of liberty and who preferred peace and security under a strong despot. To him, the worst symptom of Persian decay was the debased morality of the people; 'the Persians are ignorant, deceitful, and capricious, and above all they were vain'. The reason for their lack of progress was Islam: 'a religion adverse to all improvement'. 'What', Malcolm asked, 'but Barbarians could be the result of such a doctrine?' That is why 'there is no example of a Mahommedan nation having attained a high rank in the scale of civilisation', and hence the need for the British to intervene and forcibly civilise them. See Yapp, 'Two British Historians', p. 349. Mountstuart Elphinstone, who was in the service of the EIC from his appointment in 1795 until his retirement as Governor of Bombay in 1827, wrote his *History of India*, published in 1841, in a period when British power was expanding. Like Malcolm, he too presumed that human nature differed in different parts of the world. Europeans and Christianity, in his view, were superior to other peoples and creeds. With regard to Islam, while he considered Muhammad to be a 'reformer' and his morality, 'however [it] may appear to modern Christians', pure when compared with contemporary practices in Arabia, he nevertheless remained a 'false' prophet and 'among the worst enemies of mankind … he encouraged intolerance, fanaticism and violence'. See Mountstuart Elphinstone, *The History of India*, vol. I (London: John Murray, 1841), pp. 492–494. In one Indian historian's estimate, Elphinstone maintained an 'unconcealed contempt for all Islamic institutions in general and the Prophet of Islam in particular'. See Abdur Rashid, 'The Treatment of History by Muslim Historians in Mughal Official and Biographical Works', in C.H. Philips (ed.), *Historians of India, Pakistan and Ceylon* (Oxford: Oxford University Press, 1961), p. 140.

47 *The Philanthropist* (1814) Vol. IV, p. 117 (James Mill's review of William Gilpin's *The Lives of Reformers*) – cited by J.S. Grewal, *Muslim Rule in India* (Calcutta: Oxford University Press, 1970), p. 71.

48 Thomas Babington Macaulay (1800–1859) was a Whig politician and, in many eyes, 'the pre-eminent' nineteenth-century English historian. For him the British Empire was a rational, progressive and benevolent force; its purpose was to bring

out 'a great people sunk in the lowest depth of slavery and superstition' and make them desirous and capable of all the privileges of citizens'. Quoted in Ronald Hyam, *Britain's Imperial Century, 1815–1914: A Study of Empire and Expansion* (London: Macmillan, 1976), p. 220.

49 In his famous Minute of 2 February 1835, Macaulay claimed, 'I have never found one among them ["orientalists"] who could deny that a single shelf of a good European library was worth the whole native literature of India and Arabia.' See http://www.columbia.edu/itc/mealac/pritchett/00generallinks/macaulay/txt_minute_education_1835.html (accessed 8 April 2010).

50 See Leila Ahmed, *Edward W. Lane, A Study of his life and works and of the British ideas of the Middle East in the Nineteenth Century* (Harlow: Longman, 1978), p. 95.

51 Edward William Lane, *An Account of the Manner and Customs of the modern Egyptians*, 5th edn (London: John Murray, 1860). See also Jason Thompson, 'Edward William Lane', *Egypt, Journal of the American Research Center in Egypt*, 34 (1997), pp. 243–261. It has been suggested that his association with a group of British Egyptologists and orientalists, who had collected in Egypt in the 1820s, may have resulted in the reinforcement of some of his 'cultural preconceptions, if only unconsciously', *ibid.*, p. 255.

52 One area of Egyptian society, however, about which Lane could not write accurately, because of lack of access to the *harem*, was the female and domestic sphere. His perceptions and accounts, based mainly on conversations with Egyptian men, of inter-sexual relations, Egyptian women's sexuality and behaviour – their 'immodest freedom of conversation', their 'coarse' language, their licentiousness – were heavily shaped by his regard for and unquestioned acceptance of Victorian propriety. See Lane, *Account*, pp. 295–296. Later he was helped by his sister, Sophia Poole, who accompanied him on his third trip to Egypt, in correcting the erroneous and adding to the deficient information in his earlier account. See Sophia Poole, *The Englishwoman in Egypt: Letters from Cairo Written during a Residence there in 1842–1846*, edited by Azza Kararah (Cairo: The American University in Cairo, 2003). See also Sahar Sobhi Abdel-Hakim, 'Sophia Poole: Writing the Self, Scribing Egyptian Women', *Alif: Journal of Comparative Poetics*, 22, (2002), pp. 107–126.

53 While Charles Foster (1787–1871), for instance, accepted the traditional Christian formulations of Islam, he also affirmed Muhammad's spiritual sincerity. Sir William Muir's (1819–1905) view of Islam as an enemy of 'Civilisation, Liberty and Truth' contrasted with Reginald Bosworth Smith's (1839–1908) rejection of Muhammad's imposture and acceptance of his prophethood. See Clinton Bennett, *Victorian Images of Islam* (London: Grey Seal Books, 1992). See also Philip C. Almond, *Heretic and Hero: Muhammad and the Victorians* (Wiesbaden: Harrassowitz, 1989).

54 W. Montgomery Watt, 'Carlyle and Muhammad', *Hibbert Journal*, vol. 53 (1954–55), p. 247. Carlyle quotes Goethe (1749–1832), not entirely accurately, in his positive assessment of *Islam*: 'If this be *Islam*, do we not all live in *Islam*.' See Thomas Carlyle, 'The Hero as Prophet', in his *On Heroes, Hero Worship, and the Heroic in History* (London: Chapman & Hall, 1872), p. 52.

55 Carlyle, 'The Hero as Prophet', pp. 52–53.

56 See 'Sir William Muir, 1819–1905' in Bennett, *Victorian Images of Islam*, pp. 103–127. For Muir, 'the sword of Mahomet, and the Coran are the most fatal enemies of Civilisation, Liberty and the Truth which the world has yet known'. See W. Muir, *Life of Mahomet*, vol. 4 (London: Smith, Elder, 1861), p. 322. Muir believed that Britain's position in India carried special responsibilities – the 'enlightenment of the people of India depended on her' not neglecting her 'noble vocation' – and he saw his national mission to educate to enlighten to civilize the 'savage' natives.

57 See H.M. Elliot and John Dowson, *The History of India as told by its own Historians*, 8 vols (London: Trubner Company, 1867–1877); Grewal, *Muslim Rule in India*, pp. 170–171. See also S.H. Hodivala, *Studies in Indo-Muslim History: Critical Commentary on Elliot and Dowson's History of India as told by its own Historians*, 2 vols (Bombay:

unknown publishers, 1939–57), in which an enormous number of factual errors as well as flaws associated with reading and interpretation were identified.

58 Henry Maine, *Ancient Law: Its Connection with the Early History of Society, and Its Relations to Modern Ideas* (London; John Murray, 1861), Chapter 4.

59 Francis Henry Bennett Skrine, *Life of Sir William Wilson Hunter, K.C.S.I.* (London: Longmans & Co., 1901), pp. 468–469.

60 J.R. Seeley, *The Expansion of England: Two Courses of Lectures* (London: Macmillan, 1883). Edited and with an introduction by John Gross (London: University of Chicago Press, 1971).

61 *Ibid.*, p. 141.

62 Rudyard Kipling appositely captures the sentiment in his 1899 poem, 'The White Man's Burden'.

63 Alfred Milner, *England in Egypt* (London: Edward Arnold, 1893); George N. Curzon, *Problems of the Far East* (London: Longmans, Green, 1894); Hugh Egerton, *A Short History of British Colonial Policy* (London: Methuen & Co., 1897); Earl of Cromer, *Modern Egypt*, 2 vols (London: Macmillan & Co., 1908).

64 For a critique of the Empire, see J.A. Hobson, *Imperialism: A Study* (London: James Nisbett & Co., 1902). Another example of those dissenting from the virtues and benevolence of the British imperial mission was Lytton Strachey, *Eminent Victorians* (London: Chatto & Windus, 1918). See also A.J.P. Taylor, *The Trouble Makers: Dissent over Foreign Policy, 1792–1939* (London: Hamish Hamilton, 1957).

65 David Samuel Margoliouth (1895–1940) was Laudian Professor at Oxford until 1937, an ordained Anglican cleric and self-taught in Arabic. While Margoliouth had many good things to say about Muhammad and Islam, he considered Muhammad and his Muslim followers to be ultimately deeply flawed in several respects. See David Samuel Margoliouth, *Mohammed and the Rise of Islam* (London: G.P. Putnam's Sons, 1905).

66 In India, Arnold joined a local group of Muslim reformers who sought to bring together scientific thought with Qur'anic beliefs. Returning to London in 1904, he taught Arabic at University College London and was appointed to a chair at the School of Oriental Studies in 1921. Katherine Watt, 'Thomas Walker Arnold and the Re-Evaluation of Islam, 1864–1930', *Modern Asian Studies*, 36, 1 (February 2002), pp. 1–98.

67 T.W. Arnold, *The Islamic Faith* (London: Benn, 1928), p. 77.

68 M.A. Stein, 'Thomas Walker Arnold', *Proceedings of the British Academy*, XVI (1930), pp. 439–474.

69 'Edward Granville Brown and the Persian "Awakening"', in Geoffrey Nash, *From Empire to Orient: Travellers to the Middle East, 1830–1926* (London: I.B. Tauris, 2005), pp. 139–168.

70 Cromer, *Modern Egypt*, p. 28. See also Jennifer Kernaghan, 'Lord Cromer as Orientalist and Social Engineer in Egypt, 1882–1907', unpublished MA thesis, University of British Columbia, 1993.

71 V.A. Smith, *The Oxford History of India* (Oxford, Clarendon Press, 1919), p. 182.

72 Margery Perham (1895–1982), an Oxford University historian, in collaboration with the sometime Governor of Nigeria, Sir Frederick (Lord) Lugard (1858–1945), elaborated the theory of 'Indirect Rule' as a rationale for Britain's imperial mission in a more paternalistic mode. See Perham's *Colonial Sequence, 1930–1949: A Chronological Commentary upon British Colonial Policy especially in Africa* (London: Methuen & Co., 1967).

73 While this approach had considerable ethical and patriotic popular appeal, radical writers such as Leonard Woolf in *Imperialism and Civilization* (London: L. & V. Woolf, 1936), and Leonard Barnes, in *The Duty of Empire* (London: Victor Gollancz, 1935), mounted robust and trenchant critiques.

74 According to Norman Daniel, the 'new ideas of the Islamic world … took shape in Western Europe during the period of colonial expansion. New images came to be reflected in the old distorting mirror. The inhabitants of modern Europe inherited from their medieval fathers a large and persistent body of ideas about Islam'. See

Norman Daniel, *Islam, Europe and Empire* (Edinburgh: Edinburgh University Press, 1966), p. xiii. This book examines the images of the Muslim world in Europe in the modern period. For an example of the reliance on medieval and early modern knowledge of Muhammad and Islam, see the writings of David Samuel Margoliouth (mentioned above).

75 See H.A.R. Gibb, *Modern Trends in Islam* (first edition Chicago: Chicago University Press, 1947: reprinted, New York: Octagon Books, 1975), pp. 5–7, 106–110.

76 Irwin, *For Lust of Knowing*, p. 242.

77 See Sir Hamilton Gibb and Harold Bowen, *Islamic Society and the West: A Study of the Impact of Western Civilization on Moslem Culture in the Near East* (London: Oxford University Press, 1950).

78 Roger Owen, 'The Middle East in the Eighteenth Century – An "Islamic" Society in Decline? A Critique of Gibb and Bowen's Islamic Society and the West', *Review of Middle East Studies*, 1 (1975), pp. 113–134.

79 Caroline Finkel, '"The Treacherous Cleverness of Hindsight": Myths of Ottoman Decay', in Gerald Maclean (ed.), *Re-Orienting the Renaissance: Cultural Exchanges with the East* (London: Palgrave Macmillan, 2005), pp. 148–174.

80 Bernard Lewis, 'Communism and Islam', *International Affairs* 30, 1 (1954), pp. 1–12.

81 Zachary Lockman, *Contending Visions of the Middle East: The History and Politics of Orientalism* (Cambridge: Cambridge University Press, 2004), p. 132.

82 Bernard Lewis, 'The Roots of Muslim Rage', *Atlantic Monthly*, September 1990, http://www.theatlantic.com/doc/199009/muslim-rage (accessed 8 April 2010).

83 For a succinct critique of the historical evolution of the 'Modernisation theory', see Lockman, *Contending Visions*, pp. 133–143. Indeed, a number of scholars have demolished the thesis of the hegemonic centrality of Western modernity. S.N. Eisenstadt, for instance, has argued for 'the idea of multiple modernities'. In his view, 'the best way to understand the contemporary world ... is to see it as a story of continual constitution and reconstitution of a multiplicity of cultural programs', see 'Multiple Modernities', *Daedalus*, 129, 1 (Winter 2000), pp. 1–29. Roxanne L. Euben suggests that 'Islamic fundamentalist political thought is part of a transcultural and multivocal reassessment of the value and definition of "modernity"', see 'Premodern, Antimodern or Postmodern? Islamic and Western Critiques of Modernity', *The Review of Politics*, 59, 3 (Summer 1997), pp. 429–459. Francis Robinson more specifically identifies the 'modernising processes' – attacks on the authority of the past; the individual as the key agent on earth (human will); the accompanying transformations of the self – in 'Islamic Reform and Modernities in South Asia', *Modern Asian* Studies, 42, 2/3 (2008), pp. 259–281. In this sense, Islamic reform could, arguably, be seen as a modernising force within many Muslim societies, just as other 'modernities' operate within non-Muslim ones.

84 Bernard Lewis, in 1954, used the notion of Oriental despotism (Karl Wittfogel's 'hydraulic society') to explain the authoritarian and arbitrary character of Islamic social order: see Lewis, 'Communism and Islam', p. 9. See also Karl A. Wittfogel, *Oriental Despotism: A Comparative Study of Total Power* (New Haven: Yale University Press, 1957) for a detailed elaboration of his thesis.

85 Bernard Lewis, *From Babel to Dragomans: Interpreting the Middle East* (London: Phoenix, 2004), pp. 210, 132; Bernard Lewis, *The Muslim Discovery of Europe* (London: Weidenfeld & Nicolson, 1982), pp. 296–297; Bernard Lewis, 'The Muslim Discovery of Europe', *Bulletin of the School of Oriental and African Studies*, 20, 1/3, Studies in Honour of Sir Ralph Turner, Director of the School of Oriental and African Studies, 1937–57 (1957), pp. 409–416.

86 Nabil Matar (ed.), *In the Lands of the Christians: Arabic Travel Writing in the Seventeenth Century* (London: Routledge, 2003), p. xxii. See also Nabil Matar, 'Arab Views of Europeans, 1758–1727: The Western Mediterranean', in Gerald Maclean (ed.), *Re-Orienting the Renaissance: Cultural Exchanges with the East* (London: Palgrave Macmillan, 2005), pp. 126–147.

87 Niall Ferguson, *Empire: The Rise and Demise of the British World Order and the Lessons for Global Power* (New York: Basic Books, 2003).
88 Priyamvada Gopal, 'The Story Peddled by Imperial Apologists Is a Poisonous Fairytale', *Guardian* (London), 28 June 2006. See also Niall Ferguson, 'America: An Empire in Denial', *The Chronicle Review*, 49, 29 (28 March 2003); Vivek Chibber, 'The Good Empire: Should We Pick Up Where the British Left Off?', *The Boston Review*, February/March 2005; John S. Saul, '"Humanitarian Imperialism": Ferguson, Ignatieff and the Political Science of Good Empire', paper given on 5 February 2006 at York University, Toronto, http://www.marxsite.com/Humanitarian%20Imperialism.htm (accessed 8 April 2010); Amartya Sen, 'Imperial Illusions, India, Britain, and the Wrong Lessons', *The New Republic*, 31 December 2007.
89 Stephen Howe, 'An Oxford Scot at King Dubya's court: Niall Ferguson's "Colossus"' (22 July 2004) http://www.opendemocracy.net/democracy-americanpower/article_2021.jsp (accessed 8 April 2010).
90 Samuel P. Huntington, *The Clash of Civilizations and the Remaking of the World Order* (New York: Simon & Schuster, 1998).
91 Fukuyama argues that – with the end of the Cold War – we have arrived at 'the end point of mankind's ideological evolution and the universalization of Western liberal democracy as the final form of human government', see Francis Fukuyama, 'End of History?', *The National Interest*, Summer 1989, http://www.wesjones.com/eoh.htm (accessed 8 April 2010). He elaborates his thesis further in his later book *The End of History and the Last Man* (London: Hamilton, 1992).
92 Jonathan Powell, 'Why the West Must not Fear to Intervene', *Observer*, 18 November 2007, http://www.guardian.co.uk/commentisfree/2007/nov/18/comment.foreign-policy (accessed 8 April 2010); David Miliband, 'The Democratic Imperative', Aung San Suu Kyi Lecture, St Hugh's College, Oxford, 12 February 2008, http://www.davidmiliband.info/speeches/speeches_08_02.htm (accessed 8 April 2010).
93 'After all, civilizations and cultures do not enter into dialogue, nor do they go to war, and might not legitimately be understood anthropomorphically. What go to war are states, armies and social movements', see Aziz al-Azmeh, 'Human Rights and Contemporaneity of Islam: a Matter of Dialogue', http://www.alati.com.br/pdf/2007/the_universal_of_human_rights/pdf220.pdf (accessed 8 April 2010).
94 Gerard Delanty, 'Civilizational Constellations and European Modernity Reconsidered', in G. Delanty (ed.), *Europe and Asia beyond East and West* (London: Routledge, 2006), pp. 45–60.
95 See Jan Nederveen Pieterse, 'Oriental Globalization: Past and Present', in G. Delanty (ed.), *Europe and Asia beyond East and West* (London: Routledge, 2006), pp. 61–73, and John M. Hobson, 'Revealing the Cosmopolitan Side of Oriental Europe: The Eastern Origins of European Civilization', in G. Delanty (ed.), *Europe and Asia beyond East and West* (London: Routledge, 2006), pp. 107–119.
96 Jerry Brotton, *The Renaissance Bazaar: From the Silk Road to Michelangelo* (Oxford, Oxford University Press, 2002); Lisa Jardine, *Worldly Goods: A New History of the Renaissance* (London & Basingstoke: Macmillan, 1997); L. Jardine and J. Brotton, *Global Interests: Renaissance Art between East and West* (London: Reaktion Books, 2000); Jack Goody, *Renaissances: The One or the Many?* (Cambridge: Cambridge University Press, 2009).
97 See Brotton, *The Renaissance Bazaar*, and Lockman, *Contending Visions*.
98 Jack Goody, 'Europe and Islam', in G. Delanty (ed.), *Europe and Asia beyond East and West* (London: Routledge, 2006), p. 139.
99 B.O. Utvik, 'The Modernizing Force of Islamism', in J.L. Esposito and F. Burgat (eds), *Modernizing Islam: Religion in the Public Sphere in the Middle East and Europe* (London: Hurst, 2003), pp. 43–68.
100 John M. Mackenzie, *Orientalism: History, Theory and the Arts* (Manchester: Manchester University Press, 1995), p. 215.

101 For example, David Urquhart (1805–1877), W.S. Blunt (1840–1922), E.G. Browne (1862–1926), T.W. Arnold (1864–1930) and Marmaduke Pickthall (1875–1936) all viewed Muslim cultures positively, and argued for their integrity and autonomy. However, in their scheme, British patronage to a greater or lesser degree needed to be deployed in order to reform the Muslim societies with which they engaged. See Nash, *From Empire to Orient.*

102 Bernard Lewis, *Islam in History: Ideas, Men and Events in the Middle East* (London: Alcove Press, 1973), p. 14.

103 '[C]ultures have always been inclined to impose complete transformations on other cultures, receiving these other cultures not as they are but as, for the benefit of the receiver, they ought to be': Said, *Orientalism*, p. 67. 'Representations are formations, or as Roland Barthes has said of all operations of language, they are deformations ... The Orient as a representation in Europe is formed – or deformed ...', *ibid.*, pp. 272–273.

104 Sadik Jalal al-'Azm, 'Orientalism and Orientalism in Reverse', in A.L. Macfie, *Orientalism: A Reader* (Edinburgh: Edinburgh University Press, 2000), p. 222.

105 Said, *Orientalism*, p. 23.

Bibliography

Abdel-Hakim, Sahar Sobni, 'Sophia Poole: Writing the Self, Scribing Egyptian Women', *Alif: Journal of Comparative Poetics*, 22, (2002).

Ahmed, Leila, *Edward W. Lane, A Study of His Life and Works and of the British Ideas of the Middle East in the Nineteenth Century* (Harlow: Longman, 1978).

Almond, Philip C., *Heretic and Hero: Muhammad and the Victorians* (Wiesbaden: Harrassowitz, 1989).

Arberry, A.J., *Oriental Essays: Portraits of Seven Scholars* (London: George Allen & Unwin Ltd., 1960).

Arendt, Hannah, *On Revolution* (London: Faber & Faber, 1963).

Arnold, T.W., *The Islamic Faith* (London: Benn, 1928).

Al-Azmeh, Aziz, 'Human Rights and Contemporaneity of Islam: A Matter of Dialogue', http://www.alati.com.br/pdf/2007/the_universal_of_human_rights/pdf220.pdf (accessed 8 April 2010).

Al-'Azm, Sadik Jalal, 'Orientalism and Orientalism in Reverse', in A.L. Macfie, *Orientalism: A Reader* (Edinburgh: Edinburgh University Press, 2000).

Antonius, George, *The Arab Awakening: The Story of the Arab Nationalist Movement* (London: H. Hamilton, 1938).

Barnes, Leonard, *The Duty of Empire* (London: Victor Gollancz, 1935).

Beeston, A.F.L., *The Oriental Manuscript Collections of the Bodleian Library*, 1 (reprinted from the *Bodleian Library Record*, vol. 2, 1954).

Bennett, Clinton, *Victorian Images of Islam* (London: Grey Seal Books, 1992).

Berger, Peter L. and Thomas Luckmann, *The Social Construction of Reality: A Treatise in the Sociology of Knowledge* (New York: Anchor, 1967).

Brotton, Jerry, *The Renaissance Bazaar: From the Silk Road to Michelangelo* (Oxford: Oxford University Press, 2002).

Burman, Thomas, *Reading the Qur'an in Latin Christendom* (Philadelphia: University of Pennsylvania Press, 2009).

Carlyle, Thomas, 'The Hero as Prophet', in his *On Heroes, Hero Worship, and the Heroic in History* (London: Chapman & Hall, 1872).

Champion, Justin A.I., 'Legislators, Imposters and the Politic Origins of Religion: English Theories of "Imposture" from Stubbe to Toland', in Silvia Berti, Françoise Charles-Dubert and Richard H. Popkin (eds), *Heterodoxy, Spinozism and Free Thought in Early Eighteenth-Century Europe* (Dordrecht: Kluwer Academic Publishers, 1996), (electronic copy also available at http://digirep.rhul.ac.uk/file/3421c5d2-70b7-71fb-2ee3-9aff1d11494c/4/Champion_TRAITE2.pdf).

Chibber, Vivek, 'The Good Empire: Should We Pick Up Where the British Left Off?', *The Boston Review*, February/March 2005.

Cromer, Earl of, *Modern Egypt*, 2 vols (London: Macmillan & Co., 1908).

Curzon, George N., *Problems of the Far East* (London: Longmans, Green, 1894).

Dalrymple, William, *White Mughals: Love and Betrayal in Eighteenth-Century India* (London: Harper Collins Publishers, 2003).

Daniel, Norman, *Islam, Europe and Empire* (Edinburgh: Edinburgh University Press, 1966).

Delanty, Gerard, 'Civilizational Constellations and European Modernity Reconsidered', in Gerard Delanty (ed.), *Europe and Asia beyond East and West* (London: Routledge, 2006), pp. 45–60.

Dow, Alexander, *History of Hindostan* (London: T. Becket and P.A. De Hondt, 1772).

Egerton, Hugh, *A Short History of British Colonial Policy* (London: Methuen & Co., 1897).

Eisenstadt, S.N., 'Multiple Modernities', *Daedalus*, 129, 1 (Winter 2000).

Elliot, H.M. and John Dowson, *The History of India as told by its own Historians*, 8 vols (London: Trubner Company, 1867–1877).

Elphinstone, Mountstuart, *The History of India*, vol. I (London: John Murray, 1841).

Euben, Roxanne L., 'Premodern, Antimodern or Postmodern? Islamic and Western Critiques of Modernity', *The Review of Politics*, 59, 3 (Summer 1997).

Ferguson, Niall, *Empire: The Rise and Demise of the British World Order and the Lessons for Global Power* (New York: Basic Books, 2003).

Ferguson, Niall, 'America: An Empire in Denial', *The Chronicle Review*, 49, 29 (28 March 2003).

Finkel, Caroline, '"The Treacherous Cleverness of Hindsight": Myths of Ottoman Decay', in Gerald Maclean (ed.), *Re-Orienting the Renaissance: Cultural Exchanges with the East* (London: Palgrave Macmillan, 2005).

Foucault, Michel, *The Order of Things: An Archaeology of Human Sciences* (London: Tavistock Publications, 1970).

Foucault, Michel, *The Archaeology of Knowledge* (London: Routledge, 1972).

Fukuyama, Francis, 'End of History?', *The National Interest*, Summer 1989, http://www.wesjones.com/eoh.htm (accessed 8 April 2010)

Fukuyama, Francis, *The End of History and the Last Man* (London: Hamilton, 1992).

Gibb, H.A.R., *Modern Trends in Islam* (first edition Chicago: Chicago University Press, 1947: reprinted, New York: Octagon Books, 1975).

Gibb, Sir Hamilton and Harold Bowen, *Islamic Society and the West: A Study of the Impact of Western Civilization on Moslem Culture in the Near East* (London: Oxford University Press, 1950).

Gibbon, Edward, *The History of the Decline and Fall of the Roman Empire* (London: T. Cadell, 1837).

Goody, Jack, 'Europe and Islam', in G. Delanty (ed.), *Europe and Asia beyond East and West* (London: Routledge, 2006), pp. 138–147.

Goody, Jack, *Renaissances: The One or the Many?* (Cambridge: Cambridge University Press, 2009).

Gopal, Priyamvada, 'The Story Peddled by Imperial Apologists is a Poisonous Fairytale', *Guardian* (London), 28 June 2006.

Grewal, J.S., *Muslim Rule in India* (Calcutta: Oxford University Press, 1970).
Hale J.R., (ed.), *The Evolution of British Historiography: From Bacon to Namier* (Cleveland: The World Publishing Company, 1964).
Hamilton, Alistair, *William Bedwell, the Arabist 1563–1732* (Leiden: E.J. Brill, 1985).
Herman, Arthur, *The Scottish Enlightenment: The Scots' Invention of the Modern World* (London: Fourth Estate Limited, 2003).
Hobson, J.A., *Imperialism: A Study* (London: James Nisbett & Co., 1902).
Hobson, John M., 'Revealing the Cosmopolitan Side of Oriental Europe: The Eastern Origins of European Civilization', in G. Delanty (ed.), *Europe and Asia beyond East and West* (London: Routledge, 2006), pp. 107–119.
Hodivala, S.H., *Studies in Indo-Muslim History: Critical Commentary on Elliot and Dowson's History of India as told by its own Historians*, 2 vols (Bombay: unknown publishers, 1939–57).
Holt, P.M., 'The Study of Arabic Historians in Seventeenth-Century England: The Background and Work of Edward Pococke', *Bulletin of the School of Oriental and African Studies*, 19, 3 (1957).
Holt, P.M., *A Seventeenth-Century Defender of Islam: Henry Stubbe (1632–76) and His Book* (London: Dr. Williams's Trust, 1972).
Holt, P.M., *Studies in the History of the Near East* (London: Frank Cass, 1973).
Howe, Stephen, 'An Oxford Scot at King Dubya's court: Niall Ferguson's "Colossus"' (22 July 2004) http://www.opendemocracy.net/democracy-americanpower/article_2021.jsp (accessed 8 April 2010).
Huntington, Samuel P., *The Clash of Civilizations and the Remaking of the World Order* (New York: Simon & Schuster, 1998).
Hyam, Ronald, *Britain's Imperial Century, 1815–1914: A Study of Empire and Expansion* (London: Macmillan, 1976).
Irwin, Robert, *For Lust of Knowing: The Orientalists and their Enemies* (Harmondsworth: Penguin Books, 2007).
Israel, Jonathan I., *Radical Enlightenment: Philosophy and the Making of Modernity, 1650–1750* (Oxford: Oxford University Press, 2001).
Jacob, James R., *Henry Stubbe, Radical Protestantism and the Early Enlightenment* (Cambridge: Cambridge University Press, 2002).
Jardine, Lisa, *Worldly Goods: A New History of the Renaissance* (London & Basingstoke: Macmillan, 1997).
Jardine, L. and J. Brotton, *Global Interests: Renaissance Art between East and West* (London: Reaktion Books, 2000).
Jones, William, *The Letters of Sir William Jones*, vol. II (Oxford: Clarendon, 1970).
Kernaghan, Jennifer, 'Lord Cromer as Orientalist and Social Engineer in Egypt, 1882–1907', unpublished MA thesis, University of British Columbia, 1993.
Khairallah, Shereen, 'Arabic Studies in England in the Late Seventeenth and Early Eighteenth Centuries', unpublished PhD thesis, London, School of Oriental and African Studies, 1972.
Lane, Edward William, *An Account of the Manners and Customs of the modern Egyptians*, 5th edn (London: John Murray, 1860).
Lewis, Bernard, 'Communism and Islam', *International Affairs* 30, 1 (1954).
Lewis, Bernard, 'The Muslim Discovery of Europe', *Bulletin of the School of Oriental and African Studies*, 20, 1/3, Studies in Honour of Sir Ralph Turner, Director of the School of Oriental and. African Studies, 1937–57 (1957).
Lewis, Bernard, *Islam in History: Ideas, Men and Events in the Middle East* (London: Alcove Press, 1973).

Lewis, Bernard, 'The Question of Orientalism', *The New York Review of Books*, 29, 11 (24 June 1982).

Lewis, Bernard, *The Muslim Discovery of Europe* (London: Weidenfeld & Nicolson, 1982).

Lewis, Bernard, 'The Roots of Muslim Rage', *Atlantic Monthly*, September 1990, http://www.theatlantic.com/doc/199009/muslim-rage (accessed 8 April 2010).

Lewis, Bernard, *Islam and the West* (Oxford: Oxford University Press, 1993).

Lewis, Bernard, *From Babel to Dragomans: Interpreting the Middle East* (London: Phoenix, 2004).

Lockman, Zachary, *Contending Visions of the Middle East: The History and Politics of Orientalism* (Cambridge: Cambridge University Press, 2004).

MacKenzie, John M., *Orientalism: History, Theory and the Arts* (Manchester: Manchester University Press, 1995).

Maine, Henry, *Ancient Law: Its Connection with the Early History of Society, and Its Relations to Modern Ideas* (London; John Murray, 1861).

Majeed, Javed, *Ungoverned Imaginings: James Mill's* The History of British India and Orientalism (Oxford: Clarendon Press, 1992).

Malcolm, John, *The history of Persia, from the most early period to the present time* (London: John Murray, 1815).

Margoliouth, David Samuel, *Mohammed and the Rise of Islam*, (London: G.P. Putnam's Sons, 1905).

Matar, Nabil, *Islam in Britain 1558–1685* (Cambridge: Cambridge University Press, 1998).

Matar, Nabil (ed.), *In the Lands of the Christians: Arabic Travel Writing in the Seventeenth Century* (London: Routledge, 2003).

Matar, Nabil, 'Arab Views of Europeans, 1758–1727: The Western Mediterranean', in Gerald Maclean (ed.), *Re-Orienting the Renaissance: Cultural Exchanges with the East* (London: Palgrave Macmillan, 2005).

Miliband, David, 'The Democratic Imperative', Aung San Suu Kyi Lecture, St Hugh's College, Oxford, 12 February 2008, http://www.davidmiliband.info/speeches/speeches_08_02.htm (accessed 8 April 2010).

Milner, Alfred, *England in Egypt* (London: Edward Arnold, 1893).

Muir, W., *Life of Mahomet*, vol. 4 (London: Smith, Elder, 1861).

Mukherjee, S.N., *Sir William Jones: A Study in Eighteenth Century British Attitudes to India* (Cambridge: Cambridge University Press, 1968).

Nash, Geoffrey, *From Empire to Orient: Travellers to the Middle East, 1830–1926* (London: I.B. Tauris, 2005).

Ockley, Simon, *The History of the Saracens*, 6th edn (London: Henry G. Bohn, 1857).

'Orientalism: An Exchange', *The New York Review of Books*, 29, 13 (29 August 1982), https://www.nybooks.com/articles/6517 (accessed 8 April 2010).

Owen, Roger, 'The Middle East in the Eighteenth Century – an "Islamic" Society in Decline? A Critique of Gibb and Bowen's Islamic Society and the West', *Review of Middle East Studies*, 1 (1975).

Pailin, David A., *Attitudes to Other Religions: Comparative Religion in Seventeenth- and Eighteenth-Century Britain* (Manchester: Manchester University Press, 1984).

Perham, Margery, *Colonial Sequence, 1930–1949: A Chronological Commentary upon British Colonial Policy especially in Africa* (London: Methuen & Co., 1967).

Pieterse, Jan Nederveen, 'Oriental Globalization: Past and Present', and John M. Hobson, 'Revealing the Cosmopolitan Side of Oriental Europe: The Eastern Origins of European Civilization', in G. Delanty (ed.), *Europe and Asia beyond East and West* (London: Routledge, 2006), pp. 61–73.

Pocock, J.G.A., *Barbarism and Religion: The Enlightenments of Edward Gibbon, 1737–1764*, vol. 1 (Cambridge: Cambridge University Press, 1999).

Poole, Sophia, *The Englishwoman in Egypt: Letters from Cairo Written during a Residence there in 1842–1846*, edited by Azza Kararah (Cairo: The American University in Cairo, 2003).

Powell, Jonathan, 'Why the West Must not Fear to Intervene', *Observer*, 18 November 2007, http://www.guardian.co.uk/commentisfree/2007/nov/18/comment.foreignpolicy (accessed 8 April 2010).

Rashid, Abdur, 'The Treatment of History by Muslim Historians in Mughal Official and Biographical Works', in C.H. Philips (ed.), *Historians of India, Pakistan and Ceylon* (Oxford: Oxford University Press, 1961).

Robertson, W., *An Historical Disquisition concerning the Knowledge which the Ancient had of India* (London: printed for A. Strahan [and 2 others], 1791).

Robinson, Francis, 'Islamic Reform and Modernities in South Asia', *Modern Asian Studies*, 42, 2/3 (2008).

Rycaut, Paul, *The Present State of the Ottoman Empire* (London: John Starkey and Henry Brome, 1668: reprint, Westmead: Gregg International Publishers, 1972).

Said, Edward W., *Orientalism: Western Conceptions of the Orient* (Harmondsworth: Penguin Books, 1978: 1995 edition).

Sale, George, *The Koran, commonly called the Alcoran of Mohammed*, vol. I (London: printed for L. Hawes, W. Clarke, and R. Collins; and T. Wilcox, 1764).

Saul, John S.,'"Humanitarian Imperialism": Ferguson, Ignatieff and the Political Science of Good Empire', http://www.marxsite.com/Humanitarian%20Imperialism.htm (accessed 8 April 2010).

Seeley, J.R., *The Expansion of England: Two Courses of Lectures* (London: Macmillan, 1883). Edited and with an introduction by John Gross (London: University of Chicago Press, 1971).

Sen, Amartya, 'Imperial Illusions: India, Britain, and the Wrong Lessons', *The New Republic*, 31 December 2007.

Skrine, Francis Henry Bennett, *Life of Sir William Wilson Hunter, K.C.S.I.* (London: Longmans & Co., 1901), pp. 468–469.

Smith, V.A., *The Oxford History of India* (Oxford, Clarendon Press, 1919).

Stein, M.A., 'Thomas Walker Arnold', *Proceedings of the British Academy*, XVI (1930).

Strachey, Lytton, *Eminent Victorians* (London: Chatto & Windus, 1918).

Stubbe, Henry, *An Account of the Rise and Progress of Mahometanism – with the Life of Mahomet. And a vindication of him and his religion from the calumnies of the Christians*) (London: Luzac & Co., 1911).

Taylor, A.J.P., *The Trouble Makers: Dissent over Foreign Policy, 1792–1939* (London: Hamish Hamilton, 1957).

Teignmouth, John Shore (ed.), *Memoirs of the Life, Writings and Correspondence of Sir William Jones* (London: J. Hatchard, 1806).

Teignmouth, Lord (ed.), *The Works of Sir William Jones*, vol. I (London: John Stockdale, 1807).

Thompson, Edward and Garratt, G.T., *Rise and Fulfilment of the British Rule in India* (London: Macmillan & Co., 1934).

Thompson, Jason, 'Edward William Lane', *Egypt, Journal of the American Research Center in Egypt*, 34 (1997).

Toomer, G.J., *Eastern Wisedome and Learning: The Study of Arabic in Seventeenth-Century England* (Oxford: Clarendon Press, 1996).

Utvik, B.O., 'The Modernizing Force of Islamism', in J.L. Esposito and F. Burgat (eds), *Modernizing Islam: Religion in the Public Sphere in the Middle East and Europe* (London: Hurst, 2003).

Watt, Katherine, 'Thomas Walker Arnold and the Re-Evaluation of Islam, 1864–1930', *Modern Asian Studies*, 36, 1 (February 2002).

Watt, W. Montgomery, 'Carlyle and Muhammad', *Hibbert Journal*, vol. 53 (1954–55).

Wittfogel, Karl A., *Oriental Despotism: A Comparative Study of Total Power* (New Haven: Yale University Press, 1957).

Woolf, Leonard, *Imperialism and Civilization*, (London: L. & V. Woolf, 1936).

Yapp. M.E., 'Two British Historians of Persia', in Bernard Lewis and P.M. Holt (eds), *Historians of the Middle East* (Oxford: Oxford University Press, 1962).

2 Can the (sub)altern resist?

A dialogue between Foucault and Said

Arshin Adib-Moghaddam

> Resistance comes First.
>
> Michel Foucault

Where there is power, there is resistance. This phrase encapsulates the dialectic that Michel Foucault battled with almost throughout his scholarly life. In *Orientalism*, Edward Said took seriously Foucault's ideas about the way knowledge is implicated in power. Yet, ultimately he did not fully appreciate that for Foucault power cannot be total. When Said argues that through 'Orientalism as a discourse' European culture not only 'manages' the Orient but 'produces' it, he overemphasises the productive force of power at the expense of the creative force of resistance. According to Said, Orientalism does not only constitute a particular discourse, it produces the Orient 'politically, sociologically, militarily, ideologically, scientifically, and imaginatively during the post-Enlightenment period'.[1] For both Orientals and Europeans, then, there is no escaping the fictional world established by the Orientalist corpus. It follows, for Said, that Orientalism has muted the 'East' intellectually and discursively. The object (the Orient) is ostracised from the discourse of Orientalism; it does not speak, it is not present within its articulation. Without the power to speak, the '(sub)altern' remains trapped in a self-fulfilling prophecy.

It is this strategy of marginalisation through disciplinary power regimes that has been targeted by post-colonial theorists and 'subaltern studies', and rightly so.[2] But in the following discussion I intend to question and theoretically advance a very specific methodical premise that undergirds the argument of *Orientalism* in particular and post-colonial approaches in general. I argue that overemphasising the power of the 'west', or a discourse such as 'Orientalism', does not only threaten to contribute to muting the 'other', it confuses the way resistance affects power. To be more precise: A gigantic constellation such as Orientalism – even the 'west' for which it functions – can never really shut down modes of resistance or counter-discourses. In earlier reflections on this, I have gone as far as to say that Said's overemphasis on 'western' representations of the 'east' threatens to negate resistance to Orientalism.[3] Ultimately, Said misunderstands Foucault when, years after the publication of *Orientalism*, he adheres to the common perspective that Foucault ascribes 'undifferentiated power' to the disciplinary regime of modern society. 'With this profoundly pessimistic view', Said criticises him,

> went also a singular lack of interest in the force of effective resistance to it, in choosing particular sites of intensity, choices which, we see from the evidence on all sides, always exist and are often successful in impeding, if not actually stopping, the progress of tyrannical power.[4]

Immediately, one can return the critique and point to Said's own bias towards the power of the 'west' which he highlights almost exclusively not only in *Orientalism*, but also in *Covering Islam* and his extensive writings on Palestine. But the fact that Said does not spend much of his talent on the 'other' as an agent of history has already been sufficiently addressed. What I am rather more interested in, and what has remained marginal in the post-colonial literature, is his methodical confusion about the dialectic between power and resistance that was a part of Foucault's method throughout his career. Said undervalued, like many other critics of Foucault, that discourses and their corresponding knowledge–power dynamics cannot be possessed, organised or shut down by one social agent (e.g. individuals, institutions or disciplines). They are, in this sense, gliding phenomena; heterogeneous, rather than homogeneous, capillary rather than hierarchical, progressive rather than conservative. Said was mistaken to infer that a discursive constellation such as Orientalism can be all encompassing. Foucault draws attention to the diffusion of power, its 'relayed' locality within society, the individual and our psychological and physical existence. He clarified this view as early as in 1976 in his lectures at the Collège de France:

> Do not regard power as a phenomenon of mass and homogenous domination – the domination of one individual over others, of one group over others, or of one class over others; keep it clearly in mind that unless we are looking at it from a great height and from a very great distance, power is not something that is divided between those who have it and hold it exclusively, and those who do not have it and are subject to it. Power must, I think, be analysed as something that circulates, or rather as something that functions only when it is part of a chain. It is never localised here or there, it is never in the hands of some, and it is never appropriated in the way that wealth or a commodity can be appropriated. Power functions. Power is exercised through networks, and individuals do not simply circulate in those networks; they are in a position to both submit to and exercise this power.[5]

In the way Said uses and, at the latter stages of his career, then criticises Foucault, he ignores a range of methodical nuances. True, if there is one central theme recurring in the different phases of Foucault's scholarly life, it is his emphasis on the birth of a series of disciplinary strategies which he deems central to the making of western modernity and its modern subject. According to Foucault, a genealogy of these 'disciplines' reveals societal norms that were slowly perfected, institutionalised and enforced through a network of prisons, clinics, asylums, medical organisations, educational routines, the penal system and jurisprudential practices. 'Each society has its regime of truth, its "general politics" of truth', Foucault famously stated in an interview in June 1976. It is these colossal regimes that determine 'the types of discourse [society] accepts and makes function as true; the mechanisms and instances that enable one to distinguish true and false statements; the means by which each is sanctioned; the techniques and procedures accorded value in the acquisition of truth; the status of those who are charged with saying what counts as true.'[6] In other words, discourses (such as Orientalism) not only represent a particular issue, they do not only produce meaningful knowledge about it which in turn affects social and political practices, they are a part of the way power operates, reveals itself and is contested. Once a particular discourse sustains its effectiveness via disciplinary constellations and in practice, it can be conceptualised as a regime of truth.[7]

Ultimately then, such regimes appear as particularly overbearing power constellations. But where does that leave the power to resist? In the same interview mentioned above, Foucault seems to indicate that resistance remains viable: 'The essential political problem for the intellectual is not to criticise the ideological contents supposedly linked to science, or to ensure that his own scientific practice is accompanied by a correct ideology,'[8] he stresses at the end of the interview. The political task is to ascertain the 'possibility of constituting a new politics of truth'. It is not a matter of 'changing people's consciousness – or what's in their heads', but to tackle the 'political, economic, institutional regime of the production of truth'.[9] The main target, in other words, must be the political economy of truth making, for it is here where the subject is moulded in accordance with the reigning norms of society. The battle is to be directed against the disciplinary systems that feed into that process of wilful distortion, for instance by giving a voice to the powerless.[10]

Between the possibility to resist and the disciplinary power governing the individual, Foucault places a vast, at times enigmatically paradoxical space that needs to be overcome in order to make possible the power of the powerless. It is here where we can locate one of the nuances that were not fully appreciated in Said's interpretation of Foucault. In order to flesh them out, I investigate what I call Foucault's 'power–resistance dialectic', emancipating his statement that resistance is immanent to power from the charge that it negates individual agency. This goes to the heart of the famous statement of Foucault – 'where there is power, there is resistance, and yet, or rather consequently, this resistance is never in the position of exteriority in relation to power' – exactly calibrating the 'dimension' in which he places the forces of resistance that constantly battle against the imposition of institutionalised regimes of truth (Orientalism included). I intend to pursue this argument in two principal ways: I will start by reinterpreting the power–resistance dialectic of Foucault in close liaison with the recent literature on the topic. Some of the material marshalled has been published in English and French after his death in 1984 and has remained untapped since then. In a second step, I will shift the focus on his writings on the revolution in Iran. Via a thorough reading of those articles it is possible to achieve a better understanding of his approach to power and resistance. As such, this second part attempts to corroborate my suggestion that Foucault affirms political agency in general and the possibility of radical resistance in particular. This implies that Said misunderstood the reciprocal battles at the root of the power–resistance dialectic that is under focus here.

Power to resist, or resistance to power?

Foucault was a reluctant, yet subliminal dialectician; his concepts cannot be read in isolation from each other or within strict and uni-directional action–reaction schemata.[11] This is particularly true when it comes to the issue of 'agency', which poses a problem to Foucault in a very personal manner and permeates, as a central dilemma, the main narratives holding together the structure of *The Order of Things*: 'What must I be', Foucault asks here, 'I who think and who am my thought, in order to be what I do not think, in order for my thought to be what I am not?'[12] This dilemma, elicited by the 'outside' pressures on the making of our 'self', links up with several central questions that Foucault grappled with throughout his scholarly life: Is it possible to think in detachment from the outside world? Are we at liberty to constitute our 'self' in independence? Of course, the answers to these questions indicate the viability of resistance, for if disciplinary regimes such as Orientalism penetrate all the way down to an individual's subjective constitution, how can we act against it and defy it?

Critics of Foucault would point to his oeuvre and argue that in his writings, as opposed to his projects as an activist, he focuses almost exclusively on the strategies that mould us into subjects of power. As Said argued: For Foucault power seems 'irresistible and unstoppable'.[13] Foucault did not only describe how disciplinary constellations affect our thinking, the argument goes, but he suggests that power is both physical and metaphysical; it acts on the body *and* the cognition of the subject. 'Foucault seems sometimes on the verge of depriving us of a vocabulary in which to conceptualise the nature and meaning of those periodic refusals of control that, just as much as the imposition of control, mark the course of human history,' one feminist author complains.[14] 'From Foucault's perspective', another critic notes, 'the human sciences are a major force in the disastrous triumph of Enlightenment thinking, and the panoptical scientific observer is a salient expression of the subject-centred putatively universal reason which that thinking promotes.'[15] It is true that Foucault spilled most of his ink on alerting society about the overbearingly intrusive, carefully networked impact of disciplinary techniques that are deployed in order to contain any meaningful expression of resistance. In terms of his empirical research and theoretical treatise, Foucault prioritised disciplinary power over resistance, to the detriment of a better theory of political agency. But to conclude from this, that Foucauldian 'postmodernism' has contributed to the denial of 'both agency and causal explanations of sociocultural change' is problematic.[16] Foucault may have been more concerned with 'what is' than with 'what could be', but his theory of power and resistance does not suffocate the viability of radical dissidence. To say, as Said does, that Foucault is caught up in a paradox, that his 'imagination of power was by his analysis of power to reveal its injustice and cruelty, but by his theorisation to let it go on more or less unchecked',[17] only reveals one part of the dialectic. Criticism like this does not appreciate the theoretical thrust that Foucault ascribes to modes of resistance.

A paper authored by Gilles Deleuze provides a useful start to unravelling that accusation further. In this paper, Deleuze argues that there is no real rupture between the later and early Foucault, that he continuously theorised the prospects of change, *viz.* the viability of resistance to power. This is particularly apparent, according to Deleuze, in the way Foucault conceptualises the relationship between the subject and the outside world, which creates its own dialectically constituted dimension in which the self can act. Within this dimension, which must be treated as a theoretical category, the subject resists disciplinary power, not entirely autarkic from the political economy of knowledge, but autonomous enough to enact radical change. Deleuze is alluding exactly to the dialectics (relationships or interdependencies) of self and other, subject and object, power and resistance to make this point: 'If the outside is a relationship, the absolute of relationships,' he notes, 'then the inside is also a relationship, the relationship becoming subject.'[18] This subject has access to a dialectically constituted 'dimension' in which a form of agency can be fostered. 'If force receives a dual power from the outside, the power to affect (other forces) and to be affected (by other forces), how could there not ensue a relationship between force and itself?' It is here, Deleuze suggests, that Foucault places the 'element of "resistance."'[19] Deleuze concedes that the 'subject is always constituted, the product of a subjectivication'. But he maintains at the same time that the subject 'appears in a dimension that opposes all stratification or codification. ... [T]he relationship to the self *does not let itself be aligned* according to the concrete forms of power or be subsumed in an abstract diagrammatic function.'[20] Rather, the contrary. The self escapes into another, presumably 'third' dimension in which agency is enacted. In the words of Deleuze: 'It is as if the relationships of the outside folded to make a double [*doublure*] and allow a relationship to the self to arise that develops according to a new dimension.'[21]

Deleuze reverts to Foucault's analysis of the historical formation of the ancient Greek concept of *Enkrateia* to enunciate this fundamental dynamic further. According to Foucault, *Enkrateia* is 'a power exercised over oneself *in* the power one exercises over others'.[22] Deleuze adds that Foucault's understanding of *Enkrateia* presupposes the possibility of triumph over the subjugated self, for 'how could one claim to govern others if one could not govern oneself?'[23] From this perspective, Foucault must have accepted the viability of agency, the possibility to escape formalised forms of power that the ancient Greeks invented. 'Foucault's work was created by inventing a topology that actively puts the inside and outside in contact on the stratified formations of history,' Deleuze explains further. 'It is up to the strata to produce layers that show and tell something new; but it is also up to the relationship of the outside to call the powers in place into question, and it is up to the relationship with the self to inspire new modes of subjectivisation.'[24] It is along this dialectical *tabula rasa* that the possibility 'to show and tell something new' can reveal itself. Fold a piece of paper and you will see. The crease is a surface effect of the 'inside' and the 'outside' and it holds together both. Multiply this piece of paper and the creases infinitesimally in order to simulate the complexity of human history and the power–resistance dialectics it has provoked, and you will get an impression of the structure that Foucault imagines. It is within that topological relationship between inside and outside, subject and object, self and other, resistance and power, in other words, where the contested space in which agency unfolds itself can be localised.

There is a second pathway along which we can traverse the power–resistance dialectic under focus here. It has been said that Foucault places resistance within power. That means that power and resistance are in a constant and 'violent' battle with each other. In that sense the power of Orientalism would always also provoke resistance. Consequently, a history of Orientalism must always also be interrupted by a history of counter-discourses to it. There is no suggestion in Foucault's variant conceptualisation of this dialectical struggle that power and resistance are somehow static or oppositional forces that retain their properties when they intermingle. Neither is there a clearly demarcated inside and outside to this dialectic, where we could neatly locate either power or resistance. Rather, as I have tried to demonstrate via Deleuze, resistance is a surface effect of a dialectic between indigenous forces and exogenous impingement. 'The relationship to self is homologous to the relationship with the outside and all the contents of the inside are in relation with the outside.'[25] Applied to the power–resistance dialectic under focus here, this means that Foucault's 'genealogies of power' are implicated in 'genealogies of resistance'.[26] Recent scholarship on this issue supports this view. It is quite literally 'axiomatic that where power goes in Foucault, there is resistance as well.'[27] If resistance goes along with power, and if [p]ower is everywhere; not because it embraces everything, but because it comes from everywhere',[28] as Foucault adamantly maintains, then it must follow – quite logically – that resistance is contemporaneous with power. In short: If power is promiscuous, if the power of Orientalism is acutely penetrative as Said suggests, resistance to it must be as well.

So the charge, articulated by Said and others including Anthony Giddens, Jürgen Habermas and Michael Walzer, that Foucault sides with the non-subjective aspects of power, rather than with individual intentionality, is problematic because it is based on the false premise that power and resistance are detachable or located in different 'dimensions'.[29] The agency that unfolds itself in the dialectic between power and resistance is not a simple replication of the dialectic itself, neither is it a safe place, a Hegelian synthesis. Rather, it is an effect of power acting on resistance, which has swerved or departed from its original purpose to constrain the individual, to arrive in another dimension which opens up possibilities of agency that do not merely react to the original incentive of power, but effectively expand the boundaries of what is intentionally achievable. Agency reveals itself as a surface effect of a fundamental action–action dynamic. Foucault is very clear about this. 'When one defines the exercise of power as a mode of action upon the actions of others', he emphasises,

> when one characterises these actions as the government of men by other men … one includes an important element: freedom. Power is exercised

> only over free subjects, and only insofar as they are 'free.' By this we mean individual or collective subjects who are faced with a field of possibilities in which several kinds of conduct, several ways of reacting and modes of behaviour are available. ... Consequently there is not a face-to-face confrontation of power and freedom as mutually exclusive facts (freedom disappearing everywhere power is exercised), but a much more complicated interplay. In this game, freedom may well appear as the condition for the exercise of power (at the same time its precondition, since freedom must exist for power to be exerted, and also its permanent support, since without the possibility of recalcitrance power would be equivalent to a physical determination).[30]

For this action–action dynamic to make sense, freedom, including the viability to resist, must come first. Deleuze interprets this to mean that 'a diagram of forces presents, alongside the singularities of power corresponding to its relationships, singularities of resistance, "points, nodes, foci" that in turn act on the strata in order to make change possible'. He even goes one step further and argues that in Foucault the 'last word in the theory of power is that resistance comes first since it has a direct relationship with the outside. Thus a social field resists more than it strategizes and the thought of the outside is a thought of resistance (*The Will to Knowledge*).'[31] Consequently, a fundamental matrix is formed: Resistance precedes power ↔ resistance is a freedom that power acts upon ↔ resistance is a form of power. In other words, resistance is not only viable; it is a form of agency which necessarily exists as a part of the condition of humanity, *viz*. freedom. It is in this sense that the possibility of power *must* imply the possibility of resistance. In the words of Foucault:

> The power relationship and freedom's refusal to submit cannot therefore be separated. The crucial problem of power is not that of voluntary servitude (how could we seek to be slaves?). At the very heart of the power relationship, and constantly provoking it, are the recalcitrance of the will and the intransigence of freedom. Rather than speaking of an essential antagonism, it would be better to speak of an 'agonism' – of a relationship which is at the same time mutual incitement and struggle; less of a face-to-face confrontation that paralyzes both sides than a permanent provocation.[32]

In a well-argued article, Kevin Jon Heller attributes the widespread misinterpretation of Foucault's understanding of power to the inability of many scholars to divorce themselves from mainstream notions of power as uni-directional or inherently repressive.[33] This hierarchical effect of power seems to be what Said had in mind when he argues that Orientalism does not only create knowledge but 'reality' all the way down to the very constitution of the 'Oriental' himself. Heller points out that for Foucault power could be both repressive and productive, that it 'is a *facility* not a *thing*'.[34] His argument can be linked to Gayatri Spivak's reading of Foucault's understanding of power and the problems of translating it into English. Spivak rightly points out that *pouvoir* in French does not only (or even primarily) refer to 'repression' and 'submission' but that in its various conjugations it also refers to a form of '"can-do ness"',[35] that it relates to verbs such as 'to enable' and 'to make possible'. From this perspective, power is no longer equated with repression. Rather, power 'traverses and produces things, it induces pleasure, forms knowledge, produces discourse. It needs to be considered as a productive network that runs through the whole social body, much more than as a negative instance whose function is repression.'[36]

Foucault does not decisively answer the question whether or not such productive notions of power can be equated with resistance and what then the difference between resistance and power would be. But he does give us some clues about the battles at the root of the power–resistance dialectic. Given that Foucault believes that resistance precedes power, it must follow that power, at least in its 'first' appearance, is active, that it acts upon something pre-existing, *viz.* resistance, which is both necessary and sufficient for his theory of power to work. '[R] esistance or the possibility of resistance', it is argued in the recent secondary literature on this issue, 'constitutes the corner stone of the very definition of the "power relation", which is importantly *not* simply a relation of domination'. Rather, resistance 'comes first quite literally, resistance is what power works *on* and *through*'.[37] This does not mean that power is reactive (as much as it does not mean that resistance is reactive of course). It simply means that power and resistance are exactly coextensive. Again: Where there is power there *must be* resistance. Consequently, when Said used Foucault in order to express the discursive density of Orientalism, he should have dispersed his argument with the period before and after the colonial interlude and the modes of resistance during its heydays.

It should be noted in parenthesis that resistance is not to be thought of as a 'state of nature', or a form of primordial authenticity. Rather, resistance is not realised without power acting upon it. Power 'actualises' resistance; 'its character *as* resistance derives from its opposition to some power relation'. This should not be considered a mere semantic necessity. Rather, 'it is a fact about the ontological constitution of resistance. Without power intervening upon me, I am simply doing, not resisting.'[38] Again, this means that the power of Orientalism must provoke a powerful resistance discourse which needs to be captured analytically exactly because of the all-encompassing effects Said ascribes to the Orientalist regime. It is this inevitability of the continuous provocation of resistance that explains the rather nonchalant attitude that Foucault seemed to have towards power, as if he wanted us to ignore it altogether, forcing us to focus on the viability of resistance instead (and what a liberating utopia would that be!).[39] Don't worry about power, he seemed to say. The more powerful a particular discourse, the more intricate resistance to it: Where there is power, there must be resistance, power is not unidirectional, it cannot be monopolised, it is not a property, Orientalism can't be all encompassing, the Orient continuously resisted to be represented. Where there is reification of any powerful discourse, then, the power to narrate, to create reality, to construct meaning, to engineer Orientalism as a disciplinary regime, there must be – quite automatically – 'de-reification', the power to counter-act, to create a dissident culture.

Foucault and (sub)altern agency

Even if we allow for the previous section to counter accusations that the interest of Foucault 'in domination was critical but not finally as contestatory or as oppositional as on the surface it seems to be' as Said argues,[40] there must be something in the recurrent criticism that lends credence to such arguments against him, for even scholars sympathetic to his ideas such as Barry Smart regret that Foucault was quick to criticise Marxists for their 'loose theory' of class struggle, while 'his own conceptions of resistance, opposition and struggle remain virtually as enigmatic'.[41] It seems that indeterminacy is consciously inscribed in Foucault's theory of power and resistance exactly because of his conviction that the 'local intellectual' has to fight disciplinary power constellations not from an entrenched position or from a moral angle, but from the perspective of the 'genealogist' who is embroiled in a continuous fight against reified claims to 'truth' and 'reality'. 'I think to imagine another system', Foucault explicitly said, 'is to extend our participation in the present system.'[42] Here, the problem is not so much that Foucault attempts to approximate a 'non-position'. The problem is that his philosophy of resistance, much like the marginalisation of modes of resistance to Orientalism in the scholarship of Said, is not placed on a firm empirical footing in order to be conceptually commensurate with his detailed accounts of disciplinary regimes of truth. This is certainly the case up until 1978, when Foucault started to refer to rather more concrete forms of resistance in his lectures at the Collège de France. It is no coincidence that he moved to extrapolate more explicit historical examples during this period. He was not only responding to voices that criticised the near-total absence of genealogies of resistance in his earlier writings, but also to political developments in which he invested as an intellectual. Consequently, one finds in these lectures reference to the 'dissident' movement of the Soviet Union, Poland and Czechoslovakia which Foucault supported during that time and up until his death in 1984.[43] '"[D]issidence" in the East and the Soviet Union,' he pointed out during his lecture on 1 March 1978, 'really does designate a complex form of resistance and refusal.'[44] During that lecture, Foucault referred to the Soviet novelist, playwright and exiled dissident Aleksandr Solzhenitsyn, whose *Gulag Archipelago* had a profound influence on his views on dissident activity, in order to contextualise his *discursus* on the resistance movement in the Communist 'East':

> [T]he political struggles that we put together under the name of dissidence, certainly have an essential, fundamental dimension that is refusal of this form of being conducted. 'We do not want this salvation, we do not wish to be saved by these people and by these means.' … It is Solzhenitsyn. 'We do not wish to obey these people. We do not want this system where even those who command have to obey out of terror. We do not want this pastoral system of obedience. We do not want this truth. We do not want to be held in this system of truth. We do not want to be held in this system of observation and endless examination that continually judges us, tells us what we are in the core of ourselves, healthy or sick, mad or not mad, and so on.' So we can say that this word dissidence really does cover a struggle … [45]

Resistance is aligned here more firmly with the action–action dynamic that was covered in the first part of this discussion. (Pastoral) power (or conduct) acts upon the individual (or a community), actualising specific forms of resistance (dissidence). If power is the 'conduct of conducts and a management of possibilities',[46] resistance is a form of 'counter-conduct':

> [M]aybe this word 'counter-conduct' enables us to avoid a certain substantification [or hero worship] allowed by the word 'dissidence.' … [B]y using the word counter-conduct, and so without having to give a sacred status to this or that person as a dissident, we can no doubt analyse the components in the way in which someone actually acts in the very general field of politics or in the very general field of power relations; it makes it possible to pick out the dimension or component of counter-conduct that may well be found in fact in delinquents, mad people, and patients.[47]

Foucault's struggle to come to terms with forms of resistance in these years unfolded in various, theoretically diffuse, yet politically immediate and pertinent ways. So it came at an opportune moment that, in September 1978, he was commissioned by the Italian *Corriere della Serra* to embark on a journey to Iran in order to cover the revolution gripping the country. In the most recent appraisal of this episode of his life, his long-term companion, Paule Veyne, notes that Foucault was genuinely captivated by the events, that 'the strong personality of Khomeini fascinated him' and that 'deep down, he had been shaken by the heroism of the Iranian crowds as they stood up to the police and the army'.[48] Clearly impressed by what he saw, Foucault met with the leader of the revolution, Ayatollah Khomeini, who was in exile in Neauphle-le Château in France, before he revisited Iran at the height of the revolutionary fervour in November 1978. The 'enthusiasm' for the revolution that Foucault displayed during this period may explain why he spent a considerable amount of energy and time in reporting from Iran and in trying to understand what was happening in the country during that winter of 1978–1979.[49]

The difference was not only quantitative, however. Foucault's engagement with the revolution in Iran had distinct theoretical and empirical connotations. As indicated, it came during a period when he was developing a rather more elaborated approach to forms of resistance or 'counter-conducts'. From the perspective of Foucault, the unfolding revolution in Iran exemplified a particularly 'raw' event, the birth of an idea that may reveal a mechanism for resistance on a grand scale. 'There are more ideas on earth than intellectuals imagine', he wrote in *Corriere della Sera* in November 1978. 'We have to be there at the birth of ideas, the bursting outward of their force.'[50] There is no doubt that Foucault thought that he was witnessing exactly that, what he termed a 'political spirituality' long lost in the 'West'. Where else, then, in this, 'the first great insurrection against the planetary system, the most mad and the most modern form of revolt',[51] could Foucault find empirical substance for his inquiries into new forms of power and counter-power which could constitute the beginnings of what one observer of his termed a 'vitalist theory of resistance'?[52]

It is too far-fetched to discern major flaws in Foucault's overall thinking from his writings on Iran – for instance what Afary and Anderson term his problematic 'anti-modern' and 'anti-Enlightenment' stance.[53] Foucault can be faulted for not engaging more deeply with the history of Iran and Islam, but it should be noted in the same breath that he repeatedly stressed his role as an outsider, a European, a Westerner, a 'neophyte'[54] who is in a 'poor position to give advice to the Iranians',[55] someone who tried to understand those demonstrators who 'protested and were killed in Iran while shouting "Islamic government"'.[56] I don't think he tried to pose as an 'Iran expert' or 'Orientalist', as Afary and Anderson seem to imply.[57] Rather, he was genuinely trying to comprehend, as a self-conscious outsider with a Eurocentric upbringing, a new subjectification of power with a genealogy that he mistook as taking 'nothing from Western philosophy, from its juridical and revolutionary foundations'.[58] Ultimately, his engagement with Iran did not go beyond a 'tentative application of his more theoretical ideas to a contemporary event in a non-Western society',[59] exactly because Foucault did not qualify some of his theoretical statements with an empirical and historical analysis of the Iranian situation. On that account, Said is right to indict him for his Eurocentrism, which he found reflected in his ignorance towards alternative forms of non-Western ideas, 'as if "history" itself took place only among a group of French and German thinkers'.[60] If there was a 'different way of thinking about social and political organisation', as Foucault claimed rather grandiosely, where was this new thinking genealogically located? What was the discursive function of the mosques in contemporary Iran? What were the difference and what the commonalities between the Islamic revolution that Foucault witnessed and other revolts in Iranian history, i.e. the Tobacco uprising in 1891, the Constitutional Movement in 1906–1911, the nationalisation of the Anglo-Iranian Oil Company by Mohammad Mossadegh in 1951 and the subsequent MI6/CIA-engineered coup d'état which reinstated the dictatorship of the shah? What was Khomeini's concept of 'Islamic governance'? Addressing these questions would have set the signposts of a 'genealogy of resistance' to imperialism and the authoritarianism of the state in Iran, for it was those revolts that contributed to the perfection of anti-disciplinary counter-conducts that inscribed an infrastructure of resistance into the body politic of the country and it was this pre-existing culture of resistance that was readily exploited by the revolutionaries supporting Khomeini. To my mind, the only other time when Foucault talked about a topic without the necessary depth of empirical and historical knowledge to do so comprehensively, was with regard to the paintings of Manet, during a conference he organised in Tunis in 1971.[61]

And yet to conclude that his writings on Iran are without conceptual value stretches the criticism too far. In fact, an analysis of his articles on Iran reveals that Foucault viewed the events – unconsciously perhaps, certainly not explicitly – through the action–action dynamic that he attached to the relationship between power and resistance addressed in the first part of this discussion. There is almost a 'dialectical symmetry' from paragraph to paragraph between fascinating descriptions of resistance on the one side and strategies of power acting upon them on the other. Accordingly, in his first dispatch to *Corriere della Sera*, dated 28 September 1978, Foucault starts by describing the Iranian village of 'Tabas and forty villages' which had been 'annihilated' by a devastating earthquake. After a few introductory sentences he quickly turns his prose to the way the villagers organised themselves 'under the direction of a cleric', how they 'planted a green flag' and how Islam was already 'facing' and opposing the shah. 'Help your brothers, but nothing through the government, nothing for it,' Foucault cites a message that Ayatollah Khomeini had given from exile in Iraq.[62] Foucault then moves his attention to the urban unrests and the demonstrations, before he analyses forms of disciplinary power, in this case those sections of the army and security forces that were mobilised in order to contain the rebellion. The fundamental matrix that I tried to explain in the first part of this discussion reveals itself: Resistance precedes power ↔ resistance is a freedom that power acts upon ↔ resistance is a form of power.

A similar pattern can be discerned from Foucault's second, third and fourth articles, written during October 1978. Once again Foucault starts by describing modes of resistance, his conversations with oppositional activists, the political function of the Friday prayers, the commemoration of the 'martyrs', the imagery of Islam, Shi'ism and the role of Khomeini and intellectuals such as Shariati and their stance against the westernisation of Iran espoused by the shah. In a second dialectical step Foucault focuses on the way power acts upon these diverse and transitory points of resistance, signposted by a short history of the modernisation doctrine underlying the socio-economic policies of the Pahlavi dynasty (1925–1979), the corruption that went with it, the emphasis on Iran's Aryan, pre-Islamic heritage, the dependency on the United States, and the 'iron hand' of the shah's intelligence service, SAVAK. Here, it is striking that Foucault's emphasis on resistance increases in line with the success of the revolt. Hence, up until November, his articles strike a balance between modes of resistance and strategies of disciplinary power acting upon them, with a slight tilt towards the resources of the state, obviously because at that time its coercive power was still functional. The last article observing this balance was published in *Le Nouvel Observateur* in mid-October 1978.

In November, the discourse of Foucault changes in accordance with the success of the revolutionaries. In 'A Revolt with Bare Hands', published on 5 November, 'The Challenge to the Opposition', published on the 7th and 'The Mythical Leader of the Iranian Revolt', published on the 26th, there is a rather more pronounced emphasis on the unfolding revolutionary resistance, on the 'men and women who protest with banners and flowers in Iran',[63] on the regrouping of the opposition behind Ayatollah Khomeini,[64] his 'inflexible refusal to compromise',[65] and the 'collective will' holding the different strata of society together in opposition to the shah.[66] In November, witnessing the slow disintegration of the state, Foucault seems increasingly convinced that Iranians are enacting 'a reality that is very near to them, since they themselves are its active agents'.[67] Thus, Foucault depicts them as engineers of a revolution that was moving 'from the strikes to the demonstrations, from the bazaars to the universities, from the leaflets to the sermons, through shopkeepers, workers, clerics, teachers, and students. For the moment,' he adds at the same time, 'no party, no man, and no political ideology can boast that it represents this movement.'[68] From here, it is only one small step back to *The Will of Knowledge* and Foucault's suggestion that forms of resistance are not only 'a reaction or rebound, forming with respect to the basic domination an underside that is in the end always passive, doomed to perpetual defeat. … [N]either are they a lure or a promise that is of necessity betrayed.' Rather, most of the time 'one is dealing with mobile and transitory points of resistance'.[69]

And there is even more untapped substance in his writings on Iran. What emerges from November onwards is not only a rather more pronounced emphasis on the impingement of the revolutionary movement on the power of the shah. Foucault seems also to remain faithful to his characteristic scepticism as a critical scholar, or what I have described as his anti-synthetic (contra-Hegelian) 'negative dialectics':[70] Resistance precedes power, resistance is a freedom that power acts upon, but resistance also unfolds into a new form of power which commands its own 'regimes of truth'.[71] Foucault sees this coming. He already poses sceptical questions at the end of his articles in October 1978, that is, during the period when he is still striking a balance between descriptions of resistance and the counter-strategies of the state. Then, in mid-November 1978, in a response to an Iranian woman in exile who was opposed to the Islamists who had gathered around Khomeini, Foucault refers to the 'elements that did not seem to [him] to be very reassuring'.[72] In his article on Khomeini published on 26 November he is more defensive and points out that he 'cannot write the history of the future', that he is limiting himself to '*what is happening right now*, because these days nothing is finished, and the dice are still being rolled'.[73]

Notwithstanding this note of caution, Foucault affords a look into the future in his first article after the success of the revolution and Khomeini's return to Iran in January 1979. In this article Foucault starts by presenting a 'summary' of events, how the shah and his allies attempted to quell the revolt, how the struggle between state power and the resistance of the people revealed itself and how the situation has remained unresolved. Conscious that some of the energies of the revolution had already been channelled onto the emerging 'Islamic government', Foucault also refers to the potential of the 'revolutionary model … to overturn the existing political situation in the Middle East and thus the global strategic equilibrium. … [A]s an "Islamic" movement,' Foucault adds, 'it can set the entire region on fire'; it is a 'gigantic powder keg, at the level of hundreds of millions of men. … The Jordan', he concludes dramatically, 'no longer flows very far from Iran.'[74]

With the benefit of hindsight Foucault overestimated the potencies of the revolution, while he underestimated the power of international society to counter anti-systemic movements. Yet it is striking how loyal Foucault remains to his power–resistance model in his writings on Iran. There is even an explicit reference to the phenomenon of the double (*doublure*) that we worked out in the first part of this discussion via Deleuze. From the perspective of Foucault, the Iranian revolutionaries are acting as a 'double'; they had one foot in the politics of the day and another in the intoxicating singularity of the revolutionary movement.[75] 'What has given the Iranian movement its intensity has been a double register,' Foucault says. 'On the one hand, a collective will that has been strongly expressed politically and, on the other hand, the desire for a radical change in ordinary life.'[76] Islam promises to

> change their subjectivity … there was the desire to renew their existence by going back to a spiritual experience that they thought they could find within Shi'ite Islam itself. … Let's say then, that Islam, in that year of 1978, was not the opium of the people precisely because it was the spirit of a world without a spirit.[77]

This is what the collective will, the utopia expressed by those Iranians promises. But history strikes back with a vengeance: resistance unfolds into a new regime of truth. Let us remember that the relationship of the Iranian subject to the outside – history and other structures – folds to make a double. Thus, it allows a relationship to the self to arise that develops according to a new dimension in which agency can be enacted. This is the Islamic Republic which has not been aligned or codified according to the powers that be. But at the same time the post-revolutionary Iranian state is itself constituted: it is exactly a crease in the fabric of Iranian history that is held together by relationships to the utopia of the revolution and those pre- and post-revolutionary structures that have remained a part of the politico-cultural topology of Iran. The revolutionary event, the singularity of its intoxicating promise, was the force that made possible the crease at the top of which the Islamic Republic constituted itself, but it did not erase the historical fabric into which the new Iran was woven. 'Uprisings belong to history,' Foucault writes after the return of Ayatollah Khomeini, 'but in a certain way, they escape it. … [T]hey are thus "outside of history" and in history.'[78] In other words: Forms of resistance and political agency always retain a relationship to the outside (*viz.* history), a 'third dimension' that is neither entirely autonomous, nor entirely constituted by disciplinary power. In order to make that point clearer during his last interview on Iran, Foucault refers to François Furet's distinction between the 'totality of the process of economic and social and economic transformations', which relate to long-term structural factors that exist before and after an event such as a revolution, and the 'specificity of the Revolutionary event'.[79] In Iran, then, Foucault found confirmation of the action–action dynamic that the continuous battle between power and resistance entails. Iranians may have tried to escape history, but history remained there. In their dialectical constitution as a 'double', Iranians may have overcome the regime of the shah, but they remained caught up in its 'traditions, institutions that carry a charge of chauvinism, nationalism, exclusiveness'.[80] In his last article on the situation in Iran, written during a period when the new 'Islamic regime of truth' was already established and when news about summary executions in Iran's prisons had reached the world, Foucault offered the following explanation:

> Because of the strategic positions that Islam occupies, because of the economic importance that the Muslim countries hold, and because of the movement's power to expand on two continents, it constitutes, in the region surrounding Iran, an important and complex reality. As a result, the

> imaginary content of the revolt did not dissipate in the broad daylight of the revolution. It was immediately transposed onto a political scene that seemed totally willing to receive it but was in fact of an entirely different nature. At this stage, the most important and the most atrocious mingle – the extraordinary hope of remaking Islam into a great living civilisation and various forms of virulent xenophobia, as well as the global stakes and the regional rivalries. And the problem of imperialisms. And the subjugation of women, and so on.[81]

The revolutionary event, encapsulated in the 'extraordinary hope of remaking Islam into a great living civilisation' was singular, unmediated, it engendered the crease in the history of Iran at the top of which the Islamic Republic positioned itself. Yet the new state does not exist in a vacuum. The constitution of it unfolds within pre-existing relations to the outside of the revolutionary moment, including systems of imperialism, xenophobia, gender discrimination and so on. As Olivier Roy remarked: 'The government is the fruit of a history; the uprising is timeless; it is the rupture in the chain of causalities and determinations; consequently, it is the product neither of a history nor of a class strategy.' Rather it is 'phenomenon only'. From this perspective, then, 'Foucault rehabilitates the event, the phenomenon, as freedom, a rupture with determinisms, a rupture with history.'[82] A rupture yes, but it does not yield complete detachment. In Foucault's own words:

> The Iranian movement did not experience the 'law' of revolutions that would, some say, make the tyranny that already secretly inhabited them reappear underneath the blind enthusiasm of the masses. What constituted the most internal and the most intensely lived part of the uprising touched, in an unmediated fashion, on an already overcrowded political chessboard, but such contact is not identity. The spirituality of those who were going to their deaths has no similarity whatsoever with the bloody government of a fundamentalist clergy. The Iranian clerics want to authenticate their regime through the significations that the uprising had. It is no different to discredit the fact of the uprising on the grounds that there is today a government of mullahs. In both cases, there is 'fear,' fear of what just happened last fall in Iran, something of which the world had not seen an example for a long time.[83]

I don't think that Foucault's last comments on Iran are a belated admission of error forced upon him by the vitriol that his emphasis on the role of Islam and Khomeini provoked.[84] I think Foucault found his earlier scepticisms confirmed, both his theoretical scepticism about the viability of an absolutely new order and his notes of caution with regard to the Iranian case. After all, he dismissed the role of the clergy at quite an early stage. According to him, they were not a revolutionary force, 'even in the populist sense of the term'.[85] Rather, they were products of the revolutionary momentum which was driven by the people from below. 'The men of religion are like so many photographic plates on which the anger and the aspiration of the community are marked.' Foucault was aware that once the clerics would position themselves as the purveyors of a new regime of truth in opposition to the people they would lose that status. In the light of the mass demonstrations after the disputed re-election of President Ahmadinejad in the summer of 2009, some of which were targeted against the theocratic institutions of the Iranian state, Foucault showed foresight when he cautioned that if the clerics 'wanted to go against the current, they would lose this power, which essentially resides in the interplay of speaking and listening'.[86] From the perspective of many Iranians today, powerful segments of the clerical class stopped listening to the demands of the people a long time ago. Hence their role has contracted to one of speaking to the converted.

Penultimate conclusion

'No, Foucault was not a structuralist thinker; nor was he the product of a certain line of "1968 thinking". Nor was he a relativist or a historicist.' This is how Paul Veyne, a former student and friend of Foucault, introduces the latest testimony on his life. 'He was something that, in this day and age, is rare, a *sceptic* thinker.'[87] But despite this engrained scepticism – and that brings us directly back to the beginning of this discussion – Foucault affirms the viability of resistance, agency, political action. This is what the Iran episode taught him above anything else. 'No one has the right to say, "Revolt for me, the final liberation of each man hinges on it." But I do not agree with those who would say, "It is useless to revolt, it will always be the same." One does not dictate to those who risk their lives in the face of power.' Rather, one witnesses in silence the struggle between power and resistance which reveals itself *ad infinitum*: 'A delinquent puts his life on the line against abusive punishment, a madman cannot stand anymore being closed in and pushed down, or a people rejects a regime that oppresses it.' At the same time, '[t]his does not make the first one innocent, does not cure the second, and does not guarantee to the third results that were promised'. So there is no final judgement, no Hegelian synthesis, no end of history, no final victory. The dialectics remain negative:[88]

> No one is required to think that these confused voices sing better than others and speak the truth in its ultimate depth. It is enough that they exist and that they have against them all that strives to silence them, to make it meaningful to listen to them and to search for what they want to say. A question of morality? Perhaps. A question of reality, certainly. All the disillusionments of history will not change this. It is precisely because there are such voices that human time does not take the form of evolution, but that of 'history'.[89]

Power and Resistance *ad infinitum*. Foucault is not interested in being the judge, he does not argue from an entrenched position, either moral or deterministically theoretical. He presents himself as an open-minded outsider equipped with an 'anti-strategic' ethics, '[r]espectful when a singularity arises and intransigent as soon as the state violates universals'.[90] Foucault was interested in the Iranian revolution because it affirmed his interest in resistance to established power constellations. He was sympathetic to the emergence and viability of 'subjugated knowledge', the agency of the (sub)altern, the oppressed,[91] for he was convinced that for Europe encounters with the non-European world would be entirely productive.[92] Ultimately, however, it is his great omission that he did not take the Iranian episode as a springboard to present a viable philosophy of resistance that would be commensurate with his writings on disciplinary regimes, in terms both of historical breadth and of empirical detail. Said is right on this account. Foucault was not entirely willing to provide for enough space to the success of 'counter-discursive attempts' which have been useful in showing the 'misrepresentations of discursive power', and 'in Fanon's words, the violence done to psychically and politically repressed inferiors in the name of an advanced culture'.[93] For that Foucault stands accused until today, and perhaps rightly so. But a similar charge has been tabled against Said, whose background makes it even more emphatic and consequential. He too mentions only in passing the adversarial work of feminists and minority cultures. Those counter-discursive regimes that have lent a voice to the 'other' both here and over there in the non-western world remain fairly marginal to his scholarship. So really, the criticism should be extended to both Foucault and Said himself.

Notes

1 Edward Said, *Orientalism: Western Conceptions of the Orient* (London: Penguin, 1995), p. 3.
2 See further on this issue Robert J.C. Young, *White Mythologies: Writing, History and the West* (London: Routledge, 1991) or Zachary Lockman, *Contending Visions of the Middle East: The History and Politics of Orientalism* (Cambridge: Cambridge University Press, 2004).
3 Arshin Adib-Moghaddam, *A Metahistory of the Clash of Civilisations: Us and Them beyond Orientalism* (London/New York: Hurst/Columbia University Press, 2011).
4 Edward Said, *Reflections on Exile and Other Essays* (Cambridge, MA: Harvard University Press, 2000), p. 241.
5 Michel Foucault, *Society Must Be Defended: Lectures at the Collège de France*, edited by Mauro Bertani and Alessandro Fontana, translated by David Macey (London: Penguin, 2004), p. 29.
6 Michel Foucault, 'Truth and Power', in idem, *Power: Essential Works of Foucault, vol. 3*, edited by James D. Faubion, translated by Rober Hurley *et al.* (London: Penguin, 2002), p. 131.
7 In that sense, Orientalism is a 'regime of truth' rather than merely a 'discourse'.
8 Foucault, 'Truth and Power', pp. 132–133.
9 Ibid., p. 133.
10 See further Brent L. Pickett, 'Foucault and the Politics of Resistance', *Polity*, Vol. 28, No. 4 (Summer 1996), especially pp. 450 ff.
11 For a persuasive depiction of Foucault as a 'dialectician' see John Grant, 'Foucault and the logic of dialectics', *Contemporary Political Theory*, Vol. 9, No. 2 (Summer 2010), pp. 220–238.
12 Michel Foucault, *The Order of Things: An Archaeology of the Human Sciences*, translated by A.M. Sheridan Smith (London: Routledge, 1989), p. 354.
13 Said, *Reflections on Exile*, p. 241.
14 Sandra Bartky, 'Foucault, Femininity and the Modernisation of Patriarchal Power', in Irene Diamond and Lee Quinby (eds), *Feminism and Foucault: Paths of Resistance* (Boston: Northeastern University Press, 1988), p. 79.

15 Thomas McCarthy, 'The Critique of Impure Reason: Foucault and the Frankfurt School', *Political Theory*, Vol. 18, No. 3 (August 1990), p. 443.
16 Michael L. Fitzhugh and William H. Leckie, Jr, 'Agency, Postmodernism and the Causes of Change', *History and Theory*, Vol. 40, No.4 (December 2001), p. 60.
17 Said, *Reflections on Exile*, p. 242.
18 Gilles Deleuze, 'Michel Foucault's Main Concepts', in idem, *Two Regimes of Madness: Texts and Interviews 1975–1995*, edited by David Lapoujade, translated by Ames Hodges and Mike Taormina (New York: Semiotext(e), 2007), p. 261.
19 Ibid.
20 Ibid., p. 262 emphasis in original.
21 Ibid.
22 Quoted in ibid., p. 264. Deleuze added the emphasis.
23 Ibid., p. 262.
24 Ibid., p. 265.
25 Ibid., p. 264.
26 For a similar article see Nathan Widder, 'Foucault and Power Revisited', *European Journal of Political Theory*, Vol. 3, No. 4 (2004), pp. 411–432.
27 Jeffrey T. Nealon, *Foucault beyond Foucault: Power and Its Intensifications since 1984* (Stanford: Stanford University Press, 2008), p. 108.
28 Michel Foucault, *The Will to Knowledge: The History of Sexuality, Volume 1*, translated by Robert Hurley (London: Penguin, 1998), p. 93.
29 See among others Anthony Giddens, *The Transformation of Intimacy: Sexuality, Love and Eroticism in Modern Societies* (Stanford: Stanford University Press, 1992), pp. 24 ff.; Jürgen Habermas, *The Philosophic Discourse of Modernity* (Cambridge, MA: MIT Press, 1987), part 10; Michael Walzer, 'The Politics of Michel Foucault', in David Couzens Hoy (ed.), *Foucault: A Critical Reader* (Oxford: Blackwell, 1986), pp. 51–68.
30 Foucault, 'The Subject and Power', in idem., *Power: Essential works of Foucault, vol.* 3, edited by James D. Faubion, translated by Rober Hurley et. al. (London: Penguin, 2002), pp. 341–342.
31 Deleuze, 'Michel Foucault's Main Concepts', p. 260, emphasis in original.
32 Foucault, 'The Subject and Power', p. 342.
33 Kevin Jon Heller, 'Subjectification and Resistance in Foucault', *Substance*, Vol. 25, No. 1, Issue 79 (1996), pp. 78–110.
34 Heller, 'Subjectification and Resistance in Foucault', p. 84.
35 Gayatri Chakravorty Spivak, *Outside in the Teaching Machine* (London: Routledge, 1993), 34–35.
36 Foucault, 'Truth and Power', p. 120.
37 Nealon, *Foucault beyond Foucault*, p. 104, emphasis in original.
38 Mark G.E. Kelly, *The Political Philosophy of Michel Foucault* (London: Routledge, 2008), p. 108.
39 Foucault, *Society Must Be Defended*, p. 29.
40 Said, *Reflections on Exile*, p. 242.
41 Barry Smart, *Michel Foucault*, revised edition (London: Routledge, 2002), p. 134.
42 Foucault, 'Revolutionary Action', in idem., *Language, Counter-Memory, Practice: Selected Essays and Interviews* (Ithaca: Cornell University Press, 1980), p. 230.
43 See further Jonathan Arac, 'Foucault and Central Europe: A polemical speculation', *boundary 2*, Vol. 21, No. 3 (Autumn 1994), pp. 197–210.
44 Michel Foucault, *Security, Territory, Population: Lectures at the Collège de France 1977–1978*, edited by Michel Senellart, translated by Graham Burchell (London: Palgrave Macmillan, 2009), pp. 201–202.
45 Ibid., p. 202.
46 Foucault, *Power*, p. 341.
47 Foucault, *Security, Territory, Population*, pp. 201–202.
48 Paul Veyne, *Foucault: His Thought, His Character*, translated by Janet Lloyd (Cambridge: Polity, 2010), p. 126 and p. 128.

49 James Miller, *The Passion of Michel Foucault* (New York: Simon & Schuster, 1993), p. 309.
50 Quoted in Didier Eribon, *Michel Foucault*, translated by Betsy Wing (Cambridge, MA: Harvard University Press, 1991), p. 282.
51 Quoted in ibid., p. 287.
52 Craig Keating, 'Reflections on the Revolution in Iran: Foucault on Resistance', *Journal of European Studies*, Vol. 27, No. 2 (1997), p. 194. For a comparable point see also Georg Stauth, 'Revolution in Spiritless Times: An Essay on Michel Foucault's Enquiries into the Iranian Revolution', *International Sociology*, Vol. 6, No. 3 (1991), p. 259.
53 See Janet Afary and Kevin B. Anderson, *Foucault and the Iranian Revolution: Gender and the Seductions of Islamism* (Chicago: The University of Chicago Press, 2005), pp. 136–137.
54 Michel Foucault, 'The Mythical Leader of the Iranian Revolt', *Corriere della sera*, 26 November 1978, in Afary and Anderson, *Foucault and the Iranian Revolution*, p. 220.
55 Michel Foucault, 'A Revolt With Bare Hands', *Corriere della sera*, 5 November 1978, in Afary and Anderson, *Foucault and the Iranian Revolution*, p. 213.
56 Michel Foucault, 'Response to Atoussa H.', *Le Nouvel Observateur*, 13 November 1978, in Afary and Anderson, *Foucault and the Iranian Revolution*, p. 210. See also 'Dialogue between Michel Foucault and Baqir Parham', *Nameh-ye Kanun-e Nevisandegan* (Publication of the Center of Iranian Writers), No. 1 (Spring 1979), pp. 9–17, in Afary and Anderson, *Foucault and the Iranian Revolution*, pp. 183–189.
57 Afary and Anderson, *Foucault and the Iranian Revolution*, pp. 30–31. See also Ian Almond, *The New Orientalists: Postmodern Representations of Islam from Foucault to Baudrillard* (London: IB Tauris, 2007).
58 'Dialogue between Michel Foucault and Baqir Parham', 186. Foucault was very impressed with the writings of Ali Shariati, one of the pre-eminent intellectuals in 1970s Iran. Foucault was correct to point out the centrality of Shariati to the events in Iran, to see him as 'a shadow that haunt(ed) all political and religious life' and to observe that his 'name was the only one that was called out, besides that of Khomeini'. Michel Foucault, 'What Are the Iranians Dreaming [Rêvent] About', *Le Nouvel Observateur*, 16–22 October 1978, in Afary and Anderson, *Foucault and the Iranian Revolution*, pp. 207–208. But the Shi'ism that Foucault thought particular to Iran was a hybrid construct, not an ahistorically coded 'political spirituality'. This is particularly apparent in Shariati, where the 'West' is in the 'East', where the Shia myths and imagery were re-enacted within the frame of 'Sartrean third worldism' and a new form of Islamo-feminist militancy that positioned the daughter of the Prophet Mohammad next to Che Guevara, Abraham, Jesus and Frantz Fanon. On the hybridity of contemporary discourses of Islam see Adib-Moghaddam, *A Metahistory of the Clash of Civilisations*.
59 Michiel Leezenberg, 'Power and Political Spirituality: Michel Foucault and the Islamic Revolution in Iran', *Arcadia*, Vol. 33, No. 1 (1998), p. 76.
60 Said, *Reflections on Exile*, p. 196.
61 These have been recently published in English. See Michel Foucault, *Manet and the Object of Painting*, translated by Matthew Barr (London: Tate, 2009).
62 Michel Foucault, 'The Army – When the Earth Quakes', *Corriere della sera*, 28 September 1978, in Afary and Anderson, *Foucault and the Iranian Revolution*, p. 190.
63 Foucault, 'A Revolt with Bare Hands', p. 211.
64 Michel Foucault, 'The Challenge to the Opposition', *Corriere della sera*, 7 November 1978, in Afary and Anderson, *Foucault and the Iranian Revolution*, p. 213.
65 Ibid., p. 218.
66 Michel Foucault, 'The Mythical Leader of the Iranian Revolt', *Corriere della sera*, 26 November 1978, in Afary and Anderson, *Foucault and the Iranian Revolution*, p. 221.

It is not so much that Foucault must be criticised for identifying a 'perfectly unified collective will' in the revolution, as Afary and Anderson suggest, or for emphasising Khomeini's role as a point of fixation of the masses. Few scholars of the revolution would disagree that in the build-up to the mass demonstrations that brought down the shah, Khomeini was a unifying symbol for the protesters. See further Arshin Adib-Moghaddam *Iran in World Politics: the Question of the Islamic Republic* (London/New York: Hurst/Columbia University Press, 2008), especially part 1.

67 Foucault, 'What Are the Iranians Dreaming [Rêvent] About', p. 207.
68 Foucault, 'The Mythical Leader of the Iranian Revolt', p. 221.
69 Foucault, *The Will to Knowledge*, p. 96.
70 It is striking that Foucault refers to Max Horkheimer, one of the standard bearers of the critical theory of the Frankfurt School in Germany, in his last writings on Iran. See Michel Foucault, 'Is It Useless to Revolt?', *Le Monde*, 11–12 May 1979, in Afary and Anderson, *Foucault and the Iranian Revolution*, p. 264.
71 A reference to a Mullah 'manufacturing the Iranian truth' is emblematic for the scattered instances of critique that were slowly emerging, the closer the revolutionary ideals were turned into a new 'regime of truth'. See Foucault 'The Challenge to the Opposition', p. 219.
72 Foucault, 'Response to Atoussa H.', p. 210.
73 Foucault, 'The Mythical Leader of the Iranian Revolt', p. 220.
74 Michel Foucault, 'A Powder Keg Called Islam', *Corriera della Serra*, 13 February 1979, in Afary and Anderson, *Foucault and the Iranian Revolution*, p. 241.
75 'Iran: The Spirit of a World without Spirit' originally published in March 1979, in Afary and Anderson, *Foucault and the Iranian Revolution*, p. 256.
76 Ibid., p. 260.
77 Ibid., p. 255.
78 Foucault, 'Is it Useless to Revolt?', pp. 263–264.
79 Quoted in James Schmidt and Thomas E. Wartenberg, 'Foucault's Enlightenment: Critique, Revolution and the Fashioning of the Self', in Michael Kelly (ed.), *Critique and Power: Recasting the Foucault/Habermas Debate* (Chicago: MIT Press, 1994), p. 296.
80 'Iran: The Spirit of a World without Spirit', p. 260.
81 Foucault, 'Is it Useless to Revolt?', p. 265.
82 Olivier Roy, 'L'enigme du soulèvement (Enigma of the Uprising)', *Vacarme*, Issue 29 (Autumn 2004). English version available at http://www.vacarme.org/article1799.html [accessed 12 November 2010].
83 Foucault, 'Is it Useless to Revolt?', p. 265.
84 Afary and Anderson, *Foucault and the Iranian Revolution*, p. 129.
85 Michel Foucault, 'Tehran: Faith against the Shah', *Corriere della sera*, 8 October 1978, in Afary and Anderson, *Foucault and the Iranian Revolution*, p. 202.
86 Ibid.
87 Veyne, *Foucault*, 1, emphasis in original.
88 More work has to be done on the confluence between the negative dialectics of Adorno and Horkheimer, Foucault's power–resistance dialectic and Said's concept of 'contrapuntality'.
89 Foucault, 'Is it Useless to Revolt?', p. 266.
90 Ibid., p. 267.
91 See further Foucault, *Society Must Be Defended*, pp. 7–10.
92 See further Michel Foucault, 'Michel Foucault and Zen: A Stay in a Zen Temple (1978)', in Jeremy R. Carrette (ed.), *Religion and Culture* (Manchester: Manchester University Press, 1999), pp. 110–114.
93 Said, *Reflections on Exile*, pp. 243–244.

Bibliography

Adib-Moghaddam, Arshin, *A Metahistory of the Clash of Civilisations: Us and Them beyond Orientalism* (London/New York: Hurst/Columbia University Press, 2011).

Adib-Moghaddam, Arshin, *Iran in World Politics: the Question of the Islamic Republic* (London/New York: Hurst/Columbia University Press, 2008).

Afary, Janet and Kevin B. Anderson, *Foucault and the Iranian Revolution: Gender and the Seductions of Islamism* (Chicago: The University of Chicago Press, 2005).

Almond, Ian, *The New Orientalists: Postmodern Representations of Islam from Foucault to Baudrillard* (London: IB Tauris, 2007).

Arac, Jonathan, 'Foucault and Central Europe: A Polemical Speculation', *boundary 2*, Vol. 21, No. 3 (Autumn 1994), pp. 197–210.

Bartky, Sandra, 'Foucault, Femininity and the Modernisation of Patriarchal Power', in Irene Diamond and Lee Quinby (eds), *Feminism and Foucault: Paths of Resistance* (Boston: Northeastern University Press, 1988), pp. 61–86.

Deleuze, Gilles, 'Michel Foucault's Main Concepts', in idem, *Two Regimes of Madness: Texts and Interviews 1975–1995*, edited by David Lapoujade, translated by Ames Hodges and Mike Taormina (New York: Semiotext(e), 2007).

Eribon, Didier, *Michel Foucault*, translated by Betsy Wing (Cambridge, MA: Harvard University Press, 1991).

Fitzhugh, Michael L. and William H. Leckie, Jr, 'Agency, Postmodernism and the Causes of Change', *History and Theory*, Vol. 40, No. 4 (December 2001), pp. 59–81.

Foucault, Michel, *Manet and the Object of Painting*, translated by Matthew Barr (London: Tate, 2009).

Foucault, Michel, 'Michel Foucault and Zen: A Stay in a Zen Temple (1978)', in Jeremy R. Carrette (ed.), *Religion and Culture* (Manchester: Manchester University Press, 1999).

Foucault, Michel, *The Order of Things: An Archaeology of the Human Sciences*, translated by A.M. Sheridan Smith (London: Routledge, 1989).

Foucault, Michel, *Power: Essential Works of Foucault, vol. 3*, edited by James D. Faubion, translated by Robert Hurley *et al.* (London: Penguin, 2002).

Foucault, Michel, 'Revolutionary Action', in idem., *Language, Counter-Memory, Practice: Selected Essays and Interviews* (Ithaca: Cornell University Press, 1980).

Foucault, Michel, *Security, Territory, Population: Lectures at the Collège de France 1977–1978*, edited by Michel Senellart, translated by Graham Burchell (London: Palgrave Macmillan, 2009).

Foucault, Michel, *Society Must Be Defended: Lectures at the Collège de France*, edited by Mauro Bertani and Alessandro Fontana, translated by David Macey (London: Penguin, 2004).

Foucault, Michel, 'The Subject and Power', in idem., *Power: Essential works of Foucault, vol.* 3, edited by James D. Faubion, translated by Rober Hurley et. al. (London: Penguin, 2002).

Foucault, Michel, 'Truth and Power', in idem, *Power: Essential Works of Foucault, vol. 3*, edited by James D. Faubion, translated by Robert Hurley *et al.* (London: Penguin, 2002).

Foucault, Michel, *The Will to Knowledge: The History of Sexuality, Volume 1*, translated by Robert Hurley (London: Penguin, 1998).

Giddens, Anthony, *The Transformation of Intimacy: Sexuality, Love and Eroticism in Modern Societies* (Stanford: Stanford University Press, 1992).

Grant, John, 'Foucault and the Logic of Dialectics', *Contemporary Political Theory*, Vol. 9, No. 2 (Summer 2010), pp. 220–238.

Habermas, Jürgen, *The Philosophic Discourse of Modernity* (Cambridge, MA: MIT Press, 1987).

Heller, Kevin Jon, 'Subjectification and Resistance in Foucault', *Substance*, Vol. 25, No. 1, Issue 79 (1996), pp. 78–110.

Keating, Craig, 'Reflections on the Revolution in Iran: Foucault on Resistance', *Journal of European Studies*, Vol. 27, No. 2 (1997), pp. 181–197.

Kelly, Mark G.E., *The Political Philosophy of Michel Foucault* (London: Routledge, 2008).

Leezenberg, Michiel, 'Power and Political Spirituality: Michel Foucault and the Islamic Revolution in Iran', *Arcadia*, Vol. 33, No. 1 (1998), pp. 72–89.

Lockman, Zachary, *Contending Visions of the Middle East: The History and Politics of Orientalism* (Cambridge: Cambridge University Press, 2004).

McCarthy, Thomas, 'The Critique of Impure Reason: Foucault and the Frankfurt School', *Political Theory*, Vol. 18, No. 3 (August 1990), pp. 437–469.

Miller, James, *The Passion of Michel Foucault* (New York: Simon & Schuster, 1993).

Nealon, Jeffrey T., *Foucault beyond Foucault: Power and Its Intensifications since 1984* (Stanford: Stanford University Press, 2008).

Pickett, Brent L., 'Foucault and the Politics of Resistance', *Polity*, Vol. 28, No. 4 (Summer 1996), pp. 445–466.

Roy, Olivier, 'L'enigme du soulèvement (Enigma of the Uprising)', *Vacarme*, Issue 29 (Autumn 2004). English version available at http://www.vacarme.org/article1799.html.

Said, Edward, *Orientalism: Western Conceptions of the Orient* (London: Penguin, 1995)

Said, Edward, *Reflections on Exile and Other Essays* (Cambridge, MA: Harvard University Press, 2000).

Schmidt, James and Thomas E. Wartenberg, 'Foucault's Enlightenment: Critique, Revolution and the Fashioning of the Self', in Michael Kelly (ed.), *Critique and Power: Recasting the Foucault/Habermas Debate* (Cambridge, MA: MIT Press, 1994).

Smart, Barry, *Michel Foucault*, revised edition (London: Routledge, 2002).

Spivak, Gayatri Chakravorty, *Outside in the Teaching Machine* (London: Routledge, 1993).

Stauth, Georg, 'Revolution in Spiritless Times: An Essay on Michel Foucault's Enquiries into the Iranian Revolution', *International Sociology*, Vol. 6, No. 3 (1991), pp. 259–280.

Veyne, Paul, *Foucault: His Thought, His Character*, translated by Janet Lloyd (Cambridge: Polity, 2010)

Walzer, Michael, 'The Politics of Michel Foucault', in David Couzens Hoy (ed.), *Foucault: A Critical Reader* (Oxford: Blackwell, 1986).

Widder, Nathan, 'Foucault and Power Revisited', *European Journal of Political Theory*, Vol. 3, No. 4 (2004), pp. 411–432.

Young, Robert J.C., *White Mythologies: Writing, History and the West* (London: Routledge, 1991).

3 Edward Said and the political present

Nadia Abu El-Haj

This essay offers a reading of Edward Said's legacy. It engages Said's scholarly and political insights, on the one hand, and his vision of, and life as, an intellectual, on the other hand. The essay focuses on his broader conceptual and methodological interventions, his analysis of the politics of empire (in the Middle East), and his passionate attachment to the question of Palestine. It also contextualizes Said's work in light of the contemporary political moment, arguing that he and that for which he is seen to stand have emerged as key flash-points in the latest U.S. culture wars.

"I had absolutely no way of knowing that, a year after the book was published, Iran would be the site of an extraordinarily far-reaching Islamic revolution," Edward Said[1] wrote in a 1994 afterword to a new edition of *Orientalism*. The Iranian Revolution of 1979 marked the visible rise of "Islamic fundamentalism" on the global stage, a form of oppositional politics seen increasingly as challenging the West, in general, and the United States, in particular.[2] And that now-global challenge—the challenge of radical Islam—is generally analyzed in terms substantially different from those that framed analyses of the Cold War: Islamist movements are understood in culturalist—in Orientalist—terms. As Bernard Lewis has argued, an ongoing struggle has taken place between the "rival systems" of the Judeo-Christian and Muslim "blocks" for nearly fourteen centuries. "It has consisted of a long series of attacks and counterattacks, jihads and crusades, conquests and reconquests".[3] Borrowing Lewis's framework for this long-standing conflict, Samuel P. Huntington[4] argued that this is a "clash of civilizations"—a conflict no longer between different ideologies (as was the Cold War) but between distinct cultures, often inflected with religious overtones. And, according to Huntington, this newer global conflict is potentially far more intransigent than the Cold War had been: People tend to have deep, non-negotiable attachments to their own "civilizations".

In the post-September 11, 2001 period, Huntington is often argued to have had remarkable foresight, but it was, in fact, *Orientalism* that was the prescient work. Said's book engaged the relationship between empire and its forms of knowledge, enabling scholars to recognize in arguments such as those of Huntington an imperial vision that would work to make real the very clash of civilizations that Huntington "foresaw". After all, *Orientalism* lays out "the pattern of imperial culture"[5] that made imaginable, even natural, imperial vision(s) of the

Arab-Muslim East as a space demanding intervention, a space radically, even incommensurably, different from the West and one that had to be remade by and in the image of (European) civilization. As Said wrote in the spring of 2003, twenty-five years after its initial publication, "*Orientalism* once again raises the question of whether modern imperialism ever ended, or whether it has continued in the Orient since Napoleon's entry into Egypt two centuries ago."[6]

In this essay, I offer a reading of Said's legacy—more accurately, perhaps, I offer an account of what I think his legacy might best be, particularly in the context of the current political moment. I discuss central historical and methodological insights in his scholarly work alongside his vision of and life as an intellectual, to think about how Said sought to understand and, in turn, to intervene in a newly configured and ever more violent and interventionist US empire. In so doing, I attempt to read his work in a way that is sensitive both to Said's broader intellectual contributions and commitments—to questions about culture, power, empire, authorship, and the role and responsibility of the intellectual—and to his passionate attachment to the question of Palestine, in particular, and to the politics of empire in the Middle East, more generally. In contrast to readings of *Orientalism* that effectively both elevated and neutered Said's contribution by stripping it of its specific history and politics, interpreting the argument, instead, as being about the more universal problem of Otherness, I want to bring back into stark relief how the specific problems of representation that Said sought to address were intimately entangled with distinct colonial histories and imperial institutions of power.

Said grappled with the question of empire not just as an academic but, just as crucially, as a public intellectual, his tireless engagement with the world guided by his unfaltering humanist commitments. In short, with *Orientalism* at the core of his intellectual project, Said sought to analyze not just the history of empire but also, more urgently, the nature of power in the postcolonial world, and he sought to intervene, publicly, in debates about and struggles over that contemporary reality in which he lived. The legacy of that intellectual life, and not just his particular writings and arguments, has, if anything, become even more powerful since his death. This is not simply because Said's corpus—both academic and public—is of particular relevance for analyzing and engaging the current political moment. In addition, as Said's writings and influence come under increasing attack by neoconservatives in their battles against the academy, in general, and its purportedly biased teaching of the Middle East, in particular, so, too, has Said, and that for which he is seen to stand, emerged as a signifier in a wider cultural and political battle in which many of us— scholars and others—find ourselves enmeshed.

Reading Orientalism

The questions raised by *Orientalism* in the current political moment reach well beyond the general issue of the continuation and continuities of empire that Said raised in various fora not long before his death. The book sought to understand the specific terms, institutions, and imaginations through which imperial power operates, examining the contours of an "internally structured archive"[7] regarding the character of the Arab and Muslim East that helped to generate and to make possible U.S. imperial policies on micro- and macro-levels alike. Take one of the most striking contemporary examples: the torture of Iraqi prisoners by U.S. soldiers at the Abu Ghraib prison. Thanks in large part to the work of the *New Yorker* magazine investigative reporter Seymour Hersh, stories of abuse—much of it sexual abuse—have become public knowledge. As revealed in a series of articles and photographs that hit the U.S. press in May 2004, prisoners were subjected to various forms of sexual abuse: forced masturbation, simulating homosexual acts, mimicking sado-masochistic sex acts with female soldiers dominating male prisoners—acts of torture photographed by U.S. soldiers, with the images then passed around among themselves on computers and found in photographic collections amid other "tourist-type" pictures.

Although debates continue to rage over the question of responsibility and the chain of command, one thing seems to be clear: The character of the torture was determined by a particular vision of Arab-Muslim culture. As summed up by Hersh,

> One of the questions that will be explored at any trial, however, is why a group of Army Reserve military policemen, most of them from small towns, tormented their prisoners as they did, *in a manner that was especially humiliating for Iraqi men.*
>
> The notion that Arabs are particularly vulnerable to sexual humiliation became a talking point among pro-war Washington conservatives in the months before the March, 2003, invasion of Iraq [emphasis added].[8]

As this public debate ensued, many liberals and conservatives, pundits, journalists, and academics alike (including Hersh) shared the belief that homosexual acts would be especially humiliating for Arab men. More specifically, the source of that knowledge for those who prosecuted the war and, presumably, for those who designed this system of torture—or "information gathering"—was none other than an Orientalist scholar about whom Said wrote, Raphael Patai (see Hagopian 1977; Said 2000, 2003: 308–309).[9]

The Arab Mind, a book first published in 1973 by Patai, a Hungarian-born Jewish anthropologist who spent a decade in Palestine before moving to the United States in 1947, became "the bible of the neocons on Arab behavior".[10] As recounted by Norell B. De Atkine, the director of Middle East studies at the John F. Kennedy Special Warfare Center and School at Fort Bragg, "At the institution where I teach military affairs, 'The Arab Mind' forms the basis of my cultural instruction."[11] Written within the school of national personality studies and republished in November 2001 with a new introduction by De Atkine, the book includes a chapter on Arabs and sex—the chapter focused on during preparations for war. Deriving from a long-standing anthropological theory of honor and shame, the logic of sexual torture—and of its recording in photographic images—was intended "to create an army of informants".[12] Arab men, the theory goes, would do anything to avoid the humiliation that would accompany the photographs' public release.[13]

To confine the intellectual significance of *Orientalism* to the question of "Middle East politics *tout court*"[14] would, of course, be a gross misreading of a book that came to influence countless academic disciplines and intellectual and political debates. In Said's words, "For all its worldly reference [*Orientalism*] is still a book about culture, ideas, history, and power."[15] Nevertheless, the analysis that Said offers remains a very specific one: The question for Said, both methodological and historical, was to answer how culture, ideas, history, and power articulate within the specific contexts of unfolding empires.

As is well known, Said offers three overlapping definitions of Orientalism. First, an Orientalist is "anyone who teaches, writes about, or researches the Orient".[16] Second, Orientalism is "a style of thought based upon an ontological and epistemological distinction made between 'the Orient' and (most of the time) 'the Occident'".[17] And third, roughly since the late eighteenth century, Orientalism has referred to the "corporate institution for dealing with the Orient—dealing with it by making statements about it, authorizing views of it, describing it, by teaching it, settling it, and ruling over it: in short, Orientalism as a Western style for dominating, restructuring, and having authority over the Orient".[18] Each of these definitions engages distinct, if inseparable, aspects of his argument: the question of fields of knowledge, the question of representation, and the question of empire. Let me begin with the second, which, for many readers—and certainly in the discipline of anthropology—was and remains the most important contribution of Said's book.

Representation

It is perhaps Said's engagement with the problem of representation, in general, that has accounted for one of the widest influences of *Orientalism*. Said considers, often in passing, the question of how human societies distinguish between selves and others and with what consequences. "Can one divide human reality, as indeed human reality seems to be genuinely divided, into clearly different cultures, histories, traditions, societies, even races, and survive the consequences humanly?"[19] For many anthropologists and cultural critics, this seems to have been the main question and intellectual challenge raised by the book:[20] Is the representation of other cultures possible?[21] As James Clifford writes, *Orientalism* raises "a substantial, and disquieting, set of questions about the nature of cross-cultural discourses generally. At issue are the ways in which distinct groups of humanity (*however defined*) imagine, describe, and comprehend each other" (emphasis added).[22] Although recognizing that Said's interest in issues of representation and "cross-cultural" comprehension is rooted in his analysis of empire, Clifford nevertheless focuses on the more general point: "The key theoretical issue raised by *Orientalism* concerns the status of *all* forms of thought and representation for dealing with the alien. Can one ultimately escape procedures of dichotomizing, restructuring, and textualizing in the making of interpretive statements about foreign cultures and traditions? If so, how?"[23]

The "alien," the "foreign"—at other times, the "exotic"[24]—those are the terms most appropriate to a reading of *Orientalism* that focuses on the question of cross-cultural understanding and representation as a general, or universal, problem. And, as Said's 1987 talk before the American Anthropological Association made clear, theoretical debates concerning the "crisis in representation" were central to his work: "To represent someone or even something has now become an endeavor as complex and as problematic as an asymptote, with consequences for certainty and decidability as fraught with difficulties as can be imagined."[25] Nevertheless, Said was perhaps not quite as committed to poststructuralist understandings of language and of the (im)possibility of representation, or, more specifically, the impossibility of representing (and understanding) other cultures, as the above quotation and many readings of his work might suggest. After all, he was a great admirer of Erich Auerbach. A philologist in the best sense of that tradition, according to Said, Auerbach believed in philology precisely for

> its emphasis on the unity of human history, the possibility it granted of understanding inimical and perhaps even hostile Others despite the bellicosity of modern cultures and nationalisms, and the optimism with which one could enter into the inner life of a distant author or historical epoch even with a healthy awareness of one's limitations of perspective and insufficiency of knowledge.[26]

Both theoretically and methodologically, Said distanced himself from poststructuralist, more specifically, deconstructionist, approaches to (literary) texts (see, e.g., his discussion of Jacques Derrida[27] and of Paul de Man[28]). Said's critical interest in texts—and his methodological approach to them—moved well beyond questions of language and its undecidability and toward an understanding of their placing and effects in the world. Drawing on Antonio Gramsci's theory of culture, Said was interested in the ways in which art and culture are "connected in complex ways to doing things, to accomplishing certain things, to force, to social class and economic production, to diffusing ideas, values, and world pictures".[29] Works of art and culture are essential to what Gramsci called "elaboration"—that "ensemble of patterns making it feasible for society to maintain itself"[30]—and by focusing on such works' "affiliations", by studying and re-creating "the bonds between the text and the world",[31] Said sought to understand that essentially productive cultural and political process.[32]

The problem of representation as elaborated by Said in *Orientalism* is, thus, better understood as inseparable from the context of empire and the relations of power and subordination entailed therein.[33] He sought to understand how, in the context of specific historical encounters between Europe and the Arab Middle East, representing Otherness—demarcating the difference between East and West, between Christianity and Islam—generated imperial power in the West and helped to elaborate the patterns of thought and culture that made that imperial endeavor imaginable, sustainable, and, quite centrally, (morally) "good."[34] In short, Said was interested in the general problem of representation as it unfolded within the specific context of the history and institutions of empire.

The centrality of empire to his theoretical and historical argument is often left aside by readers of *Orientalism* for a more general engagement with the question of Othering and (the overtextual and sometimes interpersonally conceived) problems of representing "cultural difference". And the effect of such a reading is significant: It dehistoricizes and depoliticizes Said's primary intellectual intervention. As he made clear in his address to the American Anthropological Association in 1987, he was quite critical of the "textual turn" that he saw in many critiques of anthropology that had emerged of late: In focusing, for example, on the problem of ethnographic writing, anthropological critics had separated questions of ethnographic representation from the particular historical circumstances in which those representations were produced.[35] Specifically, the question of empire, generally seen as only a historical problem, was not directly engaged in the context of contemporary anthropological work. How might anthropologists, Said asked, engage more directly with and take responsibility for the imperial power of the United States in the contemporary world? And how might the present (and presence) of a new and reconfigured empire be integrated into contemporary anthropological work? In short, the affiliations between texts and the world—those that anthropologists analyze as much as those we write—were fundamental to Said, to his political commitments and to his critical method. And in seeking to track such affiliations, history stood at the very center of how he thought criticism should proceed.

The history of empire and the fallacy of Occidentalism

The key transition that Said traces in *Orientalism* was the transformation in the late nineteenth century of the "quality of geographic and spatial apprehension so far as the Orient was concerned".[36] In short, the Orient was transformed "from *alien* into *colonial* space" (emphasis added).[37] His interest is precisely in how the former—a persistent discourse about "alien" space—made possible the latter. Said traces the transformation of a largely imagined world, rooted in a long-standing and often fraught relationship between the world of Christendom and that of Islam, into a colonized one.[38] And in the context of that argument, talk of an "Occidentalist" discourse does not make epistemological, historical, or political sense, either as a way of criticizing Said's own representation of the "West" or as a way of extending his analysis to consider other essentializing discourse(s).

Many reviewers of *Orientalism*, scholars critical of as well as those sympathetic to Said's argument, raised the question of whether or not Said engaged in a reverse Orientalism, in "Occidentalism". Has Said produced a vision of the "West" that is as essentializing and ahistorical as the image he criticizes of the "East", many a critic has asked (e.g., Clifford 1980; Lewis 1982; Richardson 1990)?[39] But that question can be asked only from within a particular and partial reading of *Orientalism*: that Orientalism was and is primarily a practice of essentializing, a discursive practice stripped of its entanglement with specific forms and institutions of power in which Orientalist discourse was and remains embedded. In other words, the question requires that the specifically historical and institutional elements of Said's argument be sidelined; the question of empire must be treated as either entirely irrelevant or, at the very least, not central. And it is just such a misreading that enables criticisms of Said as himself reproducing the terms of Orientalist discourse, now in reverse. In addition, such a reading makes possible "extensions" of his argument: that there are, also, Occidentalist discourses, widespread cultural and political phenomena in the world, past and present, of which scholars need to give an account. Take, for example, Ian Buruma and Avishai Margalit's book *Occidentalism* (2004).

In summing up the nature of essentialisms regarding the "West", Buruma and Margalit invoke the term *Occidentalism*, an apparent inversion of Said's *Orientalism*, even though Said is not cited in the text. Buruma and Margalit write,

> The view of the West in Occidentalism is like the worst aspects of its counterpart, Orientalism, which strips its human targets of their humanity. Some Orientalist prejudices made non-Western people seem less than fully adult human beings. ... Occidentalism is at least as reductive; its bigotry simply turns the Orientalist view upside down. To diminish an entire society or a civilization to a mass of soulless, decadent, money-grubbing, rootless, faithless, unfeeling parasites is a form of intellectual destruction. Once again, if this were merely a matter of distaste or prejudice, it would not be of great interest. ... But when the idea of others as less than human gathers revolutionary force, it leads to the destruction of human beings.[40]

Their argument is ahistorical and pays no attention to institutional forms. Buruma and Margalit sketch Occidentalism's "particular strands"—the "idea" of the West present in four "archetypal forms": the city, the mind of the West (i.e., science and reason), the settled bourgeois (who is juxtaposed to the self-sacrificing hero), and the infidel. Those archetypes—and the hostility that they have generated—have a long and enduring history.[41] As Buruma and Margalit argue, some of them began with the ancient Greeks (e.g., fear of the city) and all of them—as expressions of anti-Enlightenment tendencies—began in Europe and then traveled, as tropes, to other parts of the world and to other fascist, nationalist, and religious movements over time: to Japan in the 1940s and to Islamists today, for example.[42] Theirs is an argument about prejudice, bigotry, and essentialisms. It is an argument not interested in the particular historical encounters and struggles that generate specific forms of (oppositional) politics or in the specific institutional structures that house those forms of politics or their discursive regimes. These archetypal forms are available tropes that somehow circulate. More specifically, Buruma and Margalit argue that particular state policies—whether of the United States, of Israel, or of elsewhere—are insufficient if not irrelevant in accounting for specific forms of radical, oppositional politics that emerge and take up these circulating themes.[43] The "rage" expressed in Occidentalisms, be it by the Japanese during World War II or by the Palestinians and Islamists today, emerges in their argument as psychological. Occidentalism itself—and, by way of extension, Orientalism—becomes a form of prejudice, of misrepresentation, of cultural reductionism, of essentialism *tout court*.

Writing about Occidentalism or reading Said's text as producing such an Occidentalist discourse is, in my opinion, to overlook Said's main arguments and intellectual and methodological contributions. It is, moreover, to elide the politics that were so central to Said's work. First, it presumes a particular reading of his text that, as argued above, separates the question of empire and its institutions from the question of knowledge (about the Orient), thus making possible the conception of a parallel Occidentalism, despite the very different histories of power and knowledge that would be involved in such a reversal (for a similar critique and a different use of the term *Occidentalism*, see Coronil 1996). Second, it requires a conflation of systematicity—Said's emphasis on patterns of knowledge and culture—with essentialization, the practice of dehistoricizing cultural forms. And within the context of critiques of culture that emerged in anthropology and cultural studies, in part, in response to Said's work in the 1980s—critiques that did the important work of retheorizing culture as never seamless, always heterogenous, and, for many anthropologists, inevitably contested or resisted—systematicity and essentialism have often come to be seen as the same thing. It is to the question of the systematicity of cultural forms that I now turn, to its centrality to Said's analysis, historical and political alike.

Said produces a genealogical account of the emergence and consolidation of modern Orientalism, one that reaches back into a history far deeper than that of the (formal) colonial period and the birth of modern Orientalism in the late nineteenth century and that stretches forward into the present with its very different configurations and locations of global power and empire. That genealogical account traces the "enormously *systematic* discipline by which European culture was able to manage—and even produce—the Orient" (emphasis added).[44] In other words, in contrast to retheorizations of culture that have emerged in anthropology and cultural studies over the past few decades that have emphasized the multivocal nature of cultural forms—questions of perspectives, of arguments, of heterogeneity, and of resistance—Said remained committed to cultural coherence, albeit, in his formulation, that coherence is continuously elaborated precisely by, or within, the forms of power that characterize, generate, and sustain particular political regimes (cf. Geertz 1973). Thus, that the text is, at times, "numbingly repetitive"[45] perhaps reveals something quite fundamental about Orientalist discourse itself. The discourse was, increasingly so as it was codified into a coherent discipline of scholarly practice and an expansive domain of cultural knowledge in the late nineteenth century, numbingly repetitive: The contours of what was said, of what could be said, about the "East" fell into an array of "statements" that could be made within the discursive regime that Said tracks. Nevertheless, Said was not insensitive to the methodological question that haunts any such genealogical account. As he writes,

> One must repeatedly ask oneself whether what matters in Orientalism is the general group of ideas overriding the mass of material—about which who could deny that they were shot through with doctrines of European superiority, various kinds of racism, imperialism, and the like, dogmatic views of "the Oriental" as a kind of ideal and unchanging abstraction?—or the

> much more varied work produced by almost uncountable individual writers, whom one would take up as individual instances of authors dealing with the Orient. In a sense the two alternatives, general and particular, are really two perspectives on the same material: in both instances one would have to deal with pioneers in the field like William Jones, with great artists like Nerval or Flaubert. And why would it not be possible to employ both perspectives together, or one after the other.[46]

Insisting on dealing with the general and the particular at the same time, Said asks, "How then to recognize individuality and to reconcile it with its intelligent, and by no means passive or merely dictatorial, general and hegemonic context?"[47] The question reveals a methodological commitment that he developed in a more sustained and nuanced manner in *Culture and Imperialism*, published over a decade after *Orientalism* and addressed far more specifically to the field of literary criticism. As he explained in the introduction to that book, his goal was to read each work "first as the great product of the creative interpretive imagination, and then to show them as part of the relationship between culture and empire".[48]

Reading *Orientalism* makes it quite clear that Said has differential respect for different Orientalist scholars and writers, recognizing the particular "creativity" of specific figures over others, the more sympathetic engagement with the East by some Orientalists than by others. For example, Said had enormous respect for Louis Massignon, a French Orientalist who worked in the best of the humanist tradition that Said saw in Auerbach, coming to empathize with Islamic traditions in a way that, albeit always Eurocentric, represented a real attempt to understand the Muslim world.[49] But I am less interested in the question of individual authorship—and, thus, the differences in "manifest" Orientalism as exhibited by particular figures[50]—than in the systematic patterns of Orientalist discourse, of "latent" Orientalism, and Said's historical account thereof. In other words, why does his account of Orientalist discourse—often read as an essentialization of the "West"—not reproduce some of the methodological failures of Orientalism itself? To address that question, I turn to think about Said's historical method.

History

In Said's account, the origins of Orientalism reach all the way back to ancient Greece (thus, opening him up to criticisms that he has dehistoricized the "West" and its forms of culture and knowledge). Focusing on the Islamic East, Europe's engagement with the Orient had long been "something more than what was empirically known about it".[51] Reading Homer's *Iliad*, Aeschylus's *The Persians*, or *The Bacchae* of Euripedes, Said finds particular "associations" that come to gather around the "East",[52] two aspects of which are persistent in images of the Orient in the European imagination: "A line is drawn between two continents: Europe is powerful and articulate; Asia is defeated and distant".[53] From the writings of the ancient Greeks through the centuries of Christianity's engagement with the menace of Islam on its borders, an archive was built up such that, not only was European engagement with the Orient (now meaning primarily Islam) self-referential, or "textual," but, moreover, the Orient itself was never wholly alien: No longer "patently distant and foreign", the Orient emerged within a "new median category"—as "versions of a previously known thing".[54]

Beginning in the eighteenth century, however, notable shifts began to occur in this long-standing archive. The European imagination of the Orient expanded beyond Islamic lands; texts were no longer written just by travelers but also by historians who tried to grapple with the Orient in novel ways. No longer judging it "inflexibly as an enemy" of the West, European engagement with the Orient was increasingly structured by historicist commitments: the belief that an outsider could "penetrate the spirit of another culture" by an "act of historical sympathy".[55] And, finally, classificatory systems were developed whereby categories of people ("the wild men", "the Asiatics", "the Europeans") emerged in correspondence with particular character traits,[56] schemes that would be refigured and consolidated in the century to come in tandem with racial theories of humankind.[57] These shifts had the effect of refiguring Europe's engagement with the Orient from "the narrowly religious scrutiny by which it had hitherto been examined (and judged) by the Christian West".[58] In sum, modern Orientalism had its origins in the "secularizing elements of European cultures".[59]

The late eighteenth century marks a second fundamental turning-point in Said's account, with Napoleon's conquest of Egypt achieving a "truly scientific appropriation of one culture by another".[60] The "Napoleonic expedition, with its great collective monument of erudition, the *Description de L'Egypte*, provided a scene or setting for Orientalism, since Egypt and subsequently the other Islamic lands were viewed as the live province, the laboratory, the theater, of effective Western knowledge about the Orient".[61] Napoleon's expedition, itself born, in part, out of a textual imagination rooted in Napoleon's "encounters" with the Orient that began with his days of adolescent reading, refigured the relationship between knowledge and power in particular ways. Napoleon prepared in advance for the encounter, relying, among others, on the work of the Comte de Volney (1959), a French traveler who published his *Voyage en Egypte et en Syrie* in 1787. Napoleon read Volney's account as a handbook of sorts for dealing with the Orient (or with Orientals).[62] Moreover, conquest and the acquisition of systematic, now-scientific knowledge emerged hand in hand: "The Institut, with its team of chemists, historians, biologists, archaeologists, surgeons, and antiquarians, was the learned division of the army."[63] As Said explains, "After Napoleon ... the very language of Orientalism changed radically. Its descriptive realism was upgraded and became not merely a style of representation but a language, indeed a means, of *creation*."[64]

Said's account of the early history of Orientalist discourse provides, in effect, a prehistory of sorts for the modern discipline of Orientalism. Not until sometime in the late nineteenth century did the birth of that discipline occur. And that birth was made possible by the convergence of Orientalism and modern colonial rule.[65] As Said points out in *Culture and Imperialism*,[66] the sheer amount of land under imperial control and colonial settlement had expanded exponentially by the late nineteenth and early twentieth centuries: Whereas in 1800 approximately 35 percent of the earth's surface was, in practice, held by Western powers, by 1878 that percentage had increased to 67 and by 1914 to 84—including lands held as colonies, protectorates, dependencies, dominions, and commonwealths.[67] Within this fully developed imperial context—and its attendant imperial contests—Said discusses Lord Cromer and Andrew Balfour, sketches the differences between English and French imperial and Orientalist visions (e.g., as evidenced in the differences between Massignon and H. A. R. Gibb), and charts the shifts in Orientalist discourse and institutional practices from the pre-World War II period to the postwar era. As Said argues,[68] that shift entailed a movement to a primarily Anglo-American discipline and a gradual shift across the Atlantic to the site of the new dominant global power—a global power that no longer speaks freely, and proudly, of itself as an empire but, rather, one for whom the question of empire is rendered invisible within an ideology of "doing good".

In my reading of *Orientalism*, Said's theoretical commitments and historical arguments are quite different from those in the essays in *The Invention of Tradition*,[69] a book that Said praised and that exemplifies a genre of historical and anthropological scholarship that often took its inspiration from Said's work. According to Said, writing over a decade later in *Culture and Imperialism*, works such as Hobsbawm and Ranger's edited volume have examined "the pure (even purged) images we construct of a privileged, genealogically useful past, a past in which we exclude unwanted elements, vestiges, narratives".[70] In search of new forms of authority, (European) ruling elites and anticolonial movements alike have manufactured rituals, ceremonies, and traditions, projecting "their power backward in time, giving it a history and legitimacy that only tradition and longevity could import".[71]

But invention is not the only—or the most useful—analytic antidote to essentialism. Although episodes of outright "invention"—or fabrication—occur (as evidenced in various essays in Hobsbawm and Ranger's volume), they do not account for very much of what goes on in the social world. The power and authority of narratives, of rituals, or of other cultural practices depend, more often than not, on resonance. And in Said's careful attention to the working and reworking of the Orientalist archive over time, it was not just its authority but, in addition, its resonance—the familiarity and, thus, the credibility of Orientalist statements and beliefs—that Said mapped.

The work of beginning

Following the publication of *Orientalism*, many in the field of Middle East studies sought to take Said's critiques seriously, generating a field of "post-Orientalist" scholarship that has struggled to grapple with the past and present of culture and religion in the Middle East without falling into the arguments and tropes that long characterized Orientalist scholarship. Take, for example, post-Orientalist writings on Islam. Concerned specifically with the problem of essentialism, of writing about Islam as a monolithic and ahistorical phenomenon—a critique that Said leveled quite forcefully in *Orientalism* (and also in *Covering Islam* [1997], a book written for a popular audience)—much of that post-Orientalist scholarship on Islam has grappled with how best to analytically engage contemporary Islamist movements. In so doing, some scholars have relied explicitly or implicitly on a notion of invented tradition. In short, they tell a story about the misrepresentation of (Islamic) history: that Islamists claim ancient roots for beliefs and practices that are, in reality, definitively modern or new.[72] In so doing, they criticize a fundamental Orientalist stereotype: that Islam is inherently anti-modern, that it has been unable to adapt to the modern world, and that Islamists are a throwback to premodern times. Nevertheless, such approaches simplify a far more complex and dynamic relationship between historical traditions and novel cultural forms in contemporary religious movements. In so doing, they ultimately fail to adequately account for or understand the actual practices and arguments through which contemporary Islamists engage Muslim histories and Islamic traditions.

Readings of contemporary Islamist movements that emphasize their invocation of false origins, a reading that in many ways Said shared, are consistent with Said's political commitments and the terms through which he understood and criticized contemporary religious movements (be they Islamist, Christian, or Jewish "fundamentalist"): his commitment to secular politics; to "worldliness" over invocations of "origins" or the divine; and his privileging of "exile" over "belonging"—topics to which I turn below. Nevertheless, *Orientalism*'s methodological and epistemological commitments can be used to consider and treat practices of piety with which Said's own secular imagination had difficulty in ways that give those who undertake them an analytic respect generally not accorded to them in Orientalist and, often, in post-Orientalist scholarship. In other words, drawing on Said's historical and conceptual analysis of Orientalism as a (scholarly) tradition, or as an internally structured archive, one might be able to produce a more complex reading of contemporary Islamist movements than those displayed in much contemporary scholarly work on the topic, a reading that entails a nuanced understanding of the relationship between continuity and change (or novelty).

In sum, Orientalism is a tradition in the classic sense of, say, a literary tradition,[73] rather than of that which opposes the modern or that which opposes change. Orientalist discourse is an archive of systematic statements and bodies of knowledge, continuously drawn on and reformulated, that converges with broader prevailing philosophical tendencies at different moments in time (e.g., race theory in the nineteenth century), all the while retaining a powerful trace of itself as Europe reexperiences the Orient but never as something wholly new or alien. *Orientalism*, after all, recounts the history of a discourse of a very long historical *durée*, albeit one that shifts as it develops within and encounters a changing world. Said is attentive to the grammar that structures this (series of) Western encounter(s) with the Orient while simultaneously tracking its reconfigurations—institutional, material, and imaginative—over time. To draw on his argument in *Beginnings*, in reading Orientalist discourse, Said is delineating "the new in the customary".[74] As Said writes of the shifts in Orientalist discourse generated by the secularizing effects of the Enlightenment in eighteenth-century Europe, for example, "This is not to say that the old religious patterns of human history and destiny and 'the existential paradigms' were simply removed [from Orientalist discourse]. Far from it: they were reconstituted, redeployed, redistributed in ... secular frameworks."[75]

Reconstituted, redeployed, and redistributed—those are the dynamics that Said seeks to understand. The strength of the Orientalist tradition lies not in its absolute sameness but in and through its transfigurations, which, nevertheless, maintain continuities with past intellectual figures and forms and from which it derives (textual and institutional) authority and, quite crucially, cultural resonance. This is an argument neither of absolute novelty (of "invention", as classically understood) nor of false origins. Rather, this is perhaps better read as an argument for a tradition as the (discursive) context within which both arguments and innovations occur.[76]

Although in a different language, many of the more hostile criticisms and reviews of *Orientalism* involve an invented tradition–type argument. Critics have argued that Said was highly selective, that he ignored those writers, national traditions, and histories that did not fit into the account that he set out to produce. In short, they argue that Said invented an Orientalist tradition—a distorted version and vision of Orientalism—that served his political perspective. (Bernard Lewis,[77] e.g., has argued that Said ignored the German and Russian Orientalists, that he focused on some individual scholars at the expense of others, and that he focused only on the Arab Middle East at the expense of other regions. Therefore, for Lewis, there is no actual, historical Orientalist tradition that corresponds with the one Said produces in *Orientalism*.[78]) But, as Said makes clear in his introduction to *Orientalism*, the question or problem of where to begin haunts all writing.

In Said's words, "There is no such thing as a merely given, or simply available, starting point: beginnings have to be made for each project in such a way as to *enable* what follows from them," a difficulty he "consciously lived" in his study of Orientalism.[79] Beginning involves an "act of delineation"—a decision to cut some things off from "a great mass of material".[80] It involves a decision about what kind of an intellectual order one seeks to delineate and describe.[81] That is the task that he undertook in writing *Orientalism*, and it involved a set of decisions that led Said to focus on the British, French, and U.S. fields of Orientalist scholarship and to choose some authors and some texts within that now more narrowly defined tradition over others. And his decision of what to focus on was guided by his interest in understanding the history of Orientalism (which, for a very long time, focused on Islam) and its entanglement with the central empires of the modern world: Britain and France "were the pioneer nations in the Orient and in Oriental studies",[82] a legacy that the United States has inherited in the post-World War II era. In sum, in choosing to focus on some Orientalist traditions, some Orientalist writers and texts and not others, Said did not invent history or a tradition. He consciously engaged the act of writing, an effort of creative intervention—of authorship—which always entails decisions about where to begin and what kinds of connections (or affiliations) one sees among texts and between texts and the world.

Beginnings (1985) was Said's first and perhaps most sustained engagement with the question of intellectual production and the sensibilities and responsibilities of the (modern) intellectual. It is a book about authorship, about the intentional act of intellectual will, a work in which one can perhaps see Said's own struggle to understand and forge his role as an intellectual within the space of modern society and politics. Drawing on Giambattista Vico's understanding of history as willed human work, Said[83] seeks to understand beginning as a productive activity and writing as an act of displacement, an effort to fashion something new. "In short, beginning is *making* or *producing* difference, but ... difference which is the result of combining the already familiar with the fertile novelty of human work in language";[84] it is "the first step in the intentional production of meaning".[85] And this act of will, as it defines the intellectual vocation for Said, requires a certain "homelessness", or exile, actual or metaphorical.[86] Once again, for Said, it was Auerbach who best exemplified the point: the importance of exile to the creative work of criticism. Auerbach wrote *Mimesis*, which Said so admired, while he was in exile in Istanbul during World War II. And by embracing that estrangement—from the libraries and traditions of European literature and culture of which he was a part and about which he wrote— Auerbach composed his most important work. The "contemporary critic," Said writes, is a "wanderer, a man essentially between homes"[87]—as evidenced by modern(ist) writers such as Friedrich Nietzsche, Sigmund Freud, Joseph Conrad, James Joyce, and Thomas Mann, to name a few—who seeks to make connections "by adjacency, not sequentially or dynastically".[88] He explains,

> The net result is to understand language as an intentional structure specifying a series of displacements. ... The series being replaced is the set of relationships linked together by familial analogy: father and son, the image, the process of genesis, a story. In their place stands: the brother, discontinuous concepts, paragenesis, construction. The first of these series is dynastic, bound to sources and origins, mimetic. The relationship holding in the second series are complementarity and adjacency; instead of a source we have the intentional beginning, instead of a story a construction. I take this shift to be of great importance in twentieth-century writing. ... The progressive advance of knowledge to which this shift belongs, displaces the burden of responsibility from origin to beginning.[89]

In juxtaposing "beginnings" to "origins," construction to mimesis, willed human work to the divine, Said defines the modern intellectual (predicament). And in his account of that modern vocation, the distinction between intellectual work, identifications, and responsibilities that rely on "dynastic" relationships versus those that rely on "affiliative" ones, the former subservient to forms of authority and the latter critical of them, is crucial. Said read modern Islamist movements, in particular, and radical religious movements, more generally, as squarely situated in a dynastic sensibility. Nevertheless, if one once again extends Said's intellectual insights—in particular, his analysis of the relationship between continuity and novelty, between the customary and the work of imagination—beyond his own decidedly secular political horizon, contemporary Islamist movements complicate his image of modern intellectual (and political) life in fundamental ways.

Many Islamist movements—movements that are, obviously, decidedly not secular, that do invoke the divine—rely precisely on the formation of communities of affiliation and not of filiation. Joining movements such as the piety movements in Cairo often involves challenging forms of authority and filiation within one's own family to embrace a different set of practices and to join a different, an affiliative, community. Moreover, the relationship of Muslim practitioners to the founding texts of Islam, the question of who reads and interprets them, in what contexts, and with what forms of authority are novel in such piety movements, effectively challenging various forms of authority and hierarchy that mark other modes of contemporary as well as historical Muslim practices. Thus, the overriding distinction between an invocation of origins (as divine) and beginning (as willed human work) cannot capture the complexity of questions of agency and creativity, individual subject and community, and the worldly and the divine that characterize such movements in the contemporary world.[90] In fundamental ways, contemporary religious movements require the work of beginning as much as does the work of any "modern" (read, secular) writer or critic.

Intellectuals and criticism

The question of intellectuals and their role in and responsibility to politics and to criticism was cardinal to Said's corpus and to the intellectual life that he fashioned for himself. As he explained in the Reith Lectures (1994), the intellectual occupies a special place and bears a particular responsibility in modern society. Drawing on Gramsci's argument in the *Prison Notebooks* (1992), Said insists that intellectuals are "pivotal to the workings of modern society".[91] Moreover, for Said, intellectuals have a "specific *public* role in society" (emphasis added), not reducible to being a professional or "competent member of a class just going about his/her business": "The central fact for me is an individual endowed with a faculty for representing, embodying, articulating a message, a view, an attitude, a philosophy or opinion to, as well as for, a public."[92] The true intellectual must be a critic—someone who is willing to raise "embarrassing questions, confront orthodoxy and dogma".[93] In addition, the intellectual vocation requires one to reach a "wide" public, not just a specialized (all too often, academic) audience.

In light of this understanding of the intellectual, Said was deeply critical both of the forms of theory that dominated literary studies and, increasingly, the fields that grew or borrowed from them (beginning in the 1980s) and of the ever-increasing disciplinary specialization, or "expertise", that characterizes intellectual life in the United States and its academy. In fact, although Said was one of the first major theorists to introduce certain French theorists—most notably, Derrida and Foucault[94]—to the U.S. (literary) establishment, he also became rapidly disillusioned with what happened when that theory crossed the Atlantic and became incorporated into distinct "American and mainly academic" circumstances. As he writes in *Culture and Imperialism*, "Cults like post-modernism, discourse analysis, New Historicism, deconstruction, neo-pragmatism transport them [intellectuals] into the country of the blue; an astonishing sense of weightlessness with regard to the gravity of history and individual responsibility fritters away attention to public matters, and to public discourse".[95] For Said, those theoretical turns—derived from readings of Roland Barthes and Levi-Strauss, and, subsequently, Foucault and Derrida—brought with them the (methodological) return of "the fairly isolated status given to the text".[96] And, as Said argues in "Secular Criticism", textuality is "the exact opposite and displacement of what might be called history. Textuality is considered to take place, yes, but by the same token it does not take place anywhere or anytime in particular."[97] Said, by way of contrast, was deeply committed to history: to reading texts—which, for Said, reached well beyond the literary—in all their "worldliness", as "to some degree events ... part of the social world, human life, and of course the historical moments in which they are located and interpreted".[98] A text's "materiality," so central to Said's understanding of (literary) criticism, required that one approach it as "a monument, a cultural object, sought after, fought over, possessed, rejected, or achieved in time".[99] In turn, he sought to produce scholarship that is, as Ann Stoler puts it, "not [just] ...'about' the world, but squarely in it".[100]

What Said saw as a cult of textuality in literary criticism was, for him, part and parcel of multiplying specialization. He saw the academy as increasingly characterized by professional competence and expertise about ever-narrower intellectual fields, often with their own "precious jargon" which limits the conversation—and audience, for whom all writers write—to a very small group of commonly trained academics. As explained in "Opponents, Audiences, Constituencies and Community", an article in which he argued that poststructural criticism was "an integral part of the currents of thought and practice that play a role within the Reagan era",[101] increasing specialization contributes to ever-increasing depoliticization of intellectual life.[102] The audience for much work within literary studies, as Said learned in a conversation with a salesperson for a major university press, is "cultural literary critics".[103] And theory itself, as Said[104] understood it, has become fetishized as an end in and of itself: Intellectuals (in the humanities, in particular) have become obsessed with the internal consistencies of a theoretical argument for its own sake, with its perfect—or exemplary—performance.

Said's humanism

It is in light of such criticism of theory and intellectual production that one might best read Said's relationship to Foucault in *Orientalism*. Although the book is often read as inconsistent or as a book with an irresolvable tension, as Clifford's insightful engagement with the work suggests, that inconsistency or tension was, perhaps, more deliberate than many readers suspect. As Stuart Hall argued at a conference in memory of Edward Said at the University of London's School of Oriental and African Studies (SOAS), *Orientalism* was perhaps Foucauldian in inspiration more than in method.[105] In fact, Said makes explicit that, although deeply indebted to Foucault, he nevertheless, "believe[s] in the determining imprint of individual writers upon the otherwise anonymous collective body of texts constituting a discursive formation like Orientalism".[106] Said rejected the "dogma" of theoretical frameworks as much as that of political ideology. (Although it does strike me that Said engages more explicitly with the tensions between Foucault and his own theoretical and methodological commitments in *Culture and Imperialism*.) Said was consciously synthetic in his approach to theory, something perhaps better understood not as inconsistency but as a sign of his maturity as an intellectual: He drew on different theorists to do very specific intellectual and political work. In short, Said's theoretical distancing from Foucault was essential to his (vision of) criticism and politics. It was critical to his understanding of the responsibility of the intellectual to politics: to maintaining a critic's "active situation in the world",[107] his or her "real opposition" to prevailing historical circumstances (as opposed to mere "oppositional debate") "conducted in political language having a direct connection with actual politics".[108]

Although seen by many as the "father" of postcolonial studies, Said was actually quite critical of the field. He distanced himself from what he saw as both its overly Foucauldian commitments as well as its oft ill-disguised identity politics.[109] As Timothy Brennan (2000) has argued regarding Said's relationship to the postcolonial field, the primary analytic category of *Orientalism* is, perhaps, not discourse but institution. Notably Gramscian in its theoretical and political commitments, *Orientalism* sought not just to map out a particular discursive formation but, just as crucially, to elaborate on how that discursive formation articulated with state power—its institutions, its economic and military imperial projects. Neither in *Orientalism* nor in his numerous subsequent writings did Said's conception of power diverge from its focus on the state and its hegemony: For example, by way of contrast with much of the postcolonial field, it was not to micropolitics, the diffusion of power throughout the social order so central to Foucault, that Said turned his attention.[110] Instead, he insisted that

> the central reality of power and authority in Western history, at least since the period from the end of feudalism on, is the presence of the State, and I think we would have to say that to understand not only power but authority—which is a more interesting and various idea than power—we must also understand the way in which any authority in modern society is derived to some degree from the presence of the State.[111]

In sum, Said's understanding of politics and authority remained committed to "what Jean Francois Lyotard famously called the grand narratives of enlightenment and emancipation".[112] His political vision was distinctly modern(ist). And that commitment distanced Said from much of Foucault's and other poststructural thinkers' theoretical armature.

So, too, of course, did his understanding of the intellectual subject. The question of "will" remained fundamental to Said's vision of the intellectual: Intention cannot be "totally domesticated by system" (which, in Foucault's formulation, is exhibited in discursive regimes), as intention is the "moving force of life and behavior".[113] Authorship was essential to Said, not in a simplistic sense of the isolated intellectual genius—all intellectuals, for Said,[114] are of a particular context, even if they do not, as critics, fully belong (with)in it. Nevertheless, their intention—their will—to engage in criticism is inseparable from his understanding of writing and, more broadly, of intellectual life and of politics and political responsibility. Said's commitment to that will, to human agency, stood at the heart of his enduring humanist commitments.

In a book published posthumously, Said engaged the question of "humanism and cultural practice". Specifically, he wanted to understand humanism as "a useable praxis for intellectuals and academics" who want to connect humanist principles to the "world in which they live as citizens".[115] He was critical of what he understood to be humanism's "abuses", in particular, of its Eurocentrism and, at particular historical moments (e.g., in the United States following World War II), of its elitism. Nevertheless, for Said, those problems were not fatal for humanism. Instead, they were problems to be addressed and redressed. Humanism remained the ground for Said's vision of the intellectual and of oppositional politics in the contemporary world. And to extend humanism's relevance in the context of a postcolonial world and increasingly multicultural societies (especially in the West), Said sought to expand and redefine humanism: to make it more "cosmopolitan", more accurately reflecting the contemporary world; to recognize other historical traditions—the practices of humanism, for example, that began "in the Muslim *madaris*, colleges, and universities of Sicily, Tunis, Baghdad and Seville in the 12th and 13th centuries"[116]—as the source of the development of Western humanist traditions and, thus, to integrate other cultural and intellectual traditions, both historical and contemporary, into what one thinks of as humanism and the humanities as taught in U.S. universities today. Within that now-revised vision, for Said, humanism was an (essential) "antidote" to the phenomenon of increasing specialization that marks the contemporary world: the transformation of knowledge into "expertise", often at the service of corporate or state interests.[117] Real humanism, as best represented for Said by the figure of Auerbach, stood against the cult of expertise that has increasingly, since the postwar period, overtaken intellectual life in the United States.

Importantly, the core of Said's humanism would always remain "the secular notion that the historical world is made by men and women, not by God, and that it can be known rationally according to the principle formulated by Vico in *New Science*, that we can really know only what we make or, to put it differently, we can know things according to the way they were made".[118] Following Vico (1970), self-knowledge, or knowledge of history as made by "man", is distinct from knowledge either of nature or of the supernatural—in particular, because it is more fully knowable. In addition, self-knowledge must entail self-criticism. Humanism, for Said, necessarily situates "critique at [its] ... very heart, critique as a form of democratic freedom and as a continuous practice of questioning and of accumulating knowledge that is open to, rather than in denial of, the constituent historical realities"[119] of the world in which people live.

Humanism can be—and has been—trenchantly critiqued on many grounds: for example, its fundamental entanglement with colonialism, its configuration of the (modern, secular) subject as normative, and its definition of "the human" (e.g., Asad 2003; Mehta 1999; Povinelli 2002). Thus, many poststructuralist and postcolonial scholars in the academy see Said's humanist commitments either as inconsistent in light of his other theoretical and political commitments or simply as a throwback to an earlier epistemological, theoretical, and political tradition too embedded in a history of Eurocentrism and its attendant forms of violence to be resuscitated today in the name of radical politics.

Nevertheless, even if one does not share Said's humanist commitments (a tradition I remain far more skeptical of than was Said), recognizing the political work that humanism did for Said is important. Said's humanism, which shaped his understanding of politics, his commitment to universal values, and his vision of the intellectual as an agent, a "maker of meaning" with a distinct public responsibility, enabled him to be the public intellectual that he was, one unparalleled by anyone else in his generation. He engaged tirelessly in public debate—in the United States most often about the struggle for Palestinian rights and, increasingly, in his last decade of life, as a critic of both Arab regimes and U.S. empire as he wrote and spoke for an Arab public throughout the Middle East. His public influence was enormous, his political effectiveness noteworthy in a country in which so many academics (including myself) have retreated into the academy and into a form of politics and political critique limited to that context. And although that role as public intellectual gained him much fame (he had almost rock-star status when he gave public talks in Beirut or in Palestine toward the end of his life, and over 1,000 participants attended the SOAS conference in his honor in London), it also made him the object of often unparalleled hostility.

Polemics

Publicly, Said was best known for his engagement with the history of the Israeli state, its multiple displacements of Palestinians, and the still-ongoing occupation. And within the domain of public polemics that emerged in response, he was often characterized in ways that seem to have no actual relationship to the person and scholar he was. Attacked relentlessly by Daniel Pipes and his organization Campus Watch, referred to as a man of violence in a eulogy written for Columbia University's *Spectator*, in which his life is summed up by the act of throwing a stone at Israeli soldiers along Lebanon's southern border, Said was often depicted as a Palestinian radical and an angry man.[120] According to an article in the conservative *Middle East Quarterly*, rather than ever providing a "serious alternative" to that which he critiqued, Said displayed "a kind of floating over-identification with political causes like Palestine, Arab nationalism and Muslim anti-imperialism",[121] a characterization of Said's political commitments that completely ignores his sustained criticism of both Palestinian and Arab nationalisms and, of course, his deep suspicion if not downright hostility toward radical Islamist movements.[122] As was often claimed in attacks on Said, "*Orientalism* could obviously have been written by no one but a Palestinian scholar with a huge chip on his shoulder and a very dim understanding of the European academic tradition".[123] Reduced to his "Palestinian identity"—or, more accurately, to other people's reading of it—Said could not have known the Western canon, his political critique could only have been that of an angry (emotional) postcolonial intellectual "writing back".[124]

Such attacks on Said and his work have, in recent years, extended well beyond a general public domain. They have entered the realm of public policy.

In congressional hearings on "International Programs in Higher Education and Questions about Bias" (Title VI-funded programs), Stanley Kurtz (a research fellow at the Hoover Institution with strong ties to Pipes, among others) testified that postcolonial studies, a field supposedly fathered by Said and one that purportedly dominates Middle East studies in the academy (as well as South Asian studies, among other area fields), is staffed by "bitter critics" of U.S. foreign policy.[125] In Kurtz's words, "The core premise of postcolonial theory is that it is immoral for a scholar to put his knowledge of foreign languages and cultures at the service of American power".[126] Seeing Said's influence everywhere, even among those who do not "directly quote him", Kurtz called for "balance", thus, asking Congress to set up a supervisory board for Title VI programs (which would put pressure on provosts and deans to achieve "balance" on college and university faculties) and to switch the funding of foreign language study (for which Title VI is largely responsible) from universities to the Defense Language Institute.[127] Congresspersons, Kurtz, and various other representatives of Title VI centers then proceeded to debate the issue—an almost amusing exchange, as one reads the transcript of this debate, with members of Congress discussing postcolonial theory and, occasionally, Foucault.[128]

Assuming that Kurtz's characterization of both Foucault and postcolonial theory was accurate, members of Congress asked whether it is true that postcolonial theory really dominates area-studies disciplines—in particular, Middle East studies—in the academy. To quote Congressman Tim Ryan (Democrat of Ohio), "We've talked a lot about postcolonial theory. Obviously it has a lot of interest. In your opinion is there a counterpoint that is being taught and if so is it being taught with as much interest, or as much energy as postcolonial theory?"[129] For Kurtz the answer was no; for others testifying before the committee the answer was yes, Said's influence has been waning in Middle East studies, although they never named a specific counterpoint. And as this battle continues—via Title VI funding, universities that fear congressional pressure, and an ongoing public campaign against Said and the so-called Saidians—what is at stake is whether or not his intellectual legacy should and will be reversed. Said—along with his continued influence (here seen in a growing faculty of postcolonial critics)—is being battled posthumously. He has become a sign of the problem of a liberal, multicultural United States, one epitomized by the presence of postcolonial scholars in the academy whose commitments both to U.S. national security and to a defense of Israel, to which U.S. foreign policy is increasingly tied, are deeply suspect.

Conclusion

Those public political battles and the manner in which they trivialize Said and his intellectual interventions return me to the seriousness of Said's work. His writings, after all, can neither be reduced to a simple anti-American polemic nor be dismissed as the work of an angry Palestinian postcolonial writing back. Said's engagement with questions of knowledge and power in the context of empire and the still-unfolding realities of a postcolonial world offer methodological, epistemological, and historical insights on which many of us in anthropology, and within the academy, more broadly, continue to draw.

In contrast to his reputation in the public domain, Said's primary legacy in the academy, and certainly in the discipline of anthropology, has little to do with either Said's critique of the Israeli state and the overwhelming support of the United States for that state or his critique of representations of Islam and their devolvement into policies of intervention abroad and policing at home.[130] In many ways, of course, that makes a lot of sense. His intellectual insights go well beyond an analysis of empire and imperial legacies in the modern—or historical—Middle East. For one thing, he made empire central to understanding the history of European culture and politics. As Hall argued during the SOAS conference, Said challenged us, as scholars, to put imperial projects at the center of the making of modernity, Western capitalism, and culture. As a cultural critic, he thought about creativity and authorship, knowledge and power, and texts and the world in ways that revolutionized many disciplines. Moreover, in fields often structured around area expertise, very few scholars work on "the Middle East", thus leaving questions about the specific forms of power and empire in Israel and Palestine or, more broadly, in the war(s) in Iraq, well outside the purview of many academics' work. (Nevertheless, in accounting for that fact, one cannot entirely elide the discomfort on the part of many Jewish academics as well as some of their non-Jewish compatriots who have varying degrees and forms of identification with the Israeli state. Moreover, the fear of being labeled an "anti-Semite" has had a chilling effect, and with renewed force over the past few years, on critical discussions of Israel within the academy and, thus, on people's willingness to engage that aspect of Said's work.)[131] Nevertheless, we face—and increasingly so—a political urgency: an ever more belligerent and expansive U.S. empire for which, if one takes Said's political and intellectual commitments seriously, we all bear responsibility as U.S. academics or as academics living and working in the United States. For, as Stoler writes in an eloquent tribute to Said, for a long time she did not fully understand why he remained critical of anthropological studies of colonialism, why he accused anthropology of allowing, as he put it, "a total absence of any reference to American imperial intervention".[132] In her "10th rereading of *Orientalism*", she realized "how much it was directed at a history of the present, not only about French and British empire in the 18th and 19th century [*sic*], but as he insisted throughout the book, about the U.S.".[133] What Said sought "to make sense of," Stoler goes on to argue, was "the political present",[134] and he did so through his historical method and commitments.

Of late, of course, that U.S. political present has become ever more fundamentally entangled with "radical Islam" and the "war on it", the Middle East having emerged as its most central locale. The War on Terror, which began in Afghanistan and has spilled over into border regions of Pakistan, now has its vortex in the U.S. occupation of Iraq. And that is not the only occupation of significance that portends a possible destabilization of the Middle East and large parts of the Muslim world, more generally; so, too, does the Israeli occupation of the Palestinian territories, with Israel's increasingly brutal policies receiving unqualified support from the U.S. administration in a way that dwarfs the support of former administrations. If we are to take Said's legacy seriously, then—if we are to learn not only from his writings but just as essentially from the intellectual life that he led—we must take responsibility, publicly, for engaging this new U.S. imperial formation and its attendant forms of violence and intimidation, both domestic and foreign. And to do so requires that we reintegrate Said's specific intellectual and political engagements with the past and present of empire in the Middle East, in general, and vis-à-vis "the question of Palestine", specifically, with his more general critique of empire—and its forms of culture, power, and knowledge—about which he wrote so much and so well.

Acknowledgments

I would like to thank Bashir Abu Manneh, John Comaroff, Virginia Dominguez, Samira Haj, Joanne Passaro, Elizabeth Povinelli, and Lisa Wedeen for their careful readings and insightful critiques of earlier versions of this article. I would also like to thank Lori Allen for collecting the materials, editing, commenting on, and putting together the bibliography for the article and Linda Forman, of the *American Ethnologist*, for her fine editorial work. I am, of course, solely responsible for all mistakes and problems that remain.

Writing a piece that does justice to Edward Said's legacy is impossible. This is but a beginning that I can only hope Edward would have thought a serious attempt to engage his work, albeit, no doubt, he would not have agreed with all of my readings of and arguments concerning his scholarly writings and his intellectual life.

Notes

1 Edward Said, *Orientalism*, 25th anniversary edition (New York: Vintage, 2003), p. 334.

2 More accurately described as "al-sahwa al-islamiyya" (the Islamic awakening), contemporary Islamist movements involve many different kinds of engagements with Islam, with piety, and with politics, only some of which are interested in challenging, at least directly, the power of the state (see Hirschkind n.d.).

3 Bernard Lewis, "The Roots of Muslim Rage", *Policy*, vol. 17, no. 4 (2001–2), p. 19.

4 Huntington, Samuel P. *The Clash of Civilizations and the Remaking of World Order* (New York: Simon and Schuster, 1996).

5 Edward Said, *Culture and Imperialism* (New York: Knopf, 1993), p. xii.

6 Said, *Orientalism*, pp. xxi–xxii.

7 Ibid.

8 Seymour Hersh, "The Gray Zone: How a Secret Pentagon Program Came to Abu Ghraib", *New Yorker* (May 24, 2004), p. 42.

9 Increasingly clear is that these forms of torture were first developed in Afghanistan and later at Guantanamo Bay in Cuba, as both argued by Hersh in his May 24 article and attested to more recently by prisoners released from Guantanamo Bay and repatriated to the United Kingdom for trial (see BBC News Online 2005; BBC Radio 4 2004).

10 Ibid, p. 42.

11 Emram Qureshi, "Misreading the Arab Mind", *Boston Globe* (May 30, 2004). In an earlier era, the book was given to U.S. diplomats serving in the Middle East.

12 Hersh, p. 42.

13 There is a notable similarity—and possibly a direct link— between these U.S. tactics regarding how to extract information from political prisoners and techniques long used by the Israeli authorities in the Occupied Territories. (For reports on similar techniques as they are used against Palestinians, see Amnesty International 1994; Human Rights Watch/Middle East 1994a, 1994b; and Public Committee against Torture in Israel 2003. For discussions of possible links between the institutions of torture in Iraq and Israel, see Abunimah 2004; Fisk 2004; and Kalman 2004.)
14 Said, *Orientalism*, p. xvii.
15 Ibid.
16 Ibid, p. 2.
17 Ibid.
18 Ibid, p. 3.
19 Ibid, p. 45.
20 Of course, the anthropological literature on colonialism and culture, one quite influenced by Said at its inception, is a notable exception to this claim (e.g., Comaroff and Comaroff 1991; Cooper and Stoler 1997; Dirks 1992).
21 For a review that critically engages anthropological readings of Said's text as raising questions about the general problem of representation, see Thomas 1991.
22 James Clifford and George E. Marcus, eds., "Orientalism", *History and Theory*, vol. 19, no. 2 (1980), p. 209.
23 Ibid, pp. 209–210.
24 Ibid, p. 205.
25 Edward Said, "Representing the Colonized: Anthropology's Interlocutors", *Critical Inquiry*, vol. 15, no. 2, p. 206. See also his discussion of Claude Levi-Strauss in *Orientalism*, in which he considers the cognitive proclivity of the human mind to divide up the world into selves and others (Said 2003: 53–54).
26 Edward Said, *Humanism and Democratic Criticism* (New York: Columbia University Press, 2004), p. 96. See *Humanism* ch. 4 for a lengthy discussion of Auerbach and his central work, *Mimesis* (2003).
27 Said, Edward, *The World, the Text, the Critic* (Cambridge, MA: Harvard University Press, 1983), pp. 178–225.
28 Ibid, pp. 162–163.
29 Ibid, p. 170.
30 Ibid, p. 171.
31 Ibid, p. 175.
32 For a more extensive discussion of what is entailed in and enabled by studying texts' affiliations with the world, see Said, *The World, the Text, the Critic*, pp. 174–175.
33 See, for example, Said's engagement with Othering in *The World, the Text, the Critic*, p.14, published just a few years after *Orientalism*, which, rather than relying on the cognitive assumptions of Levi-Strauss, engages questions of the state and its hegemonic power. See also his preface to the 25th anniversary edition of *Orientalism*, in which he writes: "What I do argue also is that there is a difference between knowledge of other peoples and other times that is the result of understanding, compassion, careful study and analysis for their own sakes, and on the other hand knowledge—if that is what it is—that is part of an overall campaign of self-affirmation, belligerency, and outright war" (Said 2003: xix).
34 Although Said was far from the first to criticize the relationship between knowledge and empire, and, certainly, that critique had been leveled by several anthropologists vis-à-vis their own discipline long before *Orientalism* was published, his argument was different insofar as he understood knowledge to be generative of forms of power (via his readings of both Gramsci and Michel Foucault) and not merely an ideological reflection of it (e.g., Asad 1973; see also Dirks 2004, who makes a similar point; of course, many of Bernard Cohn's [1987, 1996] much earlier articles argued for the generative power of knowledge within the context of empire).

35 See Said's article "Representing the Colonized: Anthropology's Interlocutors" (1989: 208; this article is the published version of the talk he gave before the American Anthropological Association in 1987). In particular, he is referring to works such as George E. Marcus and Michael M. J. Fischer's *Anthropology as Cultural Critique* (1986) and James Clifford and Marcus's *Writing Culture* (1986).

36 Said, *Orientalism*, p. 210.

37 Ibid.

38 "What we must reckon with is a long and slow process of appropriation by which Europe, or the European awareness of the Orient, transformed itself from being textual and contemplative into being administrative, economic and even military" (Said 2003: 210).

39 As Clifford, a very sympathetic critic, writes, "Indeed, his critical manner sometimes appears to mimic the essentializing discourse it attacks" (1980: 210). Or as he asks within the context of a series of questions regarding the problem of representation, more generally, "How ... is an oppositional critique of Orientalism to avoid falling into 'Occidentalism?'" (Clifford 1980: 208). A second set of critical questions raised by reviewers was whether or not Said Orientalized the (Arab) East, giving no agency to an indigenous subject and history (see Ahmad 1992). Said seems to take the latter critique to heart in *Culture and Imperialism* (1993), in which anticolonial and postcolonial intellectuals play a central analytic role in his understanding of the relationship of culture to empire. The historical dynamic through which resistance to empire is generated comes into focus in this later work. Having said that, in my opinion, this latter critique partially misunderstands Said's project in *Orientalism*. He was not interested in the nature of resistance in "the Islamic East" or in giving a historical account of the Arab-Muslim world at all. He was interested, instead, in understanding the coordinates and terms of imperial power therein, the context, one could argue, within which forms of resistance emerged.

40 Ian Buruma and Avishai Margalit, *Occidentalism: The West in the Eyes of Its Enemies* (New York: Penguin Press, 2004), p. 10.

41 Worth noting is that the four archetypal forms are different in kind: the city is an abstraction of space; the Western mind, an imaginative trope; the bourgeoisie, a sociological form; and the infidel, a figure.

42 "One way of describing Occidentalism would be to trace the history of all its links and overlaps, from the Counter-Reformation to the Counter-Enlightenment in Europe, to the many varieties of fascism and national socialism in the East and West, to anticapitalism and antiglobalization, and finally to the religious extremism that rages in so many places today" (Buruma and Margalit 2004: 11).

43 For example, in discussing the "venom" of the Palestinian intifadas, Buruma and Margalit write:

> Israel has to bear some of the responsibility for this menacing atmosphere [an atmosphere of suicide bombers, menacing to Israelis]. You cannot humiliate and bully others without eventually provoking a violent response. The daily sight of Palestinian men crouching in the heat at Israeli checkpoints, suffering the casual abuse of Jewish soldiers, explains some of the venom of the intifadas. But Israel has also become the prime target of a more general Arab rage against the West, the symbol of idolatrous, hubristic, amoral, colonialist evil, a cancer in the eyes of its enemies that must be expunged by killing. (2004: 138–139)

For their discussion of anti-Americanism, see Buruma and Margalit 2004: 8. In neither case do they provide an explanation for the remaining causes of such "venom"; rather, Occidentalism is a recurrent expression of anti-Enlightenment thinking—"hatreds and anxiety" toward the values of Enlightenment—that seems to require no historically specific explanation. Different groups, at different times, just seem to react against these values.

44 Said, *Orientalism*, p. 3.
45 Clifford, "Orientalism", p. 207.
46 Said, *Orientalism*, pp. 8–9.
47 Ibid, p. 9.
48 Said, *Culture and Imperialism*, p. xxii. His commitment to the creativity of individual authors is, of course, a theoretical and methodological commitment that diverges dramatically from Foucault's notion of discourse, on which Said also relies. I will return to this point later in the article.
49 See Said 2003: 268–269; see also Brennan 1992: 79 and Clifford 1980: 210–212.
50 Said, *Orientalism*, pp. 201–225.
51 Ibid, p. 55.
52 Ibid, pp. 55–56.
53 Ibid, p. 57.
54 Ibid, p. 58.
55 Ibid, p. 118.
56 Ibid, p. 119.
57 Ibid, pp. 120, 206–207.
58 Ibid, p. 120.
59 Ibid.
60 Ibid, p. 42.
61 Ibid, p. 43.
62 Specifically, Volney identified three "barriers" to French hegemony in the Orient, which he saw as wars that would have to be fought: "one against England, a second against the Ottoman Porte, and a third, the most difficult against the Muslims" (Said 2003: 81). On the basis of what they learned from Volney's work, according to Said, Napoleon and his troops sought to convince the Muslims that "nous sommes les vrais musulmans" [we are the true Muslims] (2003: 82) and to seek to build an alliance with the Egyptians against their Mameluk rulers.
63 Said, *Orientalism*, pp. 83–84.
64 Ibid, p. 87.
65 According to Said: During the nineteenth and twentieth centuries the Orientalists became a more serious quantity, because by then the reaches of imaginative and actual geography had shrunk, because the Oriental–European relationship was determined by an unstoppable European expansion in search of markets, resources, and colonies, and finally, because Orientalism had accomplished its self-metamorphosis from a scholarly discourse to an imperial institution. (2003: 94)
66 Said, *Culture and Imperialism*, p. 8.
67 In *Culture and Imperialism*, Said's engagement with geography takes on more explicitly materialist dimensions. Imperialism is, quite literally, a "struggle over geography"—that which entails "thinking about, settling on, controlling land that you do not possess, that is distant, that is lived on and owned by others" (Said 1993: 7). But, that struggle over geography, as Said (1993: 7) then explains, involves not only "soldiers and cannons" but, in addition, ideas, forms, images, and imaginings. More generally, his historical account in this later work—a series of essays that expand on *Orientalism* to describe "a more general pattern of relationships between the modern metropolitan West and its overseas territories" (Said 1993: xi)—is a far more materialist account than that in *Orientalism*. See, for example, his reading of Giuseppe Verdi's opera *Aida*—its development, its musical and narrative forms, and its staging in late nineteenth-century Egypt.
68 Said, *Culture and Imperialism*, pp. 8–9.
69 Eric Hobsbawm, and Terence Ranger, eds., *The Invention of Tradition* (Cambridge: Cambridge University Press, 1983).
70 Said, *Culture and Imperialism*, p. 15.
71 Ibid, p. 16.

72 For example, Al-Azmeh 1993, Eickelman and Piscatori 1996, and Zubaida 2004. For a more extended discussion of this tendency in post-Orientalist scholarship, see Hirschkind n.d.
73 Said, Edward, *Beginnings: Intention and Method* (New York: Basic Books, 1985), p. 19.
74 Ibid, p. xxiii.
75 Said, *Orientalism*, pp. 120–121.
76 See Asad 1993; Haj 2002; Hirschkind n.d.; MacIntyre 1981; Mahmood 2004.
77 Bernard Lewis, "The Question of Orientalism," *New York Review of Books* (June 24, 1982), p. 51.
78 For a collection of reviews of *Orientalism*, both critical and sympathetic, see Macfie 2000.
79 Said, *Orientalism*, p. 16.
80 Ibid.
81 Ibid.
82 Ibid, p. 17; Said, *Culture and Imperialism*, p. xxii.
83 Said, *Beginnings*, p. 66.
84 Ibid, p. xxiii.
85 Ibid, p. 5.
86 See Edward Said, *Representations of the Intellectual: The 1993 Reith Lectures* (New York: Pantheon Books, 1994), ch. 3.
87 Said, *Beginnings*, p. 8.
88 Ibid, p. 10.
89 Ibid, p. 66. The dichotomies on which Said relies could be read in classic Orientalist terms: the divine, an invocation of origins, the work of mimesis standing in for the East versus the secular, the antiauthoritative, the constructive, or the work of the imagination synonymous with the modern West. Nevertheless, these distinctions—even if taken at face value—do not need to map onto a classic "East"–"West" divide with all its attendant meanings: in sum, that the former is oriented toward origins and the latter focused on (the making of) a novel future. As I discuss later, Said (2004: 54, 58, 68–69) saw nothing inherently Western in the latter, recognizing forms of argument, agency, and creativity in Islam's history of *ijtihad* and locating humanism's origins, at least in part, in the non-West. (In Islamic law, *ijtihad* refers to the process of making a legal decision through interpretation of the Quran and the Sunna; for a discussion of *ijtihad*, see Hallaq 1984.)
90 See Mahmood 2001, 2004.
91 Said, *Reith*, p. 10.
92 Ibid, p. 11.
93 Ibid. Or, as he writes in his essay "Secular Criticism", criticism is "individual consciousness placed at a sensitive nodal point", it is "distance" (Said 1983: 15)—from belonging, from orthodoxy, and from "home".
94 See Said, *Beginnings*, ch. 5.
95 Said, *Culture and Imperialism*, p. 302.
96 Said, *Beginnings*, p. xviii.
97 Said, *World*, p. 3.
98 Ibid, p. 4; see also pp. 148–151 and Said, *Humanism*, pp. 48–49.
99 Said, *World*, p. 170.
100 Ann Stoler. "A Tribute to Edward Said" (Unpublished MS, Department of Anthropology, New School University, n.d.), p. 5.
101 Edward Said, "Opponents, Audiences, Constituencies, and Community", *Critical Inquiry*, vol. 9, no. 1 (1982), p. 135.
102 See also "Reflections on American 'Left' Literary Criticism", in *The World, the Text, the Critic* (Said 1983).
103 Said, "Opponents", p. 140.
104 Ibid.

105 The conference, "Edward W. Said (1935–2003): A Continuing Legacy Conference and Cultural Evening", was held on October 3, 2004.
106 Said, *Orientalism*, p. 23.
107 Said, *World*, p. 146.
108 Ibid, p. 160.
109 For an extended discussion of this distancing (including its relation to the question of identity politics, which I do not engage here), see Brennan 2000.
110 Although I agree with much of Brennan's argument, both in his reading of Said and in his critique of postcolonial studies, I think he goes too far in dismissing as almost superficial Foucault's influence over Said. Foucault's concept of a discursive formation is essential to Said's analysis in *Orientalism*, a debt quite evident in Said's interest in the reproduction and repetition of "form"—or, of grammar—so fundamental to Orientalism's longevity. Moreover, clearly, Foucault was also interested in institutions—the clinic, the prison, or the madhouse—even if his understanding of the nature of institutional power was quite different from Said's.
111 Ibid, p. 168.
112 Said, *Humanism*, p. 10.
113 Said, *Beginnings*, p. 319.
114 E.g., Said, *Reith*, p. 26.
115 Said, *Humanism*, p. 6.
116 Ibid, p. 54.
117 Said writes, "What is the acceptable humanist antidote to what one discovers, say among sociologists, philosophers, and so-called policy makers who speak only to and for each other in a language oblivious to everything but a well-guarded, constantly shrinking fiefdom forbidden to the uninitiated" (2004: 143). Alongside the corporatization of knowledge qua expertise, Said saw a second phenomenon contributing to humanism's demise. Recounting an argument made by Masao Miyoshi, Said argues that the humanities—which ... [Miyoshi] ... correctly presupposes, is not the province of the corporate manager but of the humanist—have fallen into irrelevance and quasi-medieval fussiness, ironically enough because of the fashionableness of newly relevant fields like postcolonialism, ethnic studies, cultural studies and the like. This has effectively detoured the humanities from its rightful concern with the critical investigation of values, history, and freedom, turning it, it would seem, into a whole factory of word-spinning and insouciant specialties, many of them identity-based that in their jargon and special pleading address only like-minded people, acolytes, and other academics. (2004: 14)
118 Said, *Humanism*, p. 11.
119 Ibid, p. 47.
120 For more on Pipes's organization, see Campus Watch n.d. According to the *Spectator* eulogy, "Said's scholarly life hit its nadir in July 2000, when he hurled a rock over the Lebanese–Israeli border toward an Israeli guardhouse. He described this act, which was undoubtedly profoundly opposed to the responsibilities of an academic, as 'a symbolic gesture of joy'" (Sebrow and Rolfe 2003).
121 Martin Kramer, "MESA Culpa", *Middle East Quarterly*, vol. 9, no. 4 (2002).
122 The journal *Middle East Quarterly* and the Campus Watch website are both programs of the right-wing think-tank Middle East Forum.
123 Michael Richardson, "Enough Said: Reflections on *Orientalism*", *Anthropology Today*, vol. 6, no. 4 (1990), p. 18, after Simon Leyes, *The Burning Forest: Essays on Chinese Culture and Politics* (London: Paladin, 1988), p. 96; for another attack on Said's knowledge and credentials, see Lewis, "Orientalism", p. 53. In *Culture and Imperialism*, Said consciously distances himself from what he calls a "rhetoric of blame", the language, he explains, "through which contemporary (post) colonial figures *are heard*"; instead, Said strives to "formulate an alternative both to a politics of blame and to the even more destructive politics of confrontation and hostility" (1993: 18, emphasis added).

124 It is worth noting that, although Said's presumed identity was fair game in public (and academic) debate and in "explaining" his intellectual and political positions, it seems to be out of bounds to comment publicly on the Jewish identity—or, perhaps more accurately, identification—of many of those driving these critiques, let alone those pushing U.S. policy into an ever-closer alliance with the Israeli state: For example, Paul Wolfowitz, Richard Perle, and Douglas Feith, who coauthored with David Wurmser at least two strategy papers for Israeli Prime Minister Benjamin Netanyahu in 1996, have all been central architects of the Bush administration's Middle East policies. In addition, Martin Kramer, Pipes, and Stanley Kurtz, seen as Said's and Middle East studies (public) intellectual critics today, all have strong ties to U.S. Jewish organizations and deep commitments to and strong identifications with the Israeli state.

125 These hearings were held on June 10, 2003, under the auspices of the Committee on Education and the Workplace, Subcommittee on Select Education. For the full transcript of the hearings, see U.S. House of Representatives 2003. See also Lori Allen et al.'s article (in press) that discusses Title VI and public intellectualism with regard to the Middle East. During the hearings, Kurtz cited Martin Kramer's book, *Ivory Towers on Sand: The Failure of Middle Eastern Studies in America* (2001) as his authoritative source. *Ivory Towers* was published by the pro-Israel Washington Institute for Near East Policy, and it "depicts academic Middle East studies as a cesspool of error, fuzzy thinking and anti-Americanism" (Lockman 2004). Kramer, formerly a research associate at Tel Aviv University's Moshe Dayan Center for Middle Eastern and African Studies and currently a senior editor of *Middle East Quarterly*, the journal that Pipes founded, is in the forefront of those leading attacks against academics who are critical of U.S. policy in the Middle East and of the Israeli state.

126 US House of Representatives 2003.

127 The question of balance has become quite central to attacks on universities, in general, and their Middle East studies programs, in particular. Among universities under the most direct attack are New York University, the University of California, Santa Barbara, and Columbia University (the former two were discussed at length during the hearings). And university administrations have become increasingly responsive to such criticisms, as I can testify to most directly regarding Columbia. (Vis-à-vis attacks on particular campuses and their Middle East faculties, the driving criticism has focused at least as much on the "problem" with a critical stance toward Israel as toward the United States; see, e.g., Feidan 2004; Fink 2004; Kleinfeld 2005; Piper 2003.) It is also worth noting that "balance" in these debates is often a code word for ethnic–religious balance and not just ideological balance (presuming the faculty of Middle East studies departments to be too heavily Arab or Muslim and completely ignoring that Jewish and Israel studies departments—a second context in which "the Middle East" is taught at universities—tend to be staffed almost entirely by Jewish faculty members). To achieve (or impose) balance, Kurtz suggested that the board supervising Title VI programs be staffed by the secretary of education, national security advisor, secretary of state, secretary of commerce, director of the National Endowment for the Humanities, commander of the National Defense University, and four additional presidential nominees.

128 I quote Kurtz, from a transcript of the question and answer period of the hearings: It's almost a reflex towards criticism of America and American foreign policy [that] has grown up within the academic community. And the folks who pervade that particular perspective themselves have critical attitudes towards traditional notions of liberty and freedom. People who take a postmodern perspective, like Professor Said, followed Michel Foucault. Michel Foucault doesn't take very seriously a tradition of democratic guarantees. (U.S. House of Representatives 2003)

129 U.S. House of Representatives 2003.

130 See Said, *Orientalism*, pp. xv–xxx.

131 The linking of criticisms of the Israeli state to the problem of anti-Semitism is part

of an organized campaign that has taken off over the past few years. For example, at its 34th Zionist Congress in 2001, the World Zionist Organization resolved to undertake steps to train its members to deal with what it described as the rise on college campuses of anti-Zionism and anti-Semitism, which it understands to be inseparable. In addition, the David Project (the group that produced the controversial documentary film *Columbia Unbecoming* [2004], which accuses members of Columbia's Middle East faculty of being biased and intimidating Jewish students) is "working on campuses to counter the hostile environment for many students and faculty who challenge the dominant paradigm about the Middle East conflict" (2005). This film equates criticism of the Israeli state with the long-standing historical problem of anti-Semitism. See also Stern 2002.

132 Stoler, "Tribute", p. 2.

133 Ibid, p. 3.

134 Ibid, p. 4.

Bibliography

Abunimah, Ali (2004) Israeli Link Possible in US Torture Techniques. *Daily Star*, May 11. Electronic document, http://www.dailystar.com.lb/ article.asp?edition_ID=10&article_ID=3446&categ_id=2, accessed June 10.

Ahmad, Aijaz (1992) Orientalism and After: Ambivalence and Metropolitan Location in the Work of Edward Said. In *Theory: Classes, Nations, Literatures*. pp. 159–219. London: Verso.

Al-Azmeh, Aziz (1993) Islams and Modernities. London: Verso.

Allen, Lori, Lara Deeb, and Jessica Winegar (in press) Academics and the Government in "The New American Century": A Conversation with Rashid Khalidi. *Radical History Review* 93.

Amnesty International (1994) *Israel and the Occupied Territories: Torture and Ill-Treatment of Political Detainees*. New York: Amnesty International USA.

Asad, Talal (1993) *Genealogies of Religion: Discipline and Reasons of Power in Christianity and Islam*. Baltimore: Johns Hopkins University Press.

——, (2003) *Formations of the Secular: Christianity, Islam, Modernity*. Stanford, CA: Stanford University Press.

Asad, Talal, ed. (1973) *Anthropology and the Colonial Encounter*. Atlantic Highlands, NJ: Humanities Press.

Auerbach, Erich (2003) [1957] *Mimesis: The Representation of Reality in Western Literature*. Willard R. Trask, trans. Princeton: Princeton University Press.

BBC News Online (2005) Abu Ghraib Inmates Recall Torture. January 12. Electronic document, http://news.bbc.co.uk/2/hi/americas/4165627. stm, accessed February.

BBC Radio 4 (2004) Today Programme Report, October 1, Letter from Guantanamo, Zubeida Malik. Electronic document, http://www. bbc.co.uk/radio4/today/reports/international/begg_20041001. shtml, accessed February 2005.

Brennan, Timothy (1992) Places of Mind, Occupied Lands. In *Edward Said: A Critical Reader*. Michael Sprinker, ed. pp. 74–95. Cambridge, MA: Blackwell.

——, (2000) The Illusion of a Future: Orientalism as Traveling Theory. *Critical Inquiry* 26(3): 558–583.

Buruma, Ian, and Avishai Margalit (2004) *Occidentalism: The West in the Eyes of Its Enemies*. New York: Penguin Press.

Campus Watch (n.d.) Campus Watch: Monitoring Middle East Studies on Campus. Electronic document, http://www.campus-watch.org, accessed February 2005.

Clifford, James (1980) Orientalism. *History and Theory* 19(2): 204–223.

Clifford, James, and George E. Marcus, eds. (1986) *Writing Culture: The Poetics and Politics of Ethnography*. Berkeley: University of California Press.

Cohn, Bernard (1987) *An Anthropologist among the Historians and Other Essays*. Delhi: Oxford University Press.

——, (1996) *Colonialism and Its Forms of Knowledge: The British in India*. Princeton: Princeton University Press.

Comaroff, Jean, and John Comaroff (1991) *Of Revelation and Revolution*. 2 vols. Chicago: University of Chicago Press.

Cooper, Frederick, and Ann Stoler, eds. (1997) *Tensions of Empire: Colonial Cultures in a Bourgeois World*. Berkeley: University of California Press.

Coronil, Fernando (1996) Beyond Occidentalism: Toward Nonimperial Geohistorical Categories. *Cultural Anthropology* 11(1): 51–87.

David Project (2004) *Columbia Unbecoming*. 53 min. David Project. Boston.

——, (2005) Campaigns. Columbia Unbecoming. Electronic document, http://www.davidproject.org/index.php?option=com_content&task=blogcategory&id=26&Itemid=28, accessed February.

Dirks, Nicholas, ed. (1992) *Colonialism and Culture*. Ann Arbor: University of Michigan Press.

——, (2004) Edward Said and Anthropology. *Journal of Palestine Studies* 33(3): 38–54.

Eickelman, Dale F., and James Piscatori (1996) *Muslim Politics*. Princeton: Princeton University Press.

Feidan, Douglas (2004) Hate 101: Climate of Hate Rocks Columbia University. *New York Daily News*, November 21. Electronic document, http://www.nydailynews.com/front/story/254925p-218295c. html, accessed June 10.

Fink, Liz (2004) Committee to Address MEALAC Controversy. *Columbia Spectator*, December 9. Electronic document, http://www. columbiaspectator.com/vnews/display.v/ART/2004/12/09/ 41b7fc1f84ed1?in_archive=1, accessed June 10.

Fisk, Robert (2004) Follow Torture Trail at Abu Ghraib. *Seattle Post Intelligencer*, May 26. Electronic document, http://seattlepi.nwsource.com/opinion/174902_fisk26.html, accessed June 10, 2005.

Geertz, Clifford (1973) *The Interpretation of Cultures: Selected Essays*. New York: Basic Books.

Gramsci, Antonio (1992) *Prison Notebooks*. Joseph A. Buttigieg and Atonio Callari, trans. New York: Columbia University Press.

Hagopian, Elaine C. (1977) The Arab Mind. *Journal of Palestine Studies* 6(4): 122–130.

Haj, Samira (2002) Reordering Islamic Orthodoxy: Myhammed Ibn Abdu Wahhab. *Muslim World* 92(3–4): 333–371.

Hallaq, Wael B. (1984) Was the Gate of Ijtihad Closed? *International Journal of Middle East Studies* 16(1): 3–41.

Hersh, Seymour (2004) The Gray Zone: How a Secret Pentagon Program Came to Abu Ghraib. *New Yorker*, May 24: 38–44.

Hirschkind, Charles (n.d.) Conceptual Challenges to Understanding Islamic Movements: Questions in Tradition, History, and Modernity. Unpublished MS, Department of Anthropology, University of California, Berkeley.

Hobsbawm, Eric, and Terence Ranger, eds. (1983) *The Invention of Tradition*. Cambridge: Cambridge University Press.

Human Rights Watch/Middle East (1994a) *Israel's Interrogation of Palestinians from the Occupied Territories*. New York: Human Rights Watch.

——, (1994b) *Torture and Ill-Treatment: Israel's Interrogation of Palestinians from the Occupied Territories*. New York: Human Rights Watch.

Huntington, Samuel P. (1996) *The Clash of Civilizations and the Remaking of World Order*. New York: Simon and Schuster.

Kalman, Matthew (2004) Were Abu Ghraib Abuses Learned from Israel? Palestinians Think So, but Shin Bet Interrogators Scoff at U.S. Methods. *San Francisco Chronicle*, June 27: A14.

Kleinfeld, N. R. (2005) Mideast Tensions Are Getting Personal on Campus at Columbia. *New York Times*, January 18: B1.

Kramer, Martin (2001) *Ivory Towers on Sand: The Failure of Middle Eastern Studies in America*. Washington, DC: Washington Institute for Near East Policy.

——, (2002) MESA Culpa. *Middle East Quarterly* 9(4). Electronic document, http://www.meforum.org/article/500, accessed February 2005.

Lewis, Bernard (1982) The Question of Orientalism. *New York Review of Books*, June 24: 49–56.

——, (2001–2) The Roots of Muslim Rage. *Policy* 17(4): 17–26.

Leys, Simon (1988) *The Burning Forest: Essays on Chinese Culture and Politics*. London: Paladin.

Lockman, Zachary (2004) Behind the Battles Over US Middle East Studies. Electronic document, http://www.merip.org/mero/interventions/ lockman_interv.html, accessed February 2005.

Macfie, Alexander Lyon, ed. (2000) *Orientalism: A Reader*. New York: New York University Press.

MacIntyre, Alisdair C. (1981) *After Virtue: A Study in Moral Theory*. Notre Dame, IN: University of Notre Dame Press.

Mahmood, Saba (2001) Feminist Theory, Embodiment, and the Docile Agent: Some Reflections on the Egyptian Islamic Revival. *Cultural Anthropology* 16(2): 202–236.

——, (2004) *Politics of Piety: The Islamic Revival and the Feminist Subject*. Princeton: Princeton University Press.

Marcus, George E., and Michael M. J. Fischer (1986) *Anthropology as Cultural Critique: An Experimental Movement in the Human Sciences*. Chicago: University of Chicago Press.

Mehta, Uday Singh (1999) *Liberalism and Empire: A Study in Nineteenth-Century British Liberal Thought*. Chicago: University of Chicago Press.

Patai, Raphael (1973) *The Arab Mind*. New York: Charles Scribner's Sons.

Piper, Michael Collins (2003) Teaching Pro-Israel Views To Lose Funding: Congress to Pass "Ideological Diversity" Legislation. *American Free Press*, April 21. Electronic document, http://www.rense.com/general37/idleg.htm, accessed May 6, 2005.

Povinelli, Elizabeth A. (2002) *The Cunning of Recognition: Indigenous Alterities and the Making of Australian Multiculturalism*. Durham, NC: Duke University Press.

Public Committee against Torture in Israel (2003) Back to a Routine of Torture: Torture and Ill-Treatment of Palestinian Detainees during Arrest, Detention and Interrogation, September 2001 – April 2003. Electronic document, http://www.stoptorture.org.il/eng/images/uploaded/publications/ 58.pdf, accessed February 2005.

Qureshi, Emram (2004) Misreading the Arab Mind. Boston Globe, May 30. Electronic document, http://www.boston.com/news/globe/ ideas/articles/2004/05/30/misreading_the_arab_mind? mode=PF, accessed June 10, 2005.

Richardson, Michael (1990) Enough Said: Reflections on Orientalism. *Anthropology Today* 6(4): 16–19.

Said, Edward W. (1982) Opponents, Audiences, Constituencies, and Community. Theme issue, "The Politics of Interpretation," *Critical Inquiry* 9(1): 1–26.

——, (1983) *The World, the Text, the Critic*. Cambridge, MA: Harvard University Press.

——, (1985) [1975] *Beginnings: Intention and Method*. New York: Basic Books.

——, (1989) Representing the Colonized: Anthropology's Interlocutors. *Critical Inquiry* 15(2): 205–225.

——, (1993) *Culture and Imperialism.* 1st edition. New York: Knopf.

——, (1994) *Representations of the Intellectual: The 1993 Reith Lectures.* New York: Pantheon Books.

——, (1997) [1981] *Covering Islam: How the Media and the Experts Determine How We See the Rest of the World.* New York: Vintage Books.

——, (2000) Shattered Myths. In *Orientalism: A Reader.* Alexander Lyon Macfie, ed. pp. 89–103. New York: New York University Press.

——, (2003) [1978] *Orientalism.* 25th anniversary edition. New York: Vintage.

——, (2004) *Humanism and Democratic Criticism.* New York: Columbia University Press.

Sebrow, Dara, and Alex Rolfe (2003) A Mixed Legacy, Editorial Dissent. *Columbia Spectator*, September 29. Electronic document, http://www.columbiaspectator.com/vnews/display.v/ART/2003/09/29/3f77dd265e154?in_archive=1, accessed June 10, 2005.

Stern, Kenneth (2002) Why Campus Anti-Israeli Activity Flunks Bigotry 101. *American Jewish Committee.* Electronic document, http:// www.ajc.org/InTheMedia/PubAntisemitism.asp?did=649, accessed February 2005.

Stoler, Ann (n.d.) A Tribute to Edward Said. Unpublished MS, Department of Anthropology, New School University.

Thomas, Nicholas (1991) Anthropology and Orientalism. *Anthropology Today* 7(2): 4–7.

U.S. House of Representatives (2003) International Programs in Higher Education and Questions of Bias. Hearing before the Subcommittee on Select Education of the Committee on Education and the Workforce, House of Representatives, One Hundred Eighth Congress, First Session, June 19. Electronic document, http://edworkforce.house.gov/ hearings/108th/sed/sedhearings.htm, accessed May 6, 2005.

Vico, Giambattista (1970) [1744] *The New Science of Giambattista Vico.* 3rd abridged ed. Thomas Goddard Bergin and Max Harold Fisch, trans. Ithaca, NY: Cornell University Press.

Volney, C.-F. (1959) [1787] *Voyage en Egypte et en Syrie.* Jean Gaulmier, ed. Paris: Mouton.

Zubaida, Sami (2004) *Law and Power in the Islamic World.* New York: I. B. Tauris.

4 New Orientalisms for old

Articulations of the East in Raymond Schwab, Edward Said and two nineteenth-century French orientalists

Geoffrey Nash

My main aim in this essay is to provide a reading of *Orientalism* that assesses its treatment of two French orientalists who are integral to Said's argument. I begin by presenting a comparative analysis of Said's *Orientalism* and Raymond Schwab's *Oriental Renaissance* with the aim of discussing how Said uses Schwab as a point of departure from which to raise his own theses about Orientalism. Schwab's incorporation of a specific image of Arthur Gobineau's ideas on Germano-Aryanism as a distortion of the Oriental Renaissance is read in conjunction with Said's placement of him, alongside Ernest Renan, as a racist upholder of "scientific" Orientalism. For Said, Renan is guilty of appropriating the new philology in order to assert European superiority over the East in the process vaunting Indo-European Aryanism against oriental Semitism. Gobineau is invoked almost exclusively in the context of his multi-volume *Essay on the Inequality of Human Races* (Essai sur l'inégalité des races humaine) and its contribution to racism, which, for Said, qualifies him as a founder figure in the establishment of "latent", or unchanging, bedrock Orientalism. However, while this work does indeed present a schema in which the rise and fall of civilisation is stimulated by the Aryan genius, Gobineau's eastern writings do very much otherwise than confirm modern European superiority over the Orient. It is my contention that, in linking Gobineau with what he also termed "scholarly" Orientalism, Said crucially mistook the orientation of Gobineau's relations with the East.[1]

Orientalism and The Oriental Renaissance

Published in 1950, Raymond Schwab's *La Renaissance orientale* pre-dated Edward Said's work by nearly three decades. In several interesting ways Schwab's career prefigured Said's own: his work was the fruit of his labours pre-1939, but he was clearly affected by the events of the Second World War, much as *Orientalism*, published soon after the end of the Vietnam War and inflected by the Arab–Israeli wars of June 1967 and October 1973, was influenced by the spread of US domination in the world. First of all, Schwab was a man of letters, not a specialist in Oriental Studies of any kind, a fact that did not go unnoticed by Anglo-American reviewers when the English version, *The Oriental Renaissance*, appeared in 1984. In *Orientalism* Said cites Schwab's as one of three "encyclopaedic works on certain aspects of the European–Oriental encounter".[2] It is obvious that the theoretical method adopted in *Orientalism* departs from Schwab's mainly narrative approach. In pointing out that his own work was neither narrative nor encyclopaedic in conception, Said adds that the three works in question lacked "the general political and intellectual context" of his own. Though in his Foreword to *The Oriental Renaissance* he praised Schwab as more "an *orienteur* than an *orientaliste*, a man more interested in a generous awareness than in detached classification",[3] it is also clear that Said was marking the distance between the Frenchman's approach and his own when he wrote: "dualities, opposition, polarities – as between Orient and Occident, one writer and another, one time and another – are converted in his writing into lines that criss-cross, it is true, but that also draw a vast human portrait … The agents and the heroes of cultural change and formation are scholars … The formula is perhaps simple, but it encompasses … the reeducation of one continent by another."[4] Notoriously, Said's method in *Orientalism* was to emphasise polarities, not so much between individuals or schools of orientalists, as between cultures, above all those apparently ontologically separated twin entities: the Occident and the Orient.

Schwab's central idea was that the Oriental Renaissance of the late eighteenth and nineteenth centuries, centred on the discovery of Sanskrit and ancient Indian religious texts, enlarged the European mind so as to take cognisance of a greater world than the Greco-Latin one opened up by the classical Renaissance. While the focus of Schwab's study is the relationship between Europe and India, and it is obviously the case that he is largely concerned with the Middle East, Said does not misunderstand the Indian dimension to the development of western Orientalism as charged by some of his critics. The emphasis in *Orientalism* is on the Islamic Middle East, but Said strongly proposed that the methodology carried over from Indology – the linguistic, classificatory ingredient – applied to both Indic and Middle East Orientalism.[5] While he devoted several pages to the achievements of William Jones and Antequil-Duperron (in Schwab's eyes the co-founders of the Oriental Renaissance), Said's handling of this crucial stage in the development of Indic studies, and indeed the Oriental Renaissance as a whole, is typical of his method in *Orientalism* in stating that the European "took from the classical Oriental past … a vision (and thousands of facts and artefacts) which *only he* could employ to the best advantage".[6] This feat was accomplished through both the acquisition of knowledge and the creation of an archive and institutions, and here Said specifically praises Schwab for his recognition of the process, foregrounding the Frenchman's openness to the emergence of disciplines such as biology and philology, and noting: "Schwab demonstrates with inexhaustible patience what it means in Foucault's sense … literally for an archive to be formed."[7] A detailed narrative of how this occurred can indeed be found in Schwab, but to understand its significance in the context of European management of the Orient one must turn to Said, according to whom the rosy picture of the Oriental Renaissance painted by his predecessor was tainted from the beginning by Europe's urge for mastery over the East.

To this effect, *Orientalism* proposes a strategic revision of Schwab concerning the proposition not only that Europeans learned from the East, but that Indian culture and religion in particular "could defeat the materialism and mechanism … of Occidental culture". Said's achievement was to demonstrate how soon the Romantic vision that envisaged a Europe revived by eastern spirituality was followed by "a swing of the pendulum" by which "the Orient suddenly appeared lamentably under-humanized, antidemocratic, backward, barbaric and so forth".[8] Structured around Flaubert's comic novel *Bouvard et Pécuchet*, Said's revision amounts to a serious caveat to, if not a wholesale dismantling of, the idea that the East acted as inspiration and tutor for nineteenth-century European artists and poets. The vision of "Europe regenerated by Asia", purloined by the mediocre copyist Bouvard, in effect stands for the entire "Romantic Orientalist project", which, Said points out, was the heart of the argument in *The Oriental Renaissance*.[9] According to Schwab the German idealists had discerned in India a "universal revelation" which they then extended to embrace the myths and mysteries of the other ancient Aryan peoples. All the legends of India and Greece, of the Scandinavians and the Persians had to be accepted as components of "a new universal religion that would regenerate a world distracted by rationalism".[10] Said uses Flaubert to fracture this idealism: "Neither 'Europe' nor 'Asia' was anything without the visionaries' technique for turning vast geographical domains into treatable, and manageable, entities. At bottom, therefore, Europe and Asia were *our* Europe and *our* Asia – our *will* and *representation*, as Schopenhauer had said."[11] Moving from the Islamic lands on to European exploration of the rest of the world, Said's argument is: "*all such widening horizons had Europe in the firmly privileged center, as main observer*". This expansion allowed for "a selective identification with regions and cultures not one's own", but the outcome – a wholesale departure from Schwab – saw the Orient "reduced to considerably less than the eminence once seen in it".[12] This process was timed to coincide with the emergence of the career orientalist, in particular the philological science of Ernest Renan.

Schwab and Said on the Orientalism of Renan and Gobineau

Alongside his predecessor Silvestre de Sacy, Renan is credited by Said with having placed Orientalism "on a scientific and rational basis". Some of Said's critics, failing to grasp the significance of Renan for his argument, contended that Renan was never a major orientalist, a fact with which Said himself agreed.[13] His inclusion within *Orientalism*, however, does not depend on the originality of his work, but on the power that his assertions commanded as a product of the sway that scientific philology held in the mid-nineteenth century. According to Cohn's summary of the methodology of comparative philology: "The theory of language implicit in the comparative method is that there are 'genetic' or 'genealogical' relations among languages that have been determined to belong to a 'family.' It is posited that there was once a single, original language from which all the languages from the family descend."[14] Said's emphasis is that philology enabled Renan to gain legitimacy for his pronouncements on race, specifically the division between Aryan and Semitic peoples. Philology's "ideological tenets encourage the reduction of language to its roots, thereafter, the philologist finds it possible to connect those linguistic roots, as Renan and others did, to race, mind, character and temperament at their roots."[15] Timothy Brennan notes that while he admired Renan's stance as an intellectual, for Said, "his misuse of language through specious analogies" to chemistry and the bogus biology of Cuvier signified a false scientism.[16] Nonetheless, Renan remains central to Said's argument about the construction of the professionalism of Orientalism: he "had a strong guild sense as a professional scholar", and the confidence to associate himself with "such philological contemporaries as Wilhelm von Humboldt, Bopp, and … Eugene Burnouf" by virtue of his mastery of the new science.[17]

While Schwab is very unlikely to have been Said's only source on Gobineau, it is important to revisit the role that Gobineau plays in *The Oriental Renaissance*. Here Gobineau appears as a young émigré student in Switzerland who developed a taste for oriental languages. Schwab accuses Schopenhauer and Gobineau of introducing a corrupting tendency within Romantic Orientalism by promoting the myth of Germanic/Aryan racial ascendancy that came "to make the Oriental Renaissance stand for the opposite of its content and its justification".[18] In *Inequality of Human Races* Gobineau had "demonstrated how a dangerous ethnic innuendo" – the Aryan myth – "could arise from a misused linguistic graph". Schwab's emphasis on Gobineau's grounding of human history in the Aryan idea – "It was, of course, a question of tall blondes"[19] – might imply that he made the common mistake of judging Gobineau on *Inequality of Human Races* alone, but in fact he refers to *Religions and Philosophies of Central Asia* (Les Religions et Philosophies dans l'Asie centrale), where Gobineau had stated: "Everything we think, and all that we think we know, have their origins in Asia." This axiom, Schwab argues, was in "exact correspondence" with what Schopenhauer "was affirming in the ontological and theological realms".[20] However, in his assessment of Gobineau overall, it is evident that Schwab's judgement had been warped by the recent war and his assumption that Gobineau would have sided with Germany against France.

Said's inclusion of Gobineau within an "official intellectual genealogy of Orientalism"[21] – alongside such academic orientalist contemporaries as Burnouf, Humboldt, Renan and Remusat – might be seen as a misconstruing of the Frenchman's tenuous connection to the French and German orientalist establishments. Moreover, his references to Gobineau in *Orientalism* do not discuss his work in any detail; he is mentioned almost exclusively in conjunction with his racial ideas. On this basis Said accorded him a systematic influence within official, scholarly Orientalism, inserting Gobineau within the category of "latent" Orientalism – the irreducible set of assumptions about the Orient "all of them converging upon such essential aspects of the Orient as the Oriental character, Oriental despotism, Oriental sensuality, and the like."[22] He cites the racial classifications to be found in Gobineau's *Inequality of Human Races*, alongside the work of Cuvier and Robert Knox, as contributing to the "theses of Oriental backwardness, degeneracy, and inequality with the West".[23] However, it seems incontrovertible that Said knew Gobineau only by his reputation as "father of racist ideology", and it is unlikely that he had read the texts that are crucial for understanding Gobineau's image of the East.[24]

Nonetheless, there is mileage in the argument that Gobineau subscribed to the pseudo-scientific racism that underpins Orientalism. On the matter of non-Aryan races, the Frenchman's writing has with some justification been construed in relation to colonial discourse.[25] Said's inference that the racial ideas evinced in *Inequality of the Human Races* could be conjoined with those advanced by Renan in his philological tomes has been frequently drawn, especially with respect to anti-Semitism. However, as Annette and David Smith point out:

> Gobineau never thought of the Jews as a *race*, since the Semites were but one branch of the original white race and the Jews but one of the Semitic groups. In contrast, Renan wrote that "the Semitic race … truly represents an inferior combination in human nature." Why is it, then, that "Renanism" did not supersede "Gobinism" as a synonym of anathema in the French language?[26]

In point of fact Gobineau's statements are rarely anti-Semitic, and while he did disparage the process of "semitisation" in the Near East he comprehended other groups besides Jews – Assyrians, Babylonians and Arabs – in the category *sémitique*. Indeed his pronouncements on Jews in *Inequality of the Human Races* are largely appreciative. As far as enrolment within the guild of orientalists of his time is concerned, Gobineau's aspirations were directed toward a similar goal to Renan's. As a youth he too desired the title of orientalist because it was a way of distinguishing himself from the detested crowd and because he believed that oriental languages were the key to deciphering the riddle of human origins.[27] If Gobineau believed in the "creed" of the orientalists, why then is Said's insistence on his impact misconstrued?

Gobineau's Romantic Orientalism

Had he taken the trouble to read Gobineau more extensively, Said might perhaps have seen the value of placing him within his category of "imaginative and travel literature". Here he chose Flaubert and Nerval as his chief prototypes of the European writer who went to the Orient to fulfil "some deeply felt and urgent project … For each … the Oriental pilgrimage was a quest for something relatively personal." While the work of each is connected to official Orientalism, it "yet remains independent of it", one reason being that "their egos never absorbed the Orient, nor totally identified the Orient with documentary and textual knowledge of it".[28] Incorporating Said's remarks within his own analysis, Ali Behdad has written of Nerval's "split discourses". On the one hand instilled with textual Orientalism, at the same time possessing a personal desire for the Orient, Nerval is disappointed by its reality – the ashes and dust of the decaying Cairo that he describes in *Journey to the Orient* (Voyage en Orient). The same response is enacted with regard to the traveller's thirst for a stereotypical sensual Orient when, sexually aroused to what lies behind the veil, Nerval realises that "the desire always lies where his subject is *not*".[29] The genius and personal complexity of Nerval caused him to borrow the "authority of a canonized Orientalist text"[30] even while, as Behdad puts it, his personal investment in the dream-like world of his Oriental *nouvelles* meant that "the narrative of the voyage becomes an imaginary tale divested of most ideological implications of a discourse on the Other".[31]

Behdad's notion of Nerval's split discourses could appropriately be applied to Gobineau's Oriental *œuvres*, which range through the genres of travelogue, dissertation, sub-standard poetry, and the Oriental short story. As a traveller in the Orient, Gobineau evinces, it is true, the type of racial observation that became almost de rigueur for later nineteenth-century travellers in the region.[32] But against the grain of race he also demonstrates a pity for, and a sense of equality with, the oppressed and exploited populations of the East.[33] Repudiating the false ideas of western travellers to Persia who were prepossessed by the superiority of their culture, he preferred to put himself in the place of the people studied before judging their ways of being or feeling.[34] Of the Gobineau who was domiciled in Tehran between 1855 and 1858 as First Secretary at the French legation, Jacques Barzun commented:

> He acclimatized himself readily and conceived a love for the "semitized" and "melanized" Persians inconsistent with his written profession of faith. His work on the history and religion of the Persians breathes sympathy and understanding in a measure that few writers wholly innocent of racial bias could achieve.[35]

Persians intrigued Gobineau in spite of their notional decadence, as can be seen in his *Asiatic Short Stories*, where, as stated in his preface, he consciously set out to broaden the orientalist dimensions of Morier's depiction in *Hajji Baba* of what came to be known as "the Persian character".[36] As he wrote to his friend Prokesch Osten: "Tout ce pays, enfin, est plein de l'idée de Dieu. La décrépitude, la vieillesse, la corruption extrême, la fin enfin, est partout dans les institutions, dans les mœurs, dans les caractères, mais cette constante et absorbante préoccupation sacrée, ennoblit singulièrement toute cette ruine."[37] In *Religions and Philosophies* we can see how he characterises Persian ways of thinking as a combination of intuitive and inductive method and distinguishes them from the practical Europeans:

> They are full of fire and are the most naturally and deeply intuitive people in the world; they excel … in splitting hairs, and from the strands they will form a bridge capable of bearing a carriage; they will see unlimited food for thought, by no means lacking in value, in the tiniest notions; but at the same time it is certain that the moral faculty we call common sense and which, let it be said in passing, depresses us at least as often as it guides us, is not in perfect equilibrium with the power of their imagination and the speed of their understanding. The truth is that they lack common sense, and in all their dealings, great and small, one sees barely a trace of it.[38]

As with Nerval's split discourses of textual and anti-Orientalism, such identification with oriental intuition answered to deep personal need; it also ensured that Gobineau did not apply race theory as the sole *power to explain* the land and its peoples – which would presumably have been Said's point in arguing "to be a European in the Orient *always* involves being a consciousness set apart from, and unequal with, its surroundings".[39] Comparable to Nerval's, Gobineau's articulation of the customs and ways of thought of Persians and other Central Asians was constructed out of personal "desire for the Orient", a need to find solace in an Other that was the antithesis of the hated Occident. Gobineau's oriental writings, too, are touched by the Oriental Renaissance, by the "idea of restorative reconstruction",[40] but – and here is his point of departure from the grand schemes of Europe's rebirth explicated by Schwab – only as related to individual quest. He placed no credence at all in the idea of the West's being re-invigorated by the East, or in the West's superiority over the East. In so far as his race theory emphasised the decline of human endeavour in the modern world, it was far too late for positive cultural exchange to occur. By expansion of western trade, the easterners would in time gain the better of the deal and eventually supersede Europe. Through the drive of western imperialism towards conquering the East, the West risked accepting a poison dish, and could only hasten its own destruction. For reasons intimately connected with his own sense of disenfranchisement, or to use the term used by Nerval, his "disinheritance", Gobineau detested western imperialism.[41]

Orientaliste manqué

Jean Boissel states: "le titre d'orientaliste lui était plus précieux et était plus satisfaisant à son ambition que celui de diplomat". But debating the question of "'l'orientalisme' de Gobineau", he poses the question: "Ne passe-t-il pas pour un touche-à-tout amateur, un esprit subtil, mais dénué de toute disposition pour la recherche scientifique et pour les sciences orientalistes en particulier?"[42] Gobineau's inability to master even one oriental language made his chances of gaining entrance to the exclusive fraternity of academic French orientalists a virtual impossibility, and in the late 1840s, exactly at the point where Renan was demonstrating his prowess in that quarter, Gobineau was forced by the pressing need of supporting a family to renounce his dreams and follow the path of popular literature, excelling in writing the *roman-feuilleton*.[43]

When, as a result of his diplomatic posting to Persia, Gobineau was given the chance to go to the East, he took the opportunity to engage in his own type of researches. In the affair of his cavalier sally into the field of the cuneiform inscriptions he found himself in open conflict with professional orientalists. The cause of his failure was, as his biographer points out, Gobineau's complete lack of scientific method.[44] Even though he adopted as his points of departure the work of specific individuals (Boissel goes so far as to suggest that Gobineau dreamed of taking over from Burnouf in the deciphering of the cuneiform inscriptions),[45] his method of depending on contemporary native Iranian sources and insistence that the ancient inscriptions could be traced down to a living Iranian dialect, together with his rash rush to publication in 1858 of his *Lecture on the Cuneiform Writings* (Lecture des textes cunéiformes), ensured either the contemptuous dismissal or studied silence of the professionals.[46]

While it can hardly be sustained that such works as those on the cuneiforms or the *Histoire des Perses*, written as they were out of genuine empathy for the Orient, can now be considered a genuine form of knowledge of the East, they at least point to the need for a revision of Said's statement: "to look into Orientalism for a lively sense of an Oriental's human or even social reality – as a contemporary inhabitant of the modern world – is to look in vain".[47] The paradoxes discussed above suggest that Gobineau was an unlikely candidate for inclusion in Said's category of scholarly Orientalism alone. His intuitional approach to sources and his reconstruction of the religious and cultural history of eastern peoples can be encapsulated as the methodological antithesis of scientific Orientalism. Moreover, those who accord pre-eminence to Gobineau as an exponent of racist Orientalism should look at the writings he composed during and after his two sojourns in Persia. The deterministic racial theory of *Inequality of Human Races* should be set alongside the greatly more sympathetic and flexible mind that produced *Three Years in Asia*, *Religions and Philosophies of Central Asia*, and *Asiatic Short Stories* (Nouvelles asiatiques). The complexity of Gobineau's writings on eastern domains, the relationship between his life, articulation of the nineteenth century's ideas on race, and intense identification with oriental peoples (above all, those of the Iranian plateau) cannot, in its entirety be comprehended within the Saidean thesis. Though I am not suggesting that Gobineau's case disables the overall message of Said's work, I am proposing that in this instance (among others) the sweep of his pronouncements concerning one of the main supports of the edifice of *Orientalism* led him to wrongly classify an author who, it should be conceded, has more often than not been misconstrued.

Notes

1 Gobineau's case should be added to what has become a varied list of revisions to the original work: e.g., Geoffrey Nash, *From Empire to Orient: Travellers to the Middle East, 1830–1926* (London: I.B. Tauris, 2005); Billie Melman, *Women's Orients, English Women and the Middle East, 1718–1918: Sexuality, Religion, and Work* (Ann Arbor: University of Michigan Press, 1995); Ali Behdad, *Belated Travelers: Orientalism in the Age of Colonial Dissolution* (Durham, NC: Duke University Press, 1994). See also A.L. Macfie, *Orientalism: A Reader* (Edinburgh: Edinburgh University Press, 2000).

2 Edward Said, *Orientalism: Western Conceptions of the Orient* (London: Penguin 1991), p. 16; the other two works besides Schwab's are by Johann Fück and Dorothee Metlitzki.

3 Edward Said, Foreword to Raymond Schwab, *The Oriental Renaissance: Europe's Rediscovery of India and the East, 1680–1880* (New York: Columbia University Press, 1984), p. ix. Said's essay first appeared as "Raymond Schwab and the Romance of Ideas" in 1976 and was reprinted in *The World, the Text, and the Critic* in 1983.

4 Ibid., pp. ix, xvi.

5 See Said, *Orientalism*, pp. 98–9.

6 Said, *Orientalism*, p. 79; my emphasis.

7 Said, Foreword, p. xvi.

8 Said, *Orientalism*, pp. 115, 150.

9 Ibid., p. 115.

10 Schwab, *Oriental Renaissance*, pp. 216–17. To confirm the great importance that Schwab attributed to the "new beginning" envisioned by Romantic Orientalism one has only to read the final paragraph of Part Three (p. 221).

11 Said, *Orientalism*, p. 115, original emphases.

12 Ibid., pp. 116–17, my emphasis; pp. 120, 150–51. Said was not alone in departing from Schwab's positive analysis. In *Black Athena: The Afroasiatic Roots of Classical Civilization, vol 1. The Fabrication of Ancient Greece 1785–1985* (New Brunswick: Rutgers University Press, 1987), Martin Bernal states: "There is no doubt about the extraordinary efforts of the early Orientalists ... Nevertheless, the growth of Orientalism did not simply go with a broadening of horizons, as Quinet and Schwab claimed. In many respects it involved a narrowing of the imagination and intensified feelings of the innate and categorical superiority of European civilization" (p. 236).

13 Said, *Orientalism*, p. 122. Said points out that Schwab has little to say about Renan in *The Oriental Renaissance*, as indeed do other nineteenth-century surveys on Orientalism, such as Müller's and Darmesteter's (ibid., pp. 338–39, n.44). However, according to Albert Hourani, Renan was "one of the seminal figures in the formation of European ideas about Islam". Albert Hourani, *Islam in European Thought* (Oxford: Oxford University Press, 1991), p. 28.

14 Bernard S. Cohn, *Colonialism and Its Forms of Knowledge: The British in India* (Princeton, NJ: Princeton University Press, 1996), p. 54.

15 Said, *Orientalism*, p. 150.

16 Timothy Brennan, "Places of Mind, Occupied Lands: Edward Said and Philology," in *Edward Said: A Critical Reader*, edited by Michael Sprinker (Oxford: Blackwell, 1992), p. 81. Elsewhere Brennan contrasts "the expansive, humane philology of Raymond Swab" with the "bad philology of Ernest Renan". Brennan, "Edward Said and Comparative Literature", *Journal of Palestine Studies*, vol. 33, no. 3 (Spring 2004), p. 33.

17 Said, *Orientalism*, p. 133–34.

18 Schwab, *Oriental Renaissance*, p. 433.

19 Ibid., pp. 184, 432.

20 Ibid., p. 431. For Gobineau's statement, see Gobineau, *Comte de Gobineau and Orientalism: Selected Eastern Writings*, translated by Daniel O'Donoghue, edited with an introduction by Geoffrey Nash (London: Routledge, 2009), p. 113. Schwab also made the curious statement that Gobineau's oft-derided *Treatise on Cuneiform Writings* (1864) was "perhaps more important" than *Inequality of Human Races.*

21 Said, *Orientalism*, p. 99.

22 Ibid., p. 203.

23 Ibid., p. 206.

24 The title of Michael Biddiss's 1970 study of Gobineau's socio-political thought. To support his notion of "the common philological and Orientalist perspective" between Renan and Gobineau (*Orientalism*, p. 150), Said refers in an endnote to an appreciative letter from Renan to Gobineau concerning, again, *Inequality of Human Races* (*Orientalism*, p. 340, n62).

25 See especially Robert J.C. Young, *Colonial Desire: Hybridity in Theory, Culture and Race* (London: Routledge, 1995), pp. 90–117.

26 Annette and David Smith *"Mademoiselle Irnois" and Other Stories [of] Arthur de Gobineau* (Berkeley, CA: University of California Press, 1988), p. 13.

27 Jean Boissel, *Gobineau: L'Orient et L'Iran, Tome I 1816–1860* (Paris: Editions Klincksieck, 1973), p. 48. According to Boissel (ibid., p. 20) "l'attitude de Gobineau à l'égard de l'Orient, ... rapprochera aisément de celle d'un Novalis ou d'un Nerval" in possessing "le caractère romantique fondamental ... de ce retour aux origines".

28 Said, *Orientalism*, pp. 158, 180–81.

29 Ali Behdad, "Oriental Desire, Desire of the Orient", *French Forum*, vol. 15, no. 1 (January 1990), p. 45, original emphasis.

30 Said, *Orientalism*, p. 184.

31 Behdad, "Oriental Desire", p. 42.
32 Comparable to Nerval's remarks in the Cairo slave market – see Behdad, "Oriental Desire", p. 51 n.15.
33 This sympathy, however, strongly contrasted with his attitudes towards the demands for democracy made by the revolutionaries of 1848 back home in Europe. See Boissel, *Gobineau*, p. 251.
34 *Gobineau and Orientalism*, pp. 23–24.
35 Jacques Barzun, *Race: A Study in Modern Superstition*, 1938, p. 79. Todorov also recognises disconnect between Gobineau's theories of race and his actual pronouncements on the East, in which "he evinces a degree of broadmindedness difficult to reconcile with his racialist reputation" (Tzvetan Todorov, *On Human Diversity: Nationalism, Racism, and Exoticism in French Thought* (Cambridge, MA: Harvard University Press, 1993), p. 129. However, in comparison with his sympathetic treatment of Central Asian peoples, Gobineau saw China as a future warning as to where democratic despotism and "progress" might lead, fearing that the Chinese, led by Russian generals, might one day invade Europe and destroy its civilization. See Gregory Blue, "Gobineau on China: Race Theory, the 'Yellow Peril,' and the Critique of Modernity", *Journal of World History*, vol. 10, no. 1 (1999), pp. 93–139.
36 Arthur Gobineau, *Œuvres*, vol. 3, pp. 305–9; Nash, *From Empire to Orient*, pp. 128–30.
37 Boissel, *Gobineau*, p. 314
38 *Gobineau and Orientalism*, p. 114.
39 Said, *Orientalism*, p. 157, original emphasis.
40 Said, *Orientalism*, p. 168.
41 Gobineau, *Gobineau and Orientalism*, pp. 105–10. Nerval's epithet is found in his poem "El Desdichado"; see also Benn Sowerby, *The Disinherited: The Life of Gérard de Nerval, 1808–1855* (London: Peter Owen, 1973).
42 Boissel, *Gobineau*, pp. 17–18.
43 Ibid., p. 57.
44 Ibid., p. 18.
45 Ibid., p. 360.
46 "*Suppositions, incertitude, doutes naturels, bizarrerie, critiques*, violà des terms qui … laissent mal augurer de l'opinion qui se fait de l'ouvrage" (Boissel, *Gobineau*, p. 374, original emphases).
47 Said, *Orientalism*, p. 176.

Bibliography

Barzun, Jacques. *Race: A Study in Modern Superstition* (London: Methuen, 1938).

Behdad, Ali. "Oriental Desire, Desire of the Orient", *French Forum*, vol. 15, no. 1 (January 1990), pp. 37–51.

——, *Belated Travelers: Orientalism in the Age of Colonial Dissolution* (Durham, NC: Duke University Press, 1994).

Bernal, Martin. *Black Athena: The Afroasiatic Roots of Classical Civilization, vol. 1 The Fabrication of Ancient Greece 1785–1985* (New Brunswick: Rutgers University Press, 1987).

Biddiss, Michael. *Father of Racist Ideology: The Social and Political Thought of Count Gobineau* (London: Weidenfeld and Nicolson, 1979).

Blue, Gregory. "Gobineau on China: Race Theory, the 'Yellow Peril,' and the Critique of Modernity", *Journal of World History*, vol. 10, no. 1 (1999), pp. 93–139.

Boissel, Jean. *Gobineau: L'Orient et L'Iran, Tome I 1816–1860* (Paris: Editions Klincksieck, 1973).

Brennan, Timothy. "Edward Said and Comparative Literature", *Journal of Palestine Studies*, vol. 33, no. 3 (Spring 2004), pp. 23–37.

——, "Places of Mind, Occupied Lands: Edward Said and Philology", in *Edward Said: A Critical Reader*, edited by Michael Sprinker (Oxford: Blackwell, 1992).

Cohn, Bernard S. *Colonialism and Its Forms of Knowledge: The British in India* (Princeton, NJ: Princeton University Press, 1996).

Gobineau, Arthur Joseph. *Œuvres*, 3 vols, edited by Jean Gaulmier *et al.* (Paris: Gallimard, 1983).

——, *Comte de Gobineau and Orientalism: Selected Eastern Writings*, translated by Daniel O'Donoghue, edited with an introduction by Geoffrey Nash (London: Routledge, 2009).

Hourani, Albert. *Islam in European Thought* (Oxford: Oxford University Press, 1991).

Macfie, A.L. *Orientalism: A Reader* (Edinburgh: Edinburgh University Press, 2000).

Melman, Billie, *Women's Orients, English Women and the Middle East, 1718–1918: Sexuality, Religion, and Work* (Ann Arbor: University of Michigan Press, 1995).

Nash, Geoffrey. *From Empire to Orient: Travellers to the Middle East, 1830–1926* (London: I.B. Tauris, 2005).

Nerval, Gérard de. *Journey to the Orient*, selected and translated with an introduction by Norman Glass (London: Peter Owen, 1972).

Said, Edward. *Orientalism: Western Conceptions of the Orient* (London: Penguin, 1991).

——, Foreword to Raymond Schwab, *The Oriental Renaissance, Europe's Discovery of India and the East 1680–1880* (New York: Columbia University Press, 1984).

Schwab, Raymond. *The Oriental Renaissance: Europe's Rediscovery of India and the East, 1680–1880* (New York: Columbia University Press, 1984).

Smith, Annette and David Smith. *"Mademoiselle Irnois" and Other Stories [of] Arthur de Gobineau* (Berkeley, CA: University of California Press, 1988).

Sowerby, Benn. *The Disinherited: The Life of Gérard de Nerval, 1808–1855* (London: Peter Owen, 1973).

Todorov, Tzvetan. *On Human Diversity: Nationalism, Racism, and Exoticism in French Thought* (Cambridge, MA: Harvard University Press, 1993).

Young, Robert J.C. *Colonial Desire: Hybridity in Theory, Culture and Race* (London: Routledge, 1995).

5 Orientalism and Sufism

An overview

Linda Sijbrand

Edward Said's *Orientalism* caused many debates in the world of Islamic Studies.[1] Alexander Knysh, however, points out that this has inspired 'surprisingly little "soul-searching" among the western "Sufiologists" of the last decades of the twentieth century'.[2] Said observed that the colonialist background of armchair academics, travellers, artists, colonial officials etc. studying 'Islam' and the 'Orient' has led to misrepresentations and stereotypes that served to define the Western Self and to legitimise the colonisation of the Eastern Other.[3] These misrepresentations were continuously reproduced in a 'self-perpetuating body of truth'.[4] It has also been said that these misrepresentations have been internalised by the 'Orientals' and have influenced their self-definition and understanding of the world as well.[5]

The question I want to explore in this essay is what influenced the scholarly attitudes towards Sufism, to what extent Western students of Sufism misrepresented Sufism and how this affected both Western and Muslim attitudes. This essay aims to be a critical exploration of the existing secondary literature, aiming to expose the gaps that need to be filled by further study in order to enhance our understanding of the study of Sufism, on the one hand, and to add to the debate on Orientalism, on the other.

Said's work has been criticised for many reasons, one being that it is too Anglocentric. Later scholars have filled this gap by writing on non-English-speaking scholars, which also led to increased knowledge of the historiography of Sufi studies.[6] Albert Hourani wrote that Said did not distinguish between different types of Orientalists.[7] Knysh distinguishes between two trends in the study of Sufism: the academic trend, which was mainly carried by 'arm-chair academics', philologists who translated, edited and commented on 'classical' Sufi texts, and the pragmatic trend, which focused on the social aspect of Sufism from the perspective of European colonial politics.[8] Edmund Burke III points out that the academics often showed a large degree of empathy towards their subjects, whereas the pragmatists, focusing on 'living Islam', with their background of sociology and ethnography, were generally less empathetic towards Sufism.[9]

Academic studies of Sufism: philology and the Aryan roots of Islamic mysticism

Several ideas and stories of Sufism first found their way into European culture in the Middle Ages. Annemarie Schimmel (1922–2003) mentions that the Catalan philosopher Ramon Lull (d. 1316) was influenced by Sufi literature, and that the legend of Rābi'a al-'Adawiyya (714/17–801) was brought to the French court in the thirteenth century and used in a seventeenth-century French treatise on Divine love. Also in the seventeenth century, the first translations began to appear, with Ibn al-Farīd's (1181–1235) poetry being translated into Latin and Sa'dī's (1213/19–1292) *Gulistān* into German.[10]

The first Europeans to come into direct contact with Sufis were travellers. Until the eighteenth century they mainly focussed on the poverty of the Sufis and the wandering lives that they led: they described the Sufi as an outsider, living outside society. The main words that they used for the Sufis were 'dervish' and 'fakir', both of which refer to the poverty that many Sufis value.[11] They often saw the dervishes as exploiting their followers' devotion. A late eighteenth-century example of this can be found in Donald Campbell's travelogue, where his Tartar guide explains how there are true holy men and impostors, leading Campbell to muse that the 'light of reason' will chase the 'monkish impostors' from the land.[12]

During the eighteenth and nineteenth centuries, travellers shifted their attention to the rituals of the Sufis, calling them 'dancing, whirling and howling dervishes', stressing 'the exotic, peculiar, and behavior that diverges from modern European norms'.[13] A well-known example is that of Edward William Lane's (1801–1876) *An Account of the Manners and Customs of the Modern Egyptians* (1836).[14] Several other travellers of the nineteenth century even travelled disguised as dervishes, e.g. Sir Richard Burton (1821–1890) and Arminius Vámbéry (1832–1913).[15]

Carl Ernst notes that most of these travellers were Protestants and that this influenced their views: they saw the Sufis as equivalent to Catholic monks, which in the eyes of these Protestant observers was not a favourable comparison.[16] This is an interesting point, but as Ernst refers only to British writers we cannot say whether the Protestant background of the travellers is an important factor in their attitude, compared to Catholic or Jewish travellers for example.

When the Ottoman Empire became less of a military threat to Europe, and the Western powers embarked on their colonial enterprise (from the eighteenth century onwards), larger numbers of Europeans journeyed to the East and they stayed there for longer periods. They learned Persian and Arabic and became interested in the literature of the East. Sufi poetry caught their interest specifically. They were intrigued by the language of love, passion, longing, drunkenness, etc.[17]

Their attitude towards Sufism was influenced by changing ideas on religion and mysticism in general in eighteenth-century Europe. These eighteenth-century ideas form the roots of our understanding of 'religion'.[18] Religions were increasingly seen as specific expressions of universal truth – even though some religions had more access to universal truth than others.[19]

The concept of mysticism first developed in the eighteenth century as the opposite of civilised, rational religion: it was seen as 'unregulated spiritual impulses', associated with the irrational and feminine. In the second half of the nineteenth century it came to be seen as the universal trend which could be found in all religions and which connected them. It was understood as the desire to achieve a direct experience of and union with the divine – in other words, with universal truth – common to all religions. As Schimmel defines it: 'the great spiritual current which goes through all religions […] the consciousness of the One Reality – be it called Wisdom, Light, Love, or Nothing'.[20] Even so, it has expressions specific to every people: 'Mysticism becomes a global species of religious experience with innumerable sub-species, historical, geographic, and national.'[21]

In this period we also see an increasing separation of the 'religious' from the public sphere. The way 'mysticism' was conceptualised – as a highly personal occupation aspiring to a personal relationship with the divine – reinforced this separation of 'religion' and 'mysticism' from the world; from the social, economic and political sphere.[22] There was no attempt to contextualise ideas and practices. 'Material practices' were 'spiritualized' which turned them 'into expressions of something timeless and suprahistorical […] it depoliticizes them'. Masuzawa calls this 'the sacralizing character of Orientalism'.[23]

Sufism was seen as the Islamic variant of mysticism: poetical, personal, and divorced from the world. The development of the concept of mysticism was 'a product of cosmopolitan literature', to which scholars writing on Sufism also added. Robert Alfred Vaughan (1795–1868), whose *Hours with the Mystics* (1856) played a major part in the definition of mysticism, referred to Ralph Waldo Emerson (1803–1882) as a modern Sufi. Leigh Eric Schmidt also mentions Edward Henry Palmer (1840–1882), an Orientalist from Cambridge, in this context.[24]

Just as all specific religions were seen as expressions of one universal truth, so all peoples (and later nations) were seen as different expressions of nature. The differences were expressed in language, myths, folk-tales, beliefs, customs, characteristics of the people in question etc., which were all expressions of the people's spirit, or *Volksgeist*. Religions were seen as part of a people's specific expression of nature. In this way, Islam was seen as the expression of the Arab spirit, and it became possible to learn things about the Arabs and Islam by studying the Arabic language.[25]

These ideas influenced the study of philology and of religion, as all aspects of a people were used to understand the other aspects and, ultimately, to understand the people's spirit, its essence. This increasingly led to a temporal and hierarchical classification of peoples and religions, giving the Europeans a comprehensive understanding of the world and of their own place in it.[26] Comparative philology developed the concept of 'language families', which was soon linked to theories on 'race'. Indo-European or Aryan languages were seen as superior to Semitic languages, due to the level to which they were capable of 'inflection', a syntactical structure which, according to the philologists, attested to creativity and a spirit of freedom.[27] Semitic languages had only partial inflection, which (according to this theory) meant that they were capable of copying ideas but not of creatively engaging with them.[28] These characteristics were also ascribed to the religions stemming from these languages, as they were all expressions of the same 'spirit'.[29]

The Aryan influences on Christianity were stressed, especially Greek influences such as 'rationality'. This Aryan/Greek rationality was the 'basis of universality' – of inclusivity, diversity and pluralism – which gave Christianity and Europe its universal legitimacy and allowed it to 'progress'. Greek rationality would improve Christianity, or even surpass it. Judaism and Islam, being Semitic religions and therefore expressions of the Semitic spirit, were seen as rigid, legalistic and stagnant, incapable of 'progress'. Their monotheism was seen as exclusive.[30]

Sufism, however – being mainly expressed in the Aryan Persian language – did not fit the idea of a rigid, legalistic Islam. As is discussed at length by Everarde Berendsen, Sufism was seen as originally Indian (Hindu or Buddhist), Persian, Hellenistic, Christian or gnostic, but not Islamic. The one thing that all these origins had in common was the fact that they were Aryan. Palmer saw Sufism as 'a flower in the desert'.[31] Europeans who could not relate to Islam did appreciate Sufism, and their main concern was how this foreign element had entered Islam.

The first scholars to write on Sufism were Sir William Jones (1746–1794) and Sir John Malcolm (d.1833), associated with the British East India Company. They saw the 'Sooffees' as 'freethinkers' who had no links with the religion of the Prophet, and were very surprised to find this 'mystical' religious movement in Islamic lands. Jones translated Ḥāfiẓ's poetry, and according to Schimmel, 'Ḥāfiẓ's poetical imagery – unfortunately mostly taken at face value – has largely colored the Western image of Sufism.'[32] Jones was the first Orientalist to write that all mystical doctrines are ultimately the same, but expressed in different languages and figures of speech. He said that they all derived from Indian mysticism.[33] Lt. James William Graham wrote the first article dealing exclusively with Sufism. He followed Jones in seeing Sufism as an expression of universal mysticism and saw influences of Indian yoga and ancient Greek philosophy. He also saw parallels with Paul's teachings and saw Sufism as approaching Christianity.[34]

The idea that Hinduism and Buddhism influenced Sufism can be found in the work of Alfred von Kremer (1873), John Porter Brown (1886), M. Horten (1927), and even still in the 1960s with R.C. Zaehner (1960).[35] According to them, the source of this contact was Abū Bāyazīd al-Bisṭāmī and his master, Abū 'Alī al-Sind. They claimed that several of al-Bisṭāmī's expressions could be found in the Upanishads, and that the idea of the *nirvana* became the idea of *fanā'* in Sufism.[36] Richard Hartmann (1881–1965) thought that Sufism derived from Hinduism, Manichaeism, Shamanism and Mithraism.[37]

Sufism's supposed Persian origins were described in R. Dozy's book *Het Islamisme* (1880), and later in Edward G. Browne's *A Literary History of Persia* (1902).[38] Browne saw Sufism as an Aryan reaction to the oppression of the Semitic religion in Persia, an idea which still echoes in Rice's work *The Persian Ṣūfis* (1964). According to him, Persians have more affinity with mysticism and religious speculation. In his view, Sufism would bring East and West together: 'The rise of Sufism will mean a return to the original religion and with that to original unity.'[39]

In 1893, Adalbert Merx argued that the name Sufism came from the Greek *sophos* (wise), which made the Sufis essentially seekers for wisdom.[40] R.A. Nicholson (1868–1945) also supported this idea in 1906, focussing on Hellenistic elements in Sufism,[41] as did Arendt Wensinck (1882–1939).[42] Margaret Smith (1884–1970) argued that Islamic and Christian mysticism share the same Hellenistic and neo-Platonic sources, which reached Islam mainly through Christian mysticism.[43] In the words of the Spanish scholar Miguel Asín Palacios (1871–1944), this led to 'un islam cristianizado'.[44] These ideas can still be found in the works of Julian Baldick, who states that mysticism cannot derive from Islam because it 'denies the possibility that God might dwell within a man' and who says that we should take the 'Indo-European and Semitic groupings' into account.[45] The Russian Orientalists Agafangel Krymskii (1871–1942) and Valentin Zhukovskii (1858–1919) also followed these ideas of the foreign origins of Sufism.[46]

Most Orientalists misunderstood the Sufi texts.[47] They saw the poetical metaphors of wine, passion and love as literal indications that Sufism was at odds with the Sharia. They thought that there was no place for mystical ideas in the legalistic Islam of the *'ulamā'*, and that there was a sharp division between Sufis and *'ulamā'*. Western students of Sufism in recent decades have shown that this distinction is difficult to make.[48]

The philologists focussed on the 'classical' period in which these texts were written, to the exclusion of other aspects of the Sufi experience. According to Said this focus on classical texts was typical of Orientalism: 'the "good" Orient was invariably a classical period somewhere in a long-gone India, whereas the "bad" Orient lingered in present-day Asia, parts of North Africa, and Islam everywhere.'[49] The idea was that texts captured the essence of a people/religion. Any move away from the texts meant that a people had lost touch with its essence and was degenerating. Orientalists saw this decline happening in the case of Sufism, an idea that was reinforced by referring to Sufi texts that complained about Sufism's decline.[50]

By divorcing Sufism from Islam and focussing on the decline of Sufism in recent times the scholars created space for themselves and their readers to appreciate Sufism without having to re-examine their racist stereotypes of the rigid and legalistic Semite/Muslim that was not prone to 'progress'. Even if the Orientalists did not create these stereotypes, their failure to challenge them made the Western students of Sufism complicit in perpetuating them. We see here how the stereotypes of Semites and Muslims are self-perpetuating, even in the face of contradictory evidence.

Even among the earliest Orientalists, however, there were scholars who disagreed with the theories of the foreign origins of Sufism on the basis of a thorough analysis of Sufi texts. Friedrich August Deofidus Tholuck (1799–1877), who wrote the first European book on Sufism in 1821, based himself on many Arabic, Persian and Turkish manuscripts from the royal library in Berlin, and concluded that the origins of Sufism should not be sought outside of Islam.[51] However, this did not enter mainstream scholarship until Louis Massignon (1883–1962) made the same argument.[52]

Massignon argued that mystical Sufism developed mainly out of ascetic trends within Islam. He based this on an analysis of mystical terminology used by the early Sufis. His main points were that most Sufi terminology and allegories derived from the Qur'an, and Sufism's most important rituals (*dhikr* and *samā'*) are centred around the recitation of the Qur'an. Apart from the Qur'an, Sufi terminology was also influenced by Islamic scientific texts (grammar, jurisprudence, science of the Hadith), Islamic theological schools and Hellenistic philosophy (on which Islamic science and theology were largely based); but these were minor influences compared to the Qur'an. He also pointed out that at the time of the Islamic conquests there was no singular Aryan/Persian culture in Iran, that Shi'ism originated among the Arabs and was spread by Arab colonists from Kufa, and that Persian scholars write about Islamic values and interests, not universal ones.[53] Even so, several scholars have pointed out that – even though Massignon saw Sufism as intrinsically Islamic – he saw it as that part of Islam that allowed it to rise beyond itself and approach Christianity, and he understood Sufism through the lens of Christianity.[54]

Ignaz Goldziher (1850–1921) also saw Sufism as part of Islam, counterbalancing the elaborate system of theology and jurisprudence that 'could stifle the desire for holiness which lies at the heart of all religions'. For him, mysticism was the way to reassert the connection with this holiness and to establish a personal connection with God. In the words of Hourani, Goldziher saw 'Islam as a living reality, […] creating and maintaining a balance between the law, the articulation of God's word into precepts for action, and mysticism, the expression of the desire for holiness, […] still living and growing'.[55]

Pragmatic studies of Sufism: colonialism and sociology

The colonial administrators were worried about rivals to their power, and they thought that the Sufi brotherhoods could be dangerous instruments to mobilise the population against them. Some of these ideas were based on academic ideas that we came across earlier: Muslims being inherently hostile to 'progress', irrational, fanatical and decadent.[56] Knysh points out that part of these fears were also based on nineteenth-century fears of 'secret societies'. They were 'privileging Sufism as a motivating force over all the other pieces of the historical puzzle'.[57] Therefore the colonial administrators asked researchers to investigate these brotherhoods, in order to devise an adequate policy to deal with them. This research has been characterised as 'a cross between the assembly of police dossiers and the analysis of dangerous cults'.[58] They saw the brotherhoods as backward, irrational and dangerous (in line with the earlier depictions of the dervishes and the fakirs), and viewed them with 'a combination of condescension and alarm'.[59] The leaders were seen as exploiting their followers, and as such it was only a religion for the lower classes. Octave Depont and Xavier Coppolani call the relationship between shaykh and follower 'a slavery both material and moral which is spread from one end of the Muslim world to the other'.[60]

Edmund Burke III shows how, in the French colonial structure, there were different types of researchers with different goals. First he mentions the officials of the Arab Bureaus, who started to work after 1844 and were linked with the royalists and aimed to protect the tribes and the Muslims by basing French policy on facts rather than 'colonial fantasy'. They displayed a rather paternalistic attitude. There also were the amateurs and explorers who supported the Republicans and the French settlers in the colonies. In general they were quite hostile to the people of the Arab Bureaus and they gained the upper hand between 1870 and 1900, but there were also instances where they worked together. The French sociologists were not interested in North Africa until the 1870s, after which they mainly focussed on folk practices of the 'natives'.[61]

The British researched the brotherhoods in India, Egypt and the Sudan for the same reasons and with similar prejudices about Muslim fanaticism. In Somalia, for example, the Sufi Sayyid Muhammad Hasan, who rebelled against British rule in 1899, was called the 'Mad Mullah', and depicted as irrational and anti-social.[62] We also see the Russians analysing the *miuridizm* movements in the Caucasus. They thought that the Sufi leaders exploited the blind fanaticism of their followers. These groups were seen as detrimental to the Russian imperialist project, and the studies legitimised the Russian conquest of the region with the aim of civilising the people.[63] After 1917 the study of Sufism was embedded in the Communist view of history and religion, with its focus on class issues, and Sufism was seen as a reactionary force. Knysh points out that these ideas were also influenced by French works on Algerian Islam.[64]

As Knysh also pointed out, the distinction made between the philologist 'armchair academics' and the pragmatic colonial sociologists is too rigid.[65] First of all, the concrete policy adopted towards the brotherhoods shows that the colonial officials might have a more nuanced view. Depont and Coppolani advised to suppress the brotherhoods' resistance.[66] But there was also the policy of co-opting the brotherhoods into the state structure.[67] This option shows that they did realise that not all brotherhoods were fanatical, anti-colonialist and anti-Western. Later, the Sufi brotherhoods came to be seen mainly as quietist, closely linked to the (colonial) government, and as 'a form of escapism which was incapable of providing solutions to political, social and economic problems'.[68]

Also, several of these 'armchair academics' were actively involved in their countries' colonial projects. At the beginning of his career, Massignon worked for the colonialist infrastructure. Later, however, he realised that the Europeans were abusing this hospitality and he became a supporter of the Algerian movement of independence. Similarly, E.G. Browne – who thought that Sufism was a Persian import into Islam – supported the constitutionalist revolution in Persia.[69]

The best example of a scholar who bridges the divide between armchair academic and practical colonial researcher is the Dutchman Christiaan Snouck Hurgronje (1857–1936). He stayed in Mecca for a year, and in Indonesia for seven years. These experiences made him aware of the fact that Islam is very different in different parts of the world. He saw the Sharia not so much as a law but as 'an ideal system of social morality, an influence on practice and a court of appeal "when times are out of joint"'. He also acknowledged how the Sufi brotherhoods participated in upholding this system of social morality: 'More important than the strict letter of the law, as an influence on the lives of people of Mecca, is the teaching of the Sufi brotherhoods in regard to practice, moral discipline and meditation leading towards a sense of the presence of God.'[70] Snouck Hurgronje appreciated that Sufism and Sharia are not mutually exclusive and that both work to form different versions of Islam in different societies.

Snouck Hurgronje occupied a research post in the colonial administration at Batavia. Hourani says that he 'used what influence [he] had in favour of a more sensitive and understanding attitude towards those whom [his] nation ruled'.[71] He hoped that the natives would eventually consent to associate themselves with the colonial regime, and in Islamic mysticism he saw 'a perfect forum for dialogue with other religious traditions',[72] not just from the organisational perspective of the brotherhoods, but also from the perspective of Sufi teachings. This paternalistic attitude came to be characteristic of the Dutch colonial Ethical Policy. Thus Snouck Hurgronje helped perpetuate Dutch rule, and his understanding of Sufism played an important part in this.

Hourani thought that the Orientalists were mainly motivated by a will to knowledge, and that they felt the 'responsibility for the way in which their governments exercised power'.[73] This attitude showed empathy, but was strongly paternalistic and supported the colonial effort. As Knysh points out, the link between the ideas of the scholars and the colonial practices is not straightforward, although in most of their thought there is the idea of 'progress' which can be used to justify these practices.[74] I think that in the example of Snouck Hurgronje we can see how the representation of Sufism as a universalist trend within Islam supported this paternalistic attitude.

In the second half of the twentieth century scholars found a paradigm to combine 'classical' Sufism and the 'living' Sufism of the brotherhoods. According to this paradigm, 'classical' Sufism was reformed in the eighteenth and nineteenth centuries into what came to be called 'neo-Sufism': a less intellectual and more activist form of Sufism than 'classical Sufism'. According to Knysh, this paradigm underwrote the idea that the essence of Sufism is 'immutable across time and space' but that its expression changed over time.[75] This paradigm has been heavily criticised, especially by R.S. O'Fahey and Bernd Radtke, who argued that the changes in Sufism were not sufficiently great to warrant a new term.[76]

We have seen how the philological studies of Sufi poetry have misrepresented Sufism as un-Islamic and degenerating, and how this combined with ideas on mysticism to add to the development of linguistic and racist theories which justified colonialism. The sociological studies of the Sufi brotherhoods were partly motivated by colonialist goals and led to a focus on their rebellious, fanatical and anti-social attitude, and led to the pacifying of the brotherhoods by force or co-optation. We have seen, however, that this distinction is not as clear as is sometimes presented, and that there were scholars who realised the link between poetry and the brotherhoods.

The question that arises is how useful the work of all these Orientalists really is: how much is the knowledge they generated really worth, taking their theoretical background into consideration? Knysh points out that they 'laid solid textual and factual foundations for the study of Sufism', but he also follows Burke in questioning how useful the facts were that they found.[77]

Beyond the opposition between West and East

Another point made about Orientalism is that, through the power structure in which knowledge is created, this created knowledge also influences the object's self-understanding. Knysh writes that '[t]hese scholars trained a cohort of "native" Muslim scholars, who disseminated western perceptions and definitions of Sufism among their coreligionists, thereby providing an alternative reading of the Sufi tradition to that of traditional Muslim theologians.'[78] Ernst writes that Modernist Islamic intellectuals became impressed by 'the scientific posture of European scholarship' and took over much of the Orientalists' critique of Sufism: they saw the Sufis as traditional and backward, opposed to progressive modernising forces. He gives the example of Muhammad Iqbal (1876–1938), Pakistan's national poet, who criticised Sufism as a foreign element in Islam, a 'recycled version of Plato', too passive and too dependent on the spiritual leaders.[79] The Salafis want to purify Islam from any foreign elements and innovations. Ernst says in this respect that they are 'echoing' and 'mirroring' the Orientalists.[80]

Rashīd Riḍā combined all these attitudes. He started his intellectual career as the student of the modernist Muḥammad 'Abduh, but became more and more influenced by the more regressive reformism of the Wahhabis. Riḍā increasingly abhorred Sufism. He also stressed the Arabic character of Islam – in line with the rising nationalist spirit of his time – and saw Sufism as a non-Islamic, non-Arab import into Islam. He pointed to the collaborationist character of many Sufi movements, which in his eyes made them the enemy of Arab nationalist resistance against the colonialists.[81]

Ernst implies that the Orientalists are in a large part responsible for this contemporary anti-Sufi attitude by misrepresenting Sufism as a foreign innovation in Islam and as degenerating since its golden age. However, many elements of the Orientalists' misrepresentations can be found in some form or other in 'Eastern' tradition as well. Ernst himself mentioned that the sources to which the British Orientalists were exposed might have influenced their ideas. Ernst mentions the *Dabistān*, a seventeenth-century Persian text written by a Zoroastrian who argued that all major philosophical and mystical ideas derived from Persian culture, which was a major influence on Jones's work.[82]

Ernst's main example is that the official Persian Shi'ite clerical hierarchy formed a major source of information. They had not been favourably disposed towards Sufism since the rise of the Safavids in the sixteenth century. The Safavids were originally a Sufi brotherhood themselves, but when they came to power their approach changed. The Iranian clergy started to distinguish between the practical aspects of Sufism – the rituals, the life-style and the social organisation – which they abhorred, and the more philosophical aspect, which they called *'irfān* and which they valued. Travellers visiting Safavid Iran were exposed to these ideas. Ernst especially mentions Malcolm, who was ambassador to the Persian court on behalf of the British East India Company in 1800 and had a close relationship with an important clergyman in Kermanshah, who was very opposed to Sufism and had persuaded the Qajar ruler to start persecuting Sufi leaders.[83]

Other examples are the Wahhabi ideas on purity and *bid'a*, which predate European influence and are strongly critical of Sufism.[84] Also, A.J. Arberry (1905–1969) refers to the works of Dārā Shikūh (1615–1659), whose work was translated in 1929 by Maḥfūẓ al-Ḥaqq. Dārā Shikūh believed that mysticism can be found in every religion, and aimed to reconcile Sufi theory with the philosophy of the Vedas.[85]

These are a few examples of 'Easterners' having ideas for which the Orientalists are later blamed. By giving these examples, I do not mean to imply that the Orientalists played no part in contemporary ideas on Sufism. I do want to say that I think the most important gap that needs to be filled when analysing the history of Sufi studies is the gap in our understanding of how the 'Easterners' themselves contributed to the misrepresentations of the Orientalists, and the concrete consequences (such as colonialism) to which they led. One of the main criticisms aimed at Said's work is that he does not let the Arabs and Muslims speak for themselves and denies them any role in the articulation of their representations, denying them agency.[86] As Edmund Burke and David Prochaska phrase it, in this way Said 'in effect imported the very dichotomies between powerful, active colonizers and passive peoples he otherwise sought to refute'.[87] As Said knowingly limited himself to the Western discourse this is a slightly unfair criticism to make, but it does show where we should put our efforts to go beyond Said and understand that 'colonized subjects were not passively produced by hegemonic projects'.[88] In the case of Sufism, we see this on both the front of representations and the front of concrete cooperation with the colonial rulers; but we also see cases of opposition. We have seen how the Orientalists were influenced not only by European ideas and power considerations, but also by 'Eastern' ideas on Sufism and by Middle Eastern power struggles (for example in the case of the Safavids). It is time to 'move beyond the polemicized rhetoric of the binary blame game'[89] and arrive at a deeper understanding of the underlying power structures in all parts of the world, not just the West.

The main problem of the Orientalist misrepresentations is that they are generalising, essentialising, reducing the 'Other' to stereotypes. This is something that we still see today, and is particularly strong in the current debates on Islam and the Middle East. Burke and Prochaska have pointed to the relevance that this discussion on Orientalism still has in our times: 'the post–9/11 terrain has seen a regrettable regression toward civilizationalist narratives. […] the "war on terrorism" and the Iraq war have acquired a discursive power to shape the political field akin to the phase of high imperialism in the nineteenth and twentieth centuries. The absence of debate over the colonial character of American presence in Iraq, and the Middle East more generally, is one telling index of the invasion of the intellectual field by the political field.'[90] In this discourse, Sufism is often portrayed as universalist and tolerant, as an antithesis to *jihādī* Islam. Some Sufis have followed the Orientalist idea that Sufism is not part of Islam. While not many contemporary Sufis go that far, the philological focus on texts, with its representation of Sufism as Islamic mysticism and an expression of a universal religious trend, combined with the practice of co-optation that many colonial (and postcolonial) rulers used, leads to the idea that Sufism is tolerant, peace loving and easy to cooperate with. Many people use it to show that there is more to Islam than *jihād*, but we should keep in mind that this image is just as much a misrepresentation of Sufism as the misrepresentation that the members of the Sufi brotherhoods are all crazed fanatics. Just as we did in the case of the anticolonial brotherhoods, we should put this view of Sufism in its historical context, focus on the power structure behind it, and see if and how academics contribute to this view.

Notes

1 See, for example, Carl W. Ernst and Richard C. Martin, 'Introduction. Toward a post-Orientalist approach to Islamic Religious Studies', in Carl W. Ernst and Richard C. Martin (eds), *Rethinking Islamic Studies. From Orientalism to Cosmopolitanism*, Studies in Comparative Religion (Columbia, SC: University of South Carolina Press, 2010), pp. 1–19.
2 Alexander Knysh, 'Historiography of Sufi Studies in the West', in Youssef M. Choueiri (ed.), *A Companion to the History of the Middle East*, Blackwell Companions to World History (Malden, MA: Blackwell Publishing, 2005), p. 121.
3 Edward W. Said, *Orientalism*, Penguin Classics (London: Penguin, 2003), pp. 43–44, 96, 202–203.
4 Albert Hourani, 'Islam in European Thought', in idem, *Islam in European Thought* (Cambridge: Cambridge University Press, 1991), p. 58; Said, *Orientalism*, p. 70.
5 Carl W. Ernst, *The Shambhala Guide to Sufism* (Boston, MA: Shambhala, 1997), p. 202.
6 E.g. Alexander Knysh, 'Sufism as an Explanatory Paradigm: the Issue of the Motivations of Sufi Resistance', *Die Welt des Islams* 42, no. 2 (2002), pp. 139–173; Hourani, 'Islam in European Thought'; Edmund Burke III, 'The Sociology of Islam: the French Tradition', in Edmund Burke and David Prochaska (eds), *Genealogies of Orientalism. History, Theory, Politics* (Lincoln: University of Nebraska Press, 2008), pp. 154–173 (first published in Malcolm H. Kerr (ed.), *Islamic Studies: A Tradition and its Problems* (Malibu, CA: Undena, 1980), pp. 73–88).
7 Gaby Piterberg, 'Albert Hourani and Orientalism', in Ilan Pappé and Moshe Ma'oz (eds), *Middle Eastern Politics and Ideas. A History from Within* (London: I.B. Tauris, 1997), pp. 78–80.
8 Knysh, 'Historiography of Sufi Studies in the West', pp. 118–119.
9 Burke III, 'The Sociology of Islam', p. 155.
10 Annemarie Schimmel, *Mystical Dimensions of Islam* (Chapel Hill, NC: University of North Carolina Press, 1987), pp. 7–8.
11 C. Ernst, 'Tasawwuf – 7. In Muslim India', *Encyclopaedia of Islam*, Vol. X (Leiden: Brill, 2000), pp. 334–337; Knysh, 'Historiography of Sufi Studies in the West', p. 108.
12 Donald Campbell, *A Journey over Land to India* (London: Cullen and Company, 1795) pp. 123–138. I would like to thank Mohammad Sakhnini for pointing me to this source.
13 Ernst, *The Shambhala Guide to Sufism*, p. 3.
14 Edward William Lane, *An Account of the Manners and Customs of the Modern Egyptians* (London: J.M. Dent & Sons Ltd, 1954; originally published London: Society for the Diffusion of Useful Knowledge, 1836), pp. 235–253.
15 Richard Burton, *Personal Narrative of a Pilgrimage to al-Madinah and Meccah, 1855–1856* (London: Darf, 1986); Armin Vámbéry, 'Voyage dans l'Asie Centrale, de Téhéran a Khiva, Bokhara et Samarkand, par Arminius Vámbéry, savant Hongrois déguisé en derviche', in Edouard Charton (ed.), *Le Tour du Monde, Nouveau Journal des Voyages* (Paris: La Librairie Hachette, 1865).
16 Ernst, *The Shambhala Guide to Sufism*, p. 3.

17 Ibid., p. 147.
18 Hourani, 'Islam in European Thought', 14; Tomoko Masuzawa, *The Invention of World Religions, or, How European Universalism was Preserved in the Language of Pluralism* (Chicago: University of Chicago Press, 2005), pp. 1–2.
19 Hourani discusses Immanuel Kant (1724–1804) and Friedrich Schleiermacher (1768–1834) to illustrate this point. Hourani, 'Islam in European Thought', pp. 23–24.
20 Schimmel, *Mystical Dimensions of Islam*, p. 4.
21 Leigh Eric Schmidt, 'The Making of Modern Mysticism', *Journal of the American Academy of Religion* 71, no. 2 (2003), pp. 277–282.
22 Ibid., p. 274.
23 Masuzawa, *The Invention of World Religions*, p. 20.
24 Schmidt, 'The Making of Modern Mysticism', pp. 283–284.
25 This idea was first developed by J.G. Herder (1744–1803). He did not think one people or nation should rule another; the goal of history was rather to achieve balance and harmony between all peoples. See J.G. Herder, *Ideen zur Philosophie der Menschheit*, 4 vols (Riga and Leipzig: Johann Friedrich Hartknoch, 1784–1791). Hourani, 'Islam in European Thought', p. 25.
26 For example, G.W.F. Hegel (1770–1831) saw Islam as an expression of the Arab spirit, whose main characteristic he thought to be its initial enthusiasm which allowed the faith to spread so fast – an enthusiasm which by his time was long gone. According to him, Islam had finished its role in history. Hourani, 'Islam in European Thought', p. 26.
27 Masuzawa, *The Invention of World Religions*, p. 25.
28 Ibid., pp. 177–178.
29 Especially Friedrich Max Müller (1823–1900), a German Sanskritist, who transferred the scientific method from the field of language to that of religion. Masuzawa, *The Invention of World Religions*, p. 24.
30 Ibid., xiii–xiv, 177–178, 191, 199, 207.
31 Everarde Berendsen, '"Als een Bloem in de Woestijn." Zes Theorieën over de Herkomst van het Vroege Soefisme', Bachelor of Arts Undergraduate Thesis (University of Leiden, 2008); Schimmel, *Mystical Dimensions of Islam*, pp. 8–9; Ernst, *The Shambhala Guide to Sufism*, p. 15.
32 Schimmel, *Mystical Dimensions of Islam*, p. 8.
33 Ernst, *The Shambhala Guide to Sufism*, p. 11; William Jones, *Collected Works of Sir William Jones* (London and New York: RoutledgeCurzon, 1993; New York: New York University Press, 1993: complete facsimile edn. of the 1807 edn. of Jones' work); John Malcolm, *The History of Persia, from the most Early Period to the Present Time: Containing an Account of the Religion, Government, Usages and Character of the Inhabitants of that Kingdom*, 2 vols (London: John Murray, 1815; new rev. edn, 1829).
34 Ernst, *The Shambhala Guide to Sufism*, 13–14; Lt. James William Graham, 'A treatise on Sufiism, or Mahomedan Mysticism', *Transactions of the Literary Society of Bombay* 1 (1819).
35 Berendsen, '"Als een Bloem in de Woestijn"', p. 25: Alfred von Kremer, *Culturgeschichtliche Streifzüge auf dem Gebiete des Islams* (Leipzig: F.A. Brockhaus, 1873; repr. Whitefish, Montana: Kessinger Publishing, 2009); John Porter Brown, *The Darvishes: or, Oriental Spiritualism* (London: Oxford University Press, 1927); Max Horten, *Indische Strömungen in der islamischen Mystik*, 2 vols (Heidelberg: Carl Winters Universitätsbuchhandlung, 1927–28); R.C. Zaehner, *Hindu and Muslim Mysticism* (New York: Schocken Books, 1969).
36 Berendsen, '"Als een Bloem in de Woestijn"', pp. 26–31.
37 Knysh, 'Historiography of Sufi Studies in the West', p. 114.
38 R. Dozy, *Het Islamisme* (Den Haag: A.C. Kruseman, 1863); Edward G. Browne, *A Literary History of Persia* (Cambridge: Cambridge University Press, 1928); R. Hartmann, 'Zur Frage nach der Herkunft un den Anfangen des Sufitums', *Der Islam* 6 (1915).

39 Berendsen, '"Als een Bloem in de Woestijn"', 16; Cyprian Rice, *The Persian Ṣūfis* (London: Allen & Unwin, 1964), pp. 12–16 and 26.

40 Schimmel, *Mystical Dimensions of Islam*, 14; Adalbert Merx, *Idee und Grundlinien einer allgemeinen Geschichte der Mystik* (Heidelberg: J. Hörning, 1893); Berendsen, '"Als een Bloem in de Woestijn"', p. 32.

41 Reynold A. Nicholson, 'A Historical Enquiry Concerning the Origin and Development of Sufism', *Journal of the Royal Asiatic Society of Great Britain and Ireland* (1906), pp. 303–348; Ernst, *The Shambhala Guide to Sufism*, p. 16.

42 Knysh, 'Historiography of Sufi Studies in the West', p. 115.

43 Berendsen, '"Als een Bloem in de Woestijn"', pp. 20–24; Knysh, 'Historiography of Sufi Studies in the West', 115–116; Margaret Smith, *Studies in Early Mysticism in the Near and Middle East* (Oxford: Oneworld, 1995), p. 244.

44 Berendsen, '"Als een Bloem in de Woestijn"', pp. 16–17; Miguel Asín Palacios, *El Islam Cristianizado: Estudio del 'Sufismo' a través de las Obras de Abenarabi de Murcia* (Madrid : Ed. Plutarco,1931).

45 Julian Baldick, *Mystical Islam: An Introduction to Sufism* (London: I.B. Tauris, 1989), pp. 2, 7.

46 Knysh, 'Historiography of Sufi Studies in the West', p. 119.

47 Schimmel, *Mystical Dimensions of Islam*, pp. 8, 12–14.

48 Knysh, 'Historiography of Sufi Studies in the West', pp. 126–127.

49 Said, *Orientalism*, p. 99.

50 Carl Ernst has pointed out, however, that these remarks should be seen as a rhetorical device rather than a real conviction that Sufism had declined. Carl W. Ernst and Bruce B. Lawrence, *Sufi Martyrs of Love: The Chishti Order in South Asia and Beyond* (New York: Palgrave Macmillan, 2002), p. 13.

51 Friedrich August Deofidus Tholuck, *Ssufismus sive Theosophia Persarum Pantheistica* (Berolini: In Libraria Ferd. Duemmleri, 1821).

52 Berendsen, '"Als een Bloem in de Woestijn"', pp. 14–15; Christopher Melchert, 'The Transition from Asceticism to Mysticism at the Middle of the Ninth Century C.E.', *Studia Islamica* (1996), p. 51; Hourani, 'Islam in European Thought', pp. 44–50.

53 Berendsen, '"Als een Bloem in de Woestijn"', pp. 14–15; Knysh, 'Historiography of Sufi Studies in the West', pp. 116–117; Louis Massignon, *Essai sur les Origines du Lexique Technique de la Mystique Musulmane* (Paris: Paul Geuthner, 1922).

54 Hourani, 'Islam in European Thought', p. 47.

55 Ibid., pp. 40–41.

56 Knysh, 'Sufism as an Explanatory Paradigm', p. 140.

57 Ibid., p. 170.

58 Ernst, *The Shambhala Guide to Sufism*, p. 5.

59 Ibid., pp. 206–207.

60 Octave Depont and Xavier Coppolani, *Les Confréries Religieuses Musulmanes* (Alger: Adolphe Jourdan, 1897), pp. 203–204, quoted in Daphne Habibis, 'The Problem of Values in Muslim Research: the Case of Sufism', *Asian Studies Review* 15, no. 2 (1991), p. 18.

61 Edmund Burke III, 'The Sociology of Islam: the French Tradition', in Malcolm H. Kerr (ed.), *Islamic Studies: a Tradition and its Problems*, Giorgio Levi Della Vida Biennial Conference (Malibu, CA: Undena, 1979), pp. 73–88.

62 Knysh, 'Historiography of Sufi Studies in the West', p. 111; Ernst, *The Shambhala Guide to Sufism*, p. 8.

63 Knysh, 'Historiography of Sufi Studies in the West', p. 111; idem, 'Sufism as an Explanatory Paradigm', p. 149–150.

64 Idem, 'Sufism as an Explanatory Paradigm', pp. 160–161.

65 Idem, 'Historiography of Sufi Studies in the West', p. 119.

66 Idem., p. 111.

67 Ernst, *The Shambhala Guide to Sufism*, pp. 205–211.

68 Habibis, 'The Problem of Values in Muslim Research', pp. 18–19.

69 Hourani, 'Islam in European Thought', p. 58.
70 Ibid., p. 42.
71 Ibid., p. 58.
72 Knysh, 'Historiography of Sufi Studies in the West', p. 113.
73 Hourani, 'Islam in European Thought', pp. 57–58.
74 Knysh, 'Historiography of Sufi Studies in the West', p. 112.
75 Idem, 'Sufism as an Explanatory Paradigm', p. 170.
76 R.S. O'Fahey and Bernd Radtke, 'Neo-sufism Reconsidered', *Der Islam* 70 (1993), pp. 52–87.
77 Burke III, 'The Sociology of Islam: the French Tradition', pp. 87–88; Knysh, 'Historiography of Sufi Studies in the West', p. 111.
78 Knysh, 'Historiography of Sufi Studies in the West', p. 121. Knysh does not give a reference to support this claim.
79 Ernst, *The Shambhala Guide to Sufism*, p. 202.
80 Idem, 'Tasawwuf – 7. In Muslim India', pp. 335–336.
81 Albert Hourani, 'Sufism and Modern Islam: Rashid Rida', in idem, *The Emergence of the Modern Middle East* (London: Palgrave Macmillan, 1990), pp. 90–102; Elizabeth Sirriyeh, *Sufis and Anti-Sufis: The Defence, Rethinking and Rejection of Sufism in the Modern World*, Routledge Sufi Series 9 (Richmond, Surrey: Curzon, 1999), pp. 98–102.
82 Ernst, *The Shambhala Guide to Sufism*, p. 11.
83 Ibid., pp. 4, 11.
84 Esther Peskes, 'The Wahhābiyya and Sufism in the Eighteenth Century', in F. de Jong and Bernd Radtke (eds), *Islamic Mysticism Contested. Thirteen Centuries of Controversies and Polemics* (Leiden: Brill, 1999), pp. 145–161.
85 A.J. Arberry, *Sufism. The Religious Attitude and Life in Islam* (London: Allen & Unwin, 1950), p. 119; Dārā Shikūh, *Majma'-ul-Bahrain: Or the Mingling of the Two Oceans*, trans. Muhammad Mahfuz ul-Haq (Calcutta: Asiatic Society, 1929). I would like to thank Carl Ernst for pointing me to this source.
86 Daniel Martin Varisco, *Reading Orientalism: Said and the Unsaid* (Seattle and London: University of Washington Press, 2007), p. xv.
87 Edmund Burke III and David Prochaska, 'Introduction: Orientalism from Postcolonial Theory to World History', in idem, *Genealogies of Orientalism. History, Theory, Politics* (Lincoln: University of Nebraska Press, 2008), pp. 2–3.
88 A.L. Macfie, *Orientalism: A Reader* (New York: New York University Press, 2001), p. 7.
89 Varisco, *Reading Orientalism*, p. xi.
90 Burke III and Prochaska, 'Introduction', pp. 50–51.

Bibliography

Arberry, A.J., *Sufism. The Religious Attitude and Life in Islam* (London: Allen & Unwin, 1950).

Asín Palacios, Miguel, *El Islam Cristianizado: Estudio del 'Sufismo' a través de las Obras de Abenarabi de Murcia* (Madrid: Ed. Plutarco, 1931).

Baldick, Julian, *Mystical Islam: An Introduction to Sufism* (London: I.B. Tauris, 1989).

Berendsen, Everarde, '"Als een Bloem in de Woestijn." Zes Theorieën over de Herkomst van het Vroege Soefisme', Bachelor of Arts Undergraduate Thesis (Leiden: University of Leiden, 2008).

Brown, John Porter, *The Darvishes: or, Oriental Spiritualism* (London: Oxford University Press, 1927).

Browne, Edward G., *A Literary History of Persia* (Cambridge: Cambridge University Press, 1928).

Burke III, Edmund, 'The Sociology of Islam: the French Tradition', in Edmund Burke and David Prochaska (eds), *Genealogies of Orientalism. History, Theory, Politics* (Lincoln: University of Nebraska Press, 2008), pp. 154–173.

Burke III, Edmund, and David Prochaska (eds), *Genealogies of Orientalism. History, Theory, Politics* (Lincoln: University of Nebraska Press, 2008).

Burke III, Edmund, and David Prochaska, 'Introduction: Orientalism from Postcolonial Theory to World History', in Edmund Burke and David Prochaska (eds), *Genealogies of Orientalism. History, Theory, Politics* (Lincoln: University of Nebraska Press, 2008), pp. 1–71.

Burton, Richard, *Personal Narrative of a Pilgrimage to al-Madinah and Meccah, 1855–1856* (London: Darf, 1986).

Campbell, Donald, *A Journey over Land to India* (London: Cullen & Company, 1795).

Charton, Edouard (ed.), *Le Tour du Monde, Nouveau Journal des Voyages* (Paris: La Librairie Hachette, 1865).

Choueiri, Youssef F. (ed.), *A Companion to the History of the Middle East*, Blackwell Companions to World History (Malden, MA: Blackwell Publishing, 2005).

Dārā Shikūh, *Majma'-ul-Bahrain: Or the Mingling of the Two Oceans*, trans. Muhammad Mahfuz ul-Haq (Calcutta: Asiatic Society, 1929).

De Jong, F. and Bernd Radtke (eds), *Islamic Mysticism Contested. Thirteeen Centuries of Controversies and Polemics* (Leiden: Brill, 1999).

Depont, Octave and Xavier Coppolani, *Les Confrèries Religieuses Musulmanes* (Alger: Adolphe Jourdan, 1897).

Dozy, R., *Het Islamisme* (Den Haag: A.C. Kruseman, 1863).

Ernst, C., 'Tasawwuf – 7. In Muslim India', *Encyclopaedia of Islam*, Vol. X (Leiden: Brill, 2000).

Ernst, Carl W. *The Shambhala Guide to Sufism* (Boston, MA: Shambhala, 1997).

Ernst, Carl W., and Bruce B. Lawrence, *Sufi Martyrs of Love: The Chishti Order in South Asia and Beyond* (New York: Palgrave Macmillan, 2002).

Ernst, Carl W., and Richard C. Martin, 'Introduction. Toward a Post-Orientalist Approach to Islamic Religious Studies', in Carl W. Ernst and Richard C. Martin (eds), *Rethinking Islamic Studies. From Orientalism to Cosmopolitanism*, Studies in Comparative Religion (Columbia, SC: University of South Carolina Press, 2010), pp.1–19.

Ernst, Carl W., and Richard C. Martin (eds), *Rethinking Islamic Studies: From Orientalism to Cosmopolitanism*, Studies in Comparative Religion (Columbia, SC: University of South Carolina Press, 2010).

Graham, James William, 'A treatise on Sufiism, or Mahomedan Mysticism', *Transactions of the Literary Society of Bombay* 1 (1819).

Habibis, Daphne, 'The Problem of Values in Muslim Research: the Case of Sufism', *Asian Studies Review* 15, no. 2 (1991), pp. 16–25.

Hartmann, R., 'Zur Frage nach der Herkunft un den Anfangen des Sufitums', *Der Islam* 6 (1915).

Herder, J.G., *Ideen zur Philosophie der Menschheit*, 4 vols (Riga and Leipzig: Johann Friedrich Hartknoch, 1784–1791).

Horten, Max, *Indische Strömungen in der islamischen Mystik*, 2 vols (Heidelberg: Carl Winters Universitätsbuchhandlung, 1927–28).

Hourani, Albert, *The Emergence of the Modern Middle East* (London: Palgrave Macmillan, 1990).

——, 'Islam in European thought', in idem, *Islam in European Thought* (Cambridge: Cambridge University Press, 1991), pp. 7–60.

——, *Islam in European Thought* (Cambridge: Cambridge University Press, 1991).

——, 'Sufism and Modern Islam: Rashid Rida', in idem, *The Emergence of the Modern Middle East* (London: Palgrave Macmillan, 1990), pp. 90–102.

Jones, William, *Collected Works of Sir William Jones* (London and New York: RoutledgeCurzon, 1993; New York: New York University Press, 1993: complete facsimile edn of the 1807 edn of Jones' work).

Kerr, Malcolm H. (ed.), *Islamic Studies: A Tradition and its Problems*, Giorgio Levi Della Vida Biennial Conference (Malibu, CA: Undena, 1979).

Knysh, Alexander, 'Historiography of Sufi Studies in the West', in Youssef F. Choueiri (ed.), *A Companion to the History of the Middle East*, Blackwell Companions to World History (Malden, MA: Blackwell Publishing, 2005), pp. 106–131.

——, 'Sufism as an Explanatory Paradigm: the Issue of the Motivations of Sufi Resistance', *Die Welt des Islams* 42, no. 2 (2002), pp. 139–173.

Kremer, Alfred von, *Culturgeschichtliche Streifzüge auf dem Gebiete des Islams* (Leipzig: F.A. Brockhaus, 1873; repr. Whitefish, MT: Kessinger Publishing, 2009).

Lane, Edward William, *An Account of the Manners and Customs of the Modern Egyptians* (London: J.M. Dent & Sons Ltd, 1954; originally published by London: Society for the Diffusion of Useful Knowledge, 1836).

Macfie, A.L., *Orientalism: A Reader* (New York: New York University Press, 2001).

Malcolm, John, *The History of Persia from the most Early Period to the Present Time: Containing an Account of the Religion, Government, Usages and Character of the Inhabitants of that Kingdom*, 2 vols (London: John Murray, 1815; new rev. edn, 1829).

Massignon, Louis, *Essai sur les Origines du Lexique Technique de la Mystique Musulmane* (Paris: Paul Geuthner, 1922).

Masuzawa, Tomoko, *The Invention of World Religions, or, How European Universalism was Preserved in the Language of Pluralism* (Chicago: University of Chicago Press, 2005).

Melchert, Christopher, 'The Transition from Asceticism to Mysticism at the Middle of the Ninth Century C.E.', *Studia Islamica* (1996), pp. 51–70.

Merx, Adalbert, *Idee und Grundlinien einer allgemeinen Geschichte der Mystik* (Heidelberg: J. Hörning, 1893).

Nicholson, Reynold A., 'A Historical Enquiry Concerning the Origin and Development of Sufism', *Journal of the Royal Asiatic Society of Great Britain and Ireland* (1906), pp. 303–348.

O'Fahey, R.S., and Bernd Radtke, 'Neo-sufism Reconsidered', *Der Islam* 70 (1993), pp. 52–87.

Pappé, Ilan and Moshe Ma'oz (eds), *Middle Eastern Politics and Ideas. A History from Within* (London: I.B. Tauris, 1997).

Peskes, Esther, 'The Wahhābiyya and Sufism in the Eighteenth Century', in F. de Jong and Bernd Radtke (eds), *Islamic Mysticism Contested. Thirteen Centuries of Controversies and Polemics* (Leiden: Brill, 1999), pp. 145–161.

Piterberg, Gaby, 'Albert Hourani and Orientalism', in Ilan Pappé and Moshe Ma'oz (eds), *Middle Eastern Politics and Ideas. A History from Within* (London: I.B. Tauris, 1997), pp. 78–80.

Rice, Cyprian, *The Persian Ṣūfis* (London: Allen & Unwin, 1964).

Said, Edward W., *Orientalism*, Penguin Classics (London: Penguin, 2003).

Schimmel, Annemarie, *Mystical Dimensions of Islam*, new edition with additional bibliography (Chapel Hill, NC: University of North Carolina Press, 1987).

Schmidt, Leigh Eric, 'The Making of Modern Mysticism', *Journal of the American Academy of Religion* 71, no. 2 (2003), pp. 273–302.

Sirriyeh, Elizabeth, *Sufis and Anti-Sufis: The Defence, Rethinking and Rejection of Sufism in the Modern World*, Routledge Sufi Series 9 (Richmond, Surrey: Curzon, 1999).

Smith, Margaret, *Studies in Early Mysticism in the Near and Middle East* (Oxford: Oneworld, 1995).

Tholuck, Friedrich August Deofidus, *Ssufismus sive Theosophia Persarum Pantheistica* (Berolini: In Libraria Ferd. Duemmleri, 1821).

Vámbéry, Armin, 'Voyage dans l'Asie Centrale, de Téhéran à Khiva, Bokhara et Samarkand, par Arminius Vámbéry, savant Hongrois déguisé en derviche', in Edouard Charton (ed.), *Le Tour du Monde, Nouveau Journal des Voyages* (Paris: La Librairie Hachette, 1865).

Varisco, Daniel Martin, *Reading Orientalism: Said and the Unsaid* (Seattle and London: University of Washington Press, 2007).

Zaehner, R.C., *Hindu and Muslim Mysticism* (New York: Schocken Books, 1969).

Part II

Art

6 Orientalism in arts and crafts revisited

The modern and the anti-modern: the lessons from the Orient

John M. MacKenzie

Edward Said's *Orientalism* was a highly seductive book exercising powerful influences well beyond Said's own literary field. To take but two examples, it became the foundation text of the group of historians known as the post-colonials; it also influenced a number of art historians who found in it new ways of interpreting Orientalist art.[1] For them, the extraordinary flowering of artistic expressions of Oriental subjects could be explained as yet another western mode for representing, and therefore mis-representing, the Orient in the era of western imperialism. Such artistic expressions could be seen as a visual form of the West's appropriation of Eastern subjects, yet another tool in the establishment of power and authority. Such slanted images of the Orient could be found not only in the canvases of large numbers of artists who travelled in and painted the East, but also in various other cultural artefacts, including performances on the stage. These performances invariably involved the art of the scene painter, another important means of presenting the East to a western public.[2] Thus, the Orient was also the setting for plays and operas, starting in the eighteenth century and fully flowering in the nineteenth.[3]

For me, my conversion from the Saidian paradigm happened as a result of hearing a keynote at an art historians' conference in which Edward Said gave a multi-media presentation on Verdi's *Aida*, the text of which was subsequently published in his book *Culture and Imperialism*.[4] This lecture surprised me, for Said seemed to be talking about a wholly different opera from the one I knew. As it happened, because of a long-standing interest in music and opera, I had given a lot of thought to *Aida*, a thoroughly intriguing opera from a cross-cultural and ideological standpoint. Although Said seemed to contextualise it impressively in terms of the history of Egypt of the time, the encroachments of the West and the opening of the Suez Canal, the activities of savants and archaeologists in the unveiling of Ancient Egypt, as well as Verdi's reactions to the commission in his extensive correspondence of the time, still something did not ring true.

My problem lay with the fact that Said never mentioned the actual text of the opera, never analysed its apparent ideology, or indeed the centres of gravity of its music.[5] The key phrase for me was that Verdi had produced, according to Said, a plot 'that ends in hopeless deadlock and literal entombment'.[6] Yet the immolation of Radames and Aida at the climactic point of the drama seemed to fit the long-standing trope of star-crossed lovers finding union in death – Hero and Leander,

Romeo and Juliet, Desdemona and Othello. I had always considered the opera to be about nationalism, about resistance to the imperialistic Egyptians, and about the relationship between landscape and patriotism. There is also a strong vein of the composer's well-known anti-clericalism, obvious in the condemnation of the hero in the final act. In all of these, Verdi was following his predilections – his celebration of figures condemned by society (like Violetta in *La Traviata*), as well as his nationalist and anti-imperial passions. The fulcrum of the opera, it seemed to me, was Aida's aria 'O patria mia', in which she invokes the great physical beauty of her homeland, Ethiopia.[7] Verdi's best music is here, and the entombment is an apotheosis, a triumphant signal of hope. In short, the Ethiopians seemed to have 'all the best tunes'.

Thus, Verdi's fascination with the 'underdog', so apparent in so many of his operas, seemed equally present here. After all, the title role is that of the Ethiopian, not the Egyptian, princess. The latter, Amneris, fails in love and seems vindictive in her vengefulness. The triumphalism of the celebrated Act 2 march and spectacle never seemed to me quite to ring true. Might it not be the case that Verdi was almost sending up such martial splendours, given the fact that it is known that he had little sympathy with either British or Italian imperialism?[8] Was it not possible that Verdi was actually offering a very back-handed compliment to the Khedive of Egypt, who had commissioned the opera, and the elite European and Egyptian members of the audience who enjoyed the spectacle in the new Cairo Opera House? And might this not offer a clue to the hidden messages – or in some cases scarcely veiled intentions – of so much Orientalist art? Might not such art convey a critique of western societies rather than of the eastern ones which it depicted?

This disenchantment with Said's *Orientalism* was confirmed when I read his Wellek lectures on music.[9] Here again he seemed to offer a severe binarism in cultural constructions of West and East, whereas the experimentation of composers with eastern forms (however artificial and rudimentary such grappling with Eastern modes was at the beginning) seemed to me to represent efforts to take western music in new directions. French and Russian composers, for example, turned to Oriental themes and rhythms in an attempt to escape stifling conventions and the dominance of the German tradition, thus producing new sensations from an exoticism which drew on Russian contacts with Central Asia, on the one hand, and French experience of North Africa and the Middle East, on the other. Moreover, it seemed to me that there were three highly significant dimensions missing from the work of Said and some of his followers. These were the key factors of social class, modes of consumption of Orientalist products, and of the market in paintings and artefacts.[10] It also seemed reasonable to argue that the victims of imperialism and of the imperial world-view somehow maintained their independent agency, however threatened, throughout the imperial experience. In maintaining such cultural independence, non-European peoples seemed to expose the essential weakness of imperial power, and to maintain processes of exchange within the patterns of dominance. It was soon apparent that some art historians, for example Emily Weeks, were indeed applying such ideas to art history.[11] They seemed to confirm the view that the way forward was in considering the reality of reciprocities even within those acknowledged patterns of inequality of power.

Imperialism, far from being the all-conquering force which some nineteenth-century contemporaries and the sub-Saidian post-colonialists seemed to imagine, in reality carried within it a great paradox. Imperialism seemed to represent the triumph of the modern, yet for many the expressions of such modernism – as in industrially produced artefacts – were a source of doubt and anxiety. The reality is that so many of the cultural expressions of the era involved the almost ubiquitous juxtaposition of the modern and the anti-modern.[12] Modernism and modernity are of course freighted with diverse and complex meanings, but for the purposes of this paper, the basic terms modern and anti-modern may be used simply to convey the nineteenth-century world of western industrial production, and of the consequent global conquest and settlement, counterposed against the anxieties about these developments which were constantly expressed in terms of the values that were being lost. Industrially produced artefacts, while capable of asserting power in striking ways (for example through the technologies of travel and of firearms), still lacked for many contemporaries the artistic worth of hand-crafted items. Much of nineteenth-century art history and comment can be seen as representing this perceived dichotomy between industrial and craft values.

Hence, the truly striking thing about expressions of the modern in the nineteenth century is that its supposed antithesis was always present. The Great London Exhibition of 1851 is a perfect example. The architectural envelope in which the exhibition was displayed seemed to represent the essence of modernity. Paxton's vast iron and glass 'Crystal Palace' owed its origins to conservatories and orangeries, but it was to become the classic – and indeed global – language of the railway station, the Victorian market building, and much else.[13] It was of course dependent on industrial-scale production of both iron and glass. But, intriguingly, the interior contained much that looked like the anti-modern. Of course the exhibition was devoted to the application of aesthetic values to industrial items, but somehow such values could be imparted only through the celebration of crafts. Thus that pure modernist envelope contained a great clutter of both crafts and industrial products. So much was this the case that one scholar, Jeffrey Auerbach, has argued that it constituted not the expression of an overweening industrial and imperial confidence, as so often suggested, but actually a sign of anxiety, a fear of weakness in the face of, for example, what were seen as superior French values.[14] Emily Weeks's reference to positive attitudes towards merchants of hand-crafted goods, relating to J.F Lewis's possible self-portrait in *The Carpet Seller*, should make us think of the transfer of such values to Europe.[15]

All subsequent Victorian exhibitions seemed to perpetuate this dichotomy between the industrial and the non-industrial, the modern and the anti-modern, in the process penetrating the significance of this paradox all the more deeply. The South Kensington Museum, later the Victoria and Albert (V&A), in London was specifically founded to attempt to raise the values of the one (the industrial) by study of the other (crafts).[16] This stimulated a major industry, as it were, of craft revival. In India, another V&A, now beautifully renovated as the Bhau Daji Lad Museum, was founded in Bombay (Mumbai), opened in 1872.[17] It was originally designed to promote precisely the same principles as those of South Kensington. One of its most influential curators was George Birdwood, who revered what he saw as the ideal craft production and aesthetic values of the Indian village. John Ruskin, while no admirer of Indian art, was also interested in the revival of craft values. Back in Britain, Birdwood became a major theorist of these notions which later fed into the work of William Morris and his associates in the Arts and Crafts movement.[18] Morris was a considerable admirer of Oriental carpets and other crafts, seeking to represent them in his ideal home at Kelmscott. He also sold Oriental ceramics and other items at his shop in London's Red Lion Square.[19] Among a number of examples, the artist Frederic Leighton sought to reproduce the crafts and the atmosphere of such work in his Arab Hall (by George Aitchison) at his home in Holland Park, London, while William Burges worked on reproducing Islamic design for the Marquis of Bute at Cardiff Castle.[20]

For most of these proponents of the revival of craft values, this was a social as well as an aesthetic movement. Crafts represented the societal relationships of the village rather than of the industrial unit. They were thus rural rather than urban. They involved what was perceived to be the dignity of individual production in closely reciprocal relationships with other craftspeople. Such producers also had closer connections with customers and patrons, even if we would now see some of those connections as being economically exploitative. This contrasted with the supposedly debased aesthetic values of the industrially fabricated artefact, in which mass production ensured that manufacturers, who had relationships with machines rather than with the genuine raw material and aesthetics of the craft, were cut off from their markets. This of course represented theorisation about an ideal rather than a reality which often ensured that craft producers received inadequate rewards for their labours, just as industrial workers did. Nonetheless, most of the celebrated exhibitions of the nineteenth century acted as showcases for crafts and their products and many of them brought craftspeople from India and elsewhere in the East to demonstrate their work in a variety of media – wood, metal, textiles, carpets, ceramics and jewellery. Often the most striking images of such exhibitions are indeed the craftspeople at work and the 'bazaars' in which their products were sold. The Austrian artist Rudolf Swoboda (1859–1914) produced a remarkable series of portraits of the Indian craftspeople who worked at the Colonial and Indian Exhibition in London in 1886.[21] These so impressed Queen Victoria that she subsequently commissioned him to go to India to paint scenes and some of her 'subjects' there.[22]

Moreover, this fascination with Oriental (and other) craft forms entered into British production. Ornamental iron-work is a case in point. The celebrated companies that produced such materials (Walter Macfarlane's Saracen iron-works in Glasgow is an excellent example) converted many oriental motifs into their work, which was exported throughout the British Empire and elsewhere. The exhibition displays of this company, such as at the Glasgow International Exhibition of 1888, had a distinctly oriental feel to them, as had its magnificent catalogue of its products.[23] This Glasgow exhibition, which was partly designed to show off the heavy industrial production of the city, took place in temporary buildings so Orientalist in style that they were dubbed 'Baghdad by the Kelvin'.[24] The exhibition also boasted a Mooresque royal reception room, Howell's tobacco kiosk, which was advertised as an Oriental smoking lounge with divans, and Doulton's Indian pavilion for the display of ceramics. Yet again, the industrial was juxtaposed against the pre-industrial arts which seemed to be represented in these Orientalist forms. But it is clear that, contra the interpretations of Said and his followers, this was not done to denigrate or down-grade the pre-industrial, but to demonstrate the necessity of staying true to its ideals even in an industrial age.

Moreover, the work of the architect Owen Jones promoted this concern with Oriental design, through his studies of the Islamic architecture of the Alhambra in Granada (a major interest in the first half of the nineteenth century), his activities in respect of the V&A Museum, and his concern with the displays in the Crystal Palace, notably after its move to Sydenham.[25] His magnificent *Grammar of Ornament* of 1856 (using a major advance in chromolithographic reproduction) sought to display examples of ornamentation from the Middle East, South Asia, and the Far East towards the same objectives.[26] These fed into the design of textiles, wallpapers, and much else. There was indeed something of a sequence of fashionable crazes in the second half of the nineteenth century, embracing North African and Middle Eastern designs, as well as examples from South Asia and the Far East. The Japonisme fascination, though much satirised by Gilbert and Sullivan and others, influenced certain areas of production, notably ceramics, over an enduring time-scale.[27] While Liberty's Store in London, somewhat more directly, made all sorts of Middle Eastern designs and artefacts highly fashionable for a season, many forms of exoticism also entered the architecture of leisure in Britain and elsewhere.[28]

This fascination with crafts connects very conveniently with Orientalist art. Yet another of the paradoxes of industrialism is the phenomenon pointed out some time ago by the American historian Martin Wiener.[29] The fact is that many industrial figures in Britain converted their wealth into wholly non-industrial practices: they invested in great country houses and estates; they attempted to join the landed aristocracy in their social practices; and, in strikingly contradictory ways, they also sought to glorify the pre-industrial. A good example is Sir William Armstrong of Newcastle, a great industrialist who made a vast fortune in engineering and munitions. But his architect, Norman Shaw, created at Cragside in Northumberland a residence which combined antique pastiche in architecture and crafts with hydraulics and other modern techniques, thereby producing a picturesque and often medievalised composition nonetheless imbued with up-to-date comforts.[30] The plunge bath there, with its blue tiles, is distinctly Orientalist in appearance, while many similar fascinations can be found around the house.

Among the pre-industrial activities that such a class pursued with fervour were a fascination with horses and hunting and shooting. Scotland became the happy hunting ground of the elite, who soon fanned out from Britain in search of new and apparently atavistic thrills around the world.[31] Modern infrastructures like steamships, railways, and the telegraph enabled them to go further and further afield in their ironic pursuit of the pre-industrial and supposedly primitive. Hunting took such travellers to Africa, North America, India, and New Zealand.

Hunting combined the modern (firearms for example) with the pre-modern, the rational with the irrational, the romance of exotic landscapes with contact with indigenous peoples. This essential cultural context helps to explain the popularity of certain themes in Orientalist painting. Eugene Fromentin's depictions of Arabs on horseback, hunting with falcons or with various forms of weaponry, fit these obsessions perfectly. (See, for example, Fromentin's *Falcon Hunt: Algeria Remembered* in the National Gallery of Ireland.)[32] And of course Fromentin (1820–76) had many lesser imitators, such as Francesco Coleman (1851–1918) and Georges Washington (1827–1910). *Arabs Travelling in the Desert* (1843) by E.J-H. Vernet (1789–1867) similarly emphasises colourful camel blankets, textiles, and firearms which are produced by craftsmen.

The travelling European hunters also desired to fill their homes with artefacts that their visitors could admire. Each great country house was invariably a private museum in which the choicest of crafts could be displayed – carpets, ceramics, metalwork, as well as carvings and paintings. These were sometimes of an antiquarian nature, but they were also often contemporary. It was an interest that can additionally be found among a wealthy white bourgeoisie in Canada, South Africa, Australia, and New Zealand. Sometimes the material displayed was quite simply imperial loot collected by officers and others on colonial campaigns, classically from Ethiopia, the Sudan, or India. Such loot might include weaponry, armour, and shields. Orientalist paintings depicting such materials are legion. This analysis is not, however, based upon questions of aesthetic value. The important facts are that a large number of artists seem to have found a ready market and, regardless of quality, their paintings display aspects of craft manufacture, connoisseurship, and purchase.

Any survey of the several exhibitions of Orientalist paintings held in recent years, of their catalogues, or of the many other books on Orientalism in the visual arts reveals many examples. Among artists of the first rank we can identify the Scots David Wilkie (1785–1841) and David Roberts (1796–1864) working in the early nineteenth century.[33] To mention but two examples, David Wilkie's *The Turkish Letter Writer* (1840), supposedly inspired by a scene he had witnessed in the courtyard of a mosque in Constantinople (Istanbul), dwells on the textiles of the garb of the letter writer himself and the two women who are looking on, but the eye is caught by a shapely glass hookah, a fluted tear-drop shape, with a brass base and other brass fitments (both a watercolour sketch and a finished oil, Aberdeen Art Gallery). One of David Roberts's celebrated lithographs is of the Bazaar of the Coppersmiths in Cairo. Later, this theme is developed further in *A Coppersmith, Cairo* (1884) by Charles Wilda (1854–1907), showing the craftsman at work on some magnificently burnished copper vessels.

The themes of crafts, connoisseurship, production, and sales can also be found in paintings such as *At the Art Dealer's Shop* by the Italian Orientalist Gustavo Simoni (1846–1926) or *The New Acquisition* (1886) by the Czech Rudolf Weisse (1859–1930 – he also painted *The Antique Shop* and the *Carpet Merchant*). These feature the textiles and patterning of the robes of the dealers and customers together with the metalwork, carpets, an occasional firearm, and fine ceramics. A similar fascination with crafts is expressed in *A Market, Cairo*, particularly featuring metalwork, by Leopold Muller (1834–1892) or in *A Bargain*, by the American artist Edwin Lord Weeks (1849–1903) with metalwork, tiles, and fabrics. The titles of many of these paintings precisely illustrate the themes mentioned above.

Arthur Melville (1855–1904) was fascinated by the Middle East and North Africa and several of his paintings are rightly celebrated. Among these are *Arab Interior*, which demonstrates the play of light through the pierced wooden screens known as *mashrabiyya*, providing striking effects for the colourful clothes of the man sitting on the divan with its patterned textiles and cushions, together with the beaten brass table top and cups.

Melville's two paintings *Waiting an Audience with the Pasha* of 1887 and *Waiting for the Sultan, Morocco*, pursue similar themes of striking contrasts of light and shade, architectural detail, carpets, and the dress of the people waiting. In the second one, the equestrian fascination of many of these paintings is represented by a beautifully realised white horse, also patiently waiting. Other paintings, such as *Hhareem Life* by J.F. Lewis (1804–76), certainly imply critiques of gender relations (a common theme of the age), but they also offer a feast of fabrics and an overdose of abstract design reminiscent of Jones's exposition of ornament.

The fascination with crafts, of which these are just a few examples, are often combined with other aspects of perceived Middle Eastern life which also had resonances for those anxious about the very industrialism which they were promoting at home. Three examples are the frequent representation of spirituality, of music, and of learning. Examples of the first are J.F. Lewis's *The Commentator on the Koran*, where ceramics, tiles, fabrics, and flowers are combined with a venerable studiousness, reflection, and religiosity, or *At Prayer* by the immensely prolific Austrian Ludwig Deutsch (1855–1935), who produced large numbers of paintings illustrating all the themes of this essay. The fascination with music is illustrated in *The Music Lesson* by Frederick Leighton (1830–96), whose artistic excursions into the Orient have been insufficiently studied, and *Two Musicians* by Osman Hamdi Bey (1842–1910), both celebrating the beauty of traditionally crafted musical instruments; while learning is admired in Ludwig Deutsch's *El-Ashar, the Arab University in Cairo* or Osman Hamdi Bey's *Young Man at Study*.

Thus, Orientalist art, far from exposing the primitive to the industrial gaze, far from producing a sense of a strict binary construction between the modern and the pre- and anti-modern, was actually revealing visual resonances which greatly appealed to Victorian contemporaries. Here was a world they had, to a certain extent, lost, and it was a world they wished to regain. It should make us think of T.E. Lawrence's reference to the 'civilisation disease'. It is a fascinating fact that considerable sales of such Orientalist art are now made through London galleries such as the Mathaf. In modern times, wealthy inhabitants of a Middle East shattered by oil, its related industries and an excess of wealth, are also in search of an older, gentler, and appealing world.[34] The Victorian middle class and the modern inhabitants of the Middle East have, surprisingly, much in common.

Notes

1 The classic statement is Linda Nochlin, 'The Imaginary Orient', *Art in America* (May 1983), pp. 118–31, 187–91. See also Rana Kabbani, *Europe's Myths of Orient: Devise and Rule* (London: Macmillan, 1986).
2 The notable Orientalist artist David Roberts started his artistic career as a theatrical scene painter, first in Glasgow and then in London.
3 John M. MacKenzie, *Orientalism: History, Theory and the Arts* (Manchester: Manchester University Press, 1995), chapter 7; Edward Ziter, *The Orient on the Victorian Stage* (Cambridge: Cambridge University Press, 2003).
4 Edward W. Said, *Culture and Imperialism* (London: Chatto and Windus, 1993), pp. 134–57. The conference was that of the British Association of Arts Historians, Brighton, 1986.
5 My critique of Said's reading of Aida was originally published in John M. MacKenzie, 'Edward Said and the Historians', *Nineteenth-Century Contexts*, special issue 'Colonialisms', vol. 18, no. 1 (1994), pp. 9–25, particularly pp. 16–18.
6 Said, *Culture and Imperialism*, p. 148.
7 'O fatherland, I shall never see you again!
O blue skies, soft breezes of my homeland,
Where I lived out the quiet morning of my life.
O grassy hills, O fragrant streams etc.'
8 Verdi was delighted when the Italians were defeated at the Battle of Adua in Ethiopia in 1896. Julian Budden, *Verdi* (London: Dent, 1985), p. 150.
9 Edward W. Said, *Musical Elaborations* (New York and London: Columbia University Press, 1991).
10 These were the elements I sought to inject in MacKenzie, *Orientalism*, chapter 3, 'Orientalism in Art'. For a powerful critique of Said and his followers on other grounds, see Robert Irwin, *The Lust for Knowing: the Orientalists and their Enemies* (London: Allen Lane, 2006). For other works on Orientalism in art, see Fine Art Society, *Eastern Encounters: Orientalist Painters in the Nineteenth Century* (London: Fine Art Society, 1978); Fine Art Society, *Travellers Beyond the Grand Tour* (London: Fine Art Society, 1980); Mounira Khemir, Ursula Prunster, and Lynn Thornton, *Orientalism: Delacroix to Klee* (Sydney: The Art Gallery of New South Wales, 1997); Gérard-George Lemaire, *The Orient in Western Art*, with a preface by Geneviève Lacambre (Paris: Konemann, 2000, English edition 2005); Donald A. Rosenthal, *Orientalism: The Near East in French Painting, 1800–1880* (Rochester: New York, Memorial Art Gallery of the University of Rochester, 1982); Mary Anne Stevens, *The Orientalists: Delacroix to Matisse, European Painters in North Africa and the Near East* (London: Weidenfeld and Nicolson, 1984).
11 Emily M. Weeks, 'A Veil of Truth and the Details of Empire: John Frederick Lewis's *The Reception* of 1873', in Timothy Barringer, Geoff Quilley and Douglas Fordham (eds), *Art and the British Empire* (Manchester: Manchester University Press, 2007), pp. 237–53; Emily M. Weeks, 'Cultures Crossed: John Frederick Lewis and the Art of Orientalist Painting', in Nicholas Tromans (ed.), *The Lure of the East: British Orientalist Painting* (London: Tate Publishing, 2008), pp. 22–32.
12 John M. MacKenzie, 'Some Reflections on Aspects of Modernity', in Trevor Harris (ed.), *Art, Politics and Society in Britain (1880–1914): Aspects of Modernity and Modernism* (Newcastle upon Tyne: Cambridge Scholars Publishing, 2009), pp. 1–19.
13 Jeffrey Richards and John M. MacKenzie, *The Railway Station: a Social History* (Oxford: Oxford University Press, 1986).
14 Jeffrey A. Auerbach, *The Great Exhibition of 1851: A Nation on Display* (New Haven: Yale University Press, 1999).
15 Weeks, 'Cultures Crossed', pp. 22–23.
16 Anthony Burton, *Vision and Accident: The Story of the Victoria and Albert Museum* (London: V&A Publications, 1999).

17 John M. MacKenzie, *Museums and Empire: Natural History, Human Cultures and Colonial Identities* (Manchester: Manchester University Press, 2009), chapter 10.
18 MacKenzie, *Orientalism*, pp. 121–4.
19 Fiona MacCarthy, *William Morris* (London: Faber and Faber, 1994), pp. 395–6, 402–6, 410, 597.
20 John Sweetman, *The Oriental Obsession: Islamic Inspiration in British and American Art and Architecture 1500–1920* (Cambridge: Cambridge University Press, 1988), particularly chapter 5. See also Louise Campbell, 'Decoration, Display, Disguise: Leighton House Reconsidered', in Tim Barringer and Elizabeth Prettejohn (eds), *Frederic Leighton: Antiquity, Renaissance, Modernity* (New Haven: Yale University Press, 1999).
21 Some of these paintings are to be found in the Durbar Dining Room corridor at Osborne, Isle of Wight.
22 Saloni Mathur, *An Indian Encounter: Portraits for Queen Victoria* (London: National Gallery, 2002). There was an exhibition of these paintings at the National Gallery, November 2002–January 2003.
23 The *Catalogue of Macfarlane's Cast Iron Manufactures* was published at least between the 1860s and the early years of the twentieth century. See also E. Graeme Robertson and Joan Robertson, *Cast Iron Decoration, a World Survey* (London: Thames and Hudson, 1977).
24 Perilla Kinchin and Juliet Kinchin, *Glasgow's Great Exhibitions 1888, 1901, 1911, 1937, 1988* (Wendlebury: White Cockade Publishing, 1988), pp. 16–53.
25 For Jones and the Alhambra, see Antonio Fernandez Puertas, *The Alhambra* (London: Saqi, 1997) and Robert Irwin, *The Alhambra* (London: Profile Books, 2004), pp. 150–59.
26 Owen Jones, *The Grammar of Ornament, illustrated by examples from various styles of ornament one hundred and twelve plates* (London: Bernard Quaritch 1868). The first edition was published in London by Day and Son in 1856; the 1868 edition is available online. See also www.vam.ac.uk/content/articles/a/a-higher-ambition-owen-jones/ (consulted December 2011)
27 Tony Birks and Cornelia Wingfield Digby, *Bernard Leach, Hamada and their Circle* (Oxford: Phaedon, 1990). See also Geneviève Lacambre, 'Le Japonisme: Exotisme et Assimilation', in Paulo Amalfitano and Loretta Innocenti (eds), *L'Oriente: Storia di una figura nelle arti occidental (1700–2000), Vol. 1, Dal Settecento al Novocento* (Rome: Bulzoni Editore, 2007), pp. 625–634.
28 John M. MacKenzie, 'Orientalism and the Architecture of Leisure in Britain', in ibid., pp. 657–672. For Liberty's Store, see Alison Adburgham, *Liberty's, a Biography of a Shop* (London: George Allen and Unwin, 1971).
29 Martin J. Wiener, *English Culture and the Decline of the Industrial Spirit, 1850–1980* (Cambridge: Cambridge University Press, 1981).
30 *Cragside, Northumberland* (National Trust 1985).
31 John M. MacKenzie, *The Empire of Nature: Hunting, Conservation and British Imperialism* (Manchester: Manchester University Press, 1988).
32 This painting was used on the cover of James Thompson, *The East Imagined, Experienced, Remembered* (Dublin: The National Gallery of Ireland and Liverpool, National Museums and Galleries on Merseyside, 1988). This accompanied an Orientalist exhibition of that year, an early example of what seems to be an enduring fascination. Other catalogues and works from which pictorial examples have been drawn can be found in the Select Bibliography. Most of the images are also available on the web.
33 For Roberts, see Helen Guiterman and Bryonny Llewellyn, *David Roberts* (London: Barbican Art Gallery and Phaidon Press, 1886).
34 Private information, Brian MacDermot, the Mathaf Gallery.

Bibliography

Auerbach, Jeffrey A. *The Great Exhibition of 1851: A Nation on Display* (New Haven: Yale University Press, 1999).

Barringer, Timothy Geoff Quilley and Douglas Fordham (eds), *Art and the British Empire* (Manchester: Manchester University Press, 2007).

Fine Art Society, *Eastern Encounters: Orientalist Painters in the Nineteenth Century* (London: Fine Art Society, 1978).

Fine Art Society, *Travellers Beyond the Grand Tour* (London: Fine Art Society, 1980).

Birks, Tony and Cornelia Wingfield Digby, *Bernard Leach, Hamada and their Circle* (Oxford: Phaedon, 1990).

Budden, Julian *Verdi* (London: Dent, 1985).

Burton, Anthony *Vision and Accident: The Story of the Victoria and Albert Museum* (London: V&A Publications, 1999).

Cragside, Northumberland (National Trust 1985).

Fernandez Puertas, Antonio *The Alhambra* (London: Saqi, 1997).

Helen Guiterman and Bryonny Llewellyn, *David Roberts* (London: Barbican Art Gallery and Phaidon Press, 1886).

Irwin, Robert *The Alhambra* (London: Profile Books, 2004).

Irwin, Robert *The Lust for Knowing: the Orientalists and their Enemies* (London: Allen Lane, 2006).

Kabbani, Rana *Europe's Myths of Orient: Devise and Rule* (London: Macmillan, 1986).

Jones, Owen The Grammar of Ornament, illustrated by examples from various styles of ornament one hundred and twelve plates (London: Bernard Quaritch 1868).

Khemir, Mounira Ursula Prunster, and Lynn Thornton, *Orientalism: Delacrois to Klee* (Sydney: The Art Gallery of New South Wales, 1997).

Kinchin, Perilla and Juliet Kinchin, *Glasgow's Great Exhibitions 1888, 1901, 1911, 1937, 1988* (Wendlebury: White Cockade Publishing, 1988).

Lacambre, Geneviève 'Le Japonisme: Exotisme et Assimilation', in Paulo Amalfitano and Loretta Innocenti (eds), *L'Oriente: Storia di una figura nelle arti occidental (1700–2000)*, Vol. 1, Dal Settecento al Novocento (Rome: Bulzoni Editore, 2007).

Lemaire, Gérard-George *The Orient in Western Art*, with a preface by Geneviève Lacambre (Paris: Konemann, 2000, English edition 2005).

MacCarthy, Fiona *William Morris* (London: Faber and Faber, 1994).

MacKenzie, John M. 'Edward Said and the Historians', *Nineteenth-Century Contexts*, special issue 'Colonialisms', vol. 18, no. 1 (1994), pp. 9–25.

MacKenzie, John M. *The Empire of Nature: Hunting, Conservation and British Imperialism* (Manchester: Manchester University Press, 1988).

MacKenzie, John M. *Museums and Empire: Natural History, Human Cultures and Colonial Identities* (Manchester: Manchester University Press, 2009).

MacKenzie, John M. 'Orientalism and the Architecture of Leisure in Britain', in Paulo Amalfitano and Loretta Innocenti (eds), *L'Oriente: Storia di una figura nelle arti occidental (1700–2000)*, Vol. 1, Dal Settecento al Novocento (Rome: Bulzoni Editore, 2007), pp. 657–672.

MacKenzie, John M. *Orientalism: History, Theory and the Arts* (Manchester: Manchester University Press, 1995).

MacKenzie, John M. 'Some Reflections on Aspects of Modernity', in Trevor Harris (ed.), *Art, Politics and Society in Britain (1880–1914): Aspects of Modernity and Modernism* (Newcastle upon Tyne: Cambridge Scholars Publishing, 2009), pp. 1–19.

Mathaf Gallery, catalogues, 1998, 2000, 2001, 2003, 2004, 2005, 2007, 2008, 2010.

Mathur, Saloni *An Indian Encounter: Portraits for Queen Victoria* (London: National Gallery, 2002).

Nochlin, Linda 'The Imaginary Orient', *Art in America* (May 1983), pp. 118–31, 187–91.

Rosenthal, Donald A. *Orientalism: The Near East in French Painting, 1800–1880* (Rochester: New York, Memorial Art Gallery of the University of Rochester, 1982).

Richards, Jeffrey and John M. MacKenzie, *The Railway Station: a Social History* (Oxford: Oxford University Press, 1986).

Robertson, E. Graeme and Joan Robertson, *Cast Iron Decoration, a World Survey* (London: Thames and Hudson, 1977).

Said, Edward W. *Culture and Imperialism* (London: Chatto and Windus, 1993).

Said, Edward W. *Musical Elaborations* (New York and London: Columbia University Press, 1991).

Said, Edward W. *Orientalism* (London: Routledge and Kegan Paul, 1978).

Stevens, Mary Anne *The Orientalists: Delacroix to Matisse, European Painters in North Africa and the Near East* (London: Weidenfeld and Nicolson, 1984).

Sweetman, John *The Oriental Obsession: Islamic Inspiration in British and American Art and Architecture 1500–1920* (Cambridge: Cambridge University Press, 1988).

Weeks, Emily M. 'A Veil of Truth and the Details of Empire: John Frederick Lewis's *The Reception* of 1873', in Timothy Barringer, Geoff Quilley and Douglas Fordham (ed.), *Art and the British Empire* (Manchester: Manchester University Press, 2007), pp. 237–53.

Weeks, Emily M. 'Cultures Crossed: John Frederick Lewis and the Art of Orientalist Painting', in Nicholas Tromans (ed.), *The Lure of the East: British Orientalist Painting* (London: Tate Publishing, 2008), pp. 22–32.

Wiener, Martin J. *English Culture and the Decline of the Industrial Spirit, 1850–1980* (Cambridge: Cambridge University Press, 1981).

Ziter, Edward *The Orient on the Victorian Stage* (Cambridge: Cambridge University Press, 2003).

7 Visual ethnography, stereotypes and photographing Algeria

Susan Slyomovics

"The imperial conquest," Edward Said writes, "was not a one-time tearing of the veil, but a continually repeated, institutionalized presence in French life, where the response to the silent and incorporated disparity between French and subjugated cultures took on a variety of forms."[1] Based on access to technology, there were vast, institutionalized inequities and disparities between conqueror and subjugated peoples, since the camera and conquest overlapped chronologically, linking French photographic representations of Algeria and Algerians to the larger phenomenon of Orientalism in its enduring historical and visual aspects. The camera was not merely a device to capture images, and photographs functioned as more than "sensorially restrained objects: mute and motionless variegated rectangles."[2] Photography contributed to creating meaning and signification through the everyday, repeated and systematic practices of picture taking by the French in Algeria. For Said, whose corpus engages with the politics of Orientalist representation in the media, photography, and advertising, it is obvious that "[t]here can be no unilateral withdrawal from ideology. Surely it is quixotic to expect photographic interpretation to serve such a purpose."[3] He alerts viewers, readers, and especially photographers to the need for "a proper schooling in the visual faculties." His insistence on the image as possessing an ideological point of view underpins his call for scholars of the visual to revisit the variety of imagined, pictured geographies of the Orient. To do so, I explore the visual, cultural form of biometric technologies that marked the French colonial bureaucratic presence through a set of colonial tourist postcards of Algeria, called *Scènes et Types* in French, and consider these images in relation to the parallel and coeval practices of French-imposed identity photographs and anthropometric classification systems. Such complex legacies of colonial French photography in Algeria re-emerge as *Scènes et Types* photographs and continue to circulate in Western museums and publications to this day, a century after their initial production and circulation. Moreover, since contemporary North Africans have become consumers of their former colonial visual histories even decades after Algeria's independence, Said's enduring question remains pertinent: "how does a culture seeking to become independent of imperialism imagine its own past?"[4]

Photographs were the pre-eminent popular media for France to know Algeria, following France's 1830 invasion of Algeria and the camera's appearance in the late 1820s (an invention claimed by the Frenchmen Joseph Nicéphore Niépce and Louis Daguerre).[5]

> The colonial photographer coded the photographs so that they were associated with certain meanings, often determined by the imperial agenda that was installed – consciously or unconsciously – in the photograph. Surveying a set of themes and ordering them into simple categories, photographers developed a "stock of signs" and "cognitive connotations" that enabled a shorthand identification of France's most significant possession *outré-mer*. ... The immediacy of photography – which differed from other illustrative techniques – furthered the colonial endeavor by helping the French public assimilate Algiers into its consciousness.[6]

Photography produced knowledge about Algeria – a knowledge characterized by Malek Alloula as merely a form of "pseudo-knowledge of the colony", spectacularly so in relation to the ways in which the French imagined Algerian women. In Alloula's path-breaking work on French postcards of Algeria, entitled *The Colonial Harem*, he describes the reach of photographic image making:

> Photography steps in to take up the slack and reactivates the phantasm at its lowest level. The postcard does it one better; it becomes the poor man's phantasm: for a few pennies, display racks full of dreams. The postcard is everywhere, covering all the colonial space, immediately available to the tourist, the soldier, the colonist. It is at once their poetry and their glory captured for the ages; it is also their pseudo-knowledge of the colony. It produces stereotypes in the manner of great seabirds producing guano, the fertilizer of the colonialist vision.[7]

Alloula compares Western and settler-colonial photographic production to great seabirds hovering high above ground with their excremental output showering Algeria because colonial French photography similarly hovered high above Algeria to estheticize, exoticize, eroticize, and stereotype Algerians. Notions about the stereotype when applied to the native, the "indigene," are best exemplified pictorially by Alloula and other critics under the rubric of *Scènes et Types*[8] (Figures 7.1 and 7.2). Many of *The Colonial Harem's* re-published and re-circulated French postcards depict photographs of Algerian *Scènes et Types*: exotic scenes and physical types mailed back to the metropole during the early decades of the twentieth century, when France's hold over North Africa from Dunkerque to Tamanrasset appeared unchallenged. *Scènes et Types* belong to a visual genre in which an individual appears within the frame, with or without background, on location or in a studio, but always in visual contexts that masked urgent political and economic realities in the colony. Alloula's focus on art history and the Algerian body passes lightly over political economy but acknowledges the colonial "double bind", defined by David Henry Slavin, as the redoubling of the ways in which "'picturesque' Algerians depend on tourism which invented the 'picturesque', while tourism perpetuates the 'backwardness' that legitimated French domination."[9]

Figure 7.1 "Algerian Photography," Alary and Geiser Advertising Sheet. Advertisement for colonial *Scènes et Types* postcards from the Alary and Geiser Studio, Algiers. Research Library, The Getty Research Institute, Los Angeles (2008.R.3).

Figure 7.2
"Types Algériens. Famille d'une femme des Ouled Nails." Library of Congress Prints and Photographs Division, Washington, DC.

Captions are an additional characteristic of the genre of *Scènes et Types* that underscore transformations of the individual into a type, while announcing a priori an act of categorization. Thus, *Scènes et Types* postcards must be accompanied by a text that is brief, broadly generic, vaguely ethnological, rarely self-explanatory, and sometimes geographically situated. Captions are conventionally placed as close as possible to the image or branded directly upon it. The text of the caption is a mini-narrative that is fragmentary and incomplete, with sentences deliberately not fully grammatical because minus the subject, verb, and object – for example, a Mauresque, a Bedouin woman, a Janissary, a Jewish woman, etc. Since photographs exist without captions but not the reverse – namely, a caption without a photograph – whatever image is considered photographable leads to what is captionable. Nonetheless, *Scènes et Types* captions are strikingly uninformative.[10] Therefore, photographs can be made to say whatever the mini-narrative caption says it should. Critic Susan Sontag, who thought deeply about captions, declared: "All photographs wait to be explained or falsified by their captions."[11] Captions provide a specific kind of legitimacy and authority to an image that itself stands in for generalities and operates synecdochically – the corporeal part standing for the entire body politic. Consequently, both caption and image work together to reinforce interpretative extremes – at one end of a spectrum concerned with the visual expression of generalities, which is what we view in *Scènes et Types* postcards, and alternatively, a focus on physical details and physiognomic typologies to the detriment of the human content of an image.

Algerian anthropologist Malek Chebel points to the significance of the postcard's visual practices by looking at its resemblance to inventories of races, peoples, and tribes. Chebel maintains that such photographs and postcards mask the deeper anxieties (*l'angoisse*) of the colonizer, who must depersonalize by speaking in terms of masses and crowds (Chebel's terms are *la masse, massificationer*). According to Chebel, each country of colonized French North Africa typified a different visual stereotype:

> In Morocco, it is above all the architecture of cities (gardens, gates, fountains, markets, *medersas*) that intrigue and hold the attention of colonial painters and illustrators. In Tunisia, the landscape and artisanat were priorities. In Algeria it was the society: "scenes and types" rained down, mouk-ères (Arab women), demi-mondaines, professions (barbers), Tuareg chiefs (*amenokals*), dancers (*nailiyate*) were at the same time occasions that permit discerning the Other in the immeasurable challenge of the image. These tendencies were obviously not neutral: they reflected the contradictions of the moment, often the will [wish or desire (*volonté*)] to find some paradigms in an ocean of uncertainties.[12]

To assuage what Chebel terms above the colonizer's "will to find some paradigms in an ocean of uncertainties", the image-plus-caption protocols of *Scènes et Types* flourished alongside physical anthropology as a racial science. Throughout the latter half of the nineteenth century, projects to compare and contrast races were realized with the help of the camera. One important example was German photographer Carl Dammann's 1876 album of approximately 642 small images entitled *Ethnological Photographic Gallery of the Various Races of Man*. Dammann adopted the use of the mug-shot protocol, consisting of frontal and profile portrait views.[13] For French colonial ethnography, influenced by Dammann's project in Germany, two key figures were Jean Louis Armand de Quatrefages de Bréau and prince Roland Bonaparte (a great-nephew of Napoleon Bonaparte), both members of the Paris-headquartered Geography Society and Anthropology Society, with Quatrefages as the first holder of the chair of anthropology in France's Museum of Natural History.[14] Algeria was their scientific laboratory in what passed for scientific experimentations, also exemplified by Roland Bonaparte's famous series of images entitled "Peaux-Rouges" ("Redskins") that depict an apparently neutral scientific pose of the frontal and profile faces of Native Americans, uniformly photographed and displayed alongside a less famous series of Arab portraits.[15]

Quatrefages' fellow French anthropologist Paul Topinard invested much effort in finding a scientific basis for European racial superiority. The latter's 1876 anthropology text was influential in France, and again in England once translated in 1890. Topinard's methodology can be examined by looking at charts that he established, for example, one to determine the "Berber type" by ranking the variety of different human ear shapes according to his estimation of a universal harmonious symmetry. He maintained that Algerian Kabyles (or Berbers) exemplified ear shapes with a "lobule … wanting" and their typical ear type, he believed, was characteristically to "project out" in ways that defined the Kabyle physiognomy.[16] Topinard's descriptions were accompanied by a drawing of an Algerian Kabyle attributed to Emile Duhousset (1863–1911), a colonial army officer and man of action who happened to be present in the rarefied precincts of the Anthropology Society in Paris during Topinard's presentation on the Kabyle ear. Duhousset's drawing (Figure 7.3) provoked a fascinating exchange between Topinard, the theorist of anthropometry, and Duhousset, the soldier-practitioner. Records of the Anthropology Society meetings reveal that Topinard insisted on the importance of distinguishing the Berber or Kabyle from the Arab Algerian according to specific, scientifically documented physical attributes, among them the characteristic Berber protruding ears. In response, Colonel Duhousset, a military officer and published ethnographer of the Berbers, asserted that the Topinard's caption of "Kabyle/Berber" in Topinard's *Anthropology* text was incorrect. Duhousset declared that as this was his own drawing, he could assert that, in fact, it depicted an Arab.[17] Topinard countered by pleading for all travelers, visitors, and military personnel to engage in the project of measuring Algerian native physiognomy with the appropriate scientific instruments. Furthermore, he asserted that anthropometry would prove that the Berbers/Kabyles were the genuine "Peaux-Rouges" ("Red Skins") of North Africa.[18] Colonel Duhousset retorted that neither his own artistic drawings nor Topinard's observations and measurements were valid. Of interest to me is Duhousset's conclusion as early as 1876 that only "photography imposes itself today as the most correct basis for all anthropological studies … the apparatus, instantly producing face and profile was less cumbersome."[19] Thus, photography documented and served as evidence

Figure 7.3 Duhousset drawing of a Berber type in Paul Topinard, *Anthropology*. London: Chapman and Hall, 1890, p. 462.

for the very stereotypes that photography created. As this exchange between Topinard and Duhousset attests – despite evidence of a wrongly captioned image in which an Arab is mislabeled a Berber because of his ear shape – colonial anthropologists abstracted racial characteristics to create racial types, which were then given visual attestation through the drawings, photographs, and captions provided by photographers and ethnographers.

ID cards: "speaking likenesses"

Colonial anthropological racial types preceded, influenced, and dovetailed with the classification and anthropometric identification system developed in the 1890 work of Alphonse Bertillon, *La Photographie judiciaire*. Bertillon, the French police clerk credited in 1872 with the invention of the standard frontal and profile shot to identify *récidivistes*, called identity photographs *portraits parlés* or "speaking likenesses".[20] Bertillon's techniques, similar to the documentation of Carl Dammann (1819–1874) and the photo albums of Roland Bonaparte, influenced the practice of visually documenting criminals as well as the colonized population of France's overseas possessions. The identity card photograph coincided and was in complicity with the advent of French colonialism that would introduce to the Maghreb the French police service, the prison system, and an anthropometric section (*service anthropométrique*). Anthropometry deployed photographs, captions, and written descriptions to establish extensive physiognomic portraits of criminals that traversed the human body section by section. As the work of Michel Foucault attests, the birth of the prison and of police photography in the 1840s are central to issues of modern disciplinary power that call for isolation, supervision, surveillance, and the imposition and recording of individualized names.[21] Thus, *Scènes et Types* photography emerges not only from colonial tourism but also from the parallel historical contexts of criminological photography and the establishment of the identity card, both pictorial processes closely associated with the overriding aims of French colonial and military administrations. The pictured colonial subject is framed within the paradigm of certainty embodied in a portrait, but "homogenized" according to the requirements of French colonial power in Algeria.[22]

In nineteenth-century Algeria, French laws governing identification cards as well as the family passbook formed part of French bureaucratic controls established over the population. This apparatus of French state control over an individual was preceded historically by registration controls for the French family, embodied in the family passbook (in French, *livret d'identité et d'état civil*, and in Maghribi Arabic, *kunnash al-tarif wa 'l-halah al-madaniyah*). Algeria was subjected to a nineteenth-century European "culture of identification" in which the personal name is the essential component of the modern state system of identification: in France, laws governing personal names (for example, the law of 1 April 1803, repealed only in 1993), restricted the French to names duly registered at birth.[23] Laws creating family documentation papers for a couple and their offspring are said to have been enacted after fires set during the 1871 Paris Commune, an uprising that burned registers of civil status in the Paris region. Demonstrators targeted for destruction official buildings, such as the Palais de Justice and the Hotel de Ville, housing birth, marriage, and death certificates. For a time, Parisians could fabricate false documents and create new identities. By 1875, however, residents of greater Paris in the Seine prefecture carried family passbooks.[24]

How does the state, whether colonial French or post-independent Algerian, contain massive population increases in new urban settings created by colonization? What are the ways that identification procedures, and therefore techniques of controlling the individual body, were used to track crowds, rioters and dissidents? How did the jurisdictional claims of the Arab–Berber–Islamic naming clash with French paper-recording technologies?[25] France extended the notion of standardized names to their Arab subjects in North Africa, beginning with Algeria, the first North African country invaded in 1830 and colonized. The law of 23 March 1882 on the civil status of Muslim natives in Algeria imposed the combined French systems of identity cards and patronymic surnames on all Algerian heads of households. In cases of Arab refusal to choose a fixed surname, article five states that French civil servants may create one of their own devising.[26] In contrast to French naming practices, pre-colonial North African names consist minimally of a first name followed by the father's name and the grandfather's name, but often include a string of names representing the holder's moral, physical, or social qualities, place of birth or ancestry, and tribal affiliation or membership in religious orders. An Arab-Berber name functions as a biography, unique to the individual and, thus, disappears with his death. Anthropologist Hassan Rachik calls this naming tradition a "beautiful labyrinth", a history of names inherited from his Moroccan forbears that changed every generation, pointing to the ways in which identity is never fixed by name but rather is to be sought through points of intersection with place, family migration, and even national consciousness:

> If I write imagining that [my grandfather] were speaking: "You know, identity cannot be totally inherited nor rejected totally. It is for you to construct your own identity multiplying endlessly your circles of belonging. In the matter of identity there is little to transmit from generation to generation, but much to invent individually and collectively. Identity is not a simple line linking an individual to a group whatever the foundation of the group – linguistic, religious or political. Identity is the actual connection that a biography has with other biographies and other groups. ... Look! I did not submit to my father's name. Can you not see what a labyrinth you become entangled in wanting to reunite in one text what I have lived successively and partially? Even for a single individual, names and identities change, fall into disuse.[27]

In the Maghreb, the French perceived onomastic chaos and discontinuity in the Arab-Berber preference for human history embodied in a biographical approach to naming. Furthermore, French officials queried how names could be individually assigned, genealogically arranged, alphabetized correctly, and made orthographically uniform. The proliferation of Ahmeds and Mohameds recurring from grandfather to father to son raised the possibility of a bewildering and uninformative genealogy comprising, for example, Mohamed ben Ahmed, son of Ahmed ben Mohamed, grandson of Mohamed ben Ahmed.[28] In addition to the French standardization of names as part of the identification process, all documentation of Muslim subjects in Algeria (including Arabic-language place names) was to be written not in Arabic but in French, Algeria's sole official language. To produce Arabic-language personal and place names accessible to users of the Latin alphabet, two French army interpreters attached to France's Ministry of War in Algeria were charged with fashioning a transcription protocol. With minor changes, William MacGuckin de Slane's and Charles Gabeau's 1866 transcription of Maghribi names remains in use in North Africa and France to this day.[29] Collective stereotyping in postcards lived alongside the creation of individual North African identity that was arbitrarily fixed, visualized, and transcribed for official confirmation purposes into a French-created and redacted document of identity. That the French colonial police force was in charge of issuing identity cards in Algeria apparently contributed to their unpopularity and the initial lack of compliance, as did the two required accompanying photographs in profile and full face, as if the bearer were a wanted criminal. Identification – a civil and legal practice in France to establish citizenship – was placed under police control in

Algeria, emphasizing its role as a criminological practice foisted on tractable colonies to circumscribe identity without granting full citizenship. Furthermore, Algerian identity documents were rightly understood by the native populace as a prelude to mass conscription.

The emergence of the ID card of the "disappeared"

French-imposed bureaucratic controls were maintained after Algeria's independence from France in 1962. Indeed, these techniques were carried over intact and deployed just as restrictively and punitively. In this essay, the techniques of identification – first, over the individual body, and then the family unit – form an intersection for complex twentieth-century histories of Algeria. In the aftermath of the Algerian war of independence (1954–1962), what linked the identification system, the criminalized body, and the criminal justice system? James Scott proposes the concept of a "legible people", a metaphor for the emergence of writing as central to the creation of nationhood and to modern forms of national control.[30] People come to legibility, can be "read", when they are under the official scrutiny of paperwork, files, dossiers, archives, records, and identity documents. The formation of a centralized, authoritarian, postcolonial Algerian state in 1962 owed much to continuities with the bureaucratic French colonial state. Family passbooks and identity cards remain constituent elements of Algerian sovereignty even as they are administrative formalities of civil identification that extend control over the population, a surveillance that was at its most efficient and rigorous in large urban settings.

Currently, the power of the identity card reaches beyond the police station, the courtroom, and even the grave to determine who we are, what names we give ourselves, and how we reconstruct the past through narrative, storytelling, and photography. The identity card, an artifact born of colonial control and post-independence repression, has been transformed into memory devices, the traces of remembrance with which to conjure the dead and missing. More than 6,000 Algerians are officially recognized as those forcibly disappeared, although international and national human rights groups estimate between 10,000 and 20,000 missing Algerians during the bloody decade of the 1990s, which claimed over 200,000 Algerian lives. To this day, many Algerian families do not know the whereabouts of family members disappeared, and where, and if, there are victims' graves. The identity card photograph is what remains. The photograph, regardless of its bureaucratic provenance, proves existence. An identity card photograph is an object that can be referred to and pointed at, the sole evidence to anchor the presence of the disappeared, as families grapple with absence. No one, especially the bereaved families, considers the photograph to be remotely related to the reality of their missing ones. The picture is all that remains.

An Amnesty International book of photographs entitled *A Biography of Disappearance: Algeria 1992* – is filled with examples of identity card portraits that have been repurposed – some images are enlarged, framed, and pasted on the wall, while others resting in their frames are brought to the dinner table and seated in the owner's former place. These images look out and speak to the audience, underlining the import of witnessing and testifying to the presence of visual likeness in the absence of the physical body[31] (Figure 7.4). Why has the ID photo become emblematic simultaneously of the visible, the invisible, and the missing body? How do some bodies come to matter (to paraphrase Judith Butler[32]) or fail to matter? Bodies formerly and formally exhibited become bodies erased and bodies denied. In many cases, the bereaved parent carries or wears the portrait of the missing child, spouse, or family member.[33]

In Algeria, as elsewhere, when the right of relatives to bury their dead is absent – a right recognized cross-culturally, no less than legally[34] – pictures represent the missing and unburied body as it was photographed when alive. In North Africa, complex funeral rites are prescribed both for the community and for the

Figure 7.4 Portrait of Amine Amrouche, brought to the table of his mother, Nacéra Dutour. Amine Amrouche, b. 1975, forcibly "disappeared" Thursday 24 October 1997, 4 p.m., close to home in Algiers. In Omar D, Tom O'Mara and Lahouari Addi, *Devoir de mémoire: A Biography of Disappearance: Algeria 1992–*. London: Autograph, 2007, p. 78. Courtesy Omar D/Autograph ABP and Nacéra Dutour. Black and white reproduction of original color image.

family unit. They begin at death with the command to wash, dress, and shroud the body, and then to lament and pray. Family and friends bear the corpse to the cemetery, and prayers are offered at the gravesite. A long period of mourning ensues, with specific ceremonial gatherings, for example, to mark the fortieth day and the first anniversary of the death. For the deceased and for the bereaved, it is considered among life's gravest misfortunes to be deprived of the observance of mourning rituals such as a funeral, and obligatory visits to care for the grave. The loss of the ability to express mourning conventionally and individually, no less than the uncertainty whether family members are in fact dead, carries with it immeasurable grief and trauma. Certainly an unforeseen use for the French identity photograph that was maintained in post-independent Algeria is as a souvenir and memorializing image to a family member, a piece of paper rendered more poignant in the case of those forcibly disappeared, unburied, and grieved over.

The circulation of Algerian ID photos in North African homes and Western museums

In 1982, French photographer Mark Garanger published a book of photos entitled *Femmes Algeriennes 1960* that consisted of ID images produced in 1960, when he was conscripted into the French army and dispatched to Algeria during the war of independence (1954–1962). A single-page introduction is the exception in this book of portraits of Algerian women that otherwise contains no words, in which Garanger describes techniques deployed to capture images:

> The French army decided to impose ID cards on Algerian natives slated for the so-called regroupement or "resettlement camps". I photographed approximately 2,000 people, 200 a day, mainly women … It was the faces of the women that impressed me greatly. They had no choice. They were forced to unveil themselves and let themselves be photographed. They had to sit on a stool, outdoors, in front of the white wall of the hamlet. I received their gaze at close range, the first witness to their mute, violent protest. I want to bear witness [*témoigner*] on their behalf.[35]

I juxtapose the fruits of Garanger's army work of the 1960s that continue to circulate widely in European and American museums with a second photograph – the 1924 official school picture of an all-girls school in Tlemcen, Algeria, one established by the Islamic reformist *Nahda* or "renaissance" movement to educate women in Arabic (Figure 7.5). The eleven-year-old child on the viewer's left, second row from the end, is Yamina Ben Yelles, my mother-in-law, whom I never met. In a series of unpublished oral history interviews collected in the 1980s towards the end of her life by her daughter, Chafika Berber, my sister-in-law, Yamina described the first time she was forced to go out in public without her veil. Her husband, Sid-Ahmed Berber, my father-in-law, had been expelled from Algeria to France for nationalist activities and, as she sat unveiled amid her bundles and young children on the pier in Marseilles in 1952, she recalled to her daughter the many ways that she felt naked, exposed, and miserable to the colonizer's gaze. The area of the school photograph containing the face of Yamina Ben Yelles was reproduced and enlarged by her family, a visual excerpt, in order to create an individual portrait for her descendants.

I bring together Garanger's ID images and my Algerian in-laws' family photos to open up an inquiry into the nature of "indigenous photography". Parallel to colonialist photography is the anthropological concept of "indigenous photography", to describe the moment when photographic techniques are disseminated to the natives (*indigènes*). Owing its introduction in Algeria to primarily French photographers, the production of "indigenous photography" represents a historically rich resource and archive. However, is the concept of indigenous photography a recognition that, as in the Arab East, many minorities were trained in photography? Scholars have profiled Arab Christians or Armenians as the visual documenters for the urban Levantine elites. In Tlemcen, Algeria, a city that was one-third Jewish until independence in 1962, among the prominent photographers in the region were the Cohen family, Algerian Jews who maintained a large photography studio. Or is indigenous photography the deployment of the rich and violent heritage of colonialist photography by the native? Does my mother-in-law's photo speak only to the formal properties of the well-known, French-imported practice of the annual school picture, or does it bring some knowledge about Algerian women's education in 1924 and the unwritten history of local Arabic language education initiatives by a populist, urban, reformist Muslim movement? What happens when these photos are cropped, detached, and framed to decorate the homes of her children and grandchildren because the school photo and the ID card are what remain visually of a beloved mother and grandmother?[36] Moreover, even in a pre-Photoshop but post-independent North Africa, there have been a variety of strategies to appropriate, repurpose, repatriate the endlessly circulating colonial images that produced and reduced categories of the Algerian to a minimum type, that evacuated any violence from the frame, and that demonstrably exhibited the empire's control over the visual archive. How do we understand when aspects

Figure 7.5 Yamina Ben Yelles, Berber family photographs, Tlemcen. Author's collection.

of the dominant colonial photographic practices, such as photocopying technologies and framing practices, are re-contextualized by the formerly colonized? How does one overcome, or avoid, seeing oneself as the French colonizers saw the Algerian natives? Activist visual anthropology came to one conventional solution by placing the subaltern and the colonized behind the camera, aiming to produce what the discipline of anthropology terms indigenous photography, an ambiguous multivalent term that no longer means photographs *of* the indigenous inhabitants but encompasses photography *by* the indigenous inhabitants. Indeed, what defines an image as indigenous?[37] Or perhaps indigenous photography is reclaiming through re-captioning the *Scènes et Types* images re-circulating on websites, as, for example, a Moroccan website that posts colonial *Scènes et Types* postcards to pose the haunting question: "Can you find your ancestor, your grandparents?"[38]

"One day captions will be needed": Dennis Adams and the Getty Exhibition, Walls of Algiers

Susan Sontag informs us in her last book, *Regarding the Pain of Other*, that "one day captions will be needed".[39] Sontag is prescient to insist that photographs do not make us understand anything; we need historical, political, cultural contexts for understanding and these a photograph cannot provide. According to the current generation of Maghribis searching for ancestors among the vast French archive of *Scènes et Types* postcards, captions are needed and names are traceable. For the moment, in addition to scholarly publications, internet postings, and domestic décor items, museums are increasingly the repository for the heritage of colonial ID photographs and *Scènes et Types* postcards, some of which are in collections privately amassed or in the archives of North African photography studios currently deposited in museums such as the Getty Research Institute in Los Angeles.[40] Museums accord value to these materials and include them in their displays, catalogs, and exhibitions. While ID photos and postcards emerged as a result of nineteenth-century anthropological and colonial notions of classifying and categorizing peoples, they also eerily mirror the social histories of museums as a site of collecting, classifying, display, and entertainment.

My essay concludes with a consideration of the recent Los Angeles Getty Museum exhibition (May–October 2009), *The Walls of Algiers*, which deployed French colonial Algerian *Scènes et Types* postcards and ID cards. The Getty exhibition was curated by Zeynep Celik, an architectural historian and professor at the New Jersey Institute of Technology, and Frances Terpak, senior curator at the Getty Research Institute.[41] My contribution to the Getty Museum exhibition was to introduce the curators to the work of American artist Dennis Adams, whom I first met during a conference in 1998 at MIT, where we both then taught. Algeria has been the focus of many projects for Adams. His artistic interrogations of post-colonial transformations in Europe and Europe's collective amnesia about its colonial pasts launched three decades' worth of his photography, video installations, and site-specific works in urban public locations such as bus shelters, pedestrian tunnels, street signs, and public urinals (*pissoirs*). Adams writes: "My idea was to crack the silence. I wanted to touch the subject of [the Algerian] war through a public intervention that went straight to the nerves.'"[42] One such project, rejected as controversial by the Dijon municipal authorities, envisioned publicly exhibiting the photographs that document the decolonizing processes in Algeria that led to dismantling statues of heroic French figures during the year 1962, when they were transported from Algeria to France upon Algerian independence. Among the objects presented in the Getty *Walls of Algiers* exhibition – another Adams effort to intervene in French-Algerian silences – was his reframing of the famous series of identity card photographs of women from the Aurès region of Algeria photographed by Marc Garanger. At considerable expense, Adams purchased ten of Garanger's ID photographs for his project entitled "Recovered 10 on 10 (Adams on Garanger)". He summarizes his project:

> Ten books were produced, each with a different portrait of an Algerian women on its back inside cover. These photographs were taken by photojournalist Marc Garanger in 1960, when he was in the French military service in Algeria. They were selected from over 2000 portraits that were ordered by military authorities for terrorist control purposes. The majority of these photographs were taken of women, all of whom were forced to remove their veils. The lower portion of each portrait has been "re-covered" with ten pages of photographs in which Adams documents social housing projects on the outskirts of various French cities. Today, many of these decaying modernist projects are occupied by Algerian immigrants, signifying the culmination of France's turbulent history with its former colony.[43]

From Adams's oeuvre of ten books, one appeared in the exhibition encased in a standard museum glass display case that permitted only a single page for display and viewing. My interest is not to unpack obvious historical and gendered ironies of Adams's complex intervention and composite image production in which, on the one hand, a French male conscript photographer, March Garanger, unveils Algerian women forcibly photographed during a ferocious anti-colonial war in 1960 Algeria[44] and, on the other hand, an American male, Dennis Adams, re-veils the same Algerian women with superimposed images depicting post-colonial views of decaying, Maghribi-inhabited social housing projects of 1993 Parisian suburbs (Figure 7.6). Indeed, in my interview with Adams (November 21, 2004, New York City), he acknowledged: "I know the implications of gender, the white male from America putting himself in the middle". Nor am I here concerned with critiques of Adams's modernist appropriations and estheticizing of Algerian women's ID photos and the presumed desolation of Algerian lives in the Parisian periphery. Perhaps, this is because I see Garanger and Adams inextricably bound in a variety of ways. For example, from the legal perspective, Adams informed me that he signed a contract agreeing not to exhibit Garanger's photographs alone, which I interpret as Garanger enforcing claims to both authorship and ownership of the ID photos that he presents as indissoluble, unchanging artifacts that nonetheless allow for modernist appropriations. Can Garanger claim ownership of the ID photographs he took, or do such images belong to the French military archives, or to the Algerian state, or to the female subjects photographed against their will?

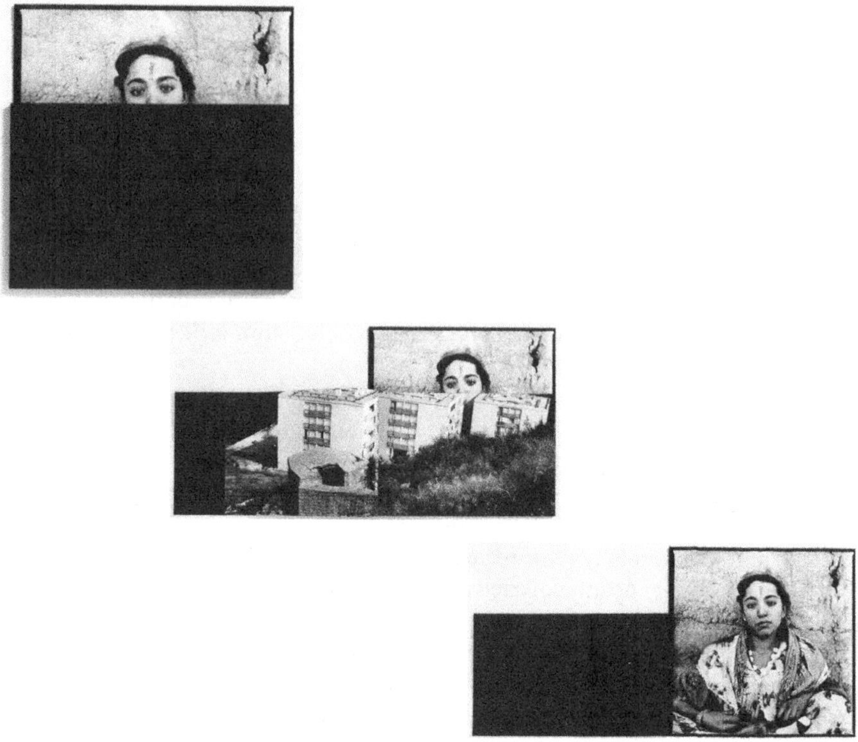

Figure 7.6 Dennis Adams, "Recovered 10 on 10 (Adams on Garanger)". Reproduced by permission of Dennis Adams.

Adams is intrigued by these confusions of authorship. An earlier 1991 installation, *Road to Victory*, is described in an online catalog: "Eight vitrines, Duratrans black anodized aluminum, wood, steel, plastic, tinted glass, mirror, fluorescent light referencing WWII aerial reconnaissance photographs taken under the supervision of Edward Steichen." During World War II, Steichen was placed in charge of American naval combat photography.[45] Adams persevered in the face of Museum of Modern Art personnel who insisted that he request permission from Steichen's estate by arguing successfully that Steichen could not claim ownership over public domain images that belonged to the US military, even though Steichen was the photographer of record. Are Garanger's images, in a sense, the "war booty" that Adams suggested to me?

Instead of theoretical approaches that draw on feminist, modernist, and copyright frameworks, I prefer to interrogate Adams's felicitous, multivalent title, "recovered," and what it might mean for family photos, ID cards, and stereotyping postcards that re-circulate in museums, homes, private collections, and the internet. Theodor Adorno's epithet "museal"[46] to describe a rupture in relations between the viewer and the object applies to Adams's "10 by 10" project, to most of the Getty museum exhibition visitors, perhaps less so to Garanger's Algerian corpus, and not at all to my Algerian in-laws and other Maghribis in search of direct genealogical links to visualizing their French colonial pasts. For this discussion, I draw on anthropology's current concern with the topic of repatriation, which includes both archives and human remains. Colonizer administrations in the post-independence era appropriated the formerly colonized archives and shipped them from colony to metropole, with the result that the archival pasts and histories of newly independent states reside elsewhere. Strengthening Algerian claims to the right to their archival past are current determinations about provenance and pertinence, meaning that though the French created the documents, they did so in Algeria (provenance), and they are about Algeria and Algerians (pertinence) in strikingly dramatic and often life-threatening ways. The international archives community has formally adopted a position on archival claims stressing the inalienability of official records and worked for restitution, which could include microfilmed copies as the mutually acceptable form of return. French jurist and legal expert Louis Joinet authored a much-quoted United Nations document, published in 1997, in which he linked his opposition to impunity for perpetrators of human rights crimes to a subsection that he entitles "the right to know", one that has become a credo for archivists worldwide and is known as the Joinet principles:[47]

> Item 17: This is not simply the right of any individual victim or closely related persons to know what happened, a right to the truth. The right to know is also a collective right, drawing upon history to prevent violations from recurring in the future. Its corollary is a "duty to remember", which the State must assume, in order to guard against the perversions of history that go under the names of revisionism or negationism; the knowledge of the oppression it has lived through is part of a people's national heritage and as such must be preserved. These, then, are the main objectives of the right to know as a collective right. Item 18: Two series of measures are proposed for this purpose ... The second is aimed at preserving archives relating to human rights violations.

Documents and photographs matter to people on all sides of former conflicts. Aside from known cultural values for history, nation building, and heritage, what lies in the archive, functionally speaking, are documents, histories, obligations, and rights. The Algerian government has repeatedly requested access to French archives to document issues more serious to the authorities than visual family histories. For example, Algeria repeatedly requested since its 1962 independence – a demand granted by France only in 2007 – the maps that determine the current placement of tens of thousands of active land mines along Algeria's eastern and western borders when the French built the 700-kilometer Challe and Morice lines during the war of independence. So potent and potentially inflammatory are the contents of archives that on April 29, 2008 French parliamentarians debated the project of a law of archives in which an increased limit to 75 years would be placed on access to government archives. Such an extension effectively places both the collaborationist Vichy French World War II archives as well as the French records of the Algerian war of independence beyond access, in defiance of the Joinet principles of the collective right to know. French legislation is at odds with parallel European legal projects on the disposition and transparency of archives. In England, the current 30-year wait is undergoing review, with proposed legislation going forward to shorten the three-decades-long waiting period; in the former Soviet Eastern bloc countries, the pressure to open Communist-era archives has led to a maximum 18- to 20-year waiting period.[48]

Objects in museums possess a history, while the museum enterprise is to sidestep, if not efface that history during the brief episode of museum display and exhibition (for example, May–October 2009 at the Getty). Recovering the histories of the museum object – in my case, studying Algerian women's ID photographs – is also an enterprise full of irony and paradox.[49] At the heart of my in-laws' domestic, intimate recovery of ID photographs is a profound gratitude for the mere existence of their grandparents' images that formerly chronicled occasions of forcible picture taking. As well, they acknowledge what Gayatri Spivak terms the "enabling violence" of colonization and what Algerians in turn have come to call "*un acquis*" (that which is acquired). What can be enumerated and viewed, the sum total of all that has been acquired voluntarily or forcibly from French-imposed culture in North Africa, defines what was acquired: these are the poisoned gifts of their colonial history that pertain to their frozen Algerian patronymic surnames, francophonie, and photography.

Notes

1 Edward Said, *Culture and Imperialism* (New York: Knopf, 1993), p. 35.
2 Victor Burgin, "Introduction," in Burgin (ed.), *Thinking Photography* (London: MacMillan, 1982), p 9.
3 Edward Said, "Bursts of Meaning," *Reflections on Exile and Other Essays* (Cambridge: Harvard University Press, 2000), p. 152. For an extended discussion of this topic, see my "Edward Said's Nazareth," *Framework: The Journal of Cinema and Media*, vol. 50, nos. 1 and 2 (2009), pp. 9–45.
4 Said, *Culture and Imperialism*, p. 214.
5 Frances Terpak, "The Promise and Power of New Technologies: Nineteenth-Century Algiers," in Zeynep Celik, Julia Clancy-Smith and Frances Terpak (eds), *The Walls of Algiers* (Seattle: University of Washington Press, 2009), pp. 87–133.
6 Zeynep Celik, "A Lingering Obsession: The Houses of Algiers in French Colonial Discourse," in Zeynep Celik, Julia Clancy-Smith and Frances Terpak (eds), *The Walls of Algiers* (Seattle: University of Washington Press, 2009), p. 142.
7 Malek Alloula, *The Colonial Harem* (Minneapolis: University of Minnesota Press, 1986), p. 4.
8 On *Scènes et Types* photography see the edited volume by Pascal Blanchard (ed.), *L'autre et nous: scènes et types* (Paris: Association connaissance de l'histoire de l'Afrique contemporaine, 1995); Leila Sebbar and Jean-Michel Belorgey, *Femmes d'Afrique du Nord: Cartes postales (1885–1930)* (Paris: Blue Autour, 2002); and Elizabeth Edwards, "Photographic 'Types': The Pursuit of Method," *Visual Anthropology*, vol. 3, nos. 2–3 (1990), pp. 235–258.
9 David Henry Slavin, *Colonial Cinema and Imperial France, 1919–1939: White Blind Spots, Male Fantasies, Settler Myths* (Baltimore: Johns Hopkins University Press, 2001), p. 20. For a critique of Alloula's absent historical and political perspectives, see the book review by Jean-Noel Ferrié and Gilles Boetsch, "Contre Alloula: le Harem colonial revisité: L'image dans le monde arabe, *Annuaire de l'Afrique du Nord*, vol. 32 (1993), pp. 299–304. On histories of French postcard production in Algeria, see David

Prochaska, "The Return of the Repressed: War, Trauma, Memory in Algeria and Beyond," in Patricia Lorcin (ed.), *Algeria and France, 1800–2000: Identity, Memory and Nostalgia* (Syracuse, N.Y.: Syracuse University Press, 2006), pp. 257–275 and Rebecca J. DeRoo, "Colonial Collecting: Women and Algerian Cartes Postales," *Parallax*, vol. 4, no. 2 (1998), pp. 143–157.

10 On captions, see Susan Slyomovics, "Edward Said's Nazareth," and Slyomovics, "Perceptions, Not Illustrations, of Sefrou, Morocco: Paul Hyman's Images and the Work of Ethnographic Photography," *Journal of North African Studies*, vol. 14, nos. 3 and 4 (2009), pp. 124–144.

11 Susan Sontag, *Regarding the Pain of Others* (New York: Farrar, Straus and Giroux, 2003), p. 4.

12 Malek Chebel, "L'image de l'autochtone maghrébine," in Nicolas Bancel, Pascal Blanchard and Laurent Gervereau (eds), *Images et colonies: Iconographie et propagande coloniale sur l'Afrique francaise de 1880 à 1962* (Paris: UNESCO, 1993), p. 272 and Chebel, "'L'Arabe' dans l'imaginaire occidentale," in *L'autre et nous: scènes et types* (Paris: Association connaissance de l'histoire de l'Afrique contemporaine, 1995), pp. 39–44.

13 Carl Dammann and Frederick Dammann, *Anthropologisch-ethnologisches Album in Photographien* (Berlin: Wiegandt, Hempel and Parey, 1873); Elizabeth Edwards, "Dammann, Carl Victor (1819–1874) and Friedrich Wilhelm (1834–1894)," in John Hannavy (ed.) *Encyclopedia of Nineteenth-century Photography* (New York: Routledge, 2008), pp. 377–378; Chrissie Iles and Russell Roberts (eds), *In Visible Light: Photography and Classification in Art, Science and the Everyday* (Oxford: Museum of Modern Art, 1997); and Anne Maxwell, *Picture Imperfect: Photography and Eugenics, 1870–1940* (Eastbourne, England: Sussex Academic Press, 2008).

14 Patricia Lorcin, *Imperial Identities: Stereotyping, Prejudice and Race in Colonial Algeria* (London: I.B. Tauris, 1995), p. 276.

15 Quatrefages was also the foremost French "acclimatizer," who drew on Algeria as proof for his racial thesis on acclimation and physiognomy in the colonies. He predicted that the French settlers of Algeria were certain to acclimate successfully and thus advocated from his scientific anthropological expertise for increased French colonization and immigration to Algeria. See Armand de Quatrefages de Bréau, *Rapport sur les progrès de l'anthropologie* (Paris: Imprimerie imperial, 1867), pp. 230–240 and George W. Stocking, "Polygenist Thought in Post-Darwinian Anthropology," *Race, Culture, and Evolution* (New York: Free Press, 1968), p. 54.

16 Paul Topinard, *Anthropology* (London: Chapman and Hall, 1890), p. 360.

17 Paul Topinard, "De la méthode d'observation sur le vivant, à propos de la discussion sur l'Algérie." *Bulletin de la Société d'anthropologie de Paris*, 3e série, no 4 (1881), p. 517. On Topinard and Duhousset, see Lorcin, pp. 155–159.

18 Paul Topinard, "De la méthode d'observation," p. 534.

19 Paul Topinard, "De la méthode d'observation," p. 536.

20 Alphonse Bertillon, *La photographie judiciaire, avec un appendice sur la classification et l'identification anthropométriques* (Paris: Gauthier-Villars 1890). See also Sandra S. Phillips, "Identifying the Criminal," in Sandra S. Phillips, Mark Haworth-Booth, and Carol Squiers (eds), *Police Pictures: The Photograph as Evidence* (San Francisco: Chronicle Books, 1997), pp. 11–31.

21 Michel Foucault, *Discipline and Punish: The Birth of the Prison* (New York: Vintage, 1977), pp. 195–228. See also John Tagg, "A Means of Surveillance: The Photograph as Evidence in Law," in *The Burden of Representation: Essays on Photographies and Histories* (Minneapolis: University of Minnesota Press, 1988), pp. 66–102.

22 Paul S. Landau, "Introduction: An Amazing Distance: Pictures and People in Africa," in Paul S. Landau and Deborah D. Kaspin (eds), *Images and Empires: Visuality in Colonial and Postcolonial Africa* (Berkeley: University of California Press, 2002), pp. 1–40.

23 Jane Caplan, "'This or That Particular Person': Protocols of Identification in Nineteenth-Century Europe," in Jane Caplan and John Torpey (eds), *Documenting Individual Identity: The Development of State Practices in the Modern World* (Princeton, N.J.: Princeton University Press, 2001), pp. 49–66.
24 On the chaos of identity brought about by burning the city records, see Alphonse Bertillon, *L'identité des récidivistes et la loi de relegation* (Paris: G. Masson, 1883), p. 5. On the French family passbook, see "Historique du livret de famille," available at http://pays-aigre.chez.tiscali.fr/genea/textes/questions/lelivretdefamille.htm.
25 Susan Slyomovics, *The Performance of Human Rights in Morocco* (Philadelphia: University of Pennsylvania Press, 2005), pp. 101–105.
26 The decree is in Robert Estoublon and Adolphe Lefébure, *Code de l'Algérie annoté: recueil chronologique des lois, ordonnances, décrets, arrêtés, circulaires, etc., formant la législation algérienne actuellement en vigueur, avec les travaux préparatoires et l'indication de la jurisprudence* (Algier: A. Jourdan, 1896), p. 500 with article five on p. 574.
27 Hassan Rachik, "Nom relatif et nom fixe," *Mediterraneans*, vol.11 (1999–2000), pp. 227–228.
28 Paul Decroux, "L'état civil et les Marocains." *Revue juridique et politique de l'union française*, vol. 6 (1952), pp. 12.
29 William MacGuckin de Slane and Charles Gabeau, *Vocabulaire destiné a fixer la transcription en français des noms de personnes et de lieux usités chez les indigènes de l'Algérie* (Paris: Imprimerie Impériale, 1868).
30 James Scott, *Seeing Like a State: How Certain Schemes to Improve the Human Condition Have Failed* (New Haven, Conn.: Yale University Press, 1998), p. 65.
31 Omar D, Tom O'Mara and Lahouari Addi, *Devoir de mémoire: A Biography of Disappearance: Algeria 1992–* (London: Autograph, 2007).
32 Judith Butler, *Bodies That Matter: On the Discursive Limits of "Sex"* (New York: Routledge, 1993), p. 16.
33 One of the earliest visual attestations of this practice that I found was Robert Capa's 1943 Naples photograph depicting women weeping at the funeral of twenty dead teen-age partisans. Capa presents an image of mothers gathered in lamentation around the unseen photographer, each one grasping a soldier's ID card of her son in uniform, their wails of sorrow almost audible.
34 See the overview of practices in Alison Dundes Renteln, "The Rights of the Dead: Autopsies and Corpse Mismanagement in Multicultural Societies," *South Atlantic Quarterly* vol. 100 (2001), pp. 1005–1027.
35 Marc Garanger, *Femmes algeriennes 1960* (Paris: Contrejour, 1982), unpaginated frontispiece.
36 Prochaska, "The Return of the Repressed."
37 Faye Ginsburg, "Indigenous Media: Faustian Contract or Global Village?" *Cultural Anthropology* vol. 6 (1991), pp. 92–112.
38 http://www.marocantan.com/2007/04/le_port_de_casa.htm
39 Sontag, *Regarding the Pain of Others*, p. 29.
40 See, for example, the Ken Jacobson collection described in his *Odalisques and Arabesques: Orientalist Photography 1839–1925* (London: Quaritch, 2007).
41 For the edited volume, *Walls of Algiers: Narratives of the City Through Text and Image*, and in the interests of full disclosure, I contributed a back cover blurb: "In this richly documented volume, the people, images, and places of the city of Algiers come alive. A group of outstanding scholars have been brought together to consider Ottoman, French colonial, and post-independence Algerian history through photography, popular culture, visual studies, religion and language. Their scholarship reveals how the inhabitants actually live in Algiers, how social relations were and are conducted, what are the symbols of political authority and the boundaries of religious space, and how the city, then and now, is delineated through memory and identity."

42 Maryanne Staniszewski, *Dennis Adams: The Architecture of Amnesia* (New York: Kent, 1989), p. 8.
43 Dennis Adams, "Recovered 10 on 10 (Adams on Garanger)," *Rethinking Marxism*, vol. 15. No. 3 (2003), pp. 350–351.
44 Gilbert Beaugé, "Portrait de femmes dans le Maghreb colonial," in Susan Ossman (ed.), *Miroirs maghrébines* (Paris: CNRS, 1998), pp. 41–56.
45 Adams's description is from the Kent Gallery, available at http://www.kentgallery.com/artists/adams_key_06.html. Much has been written on Steichen's aerial photographs held by New York's Museum of Modern Art or eventually sold commercially; see Allan Sekula, "The Body and the Archive," *October*, vol. 39 (1986), pp. 26–35.
46 For a discussion of Adorno's "museal" see Irit Rogoff, "From Ruins to Debris: The Feminization of Fascism in German-History Museums," in Daniel J. Sherman and Irit Rogoff (eds), *Museum Culture: Histories, Discourses and Spectacles* (Minneapolis: University of Minnesota Press, 1994), pp. 223–249 and Theodor Adorno, *Prisms* (Cambridge, Mass.: MIT Press, 1967), pp. 175–185.
47 Commission on Human Rights, Sub-Commission on Prevention of Discrimination and Protection of Minorities. "The Administration of Justice and the Human Rights of Detainees." Forty-ninth session Item 9 of the agenda. E/CN.4/Sub.2/1997/20/Rev.12 October 1997. See "Question of the impunity of perpetrators of human rights violations (civil and political)." Revised final report prepared by Mr. Joinet pursuant to Sub-Commission decision 1996/119. Henceforth referred to as the Joinet Report.
48 http://rue89.com/2008/04/17/archives-vichy-et-la-guerre-dalgerie-bientot-inaccessibles
49 See also on the creation of the Kafr Qasim museum dedicated to the 1956 Israeli massacre of Palestinian citizens of Israel, in Waleed Khleif and Susan Slyomovics, "Palestinian Remembrance Days and Plans: Kufr Qasim, Fact and Echo," in Kishvar Rizvi and Sandy Eisenstadt (eds.), *Modernism and the Middle East: Architecture and Politics in the Twentieth Century* (Seattle: Washington: University of Washington Press, 2008), pp. 186–217.

Bibliography

Adams, Dennis, "Recovered 10 on 10 (Adams on Garanger)." *Rethinking Marxism*, vol. 15, no. 3 (2003), pp. 350–351.

Adorno, Theodor, *Prisms* (Cambridge, Mass.: MIT Press, 1967).

Alloula, Malek, *The Colonial Harem* (Minneapolis: University of Minnesota Press, 1986).

Beaugé, Gilbert, "Portrait de Femmes dans le Maghreb colonial," in Susan Ossman (ed.), *Miroirs maghrébines* (Paris: CNRS, 1998), pp. 41–56.

Bertillon, Alphonse, *La photographie judiciaire, avec un appendice sur la classification et l'identification anthropométriques* (Paris: Gauthier-Villars, 1890).

——, *L'identité des récidivistes et la loi de relegation* (Paris: G. Masson, 1883).

Blanchard, Pascal (ed.), *L'autre et nous: scènes et types* (Paris: Association connaissance de l'histoire de l'Afrique contemporaine, 1995).

Burgin, Victor, "Introduction," in Victor Burgin (ed.), *Thinking Photography* (London: Macmillan, 1982).

Butler, Judith, *Bodies That Matter: On the Discursive Limits of "Sex"* (New York: Routledge, 1993).

Caplan, Jane, "'This or That Particular Person': Protocols of Identification in Nineteenth-Century Europe," in Jane Caplan and John Torpey (eds), *Documenting Individual Identity: The Development of State Practices in the Modern World* (Princeton, N.J.: Princeton University Press, 2001), pp. 49–66.

Celik, Zeynep, "A Lingering Obsession: The Houses of Algiers in French Colonial Discourse," in Zeynep Celik, Julia Clancy-Smith and Frances Terpak (eds), *The Walls of Algiers* (Seattle: University of Washington Press, 2009), pp. 134–160.

Chebel, Malek, "L'image de l'autochtone maghrébine," in Nicolas Bancel, Pascal Blanchard and Laurent Gervereau (eds), *Images et colonies: Iconographie et propagande coloniale sur l'Afrique francaise de 1880 à 1962* (Paris: UNESCO, 1993), pp. 272–279.

——, "'L'Arabe' dans l'imaginaire occidentale," in *L'autre Et Nous: Scenes Et Types* (Paris: Association Connaissance de l'histoire de l'Afrique contemporaine, 1995), pp. 39–44.

Dammann, Carl and Frederick Dammann, *Anthropologisch-ethnologisches Album in Photographien* (Berlin: Wiegandt, Hempel and Parey, 1873).

Decroux, Paul, "L'état civil et les Marocains," *Revue juridique et politique de l'union française*, vol. 6 (1952), pp. 1–18.

DeRoo, Rebecca J., "Colonial Collecting: Women and Algerian Cartes Postales," *Parallax*, vol. 4, no. 2 (1998), pp. 143–157.

Edwards, Elizabeth, "Photographic 'Types': The Pursuit of Method," *Visual Anthropology*, vol. 3, nos. 2–3 (1990), pp. 235–258.

——, "Dammann, Carl Victor (1819–1874) and Friedrich Wilhelm (1834–1894)," in John Hannavy (ed.), *Encyclopedia of Nineteenth-century Photography* (New York: Routledge, 2008), pp. 377–378.

Estoublon, Robert and Adolphe Lefébure, *Code de l'Algérie annoté: recueil chronologique des lois, ordonnances, décrets, arrêtés, circulaires, etc., formant la législation algérienne actuellement en vigueur, avec les travaux préparatoires et l'indication de la jurisprudence* (Algier: A. Jourdan, 1896).

Ferrié, Jean-Noel and Gilles Boetsch, "Contre Alloula: Le *Harem colonial* revisité: L'image dans le monde arabe," *Annuaire de l'Afrique du Nord*, vol. 32 (1993), pp. 299–304.

Foucault, Michel, *Discipline and Punish: The Birth of the Prison* (New York: Vintage, 1977).

Garanger, Marc, *Femmes algeriennes 1960* (Paris: Contrejour, 1982).

Ginsburg, Faye, "Indigenous Media: Faustian Contract or Global Village?" *Cultural Anthropology*, vol. 6 (1991), pp. 92–112.

Iles, Chrissie and Russell Roberts (eds), *In Visible Light: Photography and Classification in Art, Science and the Everyday* (Oxford: Museum of Modern Art, 1997).

Jacobson, Ken, *Odalisques and Arabesques: Orientalist Photography 1839–1925* (London: Quaritch, 2007).

Khleif, Waleed and Susan Slyomovics, "Palestinian Remembrance Days and Plans: Kufr Qasim, Fact and Echo," in Kishvar Rizvi and Sandy Eisenstadt (eds), *Modernism and the Middle East: Architecture and Politics in the Twentieth Century* (Seattle: Washington: University of Washington Press, 2008), pp. 186–217.

Landau, Paul S., "Introduction: An Amazing Distance: Pictures and People in Africa," in Paul S. Landau and Deborah D. Kaspin (eds), *Images and Empires: Visuality in Colonial and Postcolonial Africa* (Berkeley: University of California Press, 2002), pp. 1–40.

Lorcin, Patricia, *Imperial Identities: Stereotyping, Prejudice and Race in Colonial Algeria* (London: I.B. Tauris, 1995).

MacGuckin de Slane, William and Charles Gabeau, *Vocabulaire destiné a fixer la transcription en français des noms de personnes et de lieux usités chez les indigènes de l'Algérie* (Paris: Imprimerie Impériale, 1868).

Maxwell Anne, *Picture Imperfect: Photography and Eugenics, 1870–1940* (Eastbourne, England: Sussex Academic Press, 2008).
Omar D, Tom O'Mara and Lahouari Addi, *Devoir de mémoire: A Biography of Disappearance: Algeria 1992–* (London: Autograph, 2007).
Phillips, Sandra S., "Identifying the Criminal," in Sandra S. Phillips, Mark Haworth-Booth, and Carol Squiers (eds), *Police Pictures: The Photograph as Evidence* (San Francisco: Chronicle Books, 1997), pp. 11–31.
Prochaska, David, "The Return of the Repressed: War, Trauma, Memory in Algeria and Beyond," in Patricia Lorcin (ed.), *Algeria and France, 1800–2000: Identity, Memory and Nostalgia* (Syracuse, N.Y.: Syracuse University Press, 2006), pp. 257–275.
Quatrefages de Bréau, Armand de, *Rapport sur les progrès de l'anthropologie* (Paris: Imprimerie Impériale, 1867).
Rachik, Hassan, "Nom relatif et nom fixe," *Mediterraneans*, vol. 11 (1999–2000), pp. 223–28.
Renteln, Alison Dundes, "The Rights of the Dead: Autopsies and Corpse Mismanagement in Multicultural Societies," *South Atlantic Quarterly*, vol. 100 (2001), pp. 1005–1027.
Rogoff, Irit, "From Ruins to Debris: The Feminization of Fascism in German-History Museums," in Daniel J. Sherman and Irit Rogoff (eds), *Museum Culture: Histories, Discourses and Spectacles* (Minneapolis: University of Minnesota Press, 1994), pp. 223–249.
Said, Edward, *Culture and Imperialism* (New York: Knopf, 1993).
——, "Bursts of Meaning," *Reflections on Exile and Other Essays* (Cambridge: Harvard University Press, 2000), pp. 148–152.
Scott, James, *Seeing Like a State: How Certain Schemes to Improve the Human Condition Have Failed* (New Haven, Conn.: Yale University Press, 1998).
Sebbar, Leila and Jean-Michel Belorgey, *Femmes d'Afrique du Nord: Cartes Postales (1885–1930)* (Paris: Blue Autour, 2002).
Sekula, Allan, "The Body and the Archive," *October*, vol. 39 (1986), pp. 3–64.
Slavin, David Henry, *Colonial Cinema and Imperial France, 1919–1939: White Blind Spots, Male Fantasies, Settler Myths* (Baltimore: Johns Hopkins University Press, 2001).
Slyomovics, Susan, "Edward Said's Nazareth," *Framework: The Journal of Cinema and Media*, vol. 50, nos. 1 and 2 (2009), pp. 9–45.
——, "Perceptions, Not Illustrations, of Sefrou, Morocco: Paul Hyman's Images and the Work of Ethnographic Photography," *Journal of North African Studies*, vol. 14, nos. 3 & 4 (2009), pp. 124–144.
——, *The Performance of Human Rights in Morocco* (Philadelphia: University of Pennsylvania Press, 2005).
Sontag, Susan, *Regarding the Pain of Others* (New York: Farrar, Straus and Giroux, 2003).
Staniszewski, Maryanne, *Dennis Adams: The Architecture of Amnesia* (New York: Kent, 1989).
Stocking, George W., "Polygenist Thought in Post-Darwinian Anthropology," *Race, Culture, and Evolution* (New York: Free Press, 1968).
Tagg, John, "A Means of Surveillance: the Photograph as Evidence in Law," in *The Burden of Representation: Essays on Photographies and Histories* (Minneapolis: University of Minnesota Press, 1988), pp. 66–102.
Terpak, Frances, "The Promise and Power of New Technologies: Nineteenth-Century Algiers," in Zeynep Celik, Julia Clancy-Smith and Frances Terpak (eds), *The Walls of Algiers* (Seattle: University of Washington Press, 2009), pp. 87–133.

Topinard, Paul, *Anthropology* (London: Chapman and Hall, 1890).
——, "De la méthode d'observation sur le vivant, à propos de la discussion sur l'Algérie," *Bulletin de la Société d'anthropologie de Paris*, 3e série, no. 4 (1881), pp. 517–537.

Part III
Land

8 Revisiting Edward W. Said's Palestine

Between Nationalism and post-Zionism

Ilan Pappé

There is a tendency to separate Edward Said's theoretical work on literature and culture from his writings on Palestine. The two themes were dealt with in distinct books and essays where not only the content but also the style differed. In both fields, however, it is possible to trace a dialectical relationship between them. This is particularly true with regard to his writings on Palestine where he directs us to theoretical contexts when discussing particular issues connected to Palestine, but it is also there in his theoretical writings even where he does not mention Palestine specifically. He was both a Palestinian intellectual and a universal intellectual, and both simultaneously.

An illuminating example of this nexus is his anthology *The Politics of Dispossession*.[1] It is a collection of short interventions most of which are reactions to recent crises or junctures in the life of Palestine and the Palestinians. Each ponders not only the particular issue of Palestine but also the situation of the world in general. It is as if Said wished to contextualise every moment in Palestine's history within a universal march of history. These interconnections, however, do not hide a contradiction between Said's general ideas on culture and his practical address of the Palestine question. The former entail a sharp critique of nationalism while the latter had to be more tolerant – if not reverent – towards it. This may explain why so few other authors on Palestine employed Said's paradigms. It may also account for the paucity of Palestinian historians who followed his lead. The reasons for this are complex and understandable, but it was not until the demise of the Oslo process and the unattractive manifestation of statehood under the Palestinian Authority in the occupied West Bank and Gaza Strip that pioneering works began to de-nationalise history.[2]

I will examine in this essay Said's relationship with Israeli scholarship and academics. As I commented before, he had an important impact on what was called in Israel in the 1990s, the post-Zionist scholarship. This was an intellectual movement that since then has petered out, consisting of dozens of scholars, artists, journalists and in general producers of culture who viewed Zionism from within with critical eyes and debunked some of the foundational mythologies of the Jewish state. Throughout the 1980s and 1990s, these scholars wrote critically on Israel and Zionism. For a while their writings shook the social and human sciences in Israel. It began as a modest attempt to revisit Israeli historiography of the 1948 war – an attempt that was named at the time.

Through a description of this impact, one can understand, I will argue here, the paradoxes of Said's critique on Nationalism as a universal phenomenon and his more guarded approach to the particular case study of Palestinian nationalism.

Paradoxically, post-Zionist scholarship in Israel did find Said's paradigm immediately useful for understanding Palestine's past and present. It did not quite de-nationalise history but, at the very least, it de-Zionised it – or post-Zionised it – a process which was close to Said's general postcolonial critique of culture and nationalism. Where Said came close, towards the end of his life, to the post-Zionist critique in Israel was through his and their vision of post-conflictual Palestine. It was to be a space in the future where nationalism would be a weakened factor in the life of people, but at the same time this future would be a political outfit that would rectify some of the worst crimes committed through the years against the Palestinians, as it would end Zionist colonisation and dispossession of Palestine.

Said referred to the crystallisation of the contradictions that emerge in one's latter stage in life (and he sensed, from the discovery of his leukemia, that he was indeed in that stage). I suggest that his search for reconciliation between his universalist position of knowledge and his particular commitment to a Palestinian narrative can be viewed as part of his reconciliation of living in paradox, rather than solving it. The paradox of an exilic intellectual, as he would probably have put it. This would be in line with his general writings about the exilic intellectual. The elevation of exile into a pristine form of intellectualism defined not only a general philosophical stance vis-à-vis the modern world, but also a particular position on the Palestine question. Post-Zionism, as an intellectual position, was more limited in scope and ambition than the search for exilic intellectualism, but both fused into a joint orientation, indeed legacy, after Said's death. They can be presented together as providing guidelines to Said's 'solution' to the apparent contradiction between his general critique of nationalism and his devotion to the Palestinian cause. More importantly, they are a recommendation for the political future of Palestine.

The universalised approach towards Palestine and indeed the deductive prism used in the study of Palestine, did not, at first, win Said many followers in Israel. Academic work in Israel, until the 1990s, was primarily Zionist, or classical Zionist, comprising scholars who did not challenge the meta-Zionist narrative that the land had been empty, becoming a place only with the arrival of the first Jewish immigrants in 1882. Classical Zionist scholarship was also able to contain, for a while, the divisions within Israeli society that emerged after the occupation of the West Bank and the Gaza strip. However, after the internally disputed war in Lebanon and a bewildering first Intifada in 1987, this form of scholarship was challenged from the Left, and a group of academics began writing critically on Israel and Zionism in the early 1990s. The Lebanon war and the Intifada led them to develop a critical, a-Zionist approach to the country's past and present realities.[3]

This became an intellectual movement that shook the social and human sciences in Israel. It began as a modest attempt to revisit Israeli historiography of the 1948 war – an attempt that was named at the time as 'the new history' of Israel

– and it culminated in a scholarly internal Israeli deconstruction of the Zionist project from its beginnings to the present. It utilised theoretical and philosophical critiques that brought some scholars into the embrace of post-modernism, others to deeper Marxist convictions, while the rest remained loyal to liberal democratic notions with a hint of multiculturalism and post-colonialist deconstructivism.[4]

These scholars were challenged from the right by neo-Zionists who emulated the New Right and Neocons in the USA, and were even directly supported by them in their wish to represent the classical Zionist narrative in even more patriotic and nationalist terms. The inhibitions of classical Zionism disappeared in the works, published by a new research institute, Machon Shalem, and its journal, *Techelt* (Azure – one of the two colours of the Israeli flag). They demonised Palestinians, Arabs and Muslims and glorified the West, Jews and Zionism. They preached the takeover of the occupied territories and some indirectly advocated the transfer of the Palestinians, if need be.

These three ideological orientations within Israeli academia – classical Zionist, neo-Zionist and post-Zionist – clashed in a relatively pluralist manner in the 1990s. The years of the Oslo process enabled the Israeli Jewish public to associate criticism with the attempt to reconcile with the PLO. This was how the post-Zionist approach was heard in public meetings, university seminars and in the media. The hegemonic establishment, consisting mainly of classical Zionists, fought hard to diminish and delegitimise it, but, because it was welcomed abroad – and outside views are highly important for ascertaining the validity and quality of academics in Israel – this campaign failed. Neo-Zionists were quite marginalised in the 1990s.

During this time, it seemed that quite a few Israeli academics, media pundits and general literati could not resist Said's desire, and ability, to engage with humanity. Said's work and ideas were taken up and developed by critical Israelis affected and inspired by his thought. His impact can be detected in several major areas: in the analysis of Israel as an 'Orientalist' state, the examination of the dialectical relationship between power and academic knowledge within the local context, the introduction of the post-colonial prism into the study of the society and the critique of the present peace process and the adoption of an alternative way forward. With the collapse of Oslo in 2000 and the disappearance of the Israeli Left, however, the decade of post-Zionist impact came to an end as swiftly as it had emerged. Like the rest of Israeli society and the political scene, academia moved to the Right, namely to a neo-Zionist position of unwillingness to compromise in any significant way with the Palestinians or to allow any development of civil society that would improve the status and life of the non-Jewish, mainly Palestinian citizens. The voices of post-Zionism subsided and now are hardly present. Some of the group became neo-Zionist, most famously Morris,[5] and, while academia remained loyal to classical Zionist ideology, it allowed far more influence to neo-Zionism. The shift in the balance of power had an adverse effect upon Said's influence on the local scene. Respect for his work, and the wish to interact with it, is directly connected to the fortunes of post-Zionist critique. The surviving members of the group inevitably became more critical and would be best described today as anti-Zionist.

It would be appropriate to remark here that the distinction between post-Zionist and anti-Zionist should not be taken too seriously; these are working definitions for Israeli Jews who remain in the land, love the country and cannot tolerate their state or its policies. Still, the term is not that important; what is, is the total divorce from the consensual ideology that marginalises those who dare to criticise. In the post-2000 crises, which were presented in Israel as years of war and conflict, such deviations from Zionism are deemed tantamount to treason. Very few academics, intellectuals and cultural producers are willing to be castigated in such a way. For those who were, Said was both a friend and an inspiration.

Yet post-Zionism also reflected the wish to look more empathetically at some of the Zionist achievements in the past and to include them in a future vision. The reality on the ground, since 2000, convinced the handful of remaining critical voices in the academy and in the cultural media that only a fundamental shift from Zionist ideology towards a civil state of all its citizens can bring an end to a Zionist century of dispossession of the Palestinians.

The question of Palestine and historical 'truth'

Already in that early phase of the post-Zionist movement of critique, Said's influence could indirectly be traced. Although the main source for the revision was the emergence of new archival material in Israel and elsewhere, it is very clear that it was also influenced by the shift in attitudes towards non-Western historical perspectives to which Said, more than anyone else, contributed. The legitimisation process meant accepting as professionally valid the Palestinian version, or part of it, while at the same time exposing aspects of Israeli historiography as ideological and polemicist. Even more directly, this work was inspired by Said's *The Question of Palestine*, which appeared in Hebrew in 1984.

Another example of a direct impact was Said's presentation of the concept of a 'historical document'. When moderating a meeting between Israeli and Palestinian historians in Paris in 1998, Said discussed the meaning and significance of what constituted a 'historical document'. The Israeli historians expressed their belief that they were both ideologically and empirically just and declared that the only reliable sources for the reconstruction of the 1948 war were in the IDF archives and its documents. Said clarified that a report by a soldier from 1948 is as much an interpretation, and quite often a manipulation, of reality as any other human recollection of the same event: it was never reality itself. Through this, he pointed to the vitality and significance of oral history in the reconstruction of the past and also addressed the question of positionality. For example, the most horrific aspects of the *Nakbah* – the dozens of massacres that accompanied the Israeli ethnic cleansing of Palestine in 1948 – as well as a detailed description of what expulsion had been from the expellee's point of view can be addressed only when such a historiographical position is adopted.[6] Said wondered aloud how anyone could relate to the *Nakbah*'s real essence – as the most traumatic catastrophe that befell the Palestinian people – without showing even a modicum of solidarity with or sympathy for its victims. As he noted, Israeli historians would never have tolerated such a treatment of the history of the Holocaust.

Said's own particular interest in the Holocaust and the memory of the *Nakbah* contributed even more directly to the courage of researchers in following his call for the universalisation of the Holocaust memory, both as a critique of the Zionist manipulation of that memory and as a rejection of the Holocaust denial tendencies in the Arab and Palestinian worlds. This work won the admiration of Said himself, as he noted in his special preface to the Hebrew edition of *Orientalism*.[7] Both Palestinian and Jewish scholars expanded his basic ideas, aired for the first time in *The Politics of Dispossession*,[8] which inspired many, myself included, to look into the dialectical relationship connecting *Nakbah* and Holocaust memories on both sides.[9] As Said put it:

> What Israel does to the Palestinians it does against a background, not only of the long-standing Western tutelage over Palestine and Arabs ... but also against a background of an equally long-standing and equally unfaltering anti-Semitism that in this century produced the Holocaust of the European Jews. ... We cannot fail to connect the horrific history of anti-Semitic massacres to the establishment of Israel; nor can we fail to understand the depth, the extent and the overpowering legacy of its suffering and despair that informed the postwar Zionist movement. But it is no less appropriate for Europeans and Americans today, who support Israel because of the wrong committed against the Jews to realize that support for Israel has included, and still includes, support for the exile and dispossession of the Palestinian people.[10]

Said foretold the future: 'positionality' became no less important than archival material or available documents. In 1998, more declassified information about 1948 was revealed to historians in the Israeli military archives. But also, at that very time, oral history and Palestinian archives of memory, almost at the last moment before living witnesses of the catastrophe passed away, emerged and, far more importantly, were relocated as a vital source, no less viable than military archives. Benny Morris,[11] with the help of the new material, depicted an even more systematic expulsion of the Palestinians than he had done in his early works. But he also became, or chose to reveal himself as, a neo-Zionist. His narrative of the catastrophe was now much closer to the Palestinian narrative: it looked more like an episode of ethnic cleansing during war than an expulsion. However, unlike in his previous work, Morris justified the cleansing and advocated it as a future means to save the Jewish state, should the demographic balance disadvantage the Jewish majority.

Said did, however, also find his way to other, less professional, but more committed Israelis who focused their energy and time on countering the denial and establishing the significance of the *Nakbah*. An NGO, *Zochrot* (Remembering), for example, began in the twenty-first century to record the catastrophe of 1948 – through historical reconstruction based on memories as much as documents – and, with this, began to expose the abuse of its memory and relocate it constructively as part of a future Arab–Jewish dialogue, very much as Said – almost as a legacy – had recommended at the conference in Paris.

The Orientalist state

In its latter stages, the post-Zionist critique focused in particular on the state's early policies towards the Palestinian minority and the Jews who came from Arab countries, the Mizrachim. These were two Oriental groups, analysed, marginalised and objectified by European Jews, scholars and politicians alike. Said's influence can easily be recognised in the critical work that took the Mizrachim as its subject matter. There was an earlier attempt to deconstruct the state's treatment of the Mizrachim and the Palestinian minority within academia, even before the rise of post-Zionist critique, by Marxist sociologists in the 1970s. A decade later, the research into the plight of Arab Jews, as they were called by the more radical circles, took a more post-colonialist twist.

The focus moved away from the economic means of production and social deprivation as explanation for the discrimination against the Mizrachi Jews to questions of ethnicity, race and nation, that is, the context became mainly that of identity. This re-examination began by looking at how Zionism affected the question of Jewish identity in modern times. It argued that the transformation of Zionism from a national movement in Europe, where a Jew was defined as a non-gentile, into a colonialist project in Palestine produced a new definition of a Jew: a non-Arab person. This new, Orientalist definition of a Jew in the context of Palestine owed much to Said's claims in *Orientalism* that the Orient helped to define Europe, and the West, as its ultimate opposite in perception, in ideas, in personality and in experience.[12]

This reformulation of identity informed the Orientalist Israeli attitude to Palestinians wherever they were and created the biggest problem possible for the nascent Jewish state when one million Arab Jews were prompted to immigrate, as a result of the failure to bring enough Jews from Europe after the Holocaust. How would they be defined? The particular Orientalist Israeli praxis and discourse solved the dilemma by de-Arabising those Jews. Some of the leading works on this process of de-Arabisation owe much to Said's thought and critique – the most important of them being those by Ellah Shohat, Sami Shalom Chetrit and Yehuda Shenhav.[13] The Jewish immigrants from Arab countries were de-Arabised upon arrival in order to fit the Zionist dream of an ethnic Jewish state and to include them in the common public good from which the Palestinian citizens were excluded. By their being de-Arabised, these new immigrants contributed to the demographic balance and minimised the number of 'real Arabs' inside Israel.

It is through the works of Ella Shohat that we learn what de-Arabising meant, including her own very personal story of a young girl standing in front of a mirror and trying to lose her Arabic accent, refusing to take the kind of food to school that would identify her as an Arab and seeing how family names were Hebraicised all around her (which is why she returned to her Arabic names as part of her personal struggle).[14] And this is why any natural affiliation between the new Jewish immigrants and the survivors of the *Nakbah* was forcefully disrupted, and instead many in these communities developed particularly strong anti-Arab positions, fully exploited by the Israeli Right, as an initiation ticket to their new host society. The state rewarded them by pushing them into the social and geographical margins of society.

It is through this paradigm that questions were asked about the motives behind the immigration of the Jews from Arab and Muslim countries to Israel. Zionism was imposed as a motive in hindsight: aggressive Zionist lobbying and the emergence of an anti-Jewish local Arab nationalism were far more important. Similar revision in the official narrative appeared in the motives behind the government's abusive treatment of the immigrants – while established historiography argued for objective problems of means and security concerns, the new *Mizrachi* researchers exposed a racist attitude towards these Jews as Arabs and a wish to modernise and westernise them, with little regard for their tradition and roots.

This explains the great paradox that has accompanied the lives of the *Mizrachim* ever since their arrival: although most of the right-wing electorate comes from these communities – and with it a very racist and hostile attitude towards everything Arab – they are still seeking their Arab roots in culture and tradition as the best form of protest against the *Ashkenazi* establishment that had perpetuated their deprivation and frustration.

Said also provided a clue to the role played by Israeli academia in this policy of abuse and discrimination:

> The 'Orientalist' paradigm needed not only policy makers but also experts. The interchange between the academic and the more or less imaginative meanings of Orientalism is a constant one, and since the late eighteenth century there has been a considerable, quite disciplined – perhaps even regulated – traffic [between the two].[15]

Local academia, sociologists and anthropologists loyal to modernisation theories and 'experts' on Arab affairs, together with the local Orientalists, provided the scholarly scaffolding for the aggressive and coercive policies towards Palestinians and the Jews who came from Arab countries. It seemed that it was not only the academy in Israel that developed an 'Orientalist' interpretation of reality, but rather that the state, as a whole, also adopted this self-image. The state sells itself, even today – and more so, after the American invasion of Iraq – as an agent able to decipher the secrets of the 'barbaric' and 'enigmatic' Middle East: secrets that are open to a state which is in the area but claims not to be a part of it. This presentation of the state is the principal explanation for, and the perpetuation of, its alienating existence in the midst of the Arab world.

Common to these challenges was the underlying assumption that collective memory was constructed through the education system and the media. History and memory are acts of exclusion, as much as they could be tools of inclusion. Said's insights into the issues helped these scholars to expose the role played by the academic establishment in the nation-building process at the expense of freedom of thought and self-criticism. This followed Said's treatment of the symbols and manifestations of the Orientalist discourse in European culture: official texts, museums, ceremonies, school curricula and national emblems drew the academic community's attention to the way in which the dominant Ashkenazi group and its narrative has excised others from the national memory.

In a proper Saidian manner, these works exposed the sociological, anthropological and historiographical discourses used in research on 'Arabs' – whether Israeli Palestinians, neighbouring Arab states or Mizrachi Jews. The very grouping of Arabs, Palestinians and oriental Jews as one subject matter in scholarly research in Israel was a revolution. It could happen only if one adopted the critical paradigm of Orientalism offered by Said. In fact, for years, such a grouping or reification was taboo, as one of the first scholars employing such an approach – Ella Habib Shohat – learned when she was faced with the condemnation that forced her to leave the local academy.[16] In a fruitful dialogue with Said, Shohat debunked the Zionist myth that the Arab Jews were saved by Israel and opened up for examination the dominant discourse in academia that presented the Mizrachi and the Arabs in a similar way to that in which the Orient was introduced in the West through Orientalist discourse.[17] After Shohat, it became more common to come across work theoretically informed by Said, and the road to a bolder definition of society as a whole as Orientalism became shorter.[18]

In the spring of 2002 the journal *Theory and Critique* devoted a special issue to post-colonialism as it was understood and applied by Israeli scholars. This was a difficult title for scholarship in a state that many believed was still colonialist. Thus, a brilliant deconstruction of the Israeli Orientalist world can still be seen as constituting a colonialist, rather than a post-colonialist, reality. The continuation of colonialist imagery can also be seen in local literature, poetry and cinema.[19]

Post-colonialism seems to be a more apt categorisation when Jewish women and the *Mizrachi* Jews are the focus of this scholarly interest. Also appropriate is the connection Said made between cultural and post-colonial studies which illuminated one of the most important devices in making the state of Israel a state of denial. I refer here particularly to his notion of the possibilities of dialogue between colonisers and colonised as part of a restorative process of reconciliation. The first step in such a peaceful dialogue – and away from an alternative explosive violent clash over, and because of, history – was the question of the acknowledgement of past evils:[20] an elementary observation which was totally ignored by all those powers and individuals who were involved in peace making in Palestine and who based their vision of peace on a total absolution for Israel of its crimes in 1948 and after.

Said's journeys into the juncture between cultural and post-colonial studies produced another intriguing echo in local studies in Israel. His interest, which comes to the fore most clearly in *Culture and Imperialism*,[21] in locating the points of ambiguity where the oppressors and the victimisers are also oppressed and victimised, inspired the most original observation regarding the attitudes of the *Mizrachi* towards the Palestinians. From such a perspective, the social protest of *Mizrachi* Jews can be simultaneously supportive of, and subversive towards, the hegemonic Zionist discourse. This rather rough dichotomy between anti-colonialist tendencies in the critique and post-colonial ones can be found in Said's own reassessment of his work in retrospect (mainly in the new introduction written to *Orientalism*). The concept of Orientalism in the new version is both a concrete act of colonialist representation, anchored in a particular period, and a discursive practice, free of place or time. The latter is indeed the direction in which post-colonial studies developed after, and as a criticism of, Said's dichotomous approach, but is not part of this analysis.

Said and the exilic intellectual

The crystallisation of Said's universal humanism provided a common basis between him and post-Zionists in Israel. When this dialectical association matured, it allowed Said not only to elucidate even more forcefully than before, in political terms, his wish to bring an end to Zionist supremacy in Palestine but also to express a hope for a substitute far removed from the contemporary Arab nation-states around Palestine. This was helped by his growing critique of Arab politics. His disapprobation of Arab politics and politicians was connected in his mind with the Palestine tragedy a long time before his interest in Zionism, and particularly post-Zionists, in Israel was formed. When, in 1959, a friend of the Said family in Egypt, Farid Hadad, was murdered by the Nasserite security forces, Said divorced Arab radicalism from socialism. He continued to be dismayed by the more negative face of Arab nationalism and this discomfort was constantly linked to his vision of Palestine as a different political entity – different from Egypt as well as from Israel. This association is touchingly illuminated by the dedication of *The Question of Palestine* to Farid Hadad.[22]

In 1999, Said's friendly relationship with the Israeli academy reached a peak when he was invited, as keynote speaker, to the annual meeting of the Israeli anthropological society. He came out from that encounter with mixed feelings. On the one hand, he witnessed how his deconstructive approach to Orientalism was gladly and enthusiastically employed by post-Zionist scholars. On the other hand, he realised that the post-Zionist critics found it easier to employ his prism with regard to the cultural reality of Israel than to adopt, in any meaningful way, his political vision for the future of Palestine. In other words, they shared his narrative on *Nakbah* and dispossession, but not his vision for a bi-national state to which all refugees would be allowed to return.

In the last two years of his life, however, this situation changed. In a timely awakening, the more alert among the post-Zionists and political activists tapped into Said's recurring theme in his frequent sorties into the history and essence of the Palestine question: that the Jews and the Palestinians have chosen each other for an almost insoluble conflict, a destiny that requires mutual understanding of tragedies, national traumas and collective fears. In those two years he talked directly to the Israeli public, first in a rare and long TV interview and then in an extensive interview in *Haaretz*.[23] The questions in both cases were typically Zionist, and Said dealt with them easily and with great respect and honour, and, in the case of the television appearance, even with empathy and reverence. The running theme in the interviews – as in his memoirs, which had been translated into Hebrew – was exile.

Said 'the exiled intellectual' or, more precisely, 'the exile intellectual' was attractive to Jewish intellectuals far more than Said 'the Palestinian'. The picture, however, was more complicated as this exilic, almost Jewish intellectual, was still the voice of Palestine in the West. He was still in those days, and until his death, the sharpest critic of Oslo and its follies. Said's critical books on Oslo were not published in Israel, nor were they mentioned anywhere, and his criticisms were not addressed either in the interviews or in his memoirs (intriguingly, they were not allowed into the occupied territories by an offended Arafat, who did not take kindly to the severe criticism Said directed at him in those books). The hesitant post-Zionist embrace thus did not solve the dilemma of the man who was both the Palestinian intellectual voice – employing a national discourse and presenting a national agenda – and the universal intellectual – marginalising the importance not only of the nation but even of the homeland.

Notes

1 Edward W. Said, *The Politics of Dispossession; The Struggle for Palestinian Self-Determination, 1969–1996* (London: Chatto & Windus, 1994).
2 Issam Nassar, 'Remapping Palestine and the Palestinian Decolonizing and Research', *Comparative Studies in South Asia, Africa and the Middle East*, Vol. 23, nos.1–2 (2003), pp. 149–151; Jamil Hilal, 'Problematizing Democracy in Palestine', *Comparative Studies in South Asia, Africa and the Middle East*, Vol. 23, nos 1–2 (2003), pp. 163–172; Beshara Doumani, 'Rediscovering Ottoman Palestine: Writing Palestinians into History', in Ilan Pappé (ed.), *The Israel/Palestine Question* (London and New York: Routledge, 1999), pp. 11–40 and Beshara Doumani (ed.), *Family History in the Middle East: Household, Property, and Gender* (Albany, NY: SUNY Press, 2003).
3 Walid Khalidi, *All That Remains: The Palestinian Villages Occupied and Depopulated by Israel in 1948* (Washington DC: The Institute for Palestine Studies, 1992) and idem., *Palestine: Reborn* (London and New York: I.B. Tauris 1992).
4 Doumani, *Rediscovering* and Nassar, *Remapping*.
5 Benny Morris, *The Birth of the Palestinian Refugee Problem Revisited* (Cambridge: Cambridge University Press, 2004).
6 Edward W. Said, *The End of the Peace Process: Oslo and After* (New York: Vintage, 2001), pp. 273–277.
7 Edward W. Said, *Orientalism* (Tel-Aviv: Am Oved, 2000) Hebrew.
8 Said, *The Politics*.
9 Ilan Gur Zeev and Ilan Pappé, 'Beyond the Deconstruction of the Other's Collective Memory: Blueprints for Palestinian/Israeli Dialogue', *Theory, Culture and Society*, Vol. 20, no. 1 (2003), pp. 93–108.
10 Said, *The Politics*, p. 34.
11 Morris, *The Birth*.
12 Yerach Gover, *Zionism: The Limits of Moral Discourse in Israeli Hebrew Fiction* (Minneapolis: University of Minnesota Press, 1994).
13 Ella Habib Shohat, 'Colombus and the Arab Jews: Toward a Relational Approach to Community Identity' in B. Parry *et al.* (eds), *Cultural Identity and the Gravity of History: Reflections on the Work of Edward Said* (New York: Lawrence &Wishart, 1997), pp. 99–105 and Ella Habib Shohat, *Forbidden Reminiscences: A Collection of Articles* (Tel-Aviv: Kesher Ha-Mizrach, 2001), in Hebrew; Yehouda Shenhav, *The Arab Jews: Nationalism, Religion, and Ethnicity* (Tel-Aviv: Am Oved, 2003), in Hebrew

and Sami Shalom Chetrit, *The Mizrachi Struggle in Israel: Between Oppression and Liberation, Identification and Alternatives, 1948–2003* (Tell-Aviv: Am Oved, 2003) in Hebrew.
14 Shohat, *Reminiscences.*
15 Edward W. Said, *Orientalism* (London: Vintage, 1978), p. 3.
16 Ella Habib Shohat, 'Antinomies of Exile: Said at the Frontiers of National Narrations', in Michael Sprinkler (ed.), *Edward Said: A Critical Reader* (Oxford: Blackwell, 1992), pp. 121–143 and Shohat, *Forbidden.*
17 Shohat, *Columbus*
18 Chetrit, *The Mizrachi.*
19 See, for example, Anat Rimon-Or, 'From Silence to Voice: "Death to the Arabs" in Contemporary Israeli Culture', *Theory and Critique*, Vol 20 (June 2002), pp. 23–56, in Hebrew and Gil Eyal, 'Dangerous Liaisons: The Relations between Military Intelligence and Orientalism', *Theory and Critique*, Vol. 20 (June 2002), pp. 137–164, in Hebrew.
20 Edward W. Said, *Culture and Imperialism* (London: Vintage, 1994).
21 Ibid.
22 Moustafa Bayoummi and Andrew Rubin (eds), *The Edward Said Reader* (London: Granta, 2001), pp. xxi–xxi.
23 Ari Shavit interviewed Said in *Haaretz* on 18 August 2000 and Kobi Maidan on Channel 2 on 1 July 2000.

Bibliography

Bayoummi, Moustafa and Andrew Rubin (eds), *The Edward Said Reader* (London: Granta, 2001).

Chetrit, Sami Shalom, *The Mizrachi Struggle in Israel: Between Oppression and Liberation, Identification and Alternatives, 1948–2003* (Tel-Aviv: Am Oved, 2003), in Hebrew.

Doumani, Beshara (ed.), *Family History in the Middle East: Household, Property and Gender* (Albany, NY: SUNY Press, 2003).

Doumani, Beshara, 'Rediscovering Ottoman Palestine: Writing Palestinians into History', in Ilan Pappé (ed.), *The Israel/Palestine Question* (London & New York: Routledge, 1999), pp. 11–40.

Eyal, Gil, 'Dangerous Liaisons: The Relations between Military Intelligence and Orientalism', *Theory and Critique*, Vol. 20 (June 2002), pp. 137–164, in Hebrew.

Gover, Yerach, *Zionism: The Limits of Moral Discourse in Israeli Hebrew Fiction* (Minneapolis: University of Minnesota Press, 1994).

Hilal, Jamil, 'Problematizing Democracy in Palestine', *Comparative Studies in South Asia, Africa and the Middle East*, Vol. 23, nos 1–2 (2003), pp. 163–172.

Khalidi, Walid, *All That Remains: The Palestinian Villages Occupied and Depopulated by Israel in 1948* (Washington DC: The Institute for Palestine Studies, 1992).

Khalidi, Walid, *Palestine: Reborn* (London and New York: I.B. Tauris, 1992).

Morris, Benny, *The Birth of the Palestinian Refugee Problem Revisited* (Cambridge: Cambridge University Press, 2004).

Nassar, Issam, 'Remapping Palestine and the Palestinian Decolonizing and Research', *Comparative Studies in South Asia, Africa and the Middle East*, Vol. 23, nos 1–2 (2003), pp. 149–151.

Rimon-Or, Anat, 'From Silence to Voice: "Death to the Arabs" in Contemporary Israeli Culture', *Theory and Critique*, Vol. 20 (June 2002), pp. 23–56, in Hebrew.

Said, Edward W., *Culture and Imperialism* (London: Vintage, 1994).

Said, Edward W., *Orientalism* (London: Vintage, 1978).

Said, Edward W., *Orientalism* (Tel-Aviv: Am Oved, 2000), in Hebrew.

Said, Edward W., *The End of the Peace Process: Oslo and After* (New York: Vintage, 2001).

Said, Edward W., *The Politics of Dispossession; The Struggle for Palestinian Self-Determination, 1969–1996* (London: Chatto & Windus, 1994).

Shenhav, Yehouda, *The Arab Jews: Nationalism, Religion and Ethnicity* (Tel-Aviv: Am Oved, 2003), in Hebrew.

Shohat, Ella Habib, 'Antinomies of Exile: Said at the Frontiers of National Narrations', in Michael Sprinkler (ed.), *Edward Said: A Critical Reader* (Oxford: Blackwell, 1992), pp. 121–143.

Shohat, Ella Habib, 'Columbus and the Arab Jews: Toward a Relational Approach to Community Identity', in B. Parry *et al.* (eds), *Cultural Identity and the Gravity of History: Reflections on the Work of Edward Said* (New York: Lawrence & Wishart, 1997), pp. 99–105.

Shohat, Ella Habib, *Forbidden Reminiscences: A Collection of Articles* (Tel-Aviv: Kesher Ha-Mizrach, 2001), in Hebrew.

Zeev, Ilan Gur and Ilan Pappé, 'Beyond the Deconstruction of the Other's Collective Memory: Blueprints for Palestinian/Israeli Dialogue', *Theory, Culture and Society*, Vol. 20, no. 1 (2003), pp. 93–108.

9 Studies and souvenirs of Palestine and Transjordan

The revival of the Latin Patriarchate of Jerusalem and the rediscovery of the Holy Land during the nineteenth century

Paolo Maggiolini

During the nineteenth century the Ottoman province of Bilad al-Sham was involved in a broader political and diplomatic dynamic known as the *Question d'Orient*, becoming one of the sites of colonial encounter which lay at the intersection of European and Ottoman modernization.[1] Jerusalem and the holy places arose as one of the main theatres of conflict, not for their geopolitical and economic importance[2] but for their symbolic and spiritual significance, vividly associated in the mind of Europe with the theme of Christian chivalry and the memory of the Crusades.[3] The land of Palestine, the Holy Land *proprement dit* and not the Ottoman province, was explored, surveyed, steadily reinvented and imagined by "zealous intruders" who sought to rediscover this land to permanently reunite the East and the West.[4] This "gentle crusade"[5] favoured the emergence of the concept of the Holy Land as a region set apart, simultaneously a *terra incognita* and the well-known biblical land, that dominated the intellectual Western imagination of the nineteenth century, as evidenced by the growing usage of this term, which is remarkable, as Ben-Arieh points out, in view of the fact that it was not a separate political entity at that time.[6] Nonetheless the land of Palestine was not only a territory of exploration and pilgrimage, but also a mission land for both Catholics and Protestants. Benefitting from the favourable political climate of the *Tanzimat*, Christian missionaries increasingly flocked to the Near East, directly intervening in the local socio-political system through the foundation of many missionary establishments and religious institutions, as testified by the formation of the Anglican Bishopric of Jerusalem in 1841 and the revival of the Latin Patriarchate of Jerusalem in 1847. These new centres of religious authority played a dual role. On the one hand, they participated in the colonial encounter as important actors in a dynamic of changing and developing local balances of socio-political and religious power. On the other, encompassing their religious significance and role on the ground, their presence indirectly sustained the development of a process of intellectual acquisition of Palestine. The Holy Land *proprement dit* was not only the site and the treasure-chest of the holy places. It was a sacred and holy territory, owing to its biblical history,[7] that was inspected and checked for "evidence" of the accuracy of the Bible and, at the same time, a land that needed to be revived and rescued from neglect.[8]

Focusing on the Catholic presence in Palestine, the restoration of the Latin Patriarchate of Jerusalem involved different issues concerning the canonical aspect of the institutional controversy with the Franciscan Custody, the inter-confessional dimension and the diplomatic repercussions of the enterprise.[9] Moreover, the resurgence of the Latin Patriarchate exerted a great influence on the religious geography of Palestine, where the sacred dimension was involved with and drew meaning from social and political relationships resulting in a new geography of the Holy Land.[10] The rediscovery of Palestine, the Holy Land *proprement dit*, became part of the revival process of the Latin Patriarchate, the land being not only revealed and re-discovered, formed or constructed in its boundaries and geography, but claimed, owned and contested, giving birth to a dynamic of development of "hierarchical power relations of domination and subordination, inclusion and exclusion, appropriation and dispossession".[11] Accordingly, De Wandelbourg's *Etudes et Souvenirs de l'Orient et ses Missions*, portraying the Holy Land through "etudes et souvenirs" of his personal journey/pilgrimage and Mgr Valerga's pastoral tours, gives an interesting insight into the influence of the "revival" as a dynamic of re-sacralisation with important consequences in terms of power, religion and knowledge.[12] In his "voyage intérieur",[13] recorded in the first volume, the author visited the biblical places familiar to Western Christian culture and geographically localised biblical events, as many scriptural geographers did during the nineteenth century, whereas in his "voyage extérieur" with Mgr Valerga, recorded in the second volume, De Wandelbourg entered Transjordan, the *terra incognita* of the Holy Land, testifying to the victorious progress of "le drapeau de l'Evangile et de la civilisation chrétien"[14] thanks to the Patriarch, "restaurateur de la foi Catholique en Palestine" and "colonne des Églises d'Orient".[15] Moreover, the celebration of the "revival" of the Latin Patriarchate under the guidance of Mgr Valerga offered De Wandelbourg a way to enter into debate with European Catholic powers and their manipulation of religious issues to forward their own interests, with particular regard to France, which, from his standpoint, was choking the "real" French nation, Catholic in its essence, with atheism, secularism and modernism.[16] Following De Wandelbourg's narrative path, which echoes the encyclical *Quanta Cura* of Pius IX and its *Sillabo* of 1864, the Holy Land gains the attribute of "refuge" for the European faithful,[17] thanks to the immanent presence of the Divine and the successful revival of the Latin Patriarchate, more powerful than the transient temporality of secular politics.[18] According to De Wandelbourg, it was desirable for the Ottoman Empire, Islamic by creed but nonetheless more respectful of Catholicism and its clerics, to endure, or for Great Britain, while not yet Catholic, to triumph, since it was already able to ensure European Christians safe havens such as Malta.[19]

The poetics and narrative of Etudes et Souvenirs de l'Orient

Similarly to most nineteenth-century literature on exploring and travelling in Palestine, *Etudes et Souvenirs de l'Orient* is characterized by a deep interest in the Bible and other holy scriptures that are the lens through which the Near

East and the Holy Land are constantly viewed. Aimed at fulfilling the requests of many Catholic clerics and monks to gain new and useful insights into the ancient and modern East, biblical archaeology, interpretations of the Holy Texts and the socio-political conditions of the Near East regarding Catholic interests,[20] *Etudes et Souvenirs de l'Orient* appears to be an accumulation of literary genres on Palestine where scriptural–geographical apologetics coalescence with travellers' and pilgrims' tales, creating a "structure of feeling"[21] between the author and his audience that is deeply circumscribed within the specific cultural and institutional environment[22] of the Vatican and Catholic Europe. De Wandelbourg was not an individual or independent traveller unbacked by an institution or a government.[23] He reached Palestine, the Holy Land *proprement dite*, as a high prelate of the Roman Catholic Church, travelling in the Near East with missionaries of the Patriarchate, with its employees or with the Patriarch Mgr Valerga. Accordingly, although his individual freedom and ability to represent, portray, characterise and depict have to be respected, his resulting narrative was inevitably circumscribed and socially regulated[24] by his membership and role in the Roman Church.

De Wandelbourg was a mitred abbot, canon of the Holy Sepulchre, and a Doctor of Theology of the Pontifical University in Rome. His work was introduced by approving letters from Pope Leo XIII and the Patriarch of Jerusalem, immediately gaining in the eyes of his readers a particular authority reinforced by the fact of De Wandelbourg's being a close friend of Mgr Valerga, "one of his dearest sons",[25] and his historian during his four years of pastoral visits to the Near East.[26] Accordingly, the land of Palestine became the theologian's work field, a living biblical commentary because of being "witness" to those holy events and people[27] and the territory where the revival of the Latin Patriarchate was achieving its first successes under the guidance of Mgr Valerga, the first Latin Catholic Patriarch permanently resident in Jerusalem since the Crusades.

The figure of the Latin Patriarch is a ubiquitous presence in De Wandelbourg's work, performing a dual role. Firstly, Mgr Valerga is the main character in the second volume. In the "Avertissement", De Wandelbourg points out that one of the main purposes of his work is to "record his most intimate thoughts, and collect the memories of his glorious career and the fruits of his incomparable experience of the East".[28] Secondly, comparing his role as historian of Mgr Valerga's pastoral visits to that of Saint Luke in relation to Saint Paul, he reasserts his relationship with the Latin Patriarch, whom "Pope Pius IX appointed as his right arm to govern the Eastern Churches".[29] The Latin Patriarch fulfils the role of intermediary between the Holy Land, the author, the readers and vice-versa. In this way De Wandelbourg increased the authority of his narrative, thus reinforcing what Livingstone describes as "the crucial connection between travel experience and testimonial authority, between geographical location and sound reputation".[30]

Following De Wandelbourg's narrative path, the East "en général" and the Holy Land "en particulier" are described as the cradle of humanity, "antique rendez-vous" of all the nations, theatre of noble mysteries, revealed for the observer equally for their historical past and the secular immobility of their mores and appearance.[31] A land sought and studied because it was an inexhaustible mine of treasures for archaeologists, historians and theologians.[32] The East is thus perceived as a territory that does not change, as De Wandelbourg explained: "it is now as it was forty centuries ago, not only as a whole, but also in its details".[33]

In this regard, *Etudes and Souvenirs de l'Orient* conforms with much orientalist literature of the nineteenth century in adopting binary oppositions between an "us" and a "them", characterized by an ontological distinction between the West and the rest of the world, where the East as a whole could be intellectually acquired because of its historical immobility and passivity.[34]

This particular image of the East and the Holy Land is not only adopted but is constructed and worked out through De Wandelbourg's journey, where the "revival" is the means of establishing "continuity with a sustainable historic past".[35] This formative intellectual act perfectly explains the nature and the purpose of his work, right from the title chosen. Firstly, "Etudes" and "Souvenirs" are important narrative fictions to link the two volumes, shepherding the readers along De Wandelbourg's "voyage intérieur" and "voyage extérieur". They are also rhetorical devices of his poetics through which he animates bucolic, uplifting and peaceful biblical views of the Holy Land, inhabited by "the descendants of Sem, [that], by their instinct of fixity and stability, were predestined as assistants of the Evangelical Redemption and custodians of the oldest traditions, human and divine",[36] to which De Wandelbourg opposes European talent degenerated by secularist and atheist revolutionary attitudes.

Secondly, "Etudes" and "Souvenirs" are the outcomes of the encounter with a land that is *terra incognita*, that needs to be studied, and at the same time a place familiar to De Wandelbourg and his readers from which memories are constantly arising. This land of remembrances and studies thus became a *terra cognita* in the broad sense, thanks to De Wandelbourg's journey and the account of Mgr Valerga's pastoral visits. The result is a pseudo-pilgrimage[37] that creates a link between the reader, the biblical land and the revived diocese of the Latin Patriarchate. The contemporary Ottoman Palestine, especially with regard to its Muslim dimension, is almost ignored or, at least, relegated to the picturesque.[38] The Ottoman Empire and its Muslim subjects are mentioned only as protectors of the "refuge" of Catholicism[39] and repositories of imaginary legends that gain De Wandelbourg's interest because of their accordance with biblical traditions.[40]

Finally, "Etudes" and "Souvenirs" allow the author to move freely and without contradictions between different times and spaces, embracing both the biblical and the contemporary Holy Land that are permanently reunited through the "revival" of the Latin Patriarchate.

Tome premier: frames and memories of De Wandelbourg's journey in the Holy Land

The narrative structure of the first volume of *Etudes et Souvenirs de l'Orient* conforms with the bulk of historical–geographical literature about the Holy Land.[41] Shaped along the lines of this common model, it is composed of two sections, in fifteen chapters. De Wandelbourg organises his work geographically and historically in both of the two sections depicting the East,[42] "l'Orient", "in its respect for the memories of the past […] custodian of all things, mores and customs, names of places and ancient monuments".[43]

The first section, made up of the first six chapters – "necessary framework of the tableau"[44] – serves to introduce readers to the physiognomy, mores and customs of the East,[45] which sometimes turns out to be Syria and Palestine, with no distinction or contradiction from the author's standpoint. In these six chapters De Wandelbourg deals with the individuality of the East[46] and its correlation with the interpretation of the Holy Texts. The East is considered as a whole historical–geographical unit and this allows De Wandelbourg to embrace an extensive period of time that runs from the biblical period through the immanent time of the Oriental culture to the contemporary age of the revival of the Latin Patriarchate. Ottoman Palestine is analysed only according to the condition of the Catholic Church within the Empire and its interests on the ground.[47] Accordingly, readers became familiar with the historical development of the Holy Land, shown to be closely tied to its physical–geographical structure[48] and thereby a solid interrelation between the Book of Nature and the Book of Scripture was established.[49] Moreover, in the third chapter, De Wandelbourg outlines a tableau of the "different races, religions, social classes of Palestine and Syria" under the Ottoman government.[50] The author does not fail to introduce his readers to the obstacles that Catholicism and the Latin Patriarch had to face in the Holy Land. Echoing the competition between different missionary activities in the Near East, he stigmatises Protestant and Greek Orthodox oppositions, upholding the vitality and superiority of the Latin rite over the Oriental because of clerical celibacy.[51] Accordingly, he introduces another element to the ontological distinction between the West and the East, lowering it into the Catholic dimension.[52] This section ends with an attack on the European powers – responsible because of their inexpèrience and arrogance for most of the troubles that Catholics have to face – in which they are contrasted with "the civilizing influence of the Church" embodied by the wisdom of Mgr Valerga.[53]

The second section, made up of nine chapters, contains a detailed description of the regions,[54] localities and towns that De Wandelbourg visited during his travels, from his departure from Marseille until his arrival in Jerusalem and its environs, to which he dedicates five chapters.[55] This section conforms to the polemical scriptural–geographical narrative, in which the author sought to limit science's role in the explanation of places and biblical traditions.[56] De Wandelbourg's narrative and imaginative understanding proceed along a precise structure, as Aiken describes in analysing Josias Leslie Porter.[57] During his visits, De Wandelbourg sketches a series of tableaux in which the landscape is a stage where past events can be played out, a *religio loci*.[58] His work, however, is distinctive from other forms of scriptural geography because the Holy Land of the present is not only subservient to the holy landscape's biblical past,[59] but is also the place where the "revival" is achieving success. This aspect modifies the perception of the territory as unchanging and timeless, in favour of a circular dimension of time.

Scientific fieldwork only proved what the Bible had already said, as Aiken points out.[60] Accordingly, his experience of the Holy Land as archaeologist, theologian and traveller results in what De Wandelbourg regularly recalls as the verification of "how this Biblical phrase is strictly accurate [...] as photographed on the situation and the outskirts"[61] of the places visited, as testified to by the passage on Sodom or the statue of Lot, where he sought to re-establish a proper understanding on the basis of his inspection and knowledge of the scriptural and historical accounts.[62]

Tome deuxième: visiting the Bilad a-Sham with Mgr Valerga

In the second volume of *Etudes et Souvenirs de l'Orient* De Wandelbourg continues the description of his excursions to different biblical towns and regions in the Near East. Defending the "positive and inevitable [...] historical truthfulness" and "accuracy"[63] of the Holy Texts, the polemical tone of his narrative does not change, nor does his purpose of establishing a relationship between geography and theology. The narrative path proceeds along the same structure of the first volume until chapter twenty-six, where De Wandelbourg begins to perform the role of historian and biographer of the Patriarch, with an account of his visits to Rome, Beirut, Damascus and Transjordan, "l'Arabie désert", which represented the last pastoral visit of Mgr Valerga before his death.

The landscape, never imagined, is holy, sacralised, bucolic and secure, imbued with biblical perfume[64] and the "melancholic and unfamiliar melody" of muezzins.[65] Nevertheless, De Wandelbourg tempers this understanding of the Holy Land's landscape, reminding his readers that he is passing through a land where danger seems to be immanent.

The entrance of the author with Mgr Valerga into the *terra incognita* of the Holy Land, "l'Arabie désert" – Transjordan – marks the triumph of the picturesque and the "baroque in the desert",[66] manifested and evoked through a succession of reminiscences, mirages, Bedouin war chants and equestrian fantasies to celebrate the passage of the Patriarch,[67] "the keystone and the cornerstone" of Catholicism in the Holy Land.[68] Accordingly, De Wandelbourg works out a series of tableaux, dignified by the presence of the Patriarch, in which the biblical past coalesces with the history of the Crusades and the Oriental exotic.[69] As Mgr Valerga's pastoral visit progresses, De Wandelbourg gets acquainted with a population that lives "entirely in the traditions of the past [...] that have not changed by the introduction of European customs".[70] The Bedouin women are depositary of a nature "naïve and wild",[71] part of a community characterised by "piety and fervour [...] far more zealous in their faith than the inhabitants of Arab towns and villages of the interior of Palestine" that De Wandelbourg describes as "sometimes fickle and lukewarm".[72]

The slow pace of De Wandelbourg's narration in the wake of Mgr Valerga's pastoral visit seems to re-enact the successful progression of the "revival". The Patriarch, as Possetto outlines in his work,[73] meets Transjordanian tribes and becomes acquainted with local social and cultural climates, sowing the seeds of conversions that the new generation of Catholic missionaries would collect over the years after his death.

Similar to the euphoria that De Wandelbourg feels in witnessing the first celebration of the *Corpus Domini* through Jerusalem's streets – heart of the Holy

Land and headquarters of the revived Latin Patriarchate – which is described by the author as the "Catholic victory offsetting in the infidels' countries the afflictions and persecutions that the Church suffered in Christian countries",[74] the reception of Mgr Valerga in Salt, "wonderful and magical spectacle",[75] marks the triumph of Catholicism and the Latin Patriarchate in the *terra incognita*. Salt, "the famous Ramoth-Gilead, impregnable capital of Jophté and most formidable stronghold of the kings of Syria"[76] and "the great fortress of Bedouins, real eagle's nest, still repair of thieves",[77] welcomes Mgr Valerga, "the Supreme Pontiff of the Roman Church",[78] with ovations. The Patriarch enters the village by "riding side by side with the lieutenant of the Sultan, who comes to respectfully escort him as the Christian kings had escorted popes and their legates when Europe was proudly claiming to be Catholic".[79] The tableau of the reception in Salt ends with Mgr Valerga leaving the town in harmony and peace, heading for Jerusalem after having visited the ruin of Rabbath-Ammon, the contemporary Amman.

The epilogue of *Etudes et Souvenirs de l'Orient* is dedicated to De Wandelbourg's return in Europe and to an elegy to Mgr Valerga, who died shortly after his arrival in Jerusalem. The death of the Patriarch, martyr of the Catholic Church who donated his life to bringing the Revelation to the remotest lands of the Holy Land, represents the apex of De Wandelbourg's narration and the end of his work. The celebration of the "revival" is now performed.

Conclusion

As emerges from reading *Etudes et Souvenirs de l'Orient*, De Wandelbourg's understanding of the Holy Land was Western and Catholic, leading him to record little of the Ottoman and Muslim dimensions except for their correlations with the activities of missionary establishments and Catholic interests in the East or their relations to biblical traditions and old mores and customs. His narrative path, which proceeds through the fictional devices of personal *souvenirs* inspired by touching the Holy Land's landscape and a synoptic tableau of a significant portion of the "Christian or Muslim East",[80] pursues the relationship between geography – frequently informal in his description, as in a traveller's tale – and theology.[81] The Holy Land arises as *religio loci*, the land of the "revival" and a secure "refuge" for Catholicism. Accordingly, De Wandelbourg delineates a "moral geography"[82] of the Holy Land, a territory holy due its biblical past and, at the same time, a land re-sacralised through the account of the life and the pastoral visits of Mgr Valerga, "priest, diplomat and soldier of Catholicism"[83] in the East. Consequently, De Wandelbourg's Holy Land appears as a product of the intertwining of precise forms of poetics with sacred and power relations.[84] On the one hand, the theme of the "revival" and "refuge" describes the re-sacralisation process through the "revival", involving politics of position, property, exclusion and exile.[85] On the other hand, the relationship between geography and theology shown through De Wandelbourg's visits and inspections explains the creative dynamic of working out the Holy Land's landscape by imagining it promotionally, intuitively and aesthetically.[86]

Notes

1 Ussama Makdisi, *The Culture of Sectarianism: Community, History, and Violence in Nineteenth-Century Ottoman Lebanon* (Berkeley and Los Angeles: University of California Press, 2000), p.7.
2 Hain Goren, "Sacred, but not Surveyed: Nineteenth-Century Surveys of Palestine", *Imago Mundi: the International Journal for the History of Cartography*, Volume 54, Issue 1 (2002), pp. 87–88.
3 Naomi Shepherd, *The Zealous Intruders: The Western Rediscovery of Palestine* (San Francisco: Harper & Row, 1987), p. 12.
4 Ibid., p. 15.
5 Ussama Makdisi, *The Culture of Sectarianism*, p. 14.
6 Yahosua Ben-Arieh, "Nineteenth Century Historical Geography of the Holy Land", *Journal of Historical Geography*, Volume 15, Issue 1 (1989), p. 70.
7 Ibid., p. 71.
8 Naomi Shepherd, *The Zealous Intruders*, p. 73.
9 Paolo Pieraccini, *Il Ristabilimento del Patriarcato Latino di Gerusalemme e la Custodia di Terra Santa, la dialettica istituzionale al tempo del primo patriarca Mons. Giuseppe Valerga (1847–1872)*, Studia Orientalia, Monographiae, no. 15 (Cairo, Jerusalem: The Franciscan Centre of Christian Oriental Studies, 2006), p. 4.
10 Lily Kong, "Mapping 'New' Geographies of Religion: Politics and Poetics in Modernity", *Progress in Human Geography* (2001), p. 213.
11 Ibid.
12 Edward Said, "Orientalism Reconsidered", *Cultural Critique*, No. 1 (Autumn 1985), p. 91.
13 Irene Maffi, 'Orientalisme et Temporalité de l'Autre, Quelques Clés pour une Lecture de Jaussen et de Robertson-Smith', in G. Chatelard and M. Tarawneh (eds), *Antonin Jaussen: Sciences Sociales Occidentales et Patrimoine Arabe* (Beirut: Cermoc, 1999), p. 98.
14 A. H. De Wandelbourg, Études et Souvenirs sur l'Orient *et Ses Missions: Palestine, Syrie et Arabie, Visitées avec Mgr Valerga, Patriarche De Jérusalem, Vicaire Apostolique d›Alep, Délégat De Syrie* (Lyon: Berche et Tralin, 1883), p. 2.
15 Ibid. p. 3.
16 Ibid., p. 110. Naomi Shepherd, *The Zealous Intruders*, p. 184. A. Latreille, A. Delaruelle and J.-R. Palanque, *Histoire du Catholicisme en France* (Paris: Edition Spes, 1960), p. 408.
17 Ussama Makdisi, *The Culture of Sectarianism*, pp. 18–19.
18 A. H. De Wandelbourg, Études et Souvenirs sur l'Orient et Ses Missions, p. 109.
19 Ibid., pp. 123–124.
20 Ibid., p. 2.
21 Edward Said, *Culture and Imperialism* (New York: Vintage Books, 1994), p. 14.
22 David N. Livingstone, "Oriental Travel, Arabian Kinship, and Ritual Sacrifice: William Robertson Smith and the Fundamental Institutions", *Environment and Planning D: Society and Space*, Volume 22, Issue 5 (2004), p. 639.
23 Hain Goren, "Sacred, but Not Surveyed", p. 87.
24 Edward Said, *Culture*, p. 95.
25 A. H. De Wandelbourg, Études et Souvenirs sur l'Orient et Ses Missions, p. 2.
26 Ibid.
27 Edwin J. Aiken, *Scriptural Geography, Portraying the Holy Land* (London: I. B. Tauris, 2009), pp. 5–6.
28 A. H. De Wandelbourg, Études et Souvenirs sur l'Orient et Ses Missions, p. 3.
29 Ibid.
30 David N. Livingstone, "Text, Talk and Testimony: Geographical Reflections on Scientific Habits", *British Journal for the History of Science*, Volume 38 (2005), p. 97.
31 A. H. De Wandelbourg, Études et Souvenirs sur l'Orient et Ses Missions, p. 1.

32 Ibid.
33 Ibid., p. 23.
34 Edward Said, *Culture*, p. 129.
35 E. Hobsbawm and T. Ranger, *Invention of Tradition* (Cambridge: Cambridge University Press, 1992), p. 1. See also Edward Said, *Culture*, p. 36.
36 A. H. De Wandelbourg, Études et Souvenirs sur l'Orient et Ses Missions, p. 23.
37 Edwin J. Aiken, *Scriptural Geography*, p. 79.
38 Naomi Shepherd, *The Zealous Intruders*, p. 72.
39 A. H. De Wandelbourg, Études et Souvenirs sur l'Orient et Ses Missions, p. 89, p. 110.
40 Ibid., p. 262.
41 Yahosua Ben-Arieh, 'Nineteenth Century Historical Geography', p. 74.
42 Butlin Robi, "George Adam Smith and the Historical Geography of the Holy Land: Contents, Contexts and Connections", *Journal of Historical Geography*, Volume 14, Issue 4 (1988), p. 386.
43 A. H. De Wandelbourg, Études et Souvenirs sur l'Orient et Ses Missions, p. 25.
44 Ibid., p. 3.
45 Ibid.
46 Yahosua Ben-Arieh, "Nineteenth Century Historical Geography", p. 74.
47 See the "Table des Matiers", A. H. De Wandelbourg, Études et Souvenirs sur l'Orient et Ses Missions, p. 1, p.5, p. 23, p. 49, p. 70, p. 97, p. 125.
48 Yahosua Ben-Arieh, "Nineteenth-Century Historical Geography", p. 74.
49 Edwin J. Aiken, "Scriptural Geography", p. 19.
50 A. H. De Wandelbourg, Études et Souvenirs sur l'Orient et Ses Missions, p. 49.
51 Ibid., pp. 54, 291.
52 Joseph Hajjar, *Les Chrétiens Uniates du Proche-Orient* (Paris: Éditions de Seuil, 1962), p. 274.
53 A. H. De Wandelbourg, Études et Souvenirs sur l'Orient et Ses Missions, p. 54, p. 81.
54 Yahosua Ben-Arieh, "Nineteenth Century Historical Geography", p. 74.
55 See the "Table des Matiers", A. H. De Wandelbourg, Études et Souvenirs sur l'Orient et Ses Missions, p. 166, p. 179, p. 194, p. 211, p. 228, p. 245, p. 264, p. 293, p. 302.
56 Edwin J. Aiken, *Scriptural Geography*, p. 27.
57 Ibid., p. 99.
58 Ibid.
59 Ibid., p. 100. Naomi Shepherd, *The Zealous Intruders*, p. 73.
60 Edwin J. Aiken, *Scriptural Geography*, p. 95.
61 A. H. De Wandelbourg, Études et Souvenirs sur l'Orient et Ses Missions, p. 7.
62 Naomi Shepherd, *The Zealous Intruders*, p. 73.
63 A. H. De Wandelbourg, Études et Souvenirs sur l'Orient et Ses Missions, p. 331.
64 Ibid., p. 198.
65 Ibid., p. 255.
66 Edwin J. Aiken, *Scriptural Geography*, p. 45.
67 A. H. De Wandelbourg, Études et Souvenirs sur l'Orient et Ses Missions, p. 292.
68 Ibid., p. 379.
69 Ibid., pp. 301–302.
70 Ibid., p. 306.
71 Ibid, p. 255.
72 Ibid., p. 323.
73 Alessandro Possetto, *Il Patriarcato Latino di Gerusalemme (1848–1938)* (Milan: "Crociata", 1938), pp. 78–88.
74 A. H. De Wandelbourg, Études et Souvenirs sur l'Orient et Ses Missions, p. 186.
75 Ibid., p. 337.
76 Ibid.
77 Ibid.
78 Ibid.
79 Ibid., p. 338.

80 A. H. De Wandelbourg, Études et Souvenirs sur l'Orient et Ses Missions, p. 380.
81 Edwin J. Aiken, *Scriptural Geography,* p. 43.
82 Amy Derogatis, "Moral Geography: Maps, Missionaries and the American Frontier", *Journal of Religious History*, Volume 32, Issue 1 (2008) p. 124. See also David N. Livingstone, *Text, Talk and Testimony*, p. 97.
83 A. H. De Wandelbourg, Études et Souvenirs sur l'Orient et Ses Missions, p. 134.
84 Lily Kong, "Mapping 'New' Geographies of Religion", p. 213.
85 Ibid., p. 213.
86 John K. Wright, "Terrae Incognitae: The Place of the Imagination in Geography", *Annals of the Association of American Geographers*, Volume 37, Issue 1 (1947), p. 5.

Bibliography

Aiken, E. J., *Scriptural Geography, Portraying the Holy Land* (London: I. B. Tauris, 2009).

Ben-Arieh, Y., "Nineteenth Century Historical Geography of the Holy Land", *Journal of Historical Geography*, Volume 15, Issue 1, January 1989, pp. 69–79.

De Wandelbourg, A. H., *Études et Souvenirs sur l'Orient et Ses Missions: Palestine, Syrie et Arabie, Visitées avec Mgr Valerga, Patriarche De Jérusalem, Vicaire Apostolique d›Alep, Délégat de Syrie*, Tomes I–II (Lyon: Berche et Tralin, 1883).

Derogatis, Amy, "Moral Geography: Maps, Missionaries and the American Frontier", *Journal of Religious History*, Volume 32, Issue 1 (2008), pp. 124–125.

Goren, H., "Sacred, but not Surveyed: Nineteenth-Century Surveys of Palestine", *Imago Mundi: the International Journal for the History of Cartography*, Volume 54, Issue 1, 2002, pp. 87–110.

Hajjar, J., *Les Chrétiens Uniates du Proche-Orient*, Collection Les Univers (Paris: Seuil, 1962).

Hobsbawm, E. and T. Ranger, *Invention of Tradition* (Cambridge: Cambridge University Press, 1992).

Kong, L., "Mapping 'New' Geographies of Religion: Politics and Poetics in Modernity", *Progress in Human Geography*, Volume 25, Issue 2, 2001, pp. 211–233.

Latreille, A., A. Delaruelle and J. R. Palanque, *Histoire du Catholicisme en France* (Paris: Edition Spes, 1960).

Livingstone, D. N., "Oriental Travel, Arabian Kinship, and Ritual Sacrifice: William Robertson Smith and the Fundamental Institutions", *Environment and Planning D: Society and Space*, Volume 22, Issue 5 (2004), pp. 639–657.

Livingstone, D.N., "Text, Talk and Testimony: Geographical Reflections on Scientific Habits", *British Journal for the History of Science*, Volume 38 (2005), pp. 93–100.

Maffi, I., "Orientalisme et Temporalité de l'Autre. Quelques Clés pour une Lecture de Jaussen et de Robertson-Smith", in G. Chatelard and M. Tarawneh (eds), *Antonin Jaussen: Sciences Sociales Occidentales et Patrimoine Arabe* (Beirut: Cermoc, 1999).

Makdisi, U., *The Culture of Sectarianism: Community, History and Violence in Nineteenth-Century Ottoman Lebanon* (Berkeley and Los Angeles: University of California Press, 2000).

Pieraccini, P., *Il Ristabilimento del Patriarcato Latino di Gerusalemme e la Custodia di Terra Santa, la Dialettica Istituzionale al Tempo del Primo Patriarca Mons. Giuseppe Valerga (1847–1872)*, Studia Orientalia, Monographiae no. 15 (Cairo, Jerusalem: The Franciscan Centre of Christian Oriental Studies, 2006).

Possetto, A., *Il Patriarcato Latino di Gerusalemme (1848–1938)* (Milan: "Crociata", 1938).

Robi, B., "George Adam Smith and the Historical Geography of the Holy Land: Contents, Contexts and Connections", *Journal of Historical Geography*, Volume 14, Issue 4 (1988), pp. 381–404.

Said, E., Orientalism Reconsidered, *Cultural Critique*, No. 1 (Autumn 1985), pp. 89–107.

Said, E., *Culture and Imperialism* (New York: Vintage Books, 1994).

Shepherd, N., *The Zealous Intruders: The Western Rediscovery of Palestine* (San Francisco: Harper & Row, 1987).

Wright John K., "Terrae Incognitae: The Place of the Imagination in Geography", *Annals of the Association of American Geographers*, Volume 37, Issue 1 (1947), pp. 1–15.

10 Arabizing the Bible

Racial supersessionism in nineteenth-century Christian art and biblical scholarship

Ivan Davidson Kalmar

Between the Renaissance and the middle of the twentieth century, the Israelites of the Bible came to be imagined in the West as a people similar to the modern inhabitants of Muslim West Asia and North Africa. A near-equation of ancient Jew and contemporary Muslim followed from the typical orientalist assumption that the "Orient"[1] was ahistorical and monolithic. The current peoples of the Orient, it was thought, lived in the same kind of civilization as their "ancestors." And, as one oriental was like another, it mattered little if these ancestors had been Jews, Turks, or Arabs. The record of this orientalization of the Bible is pervasive and extensive. I will have space to illustrate it with only a few almost randomly chosen examples. My focus is on the long nineteenth century. My examples are from two areas that have still not quite received all the attention they deserve in the literature on orientalism: Christian art, and biblical scholarship.

The orientalization (eventually, Arabization) of the Bible was part of a general transformation of Christian notions that is commonly but rather imprecisely referred to as secularization. I would like to show how inherited Christian notions were developed into newer ideas about the Orient. These ideas were expressed in the ostensibly secular, pseudo-scientific vocabulary of "race." But racial "thought" in the nineteenth century did not replace inherited Christian conceptions. Rather, it reinvigorated and gave support to them.

I argue that the relationship imagined to hold between the "Aryan" races of Europe and the "Semitic" races of Asia was the latest manifestation of a long, theological tradition of Christian supersessionism. Christian supersessionists believe that the Christian gospels announced the replacement of Judaism and the Old Testament as the vanguard of sacred history, with the place of Israel taken by the Christian Church. Racial supersessionists of the long nineteenth century believed that the peoples of the West had similarly taken over from the peoples of the Orient, a project that was referred to as progress and the civilizing mission. To many, however, progress in civilization remained fundamentally related to progress in religion.

There were, to be sure, those who distanced themselves from Christian traditions, or even saw "progress" as a form of degeneration rather than advance. Yet even most of these agreed that a more primitive, Semitic or "Arabian" spirit infused the Old Testament, while Christianity was the product of a more modern race.

This reformulation of the religious tradition was part of a wider racialization of history, which legitimated the rule of the Aryan Christians, as the most advanced race, over those who were more backward. But beyond that, the specific contrast between Aryans and Semites had some more or less unintended side effects. These included racial anti-Semitism and calls for the Jewish people to resettle, or be resettled, in their oriental homeland outside of Europe and the West.

Before the long nineteenth century

Imagining the Bible in terms of contemporary information about the Orient became common only towards the end of the fourteenth century. Neighboring Asia was then becoming stranger than ever to western Christians. All of West Asia became a Muslim dominion with the Ottoman conquest of Christendom's ancient capital, Constantinople, in 1453. Around this time many Christian artists in the West began to model biblical characters on what they knew of contemporary "Turks" (a rather generic term used more or less for all residents of the Ottoman Empire). The most striking, and most enduring, iconographic legacy from this period is the use of turbans on biblical personages.[2]

This Israelites-in-turbans convention was still in evidence in the biblical canvases of Rembrandt. Most of his biblical paintings, such as *Saul and David* or *David and Uriah*, as well as some of his self-portraits as a biblical prophet, feature the turban. There is no evidence that such headwear was worn in ancient Israel, and Rembrandt's portraits of Jewish Amsterdamers show that it was not worn by Jews there, either. Rather, Rembrandt, a collector of exotic artifacts,[3] visualized Saul and David's attire as what was worn, he imagined, by the Muslims of the Ottoman Empire.

In Rembrandt's time, information about non-Jewish "orientals" also served scholars who studied the Bible, although here Arabs rather than "Turks" were the model, because of the kinship between the Arabic and Hebrew languages that was already well recognized. Biblical scholarship was probably the major motivator of a resurgence in Arabic studies in the seventeenth and early eighteenth centuries. The first scholar to hold the new chair of Arabic at Oxford, Edward Pococke (1604–1691), was a Hebraist, who published commentaries on several books of the Bible.

In 1706, Rembrandt's countryman Albert Schultens would advocate explicitly the use of Arabic in interpreting Scripture. To him, it was not only Arabic language but also what we would now call Arabic culture that provided a key to the world of the Old Testament. Arabic philosophy and popular proverbs illustrated, to Schultens, facets of biblical thought.

Eighteenth-century English scholars, also, believed that the Hebrew Scriptures embodied the spirit of a wider, oriental world. This attitude was in fact probably responsible for the introduction of the term "orientalism" into the English language. If Joseph Spence, who used it in his *Essay on Pope's Odyssey*, published in 1726, is to be trusted, "orientalism" was his own "new word." In Spence's *Essay* one of his characters comments as follows on a Homeric passage that he says is his "particular favourite:"

> now you repeat it in English, I seem to want something of the strong pleasure it used to afford me, where the Greek speaks "Of the sun being perished out of Heaven, and of darkness rushing over the Earth!" I cannot express the fullness of the words – But you know the original; and, I fear, will never see a translation equal to it. This whole prophetical vision … is the True Sublime; and in particular, gives us an higher Orientalism than we meet with in any other part of Homer's writings. You will pardon me a new word, where we have no old one to my purpose: You know what I mean, that Eastern way of expressing Revolutions in Government, by a confusion or extinction of light in the Heavens.[4]

Clearly, the reference to the sky and government is only one specific example rather than an exhaustive definition; "orientalism" is not merely "a way of expressing Revolutions in Government," but rather the "Eastern way of expressing" such Revolutions is one particular example of orientalism as a broader category. The implication is that there are other examples, and that it is the broader category of orientalism in general that is capable of expressing the "True Sublime." (That Homer was subject to oriental influences was a common belief at the time.)

The English biblical scholar Robert Lowth (1710–1787) frequently drew on Arabic to elucidate elements of the biblical Hebrew text. This practice was in conformity not only with Schultens' program, but also with the German school of biblical criticism that was beginning to come to prominence at the time. The influential German orientalist scholar Johann David Michaelis (1717–1791), whose comments on Lowth's *Sacred Poetry* were included in its successive republications, was a major believer in using Arabic as a key to the Hebrew Bible. One of Lowth's propositions that Michaelis espoused enthusiastically was that the Book of Job was the oldest of the Bible and that it "seems to have little connexion with the other writings of the Hebrews, and no relation whatever to the affairs of the Israelites." Its characters are "Idumaeans, or at least Arabians of the adjacent country, all originally of the race of Abraham." The book of Job was written "before Moses, and [is] probably contemporary with the patriarchs." Michaelis added approvingly regarding the characters of Job that "As to the manners, they are what I called *Abrahamic*, or such as were at that period common to all the seed of Abraham at that time, Israelites, Ishmaelites, and Idumaeans." In fact, "most of the peculiar customs of the Israelites, those I mean which distinguished them from other descendants of Abraham, were either derived from the Egyptians, or were taught them by Moses."[5] In other words, Michaelis believed that the Israelites had brought to Egypt nothing peculiar to themselves, as opposed to oriental peoples in general.

Traveling in search of the Bible

One logical, and probably intended, consequence of this denial of a distinctive Jewish cultural character of the Bible was to refuse to contemporary Jews the mantle of modern-day carriers of the biblical spirit. Instead, to find a still-living biblical culture one needed to look for a people who shared that achievement but had *not* changed. And these, Michaelis believed, were the Arabs. In Michaelis' mind,

> One will hardly find a people that has kept its customs the same for so long as the Arabs; which is a result of their never having been brought under the yoke of other peoples. Everything we know about these customs coincides so exactly with the most ancient customs of the Israelites and thus gives the richest and most beautiful elucidations to the Bible. In contrast, the customs of the Jews themselves among the Persians, Greeks and Romans, and since their European Diaspora, have changed so much that one can no longer see in them the descendants of the people of whom the Bible speaks.[6]

Michaelis convinced the enlightened King of Denmark to send five men to "Arabia and other Countries of the East" in order to study the local population as well as the local flora and fauna, which, too, Michaelis thought would closely resemble the biblical environment.[7] The expedition achieved great fame in Europe[8] and became the mother of all expeditions to the East and of that branch of scholarly orientalism – Middle and Near Eastern ethnography and archeology – that relies on them.

The history of expeditions to the Orient in search of studying what might be called the "historical Bible" needs to be far more fully investigated and documented than scholars have done to date. Suffice it to say that such travel, even for short periods, became almost *de rigueur* for people claiming expertise on the Bible that was more than just strictly philological. Among the long list of nineteenth-century travelers who shared their insights into biblical culture, one might rather arbitrarily mention the French author and diplomat François-René de Chateaubriand (in the Orient in 1806);[9] the author–politician Benjamin Disraeli (traveled 1830–1831);[10] the orientalist and author of a major book on the historical Jesus, Ernest Renan (1860);[11] and the dean in his day of all orientalists, Ignaz Goldziher (1873–1874).[12] Although travelers often devoted special attention to the local Jews, their musings about resemblances between the contemporary Orient and the Bible were usually based on their encounters with Muslim and Christian Arabs.

True, the most celebrated biblical scholars never set foot in the Orient. The list includes Michaelis' student Johann Gottfried Eichhorn (1753–1827), conventionally considered the founder of the new biblical criticism, whose thesis was on Arab uses of money; Julius Wellhausen (1844–1918) who, too, was an Arabist as well as a daring revisionist of biblical scholarship; and William Robertson Smith (1846–1894), a professor of Arabic who wrote in English on both the Bible and Arab customs. However, these armchair experts relied frequently on the reports of Orient travelers.

The same cachet of special knowledge that oriental voyaging gave to popular and scientific authors was acquired by the many artists who traveled to, or even lived in, the Orient. *Orientalisme* was a recognized genre of visual art in the long nineteenth century.[13] A decisive influence on the manner in which the Orient was depicted and orientalist art distributed was Jean-Léon Gérôme (1824–1904). This academic painter traveled to the Orient on a number of occasions. He married the daughter of Adolphe Goupil, one of the most important and innovative art merchants of the period. Goupil seized the potential of new reproductive technologies, and had the full cooperation of his son-in-law. In particular, the Goupil firm was instrumental in selling volumes of photographic reproductions of Gérôme's art in the United States.[14]

As in biblical criticism, there was in biblical art a fertile cross-referencing among representations of the contemporary Orient and of biblical Israel. No doubt the scholarly Arabization of the Bible reinforced the artistic and vice versa. (It must be assumed that the scholars, no less than other educated people, spent their time surrounded by the orientalist art and bric-a-brac that was required in period homes to certify bourgeois status.) In the long nineteenth century, art and biblical criticism came even closer to one another in the way they orientalized the Bible. Earlier, artists tended to portray biblical Israelites as if they were "Turks." Biblical scholars (who came on the scene later than the artists), as we have seen, took Arabs, instead, as their model. But – given the relative decline of the Ottoman government and greater western familiarity with, and imperial designs on, its Arab subjects – even in art the default sartorial representation of biblical Jews changed from "Turkish" to (Bedouin) "Arabic." On the heads of male Israelites in Christian art, the turban did not entirely disappear, but was often replaced by the flowing *kaffiyeh.*

The prime example of this is the best-selling illustrated Bible of the nineteenth century, by Gustave Doré (1832–1883). His images of biblical personages are ethnographically relatively faithful renderings of contemporary Arab costume in Palestine and beyond. The implicit supersessionism here as elsewhere, however, does not permit depicting Jesus himself as an Arab.[15] He always wears "classic" European garb. In fact, the rather amusing sequence of the *Ascension* (Figure 10.1) followed by the *Descent of the Spirit* (Figure 10.2) has Jesus' disciples dressed as Bedouin in the first and as European monks in the second. Having received the Spirit, it seems that the apostles also managed to supersede their identity as orientals.

Racial supersessionism

To recapitulate, the relationship between this oriental spirit and that of the Christian West came in the nineteenth century to be associated to a large extent (though never exclusively) with the relationship between an alleged Semitic and an alleged Aryan race. The development of the race concept here and elsewhere is closely tied to the development in the West of various forms of evolutionary thought. Within human society, evolutionist schemes represented the civilization of the ascendant West, with its Christian heritage, as the pinnacle of lawful historical processes. A new concept of time took hold, dubbed "mundane time" by Johannes Fabian. The term refers to a revised concept of time not as an abstract entity independent of cultural content, but as a sequence of "ages and stages," one following the other.[16]

Figure 10.1
Gustave Doré, *The Ascension*, woodblock engraving (Figure 223, *Doré Bible Illustrations*, ed. by Millicent Rose, New York, Dover, 1974)

Figure 10.2
Gustave Doré, *The Descent of the Spirit*, woodblock engraving (Figure 224, *Doré Bible Illustrations*, ed. by Millicent Rose, New York, Dover, 1974)

The weightiest example is the evolutionary scheme propounded by Hegel. Hegel posited several stages of religious civilization, each the property of a distinctive population. He classified Judaism and Islam together as "religions of the sublime": sublime in his view because they subordinated all reality to the concept of an external One God.[17] This was not a complement. Hegel explained that in the Jewish religion consciousness of the self was no more than an element of being conscious of divine power, i.e.

> my consciousness knows itself through and through as dependent, as unfree. The relationship [is that] of the servant to a Lord; the fear of the lord is what defines it. In any religion, *such as Judaism or Islam*, where God is comprehended only under the abstract category of the one, this human lack of freedom is the real basis, and humanity's relationship to God takes the form of a heavy yoke, of onerous service. True liberation is to be found in Christianity, in the Trinity.[18]

Elsewhere Hegel suggests that the proposition that there is only one God and "he is a jealous God who will have no other gods before him" is "the great thesis of the Jewish, of overall Arab religion of the western Orient and Africa."[19] Notice that Hegel speaks here of "Arab," not "Islamic" religion. He may be conceptualizing "Jewish" as an instance of "Arab," a usage that notably occurs, though some decades later, in Benjamin Disraeli's fiction.[20] At any rate, in Hegel's conception of history as one tremendous dialectic, major stages chart the evolution from self-alienating slavery to self-realizing citizenship, and the Jewish–Islamic stage occupies a stage lower than that of western Christianity.

Hegel's writing on the progress of the *Geist* from "Arabic" Judaism and Islam to Christian and "Germanic" Protestantism is racist in the cultural but not yet the biological sense. However, he was writing at a time when cultural racism and biological racism were already allied in contemporary debates about slavery, which connected skin color to one's cultural capacity to live free.[21] His evolutionary scheme of civilizations is implicitly a part of an effort to find independent justification for Northern European imperialism, which was on the surge during his lifetime.

Looked at specifically in the context of the relationship between Christianity and Judaism, Hegel's scheme was also a sort of secularization of the classic Christian attitude to the difference between the two religions, and between the Hebrew Old Testament and the Greek New: supersessionism. A supersessionist attitude does not reject the earlier stage as worthless. On the contrary, it sees it as essential, and may even romanticize it as glorious.

The Aryanization of Jesus

Some western Christians took this racial supersessionism to yet another degree, rejecting not only Judaism but to some extent also classic Christianity itself as a defunct stage in intellectual development, superseded by a higher western sensibility.

The influential French orientalist and author Ernest Renan (1823–1892) is probably the person who popularized the term "Semite" as referring to a racial grouping rather than just a language family. In his *Histoire générale et système comparé des langues sémitiques*, published in 1855,[22] the racialization of civilizational stages and their supersessionist interpretation is clear.

At times Renan seemed unsparing in his compliments. "It is the Semitic race," he would write, "which has the glory of having made the religion of humanity. Far beyond the confines of history, resting under his tent free from the taint of a corrupted world, the Bedouin patriarch prepared the faith of mankind."[23] Yet the *Histoire* abounds with apparent insults such as "The Semitic people lack curiosity almost completely" (10), "In general, the perception of nuances is deeply absent among the Semitic peoples" (11), "polygamy, consequence of an original nomadic way of life, has blocked among the Semites the development of all that we call society, and has formed a race that is exclusively virile, without flexibility or *finesse*" (11), "The military inferiority of the Semites is due to this total lack of ability for discipline or subordination" (14), or "Morality has always been understood by this race in a manner very different from ours" (15). Obviously, the admirable qualities of the Semites do not compare with "ours."

Shlomo Sand suggests that the young Renan who wrote the *Histoire générale et système comparé* with its negative judgments of the Semites had a change of heart later, which would account for his apparently contradictory, positive assessment.[24] But Renan never renounced the opinions made in this early tome. Rather than considering admiration and condemnation as a contradiction here, it is more useful – as it is in the case of orientalism in general – to think of consistent supersessionism. One can admire the contribution of a relatively primitive race to a civilization that would then be developed by a more advanced race. But from the vantage point of the more advanced the achievement of the less advanced, though valuable and praiseworthy, ultimately fails to arrive at the goals to which history has tended.

Renan was no more a biological racist than was Hegel: both posited a cultural/civilizational latter of how the human spirit developed, and not necessarily a physiological one. But that said, Renan's Aryan racism goes well beyond Hegel's. Monotheism is Renan's *bête noire*. He is able to write, for example, that "The intolerance of the Semitic peoples is a necessary consequence of their monotheism" (7). The attempt is openly to devalue the Semitic monotheism that underlies Christianity, and to identify instead with the Indo-European mind, which is based in a polytheist tradition but which, Renan thinks, is better suited than Judaism to evolve a rational religion.

> Research that is reflexive, independent, rigorous, courageous, philosophical – in a word, the search for truth – seems to have been the heritage of that Indo-European race that has, from deep India to the northern extremities of the West and of the North, from the remotest centuries to modern times, sought to explain God, man and the world by a rational system, and left behind, like rungs to different levels (*echelonnées aux divers degrés*) of its history, philosophical creations that have always and everywhere been submitted to the laws of logical development. But to the Semitic race belong those firm and certain intuitions that have been first to free the divinity of its veils and, without reflection or reasoning, attained the most purified religious form that antiquity has known.
>
> (3)

Later, in his famous *Life of Jesus* published in 1860, Renan made an effort to rescue Christianity from its Hebraic roots and to show whatever is left as the product of the non-Semitic, Aryan genius. Renan did travel to the Holy Land. He used his field work as the basis for describing Jesus as completely human, but also a human who rises radically above his oriental environment. Renan insisted that Jesus, a native resident of the ethnically mixed Galilee, was hardly a Semite.[25] Here, arguably, Jesus supersedes Christianity, which supersedes Judaism but remains marked by Semitism. More radical developments of this theme later included the hugely popular *Foundations of the Nineteenth Century* (1899) by Houston Chamberlain.[26]

The Aryanization of Jesus played an important role in establishing, during the long nineteenth century, the extra-European character of the imagined Semitic "race." As such, it was one of the cornerstones of the argument, by both friends and enemies of the Jews, for resettling them outside the Christian continent, preferably in their ancient oriental homeland. And, of course, it was a cornerstone on which the appalling history of anti-Semitism was built.[27] But the Aryanization of Jesus was itself a consequence of an earlier Arabization of the Bible, whose contours I have sketched out in this essay.

Notes

1 I am using the term "Orient" in the old-fashioned way, as did Edward Said in *Orientalism* (New York: Vintage Books, 1978, 2003). The focus is not on China or Japan but on Muslim West Asia and North Africa.
2 Ivan Davidson Kalmar, "Jesus Did Not Wear a Turban: Orientalism, the Jews, and Christian Art," in Ivan Davidson Kalmar and Derek Penslar (eds), *Orientalism and the Jews* (Hanover, NH: University Press of New England, 2005).
3 This is known from an inventory of his possessions taken at the time of his death: "Inventaris van de schilderijen mitsgaders meubilen en de huijsraet bevonden in den boedel van Rembrandt van Rijn," Amsterdam Municipal Archives, Register of Inventories B, DBK 364, fos. 29r–38v. Reproduced, with a translation, by Walter L. Strauss and Marjon van der Meulen, *The Rembrandt Documents* (New York: Abaris, 1979), item 1656/12.
4 J. Spence, *An Essay on Mr. Pope's Odyssey, in Five Dialogues* (London: Wilmot, 1737), pp. 214–215; Brian Hepworth, *Robert Lowth* (Boston: Twayne Publishers, 1978), pp. 26, 58–69, 68.
5 Robert Lowth, *Lectures on the Sacred Poetry of the Hebrews*. [Translated from the Latin by G. Gregory with the Notes of Professor Michaelis and Others] (New York: Garland Pub, 1971), p. 362.
6 Letter from Michaelis to Baron von Bernstorff of August 30, 1756, *Literarischer Briefwechsel von Johann David Michaelis*, ed. by Johann Gottlieb Buhle (Leipzig: Weidmannsche Buchhandlung, 1794–96, vol.1, p. 305, quoted here as translated in Jonathan M. Hess, *Germans, Jews and the Claims of Modernity* (New Haven, Conn.: Yale University Press, 2002), p. 76.
7 Michaelis, *Literarischer Briefwechsel*, pp. 302–304.
8 See the papers in Josef Wiesehöfer and Stephan Conermann (eds),*Carsten Niebuhr, 1733–1815, und seine Zeit* (Stuttgart: F. Steiner, 2002).
9 François René de Chateaubriand, *Travels to Jerusalem and the Holy Land*, Vol. 1, p. 1 (London: Henry Colburn, 1835); Alain Guyot, *Itinéraire de Paris à Jérusalem de Chateaubriand: L'invention du voyage romantique* (Paris: Presses de l'Universite Paris-Sorbonne, 2006).
10 Robert Blake, *Disraeli's Grand Tour: Benjamin Disraeli and the Holy Land, 1830–31* (London: Weidenfeld and Nicolson, 1982).
11 Maurice R. Hayoun, *Renan, la Bible et les Juifs* (Paris: Arléa, 2008).
12 Ignaz Goldziher, *Ignaz Goldziher and His Oriental Diary: A translation and psychological portrait*, edited by Raphael Patai (Detroit: Wayne State University Press, 1987).
13 See, for example, Nicholas Tromans and Rana Kabbani (eds), *The Lure of the East: British orientalist painting* (London: Tate, 2008); Kristian Davies, *The Orientalists: Western artists in Arabia, the Sahara, Persia and India* (New York: Laynfaroh, 2005); Christine Peltre, *Orientalisme* (Paris: Terrail, 2004).
14 Hélène Lafont-Couturier (ed.), *Gérôme & Goupil: Art et entreprise* (Bordeaux: Musée Goupil, 2000).
15 Kalmar, "Jesus did Not Wear a Turban."
16 Johannes Fabian, *Time and the Other: How anthropology makes its object* (New York: Columbia University Press, 2002), p. 22.
17 Ivan Kalmar, *Early Orientalism: Imagined Islam and the notion of sublime power* (London and New York: Routledge, 2012), ch. 8. "The sublime is not enough: The hard orientalism of G.F.W. Hegel," pp. 76–87.
18 Georg Wilhelm Friedrich Hegel, *Lectures on the Philosophy of Religion*, edited by Peter C. Hodgson, vol. 2 (Berkeley: University of California Press, 1987), p. 156. Emphasis added.
19 That, in any case, is the most literal translation; the German reads *großer Satz der jüdischen, überhaupt arabischen Religion des westlichen Morgenlandes und Afrikas.*

Peter C. Hodgson translates it as "the great thesis of Jewish and of Arab religion generally" (*Philosophy of Religion*, p. 129).

20 See Ivan Davidson Kalmar, "Benjamin Disraeli: Romantic Orientalist," *Comparative Studies of Society and History* 47, no. 2 (2005).

21 Audrey Smedley, *Race in North America: Origin and evolution of a worldview*, edited by Brian D. Smedley, 4th edn. (Boulder, CO: Westview Press, 2012).

22 Ernest Renan, *Histoire générale et système comparé des langues sémitiques*: 1. Ptie. 4th ed. (Paris: Lévy, 1863).

23 Ernest Renan, *The Life of Jesus* (New York: A.L. Burt, 1894), p. 70.

24 Shlomo Sand, *On the Nation and the "Jewish People"*, (New York: Verso, 2010), p. 25.

25 Ernest Renan, *The Life of Jesus,* p. 83.

26 Houston Stewart Chamberlain, *Foundations of the Nineteenth Century* (New York: H. Fertig, 1968).

27 Susannah Heschel, *The Aryan Jesus: Christian theologians and the Bible in Nazi Germany* (Princeton, N.J.: Princeton University Press, 2008).

Bibliography

Blake, Robert, *Disraeli's Grand Tour: Benjamin Disraeli and the Holy Land, 1830–31* (London: Weidenfeld and Nicolson, 1982).

Chamberlain, Houston Stewart, *Foundations of the Nineteenth Century* (New York: H. Fertig, 1968).

Chateaubriand, François René de, *Travels to Jerusalem and the Holy Land* (London: Henry Colburn, 1835).

Davies, Kristian, *The Orientalists: Western artists in Arabia, the Sahara, Persia and India* (New York: Laynfaroh, 2005).

Fabian, Johannes, *Time and the Other: How anthropology makes its object* (New York: Columbia University Press, 2002).

Goldziher, Ignaz, *Ignaz Goldziher and His Oriental Diary: A translation and psychological portrait*, edited by Raphael Patai (Detroit: Wayne State University Press, 1987).

Guyot, Alain, *Itinéraire de Paris à Jérusalem de Chateaubriand: L'invention du voyage romantique* (Paris: Presses de l'Université Paris-Sorbonne, 2006).

Hayoun, Maurice R., *Renan, La Bible et les Juifs* (Paris: Arléa, 2008).

Hegel, Georg Wilhelm Friedrich, *Lectures on the Philosophy of Religion*, edited by Peter C. Hodgson (Berkeley: University of California Press, 1987).

Hepworth, Brian, *Robert Lowth* (Boston: Twayne Publishers, 1978).

Heschel, Susannah, *The Aryan Jesus: Christian theologians and the Bible in Nazi Germany* (Princeton, N.J.: Princeton University Press, 2008).

Hess, Jonathan M., *Germans, Jews and the Claims of Modernity* (New Haven, Conn.: Yale University Press, 2002).

Kalmar, Ivan Davidson, "Jesus Did Not Wear a Turban: Orientalism, the Jews, and Christian art," in Ivan Davidson Kalmar and Derek J. Penslar (eds), *Orientalism and the Jews* (Hanover, NH: University Press of New England, 2005).

Kalmar, Ivan Davidson, "Benjamin Disraeli: Romantic Orientalist," *Comparative Studies of Society and History* 47, no. 2 (2005).

Kalmar, Ivan, *Early Orientalism: Imagined Islam and the notion of sublime power* (London and New York: Routledge, 2012).

Lafont-Couturier, Hélène (ed.), *Gérôme & Goupil: Art et enterprise* (Bordeaux: Musée Goupil, 2000).

Lowth, Robert, *Lectures on the Sacred Poetry of the Hebrews* (New York: Garland Pub, 1971).

Michaelis, Johann David, *Literarischer Briefwechsel von Johann David Michaelis*, edited by Johann Gottlieb Buhle (Leipzig: Weidmannsche Buchhandlung, 1794–96).
Peltre, Christine, *Orientalisme* (Paris: Terrail, 2004).
Renan, Ernest, *Histoire générale des langues sémitiques*, 4th edn. (Paris: Lévy, 1863).
Renan, Ernest, *The Life of Jesus* (New York: A.L. Burt, 1894).
Said, Edward, *Orientalism* (New York: Vintage Books, 1978, 2003).
Sand, Shlomo, *On the Nation and the "Jewish People"*, (New York: Verso, 2010).
Schultens, Albert, *Liber Jobi: Cum nova versione ad hebræum fontem et commentario perpetuo: in quo veterum & recentiorum interpretum cogitat præcipua expenduntur: Genuinus sensus ad priscum linguæ genium indagatur, atque ex filo, & nexu universo, argumenti nodus intricatissimus evolvitur* (Leyden: Johannes Luzac, 1737).
Schultens, Albert, *Oratio de linguæ arabicæ antiquissima origine, intima ac sororia cum lingua hebræa affinitate, nullisque seculis præflorata puritate* (Franeker: Willem Coulon, 1729).
Smedley, Audrey, *Race in North America: Origin and evolution of a worldview*, edited by Brian D. Smedley, 4th edn. (Boulder, CO: Westview Press, 2012).
Spence, J., *An Essay on Mr. Pope's Odyssey, in Five Dialogues* (London: Wilmot, 1737).
Strauss, Walter L. and Marjon van der Meulen, *The Rembrandt Documents* (New York: Abaris, 1979).
Tromans, Nicholas and Rana Kabbani (eds), *The Lure of the East: British orientalist painting* (London: Tate, 2008).
Wiesehöfer, Josef and Stephan Conermann (eds), *Carsten Niebuhr, 1733–1815, und seine Zeit: Beiträge eines interdisziplinären Symposiums vom 7.–10. Oktober 1999 in Eutin* (Stuttgart: F. Steiner, 2002).

11 Orientalism and bibliolatry

Framing the Holy Land in nineteenth-century Protestant Bible customs texts

Daniel Martin Varisco

> The Orient was almost a European invention, and has been since antiquity a place of romance, exotic beings, haunting memories and landscapes, remarkable experiences.
>
> Edward Said, *Orientalism*, 1979

> In a word, Palestine is one vast tablet whereupon God's messages to men have been drawn, and graven deep in living characters by the Great Publisher of glad tidings, to be seen and read of all to the end of time.
>
> William M. Thomson, *The Land and the Book*, 1859

This essay begins with a famous opening phrase from Edward Said's *Orientalism* not because there is a need to validate or dispute it, but because of what it leaves out. Indeed, Said's caveat of "almost" is telling, since his text describes only the "Orient" invented through the writings of Western writers. What is remarkable about Said's styling of the Orient as a form of politicized discourse is that the most important part of this invention is missing: the Orient invaded by Napoleon is also the Holy Land, the "vast tablet," as American missionary William Thomson phrases it, which brings the Bible to life. Napoleon may have initiated Western imperialist ambitions in this Holy Land, but the ultimate failure of his military mission stands in stark contrast to the perpetual array of Christian pilgrims, scholars and missionaries who visited this holiest of Holy Lands for Christians and Jews. Absent from Said's text is the genre that was most widely read in nineteenth-century Europe and America, specifically Holy Land travel texts that cited contemporary customs and manners of Arabs and other groups encountered as illustrations of Bible characters for popular consumption, especially among Protestants.

Said's genealogy of the discourse he identifies as Orientalism is a thoroughly academic one. Although Said speaks of biblical text and biblical lands as part of the "disparate realms" that this discourse encompasses, he fails to discuss any travel accounts by Protestant biblical scholars. Also missing in *Orientalism* is any reference to the vast number of texts about the nineteenth-century archaeological discoveries that were claimed to offer confirmation of Bible history.[1]

Said's oblique references to the Bible indicate he was unaware of the extent to which devout Protestant travelers believed accurate information about the local cultures and their history would validate their interpretations of the Bible against the nascent literary critique of biblical literalism. His discussion of the Sanskrit scholars Anquetil-Duperron and William Jones is preceded by the notion that the efforts of these two scholars were "made to invade the Orient by stripping it of its veils and also by going beyond the comparative shelter of the Biblical Orient."[2] This shelter, however, was where most of the travel was conducted in the nineteenth century, at a time when the so-called Bible lands were not under European control. It has been estimated that at least 2,000 individuals recorded their visits to Palestine alone between 1800 and 1870.[3] While the majority of these authors reflected a Christian bias against the dominant religion of Islam in the Holy Land, they also viewed the current inhabitants as a kind of "ethnographic" window for Biblical interpretation.

Said's sweeping generalization of a recognizable Orientalist discourse from Aeschylus to Karl Marx (and indeed to Henry Kissinger) has been criticized as inventing an "Orientalism in reverse."[4] To the extent that anyone teaching, writing about or researching the so-called Orient is part of this ideological trajectory, as Said claims, the usefulness of the concept is diminished. Two millennia-worth of texts, starting before an imaginary European space had evolved, reflect not only the universal prejudices of ethnocentrism but also a wide range of individual variation. The polemical claim that all of the "generous number of books" selected by Said represent a specific "Western style for dominating, restructuring, and having authority over the Orient" becomes through his mode of rhetoric an equally invented style stemming from the textual attitude of its author.[5] More than three decades after Said's important, but flawed, intellectual reconstruction of Orientalism, the discussion is shifting to fleshing out the nuances of an admittedly imagined East vs. West dichotomy. My aim in this essay is to analyze a secret sharer of Said's Orientalism, the bibliolatry of nineteenth-century Protestant Holy Land and Bible customs texts.

Said's text deals at length with the rhetorical conflict between Christians and Muslims, but ignores the significant cleavages that evolved within Europe after the Renaissance. From the sixteenth century on, Protestants and Catholics fought each other bitterly, even with the ominous presence of Ottoman armies in the Balkans. Far more Christians died in these internecine religious wars than at the hands of any invading Muslim armies. By the end of the eighteenth century another theological squabble pitted scholars of a new literary criticism of the Bible against orthodox defenders of sacred writ. Said admitted that his discussion would not do justice to "the fact that one of the impulses toward the study of the Orient in the eighteenth century was the revolution in Biblical studies," but he ignored the fact that popular interest in the so-called "Near Orient" as a window to interpreting the Bible generated far more writing and teaching than the few academic tomes produced.[6] Ironically, many of the Protestant travelers wrote about their observations of the geography, archaeology and current populations of the Bible lands in opposition to those biblical interpreters who relied on literary analysis.

The Bible and the Orient

> As an humble contribution to the department of Bible history, this work is offered to Christian readers, and especially to the young, with the prayer and the hope that it may not only contribute something towards a popular and attractive illustration of the Historical Scriptures, but create an increased interest in the sacred book given of God for the edification, enlightenment, and spiritual benefit of all nations and all ages.
>
> Alvan Bond in John Kitto, *An Illustrated History of the Holy Bible*, 1871

The quintessential "Oriental" text, at least for the part of the Orient that Said focuses on in his *Orientalism*, is the Bible. The interpretation of this essential Christian text was channeled through an official ecclesiastical structure up until the Protestant revolution. Martin Luther and John Calvin challenged the magisterial authority of the Catholic church and advocated reading of the Bible in the emerging vulgar dialects as opposed to solely in the Vulgate. As Calvin argued, "Scripture bears upon the face of it as clear evidence of its truth, as white and black do of their colour, sweet and bitter of their taste."[7] Access to the Bible, facilitated by Gutenberg's printing press, insured that interpretation was now open to any sincere Christian tuned in to the Holy Spirit. Luther's German edition of the Bible, first printed in 1534, followed the Middle English manuscripts attributed to John Wycliffe by more than a century. In 1611 the appearance of the newly authorized King James version made the Bible available to just about anyone.

Expanding the interpretive pool of Holy Scripture did not in itself constitute a shift in the orthodox belief that the texts were divinely inspired. Biblical literalism in historical matters stood largely unchallenged until the rise of literary criticism in the eighteenth century. Within Protestantism the authority of the text, coupled with the revolutionary notion of the priesthood of all believers, hindered the hegemony of an ecclesiastical system. The more extreme adherence to the primacy of the Bible led to what can justifiably be called a form of bibliolatry. Indeed, before the emergence of the historical and archaeological research that Said subsumed under the rubric of Orientalism, the Bible was seen as both a spiritual and a historical text. Those who believed in the inerrancy of the original biblical writings did not view their reverence of these texts as a form of worship. But when biblical exegetes refuse the idea that the canonized scriptures could contain historical or theological errors, then the revealed text must trump all human opinions and discoveries.

Is this Protestant bibliolatry, this theologic-centric companion to the ethnocentric bias Said suggests was inherent in Western writing about the Orient, simply a species of the discursive genus? Should Ernest Renan, who clearly rejected the idea of biblical inerrancy, be read in the same way as a defender of biblical accuracy? The genre of Bible lands writings is an apt category for Said's trenchant argument, especially given the widespread distribution of such texts and their impact in Protestant sermons and Sunday school lessons. At first glance such texts might seem a good fit, for they start with a bias. But the bias is not of a generic Western view of the Orient; rather, the guiding principle is that the observable customs of people living in Bible lands would serve to both validate and illuminate Scripture. In this sense the Orient of biblical interest was approached as a reality that God had preserved for his faithful followers to refute those in the West who challenge the Bible's divine authority. The Orient is not mute; the dead stones speak.[8]

Rather than provide a survey of the genre, I focus on two widely read nineteenth-century Protestant texts: Henry J. Van-Lennep's *Bible Lands: Their Modern Customs and Manners Illustrative of Scripture* (1875) and William Thomson's *The Land and the Book* (first published in 1859). Van-Lennep provides an encyclopedic compilation of contemporary customs in Bible lands illustrative of Scripture, and Thomson an entertaining armchair travel through the "land where the Word-made-flesh dwelt with men."[9] I have chosen the title for this essay quite deliberately: "Framing the Holy Land." Both texts include line drawings to illustrate the verbal commentary. This visual representation, hardly in the same colorful genre as Ingres' or Gérôme's odalisques, is an important part of the documentation. While Orientalist art has been the subject of analysis beyond the literary focus on Said, the circulation of popular art illustrating Bible customs has been ignored.[10] The illustrations in these texts are not in themselves neutral, but always the result of the artist's choice of what is to be represented and how it is to be represented. In this sense, the illustrations channel the romantic notions of readers with obvious subjective representations rather than the theoretically "objective" snapshot of a moment in reality afforded theoretically by a photograph.

Yet, there is another sense of "framing" here, the politically biased one that Said deconstructs in his *Orientalism*. I argue that the framing in these Bible lands texts goes beyond "political" in the usual sense of imperialist and colonialist ideologies, to the highly contested hermeneutics of biblical scholarship. For example, Lord Cromer clearly viewed the Egyptians whom he oversaw as inferior subjects and totally irrelevant for making sense of his history or affecting social change in Britain,[11] while William Thomson viewed the contemporary Bedouin, Jews, Christians and other groups as subjects that could teach him the truth about the lives of Bible characters. In this sense, the images constitute a double framing – that of the Westerner who has the ability to draw the people he sees as he wishes and, at the same time, does so to validate a specific interpretative approach to the Bible.

I view this double framing as an art, in the sense that Aristotle defines the art of rhetoric as a political act, and note that Aristotle suggests that the schema of politics are wide enough to include its aspiration through "ignorance, humbug or other human reasons."[12] The emphasis, in previous text-based studies of "Orientalism," on imperialism as a material quest via conquest is understandable, but there is more to reading between the lines of literary works than adding contrapuntal spoonfuls of slave-labor sugar. The humbug factor so prevalent in previous scriptural interpretation is no less relevant for understanding how a culturally Christian West has imagined an ascribed Muslim East. Visitors to the Holy Land not only returned to the land where their most sacred texts were created, but also saw it as the locus for continual recreation of meanings from an idealized past for a theologically satisfying present. Most visitors saw what they wanted to see, which is why their literal drawings are worth comparing to the rhetoric artfully deployed through words. Thus, it should not be surprising that the missionary author and artist Henry J. Van-Lennep describes his *Bible Lands* as a way "to throw light upon the Scriptures by tracing such a picture of Bible lands as lies before the mind of an intelligent Oriental."[13]

Drawing on a personal trip through the Holy Land is no more a substitute for reality than drawing that reality with pen and ink. The two Protestant Christian authors discussed here not only ground their arguments with a theological axe, but used an entire hermeneutic tool kit. It is worth remembering that these authors did not view Bible history as unique to a given people or land, but as the explanatory text for all of history: the past from Eden to the apostles, the present world of Satanic dimensions and the impending apocalyptic future at Armageddon. It hardly matters that their view of the world spanned less than four millennia back, since this was assumed to be the entire sum of world history. Bias pervades their writing, although at times the description of places, people and customs has value even today as documentation of conditions no longer observable.[14] My concern is not with "truth" either in the BIBLICAL or scientific sense, but with how the supposed "Truth" central to the religion of the authors was framed with real "Orientals" for those who read their texts and viewed their illustrations.

The numerous illustrated texts of biblical history and natural history were best sellers in the nineteenth century, thus literally shaping the imagination of readers on the places and inhabitants of the region. In an era before modern cinema and with limited photography, drawings were the main visual props for texts. Obviously, not everything could be illustrated, so the choice of drawings, whether embedded within the narrative or as separate plates, framed the visual experience. Unfortunately, the "textual attitude" of many critics researching the intellectual history of Oriental and Biblical Studies has biased the record by sidelining the persuasive power inherent in visual images alongside narratives. This is especially the case for the nineteenth-century Bible customs texts.

Accustomed to Bible lands

> How important, then, to the Biblical scholar is the study of the modern East, not only of its antiquities, intensely interesting as they are, but of the manners and customs of its present inhabitants!
>
> Henry J. Van-Lennep, *Bible Lands: Their Modern Customs and Manners Illustrative of Scripture*, 1875

In Europe the Higher Criticism of the Old Testament books by German scholars such as Johann Gottfried Eichhorn (1752–1827) marked a change in the approach to the Bible as a sacred text, but this in no way lessened the ardent interest of Christians apologists who viewed the Bible as literally true. During the nineteenth century a variety of archaeological discoveries in Bible lands brought aspects of biblical history to light. While many of these finds clearly illustrated biblical customs, conservative theologians also saw them as a modern confirmation of the historicity and accuracy of the Bible. The archaeologist's spade, I have argued elsewhere, served as a perfect tool for the rhetoric inherent in the apologist's stacked deck.[15] Inscriptions, potsherds and tumuli were only part of the interest in the biblical portion of the Orient. As noted in the quote above from Reverend Henry J. Van-Lennep, the "present inhabitants" of the Holy Land were even more important for the biblical scholar. Van-Lennep provided one of the most exhaustive (832 pages) compilations of contemporary customs said to be "illustrative of scripture." The popularity of the "Bible customs" genre, which included many of the travel accounts of ministers, missionaries and lay Christians, served as an antidote to both the Higher and Lower Criticism of the Bible. Thus, Van-Lennep has no doubt that the "remarkable reproduction of Biblical life in the East of our day is an unanswerable argument for the authenticity of the sacred writings."[16]

At first glance, it might be argued that this genre is little different from the overarching discourse of Orientalism posited by Said. While the bias of these Christian writers is clear, it flows more from a desire to better understand the revered text of their tradition than from a latent desire to denigrate or subjugate the people being studied. Because writers like Van-Lennep believed that current customs of the Arabs, in particular, had been preserved by God as a testimony to the truth of Scripture, these customs needed to be properly understood. While I hesitate to label the efforts of these texts as ethnography in the contemporary anthropological sense, Van-Lennep is proud of the fact that he "enjoyed unrivaled opportunities of intercourse with all classes of people."[17] Rather than using his text to criticize the "Orientals," Van-Lennep in several respects counters existing stereotypes of his day. Consider his rationale for recognizing how Muslims saw themselves: "On the other hand, we have not called the religion of Mohammed Mohammedanism, but Islam, its universal name in the East (not *Islamism*, nor the *religion* of Islam); and his followers not Mohammedans, but, as they call themselves, Muslims (not Mussulmans); Muslimin is the plural of Muslim."[18] To the extent that Van-Lennep believed that God had preserved these customs as a testimony, it was important to describe them as accurately as he could, starting with the proper terminology.

Van-Lennep's *Bible Lands* rests on first-person experience as a missionary in the Ottoman world as well as on information from earlier travel accounts. The author was born in Smyrna in 1815 and came to the United States in 1830, graduating from Andover Theological Seminary in 1837. He began his missionary work in 1838, bringing his young wife Mary, also a seminary graduate, to Constantinople in 1843; she died of dysentery within a year and he married twice again. He traveled extensively throughout the Holy Land, including Egypt, and was said to preach in five different Arabic dialects. In addition to his missionary work, Van-Lennep was an excellent artist. In 1862 he published twenty original chromolithographs of life in Ottoman Turkey.[19] Although he lost his sight in 1869, he was still able to publish the results of his travels, first in 1870, and then in his monumental *Bible Lands* (1875), passing away in 1889.

In postmodern hindsight Van-Lennep is to be faulted for assuming that there is a pure type of surviving people who practice identical customs to those mentioned in the Bible. He rejected the idea of interpreting Scripture by the Jewish customs of his day, reasoning that those who still live in the land are the closest to the originals:

> Since the descendants of the ancient Israelites have so far departed from the type of their ancestors as to offer but little aid to our imaginations in forming a correct idea of the Hebrew of Joshua's or David's time, may there not be remnants of the vanquished nations of Canaan still dwelling in the land, and retaining something of the physical characteristics, the dialect, or the manners of the ancestors?[20]

The author is very much a product of his time. He assumes that traditions would change but little in their natural environment and he is convinced that some of the local "races" have remained pure because of not marrying outside. Ironically, it is the "Arabs" who are thought to be the closest racially and culturally to the ancient Hebrews. "In their language, manners, and customs, however, these people [Arabs], more perhaps than any other, vividly remind us of the social life and political institutions of God's ancient people," he assures the reader.[21] As a result, Van-Lennep devotes barely a mention to the Ottoman Turks, whom he recognizes as "the present ruling race", and rightly notes that they refer to themselves as Osmanlis rather than the disparaging term "Turks".[22]

Despite his clear preference for certain peoples having the most authentic customs, Van-Lennep also follows the homogenizing rhetoric of the day in applying "Oriental" as a generic term. Thus, the actual information provided in his text is not always provided in context. When he writes: "Oriental women never show themselves unveiled before men other than their relatives"[23] or that the "Oriental theory is that love comes after marriage,"[24] the type of overarching Orientalist discourse criticized by Said is evident. Yet, such phrasing, no matter how problematic, should not obscure the points made in an entire passage. After the description of a full-length veil in some detail, differences are noted within Lebanon and between Lebanon and Egypt. "Let it now suffice to remark," concludes Van-Lennep, "that the large veil just described is almost exclusively worn by the inhabitants of the larger towns … "[25] A footnote informs the reader that this kind of veiling was also found in ancient Thebes. The presence of bias does not negate the nuance to be found in the narrative, although it clearly calls for caution in the sense that rigorous historiographic method demands.

Picturing the land and the Book

> Stop a moment. A city gate is a novelty to me, and I must examine in detail an apparatus so often mentioned in the Bible.
> Well, what is there in a mere gate to attract attention?
> Very little, perhaps, to one who has passed in and out daily for twenty years; but a hundred Biblical incidents connect themselves in my mind with gates.
> W. Thomson, *The Land and the Book*

A key element to Edward Said's Orientalism thesis is that Western narratives invariably treat the Orient as "all absence" so that "we must not forget that the Orientalist's presence is enabled by the Orient's effective absence."[26] But what about those texts in which the key objective is presence in the land in order to write the book and in which there is a sacred dimension of that land that transcends the author and those he or she describes. To illustrate my point, return with me to Reverend William M. Thomson, an American Protestant missionary who arrived in Syria in 1834 at age 28. Only fifteen years after the first American missionary activity here in 1819, the Ohio-born Thomson came with a twofold goal far removed from antebellum American foreign policy at the time. He certainly was commissioned to bring the Gospel as he knew it back to the land of its origin, but he also came to settle for the spiritual experience itself. He settled in for several decades, a choice made bittersweet by the death of his wife soon after his arrival. His goal, as stated at the very start of his book, was to walk through the Land of Promise not just as a pilgrim but in order to make the Holy Land his as a spiritual quest; this was fueled by a healthy curiosity.

It would be easy to dismiss Thomson's text as the bias of a missionary who only cared about the Holy Land for its biblical past. Yet, he is also an enthusiastic consumer of the contemporary culture. In visiting the Dome of the Rock and al-Aqsa Mosque in Jerusalem, he foregoes describing the architecture in detail, noting "I ran about, half wild with excitement, until I was quite exhausted."[27] Here was a Muslim shrine on a biblical site, but it was the present that most enamored Thomson. Ironically, it was the Christian "buffoonery and the profane orgies performed by the Greeks around the tomb on the day of the Holy Fire" that disgusted Thomson, rather than the religious devotions of the Muslims.[28] Near the beginning of his narrative, Thomson gives a straightforward description of Muslim prayer, noting that in large outside assemblies it can be "quite impressive."[29]

As a devotional travel guide for the English-speaking Christian, *The Land and the Book* does not leave out the people along the way. For Thomson the Holy Land is populated by people worthy of being saved, unlike the Canaanites of old, who were to be wiped out. The current customs of the people encountered along the author's excursions continually provide illustrations of Bible characters; this is a major theme for *The Land and the Book* and no doubt the most important aspect of its success as a text. Even the author's confrontation with "a troop of the most savage Bedawîn" provides a devotional lesson for the thousands of allusions to robbers in the Bible.[30] Yet Thomson lives to tell the story because he was under the protection of a guide from the tribe of an important shaykh noted for his "dignified manner and intelligence." For this Buckeye State Yankee, all Bedawîn are not the same. Some of the Bedawîn encountered, not surprisingly, fail to fit the author's *beau ideal* as living testimonies of the biblical patriarchs. "Pshaw!" he humphs, "the Bedawîn are mere barbarians – rough when rational, and in all else coarse and vulgar."[31] Yet Thomson as narrator adopts a contextual rationale that does not view the Bedouin as inferior by nature: "the ancient, generous customs of the Bedawîn were being corrupted by Turkish oppression."[32]

It would be a mistake to only read Thomson's text, since the original consumers were guided by the illustrations that framed the text from start to finish. The frontispiece, opposite the title page, draws the reader visually into a land with contemporary inhabitants; the scene is "Fords of the Jordan" (Figure 11.1) and shows a number of Arabs resting beside and bathing in the Jordan river. There are no Westerners yet in sight; in this sense the reality of the present culture is not denied or denigrated, since it is that very pristine and obviously imagined reality that is proclaimed as divine testimony to the sacred text. The presence of real Arabs is necessary, because a vacant landscape would not serve as a testimony.

In the 1901 edition of Thomson's text there are 135 illustrations; fifty of the scenes and objects show people. These include two maps and fourteen insert plates with wrappers; of the latter, twelve show contemporary people. The emphasis on inclusion of the people living in the Holy Land, especially in the insert plates, shows that their presence is central to the purpose of the text. Most of the illustrations show people going about their daily life. For example, the frequent biblical mention of grinding stones is illustrated with a contemporary scene (Figure 11.2).

The close portraits of a Syrian man and woman (Figure 11.3) do not exoticize but are meant to document typical dress, as in the manner of Edward Lane's well-known account of Egyptian life. Even the exotic scene of dancing girls (Figure 11.4) is tame for the genre. The two dancers are shown standing straight, with a male and a female musician seated in the background in what is clearly an outdoor format.

Figure 11.1 "Fords of the Jordan" (frontispiece in William H. Thomson, *The Land and the Book* (1901))

Figure 11.2 Women grinding at a mill (Thomson, p. 527)

"We see little to admire in their performances," reports the staid American missionary, lamenting that the dancing was "sometimes indecent" but at the same time appreciating that "the different sexes do not intermingle in those indecorous sports."[33] The ultimate aim of Thomson's travel book is to convince the reader that life in the Holy Land of his day provided divinely guided evidence of the truth of the Bible. The Bible could be trusted as theology because it could be verified as history through what the current inhabitants still practiced.

All Arabs present and accounted for

> In personal appearance the inhabitants of what are usually denominated Bible lands, probably offer a greater variety than those of any other part of the globe.
>
> Henry Van-Lennep, *Bible Lands*, 1875

The two texts examined here illustrate a genre of Orientalism that is as much a "secret sharer" of Edward Said's politically charged Orientalist discourse as

Figure 11.3a
Syrian gentlemen in full dress
(Thomson, pp. 116)

Figure 11.3b
Dress of Syrian or Egyptian lady
(Thomson, pp. 119)

anti-Semitism.[34] The authors carried with them an obvious bias as Christian missionaries devoted to a literal interpretation of the Bible as history. Their description should not be accepted as "objective" in the modern scientific and secular sense, although at times their commentary is sympathetic and avoids denigration. Each of the texts presents both the contemporary people of the Holy Land and the emerging historical evidence about biblical cultures as a divine sign for accepting the authenticity and truth of the Bible. In this sense Said is correct in arguing that "what the Orientalist does is to confirm the Orient in his readers' eyes."[35] But the issue is not simply one of creating an imaginary, which is hardly unique to any culture or its intellectuals, but the purpose for imagining an "Orient" at all. Observable peasant customs trump the literary characters of *Arabian Nights* dimension.

For Said, the "Orient" of Gustave Flaubert and of Lord Cromer connects only in the imagination, fueled by the words left on the pages of their texts. A poet and a colonial administrator may share embedded cultural prejudices, but the nature of their encounter and the incentive for commenting on it are certainly not the same. Similarly, the numerous missionaries and pilgrim travelers who moved about Palestine during Ottoman rule had a different motive for writing their texts than did Nerval and Burton, whom Said places in the service of European imperialism. For writers in the Bible customs genre the Orient was not the political issue that it was for the administrative and military officials. Nor, I argue, was the primary aim to denigrate and look down upon the contemporary people living in the region. If we simply stop our analysis when we encounter obvious examples of cultural bias, there is little to be learned from the texts or about the reception of these texts when they were published. What is unique about the texts described here is that the continued presence of local inhabitants, notably the Arabs and Bedouin, is necessary for them to serve as a symbol of divine authority.

For William Thomson the landscape must be peopled with individuals whose daily acts illustrate the kind of biblical custom which "confounds us simple Americans."[36] Thus, he repeats over and over again a common refrain: "A custom prevails among the Bedawîn Arabs, and especially those around the Hûleh, which illustrates this whole subject."[37] Whether grinding wheat, making a pot, building a house or any of the normal processes of social life, there was an expectation that what contemporary "Arabs" did provided a key to illustrate biblical customs. It is the presence of Arabs that validates Thomson's ability to interpret the Bible. Whatever regard he has for certain groups he encounters, admiring some and despising others, he would not be interested in removing the contemporary Arabs from the scene. As a seasoned missionary he was well aware of the difficulty of converting the local inhabitants, especially Muslims, to Protestant Christianity. Yet their active presence, which he recognizes is undergoing change, remains vital to his spiritual mission.

The "presence" of Arabs in these texts is, of course, an imposed one, not an indigenous narration, although local folklore can be found.[38] This is true for any narrative, which can only represent a presence. The significant issue becomes the kind of presence articulated. The personal bias of cultural superiority for the authors is evident, but at the same time there is an admiration of even the most mundane contemporary customs. To the extent that the Bible frames their entire worldview, the Holy Land is less an "Orient" to be conquered or recreated in a Western image than a spiritual laboratory for expounding and defending the faith. Thus, by inclusion of the local inhabitants in most of the illustrations, readers (and thus viewers) are guided to recognize the importance of the assumed cultural continuity. Contrast this to the exploitation of the Americas, where the indigenous peoples were denied humanity and literally removed from the landscape through slavery, disease and outright slaughter.

Do any "real" Arabs appear in these texts or are they simply the sanitized images that fit the hermeneutic of the authors? It is important to remember that this is not a modern genre proposing, as in Malinowskian ethnography, to

Figure 11.4 Dancing Girls (Thomson, p. 555)

provide the "native point of view." Both Van-Lennep and Thomson are quite conscious of the differences in social and ethnic groups encountered. Thomson, for example, has no qualms in calling out scoundrels and thieves among the Bedawîn, but he also encounters individuals, including imams, whom he fully respects. To the extent that these authors assumed that the customs were kept intact by God as a sign of the authenticity of the Bible, the main concern was finding parallels with biblical customs that often made little sense in King James English. Given the emergence of archaeological data, which initially seemed to support biblical history, it is not surprising that the authors were confident in such a loaded presupposition.

So the answer is no; the Arabs encountered are presented as real but they do not speak for themselves. But when do real people ever speak for themselves? Is a biographical text in Arabic more "real" because it is written by an Arab author in Arabic? Once it is accepted that all textual description, and most visual documentation, is re-presenting, it is obvious that any published presence must be second hand. It is easy to find examples of bias in the Bible customs genre, but if some level of bias is inevitable the question becomes less its mere presence than the trajectory of its role in shaping opinions. The reader of Thomson or Van-Lennep would not be challenged to send the troops and take political control of the region and its resources, nor would they dismiss the local inhabitants as terrorists to be denied humanity. The key assumption is that God has preserved customs in the quotidian existence of current inhabitants as a sign, as part of the divine plan for their own lives. Such apologetic requires real Arabs to be present, not in the role of Canaanites occupying the Promised Land, but as evidence divinely provided to counter the growing rationalist attacks on scripture from within Western intellectual tradition.

The texts by Thomson and Van-Lennep provide a number of accurate details and positive comments on Islam. In his tour of the Temple Mount in Jerusalem, Thomson notes that "The Moslems have become suddenly very fanatical in regard to this holy Harem," but he observes that this is "owing in part to the injudicious behavior of travellers."[39] He further remarks how the "old sheikh of the harem treated us with great respect, showing everything about the Mosque without reserve, and allowing us afterward to ramble as we pleased in the vaults below, and all over the area above, without any surveillance whatsoever." Van-Lennep provides a description of Islamic shrines and mosques that is devoid of cultural denigration, although he clearly wishes that Muslims would convert to Christianity.[40] He provides a full-page print of the ka'ba in Mecca and a scene of Muslims at prayer (Figure 11.5). I focus on this image as a visual counterpoint to the condescending Orientalist art of Gérôme which graces the cover of Said's *Orientalism*.[41] In this black-and-white graphic there is no voyeuristic gaze, no hint of sexual impropriety, no denigration of the act of worship. Four men in various positions in the prayer ritual are shown in an ornate mosque interior. This and the other visual representations of Islam draw attention to the reality of the present in the Holy Land.[42]

After three decades of debate over the nature of an East/West divide, it is time to forge a path out of the rhetorical quagmire in which most discussion of Orientalism in Western scholarship has been mired. Today, the preponderance of contemporary academic scholarship, despite the partisan political views of individual scholars, does not operate on the basis of an attainable and unassailable objectivity, nor do I believe that the best scholars of the past were as dogmatic as some excerpts from their writings might suggest. Critical scholarship, and I can think of no other kind worthy of being called scholarship, seeks to advance understanding based on available information and not to hermetically seal interpretation as dogma. May we all be liberated from the dogma-eat-dogma mentality where *ad hominem* arguments inevitably sink to the level of *ad nauseam* rhetorical whining. Rhetoric is indeed a political art, no matter who is doing the framing, but it is well to remember that it is primarily an art of persuasion. And in the final analysis, despite the inevitable disagreements, persuasion is the *raison d'être* for all texts, no matter the extent of their bias.

Figure 11.5 "The mihrab, pulpit, and candlestick in the mosk" (Van-Lennep, p. 719)

Notes

1 Edward Said, *Orientalism* (New York:Vintage Books, 1979), p. 4.
2 Ibid., p. 76.
3 Yehoshua Ben-Arieh, "The Geographical Exploration of the Holy Land," *Palestine Exploration Quarterly*, 1972, p. 83. An early, but comprehensive, bibliography of travel accounts of Palestine is provided by Reinhold Röhricht, *Bibliotheca Geographica Palaestinae* (Berlin: H. Reuther's, 1890).
4 Said, *Orientalism*, p. 76; Sadiq Al-'Azm, "Orientalism and Orientalism in Reverse," in Jon Rothschild (ed.), *Forbidden Agendas: Intolerance and Defiance in the Middle East* (London: Saqi, 1984), pp. 349–376. Al-'Azm's essay was first published in *Khamsin*, no. 8, 1981, pp. 5–26 and is also reprinted in Alexander L. Macfie (ed.), *Orientalism: A Reader* (New York: NYU Press, 2000), pp. 217–238.
5 Said, *Orientalism*, pp. 2–3. I published a survey of the debate over Said's Orientalism in my *Reading Orientalism: Said and the Unsaid* (Seattle: University of Washington Press, 2007).
6 Said, *Orientalism*, p. 17.

7 John Calvin, "Institutes of the Christian Religion," in A.D. Galloway (ed.), *Basic Readings in Theology* (Cleveland: Meridian Books, 1964), p. 166.

8 Quoting the Biblical prophet Habbakuk, William Thomson (*The Land and the Book; or, Biblical Illustrations Drawn from the Manners and Customs, the Scenes and Scenery of the Holy Land*, London: T. Nelson & Sons, 1901, p. 64) said: "The stone cries out of the wall, and the beam out of the timber will answer. We only need to know how to put them to the question."

9 Thomson, *The Land and the Book*, p. 1.

10 Said's approach was applied uncritically to the fine arts by Linda Nochlin, "The Imaginary Orient", *Art in America*, no. 71, May 1983, pp. 118–131, 186–191. For a more nuanced survey of Orientalist art, see John M. MacKenzie, *Orientalism: History, Theory and the Arts* (Manchester: Manchester University Press, 1995) and Roger Benjamin, *Orientalist Aesthetics: Art, Colonialism, and French Africa, 1880–1930* (Berkeley: University of California Press, 2003).

11 See Said, *Orientalism*, pp. 36–42 for his analysis of Cromer as an archetypal Orientalist.

12 Aristotle, *The Art of Rhetoric*, trans. H.C. Lawson-Tancred (London: Penguin Books, 1991), p. 75.

13 Henry J. Van-Lennep, *Bible Lands: Their Modern Customs and Manners Illustrative of Scripture* (New York: Harper & Brothers, 1875), p. 7.

14 In his study of the twentieth-century folklorist Tawfiq Canaan, who also accepted the notion that Palestinian folklore was a reflection of Biblical customs, Salim Tamari ("Lepers, Lunatics and Saints: The Nativist Ethnography of Tawfiq Canaan and his Jerusalem Circle", *Jerusalem Quarterly*, no. 20, 2004, p. 29), observes: "These essentialist assumptions did not prevent Canaan and his circle from producing an ethnographic corpus that was rich in empirical detail and textured in the manner it examined regional variations in peasant lore all over Palestine." It is the quality of the observer and not just the specific assumptions held that needs to be assessed in judging the value of the data.

15 Daniel Martin Varisco, "The Archaeologist's Spade and the Apologist's Stacked Deck: The Near East through Conservative Christian Bibliolatry", in Abbas Amanat and Magnus T. Bernhardsson (eds), *The United States and the Middle East: Cultural Encounters* (New Haven: YCIAS Working Paper Series, 2002), pp. 57–116.

16 Van-Lennep, *Bible Lands*, p. 5.

17 Ibid., p. 6.

18 Ibid., p. 7.

19 Idem., *The Oriental Album: Twenty Illustrations, in Oil Colors, of the People and Scenery of Turkey* (New York: Anson D.F. Randolph, 1862). These include two scenes of Jewish life in the Ottoman Empire, "A Turkish Effendi", "Armenian Lady (at home)", "Turkish and Armenian Ladies (abroad)", and "Turkish Scribe".

20 Van-Lennep, *Bible Lands*, p. 341.

21 Ibid., p. 351.

22 Ibid., pp. 373–374.

23 Ibid., p. 537.

24 Ibid., p. 539.

25 Ibid., p. 538.

26 Said, *Orientalism*, p. 208.

27 Thomson, *The Land and the Book*, p. 688.

28 Ibid., p. 679.

29 Ibid., pp. 24–25. In describing a typical prayer sequence, he states: "There is certainly an air of great solemnity in their modes of worship, and, when performed by a large assembly in the mosques, or by a detachment of soldiers in concert, guided in their genuflections by an imam or dervish, who sings the service, it is quite impressive" (p. 25). After noting that not all this ceremony should be interpreted as "hollow-hearted

hypocrisy", he exclaims: "What opposite conclusions different persons can and do draw from the same premises!"

30 Thomson, *The Land and the Book*, p. 369.
31 Ibid., p. 255.
32 Ibid., p. 369.
33 Ibid., p. 556.
34 See Said, *Orientalism*, p. 27.
35 Ibid., p. 65.
36 Thomson, *The Land and the Book*, p. 102.
37 Ibid., p. 105.
38 An example would be the two appendices in Van-Lennep, *Bible Lands*, pp. 813–816, on proverbs and translation of an Arab poem.
39 Thomson, *The Land and the Book*, p. 687.
40 Van-Lennep, *Bible Lands*, pp. 714–725.
41 See the discussion on the cover art in my *Reading Orientalism*, pp. 24–27.
42 An exception is the image of "Self-Torture of Religious Devotee" (Van-Lennep, *Bible Lands*, pp. 765, 769), but Van-Lennep notes that these frenzied practices are also found among Christians and Druze, not just Muslim dervishes. Even here the example is said to illustrate the blood-letting of the prophets of Baal in 1 Kings xviii: 28.

Bibliography

Al-'Azm, Sadiq, "Orientalism and Orientalism in Reverse," in Jon Rothschild (ed.), *Forbidden Agendas: Intolerance and Defiance in the Middle East* (London: Saqi, 1984), pp. 349–376.

Aristotle, *The Art of Rhetoric*, trans. H.C. Lawson-Tancred (London: Penguin Books, 1991).

Ben-Arieh, Yehoshua, "The Geographical Exploration of the Holy Land", *Palestine Exploration Quarterly*, no. 104, 1972, pp. 81–92.

Benjamin, Roger, *Orientalist Aesthetics: Art, Colonialism, and French Africa, 1880–1930* (Berkeley: University of California Press, 2003).

Calvin, John, "Institutes of the Christian Religion" in A.D. Galloway (ed.), *Basic Readings in Theology* (Cleveland: Meridian Books, 1964), pp. 164–186.

Kitto, John, *An Illustrated History of the Holy Bible* (Social Circle, Georgia: E. Nebhut, 1871).

Lane, Edward, *An Account of the Manners and Customs of the Modern Egyptians* (London: Murray, 1860).

Macfie, Alexander (ed.), *Orientalism: A Reader* (New York: NYU Press, 2000).

MacKenzie, John M., *Orientalism: History, Theory and the Arts* (Manchester: Manchester University Press, 1995).

Nochlin, Linda, "The Imaginary Orient", *Art in America*, no. 71, May 1983, pp. 118–131, 186–191.

Röhricht, Reinhold, *Bibliotheca Geographica Palaestinae* (Berlin: H. Reuther's, 1890).

Said, Edward, *Orientalism* (New York: Vintage Books, 1979).

Tamari, Salim, "Lepers, Lunatics and Saints: The Nativist Ethnography of Tawfiq Canaan and his Jerusalem Circle", *Jerusalem Quarterly*, no. 20, 2004, pp. 24–43.

Thomson, William H., *The Land and the Book; or, Biblical Illustrations Drawn from the Manners and Customs, the Scenes and Scenery of the Holy Land* (London: T. Nelson and Sons, 1901).

Van-Lennep, Henry J., *Bible Lands: Their Modern Customs and Manners Illustrative of Scripture* (New York: Harper & Brothers, 1875). Online pdf at http://www.archive.org/search.php?query=creator%3A522Van-Lennep%2C%20Henry%20John%2C%20 1815-1889%22.

Van-Lennep, Henry J., *The Oriental Album: Twenty Illustrations, in Oil Colors, of the People and Scenery of Turkey* (New York: Anson D.F. Randolph, 1862). Online at the NYPL Digital Library: http://digitalgallery.nypl.org/nypldigital/dgkeysearchdetail.cfm?trg=1&strucID=112066&imageID=82944&total=13333&num=100&word=div_id%3Aha&s=1&notword=&d=&c=&f=&k=)&1Word=&1Field=&sScope=images&sLevel=&sLabel=NA&imgs=20&pos=110&e=r.

Varisco, Daniel Martin, "The Archaeologist's Spade and the Apologist's Stacked Deck: The Near East through Conservative Christian Bibliolatry," in Abbas Amanat and Magnus T. Bernhardsson (eds), *The United States and the Middle East: Cultural Encounters* (New Haven: YCIAS Working Paper Series, 2002), pp. 57–116.

Varisco, Daniel Martin, *Reading Orientalism: Said and the Unsaid* (Seattle: University of Washington Press, 2007).

Part IV
Voyage

12 The Orient's medieval 'Orient(alism)'

The *Riḥla* of Sulaymán al-Tájir

Nizar F. Hermes

And whoever sees himself really free.
Let him experience the meaning of the word!
Away from home, I spent most of my life,
Witnessing wonders of ancient times.
My adventurous soul finds peace in alien things.
Not in the comfort of the known world.
For indeed we are people of lands and seas,
Amassing poll taxes from Egyptians and Chinese.
In Tangiers, indeed in all corners, our horses race.
If bored in a space, we leave it for another place.
Muslim and non-Muslim lands are at our hands,
In summers we resort to snow.
In winters the oasis we enjoy![1]

Abu Dulaf (d. 1012)

Nabil Matar is not totally wrong when he deplores the fact that Anthony Pagden's voluminous collection of articles published under the title *Facing Each Other: The World's Perception of Europe and Europe's Perception of the World* fails to include "a single entry about the perception of or by any of the civilizations of Islam".[2] He has, however, overlooked a "single" exception: it is Jacques Le Goff's reference to the medieval Arabs' perception of the Indian Ocean in his seminal article "The Medieval West and the Indian Ocean: An Oneiric Horizon".[3] For the erudite Le Goff, medieval Westerners' ignorance of the Indian Ocean and India in particular was in part the result of a negative Arabic influence. To the medieval Arabs, Le Goff states, "it is possible that the Indian Ocean was a forbidden and unknown world".[4] This lack of information about the Indian Ocean on the part of medieval Arabs, Le Goff goes on to observe, did nothing but reinforce the "illusions" of medieval Western writers and merchants who "sometimes turned to them for information."[5] Fortunately, Le Goff's statement does not represent the scholarly attitude of the vast majority of Western Arabists, many of whom have made efforts that have been instrumental in both introducing and safeguarding the rich heritage of medieval Arab-Islamic geo-cosmographical, historiographical, and travel literature.[6]

It would hardly be an overstatement to say that during their own age of discovery and expansion, poetically captured by the aforementioned lines of the poet/traveler Abu Dulaf, medieval Muslims showed an enormous interest in their own 'Orient' especially after the conquest of the region of *al-sind* (modern Pakistan) in 711 by Muhammad ibn Qasim.[7] "By the 8th Century," Peter Boxhall notes, "Arabian seafarers were traveling frequently, in the wake of the great Islamic incursion by land into the Sind Province, and by sea along the Malabar Coast, to far-distant '*As-Sin*' [China]."[8] In a general sense, outside the borders of *dar al-islam*, it was mainly *al-hind* (India) and *al-sin* (China) that drew the closest attention of Muslim politicians, geographers, merchants, and travelers alike.[9] Although this "Orient" was predominantly conceived as "an actual space", to use Iain Macleod Higgins's phrase, some elements of "the imaginary and the conceptual" were unquestionably present, without, however, attaining the imaginary and the conceptual Orient "envisioned, elaborated, and encountered in the corpus of western writing about the East."[10] Indeed, in addition to the economic, political, and religious motives behind the interest in *al-sharq* (East), the Indo-Chinese inspiration of *al-'ajib*/*al-gharib* (the marvelous/the unfamiliar) made the Indian Ocean rather a desirable destination and not a "taboo", as Le Goff has assumed.[11]

The interest of Muslims in the East dates back to the early days of Islam wherein "the caliphs, were probably for political reasons, interested in acquiring information about different countries, their inhabitants and special features of their lands."[12] It was with the Abbasids, however, that this interest reached its historical climax through the expedition sent to India by Yahya ibn Khalid al-Barmaki (d. 805), the competent *wazir* of Harun al-Rashid. According to Muhammad Zaki Hassan, the expedition was the direct result of the "intellectual awakening and frequent religious debates encouraged by the Abbasid caliphs", which, in his own words, "stimulated an urge in the hearts of the Arabs to make enquiries and researches into the religion of the Hindus."[13] Seen in this light, this expedition to study the East's own East, in spite of the almost ten centuries that separate them, conjures up to some extent the French expedition to Egypt in 1789. The outcome of this older nonmilitary expedition was an intriguing report "that covered various arts, skills and scientific achievements of the Indians and a detailed account of the castes and religious practices."[14]

In this same period, an independent traveler by the name of 'Abd Allah Muhammad ibn Ishaq made his way as far as Khmer (Cambodia), where he lived for two years. Although Ishaq's report is mostly lost, he is credited with leaving a number of valuable comments not only on the ancient kings of India but also on Ceylon and Khmer that were used by later historians and geographers.[15] Years later, the Abbasid polyglot/translator Sallam al-Turjuman is reported to have reached the Great Wall of China.[16]

In his geographical encyclopedia *Kitab al-Masalik wa'l-Mamalik*, Ibn Khordadbeh reported, on the authority of al-Turjuman himself, that the latter left for China at the request of the caliph al-Wathiq (d. 847), who was terrified by a nightmare in which he saw a hole in *al-sudd* (the dam) that the Quranic character *dhu al-qarnayn* is said to have built to prevent the apocalyptic nations of *ya'juj wa ma'juj* (the biblical Gog and Magog) from invading and ravaging the adjacent territories.[17] Although one cannot totally exclude the story of the nightmare, Malallah has argued convincingly that this nightmare was rather used by al-Wathiq as a pretext to expose his political and military power by showing that he could reach any corner he wished to reach.[18]

In defense of the historical accuracy of the trip against the doubt leveled by some Western Arabists—such as Sprenver, Grigorev, and mainly Minorski, who described al-Turjuman's trip as "a wondertale interspersed with three or four geographical names"—Zaki Muhammad Hassan has argued that what people should doubt is rather some of the mythical descriptions found in certain reports on the trip and whether Sallam reached the Great Wall of China or just stopped in modern Dagestan. As pointed out by Hassan, this is the position espoused by the French Arabist Carde Vaux, who, although he defended ardently the authenticity of the trip, used to argue that al-Turjuman did not see the Great Wall of China, his prime objective.[19] Referring to Arabists such as De Goje, Tomashek, and Vasmev, who confirmed the authenticity of the trip, Malallah has asserted that the very fact that Ibn Khordadbeh (who was one of the closest advisers of al-Wathiq) mentioned that he heard directly much of the report from his friend al-Turjuman appears to prove that the latter had indeed embarked on such a trip.[20]

This fascination with India and China manifested itself in the publication in 916 of *Silsilat al-Tawarikh* (Chain of Histories), the first 'anthology' of Arabic accounts of India and China, by Abu Zayd al-Hasan al-Sirafi (d. 950), who most likely traveled to both countries.[21] Because he was also "an ardent collector of information from travelers visiting in India and China and other parts of the East",[22] al-Sirafi (after exhaustive editing and correcting) incorporated in *Silsilat al-Tawarikh* a number of accounts and reports of Muslim travelers, sailors, and merchants who had visited India and China.[23] The most interesting of these accounts is *Akhbar al-Sin wa'l-Hind* (Account of China and India), still attributed by the majority of Middle Eastern scholars to Sulayman al-Tajir. Al-Tajir's account of China and India, according to Hassan, is not only one of the world's most interesting and authentic texts concerning medieval India and China but also "the earliest known travel diary of an Arab that has come to us."[24, 25]

Little is known about Sulayman al-Tajir other than his own text and the fact that he was, as the second part of his name confirms, a *tajir*, that is to say a merchant. Indeed, what strikes the reader most on reading the opening pages of *Akhbar al-Sin wa-'l-Hind* is the remarkable reticence of the author on the subject of his own life and career during his journey in the East. Most probably, however, like his editor Abu Zayd al-Sirafi, he was from the coastal city of Siraf. From there, as mentioned by some reports, he sailed across the Indian Ocean before reaching India and journeying into China. Al-Tajir's account is a mine of sociocultural, religious, political, and economic information about India and China in the ninth century. In fact, from the beginning of his journey the merchant seems to abandon his initial trade and become a keen observer and a preoccupied explorer who finds himself captivated not only by the spectacle of the Oriental Other he will soon meet but also by the authentic *'aja'ib/ghara'ib* (marvels/wonders) of the Indian Ocean.

The opening pages of the account are full of rich maritime information about "this sea", as he calls it. It is the detailed and fascinating description of the sperm whale that proved the most valuable in his entire account of the Indian Ocean. "In this sea is found a fish that appears occasionally," he tells us in his opening paragraph. "It has herbs and shells growing on its back. The captains of boats, sometimes, lay anchor against it thinking it to be an island, but when they realize their mistake they set sail from it."[26] Without the necessity of calling (him) Ishmael, for certainly he was, *Moby Dick* must have loomed large in the oceans of our memory, conjuring up the harpoons of Queequeq, the destructive revenge of Captain Ahab, and more importantly *le plaisir* of navigating through foreign texts.

Perhaps it is not going too far to state that the remainder of the description of al-Tajir's factual Moby Dick, however, appears too classical to fit into the novelistic structure, if not the colonialist discourse, of Herman Melville, for it is Longinian in essence. Capturing the Muslim sailors' feelings of the "sublime" whenever they encounter the sublime sperm whale, al-Tajir writes:

> Sometimes, when this fish spreads out one of its two wings on its back, it appears like the sail of a ship. When it raises its head above water, you can see it as an enormous object. Sometimes it blows out water from its "mouth," which resembles a lofty tower. Whenever the sea is calm and the fish gather together, it collects them round with the help of its tail. Then it opens its mouth and the fish dive into its belly as if diving into a well. The boats sailing on this sea are scared of it, so during the nightfall they blow the trumpets resembling those of the Christians, for they are afraid that it might lean heavily against their boat and cause it to be drowned.[27]

The "un-Ahabian" al-Tajir was fully aware of the tragic doom of chasing the sperm whale. Hence, he opted for a comic Sindbadian adventure that uses the sea as a means and never an end per se. Apart from the rhapsodic reference to the cannibalistic Andaman, to which we will return later, the awkward opening of *Akhbar al-Sin wa-'l-Hind* resembles closely the medieval and Renaissance Western *isolari* (catalog of islands), especially when al-Tajir consumes many pages to list clumsily the numerous islands of the Indian Ocean. Fortunately, however, with the approach to the nearest Indian shore, al-Tajir embarks on a rather pleasant Oriental journey wherein he gratifies the curious reader with a mine of information about ninth-century India and China.

Throughout the remaining pages, al-Tajir engages in a comparative description of the religious, social, political, economic, and cultural conditions of the Indians and the Chinese. He has proved particularly keen in exploring and mapping the topos of difference and sameness between these two non-Muslim peoples most of the time, as his comments are without polemical addition or omission. Yet, at other times, he is quick in reporting with implied disapproval, but without much moralizing, what he deems to be religious aberrations and social vices that utterly contradict his own religion and his cultural traditions.

It goes almost without saying that al-Tajir, as is the habit of the "religious minded" Arabs to use Zaki's phrase, seems to be particularly interested in Indian religions and sects.[28] Relatively aware of the differences among the major Hindu castes and main sects such as the Brahmans, Samanis, and Buddhists, al-Tajir (unlike more scholarly medieval Muslim writers on Indian religions) does not explain in detail many of the Hindu tenets and beliefs. Nevertheless, he has filled his account with valuable information on common Hindu religious and social practices, rituals of death, marriage, asceticism, women, justice, and politics. In several important respects, the most salient aspect of his commentary is the comparative mode that dominates the entire account. This can be seen in the traveler's thorough analysis of a number of similarities and differences between the Indians and the Chinese. These latter—in spite of their "superiority" in matters of education, culture, and civilization—in general are, religiously speaking, depicted by al-Tajir as "blind" followers of the Indians. This apparently led to the existence of several sociocultural similarities between the two otherwise different peoples.

In Hindu Serendib (Sri Lanka), which he describes as "the last of the islands and one of the lands of India", al-Tajir informs us that when a Hindu king dies and before his cremation, a woman engages in a number of sacramental rituals wherein she pronounces a moving *tadhkira*, a type of a short but very meaningful admonition on the ineluctability of death. After the cremation, she repeats the same admonition for three consecutive days.[29] Significant too is al-Tajir's accurate exposition of the Hindu practice of *sati*, or the burning of wives with the bodies of their dead husbands. Shunning hasty conclusions and easy generalizations, he proves himself objective in emphasizing the fact that Hindu wives have the final decision when it comes to this highly valued Hindu practice. Evidently, he could have easily made us believe that all Hindu wives must be burnt along with their dead husbands.

Centuries later, this same detail is highlighted almost verbatim by Marco Polo (d. 1324) and Ibn Battuta (d. 1369), the world's best-known globe-trotters: "When a man is dead and his body is being cremated," Marco Polo tells us, "his wife flings herself into the same fire and lets herself be burnt with her husband. The ladies who do this are highly praised by all. And I assure you that there are many who do as I have told you."[30] Similarly, Ibn Battuta notes, "The burning of the wife after her husband's death is regarded by them [Indians] as a commendable act, but is not compulsory, for when a widow burns herself her family acquires a certain prestige by it and gains a reputation for fidelity." Soon, however, he emphasizes the enormous social pressure on all women to practice the *sati*, for, as he concludes, "a widow who does not burn herself dresses in coarse garments and lives with her own people in misery, despised for her lack of fidelity."[31] It should be mentioned that, at least in this religious cult of burial and self-immolation, the Hindus have not changed much between the time al-Tajir visited India in the ninth century and the time Marco Polo and Ibn Battuta were there. Even more interesting is this rare medieval moment of agreement among two Mashriqi and Maghribi Muslims and a Euro-Christian on the crucial issue of religious Otherness.

Among the several factual wonders that drew the keen eyes of al-Tajir is the life of a number of Hindu gurus (enlightened masters). These mystics, al-Tajir tells us, dedicate their lives to wandering in uninhabited places such as forests and mountains without having any connections or communication with other human beings. They starve themselves as much as they can, and it is understood that they are strict vegetarians, for they survive by feeding occasionally on herbs and fruits. They also abstain from sexual congress with women by covering their penises with iron rings.[32] Al-Tajir's testimony can perhaps be seen as evidence for a Hindu influence on the rise of Sufism in medieval Islam. Among other things, this is especially significant when it comes to the cults of *siyaha* (wandering) and *khalwa* (isolation) that bear close similarities to the aforementioned Hindu cults as reported by al-Tajir.

Indeed, in addition to a number of monistic and pantheistic tendencies among some Sufi *shuyukh* (masters) such as al-Hallaj (d. 922), Ibn 'Arabi (d. 1240), Ibn Sab'in (d. 1269), and Ibn al-Faridh (d. 1353), Sufi *shuyukh* and *murids* (disciples) chose to wander for years, in some cases for life, in the *sahra'* (desert) and *khala'* (uninhabited places), without taking provisions, in search of *kashf* (enlightenment), *haqiqa* (inner truth), and other mystical *karamat* (miracles); this practice continues today in some Muslim countries. This is in addition to the spread of *'uzubiyya* (celibacy) and *tabattul* (sexual abstinence) among some of these masters and disciples.[33]

In al-Tajir's view, the religious influence of the Indians over their eastern neighbors the Chinese is uncontested. Acknowledging some small differences in minor practices, he calls them *furu'* (Arabic for "minor issues") and observes that the sciences of religion never developed in China, for "their religion originated in India";[34] this is an apparent reference to the fact that the predominant religion of the medieval Chinese was Buddhism, which is Sanskrit for "enlightenment", again a concept of fundamental importance in Sufism. Owing to the religious dependence of the Chinese on the Indians, several social customs related to marriage, hygiene, and food are similar in both countries. Marriage, for instance, is enacted in the same way: "When the Indians and the Chinese wish to perform a marriage," al-Tajir remarks, "they felicitate each other, then exchange presents, and then they make the marriage public by playing on cymbals and drums. Their present consists of money, according to their means."[35] In a similar fashion, he informs us that neither of them practices circumcision, nor do they take a bath after *janaba* (sexual intercourse). This is in addition to the fact that the Chinese and the Indians do not slaughter their animals as Muslims do. Instead, they kill them by a blow to the skull. The Indians and Chinese, however, have different views in other issues of hygiene.

All in all, al-Tajir does not hesitate to imply that the Indians are not only clean, but are unquestionably "cleaner" than the Chinese for a number of reasons that are intrinsically inspired by his own culture, such as the Indians' daily bathing and teeth cleaning. Others are quite obvious, despite slight differences from Islamic practice. This recalls his statement that, contrary to the Chinese, who have sexual intercourse with menstruating women, the Indians—more similar to the Jews than to Muslims—not only do not cohabit with them, but "they make them leave their homes and keep away from them".[36, 37]

We may say, then, that when it comes to the matters of conjugal and sexual life of the Indians and the Chinese, al-Tajir never seems indifferent. Of significance is his accurate statement that the Hindus, contrary to the Muslims, consider marriage a religious sacrament that joins the Hindu couple not only for life but, as we saw earlier, in the afterlife. Divorce is therefore not allowed, and at the death of husbands, wives who do not practice the *sati* are not allowed to remarry.[38] This is because, in stark contrast to Marco Polo's affirmation that the Indians "do not regard any form of sexual indulgence a sin",[39] *zina'* (adultery/fornication) is considered an extremely serious crime that can end with death. Throughout India, as observed by al-Tajir, consensual adultery among married couples is punished by death for both men and women.

Interestingly, al-Tajir mentions that if a married woman is forced to engage in adultery, she is saved and only the man is killed. The severe punishment of adulterous married couples does not mean that other forms of sexual relations are nonexistent in India. Indeed, prostitution among both the Indians and the Chinese is tolerated. As he tells us, in China prostitution as well as *liwat* (sodomy) with young boys is widely practiced in places built for the purpose. In India, legal prostitution is common in Hindu temples through the *devadasis* (temple girls).[40] According to Zaki and others, these women were not only "attached with the temple", but they also "traded in flesh and offered their income to the custodians of the temples."[41] Interestingly enough, al-Tajir does not describe the *fitna* (sexual temptation) of the temple *devadasis* as does Marco Polo, who in his account mentions that the Hindu temple girls were "completely naked except for their private parts."[42] "Marco was quite taken with the temple girls," Jonathan Clements humorously tells us, "and noted with great interest their pert, firm bosoms and their taut, tight flesh—*for a penny they will allow a man to pinch them as hard as he can*, he [Polo] adds, without daring to suggest that he had the right change."[43]

In general, if the Indians encountered by al-Tajir were, in his eyes, far superior to their Chinese neighbors in matters related to spirituality, wisdom, hygiene, and to some extent morality, the Chinese excelled over their spiritual masters in matters related to culture. This impression was the outcome of al-Tajir's fascination with ninth-century China's "Universal literacy", political justice, social equality, agricultural and economic abundance, and the people's unequalled artistic skills in craftsmanship and painting. For obvious reasons, al-Tajir notes with fascination what he saw of widespread literacy among Chinese men and women. Whether poor or rich, young or old, he tells us, the Chinese learn calligraphy and the art of writing.[44] This was the outcome of an effective political policy of decentralized promulgation of education on the part of the Chinese politicians. "In every town," al-Tajir writes, "there are scribes and teachers who impart education to the poor and their children; they receive their maintenance from the treasury."[45]

Since everybody knows how to read and to write, all the disputes and complaints must reach the king not only in documents written by a *katib* (scribe) licensed by the *hikam* (laws) but—to our surprise and amazement—in perfect spelling. "[And] before the plaintiff [*sahib al-qiss*] is presented in the audience of the king," al-Tajir says, "a person who is stationed at the gate of the house looks into the written [complaint] of the person. If he finds that there are some mistakes in it he rejects it" (51). Universal literacy does not seem to be the invention of our modern times, and "the Literall advantage", to the detriment of the seventeenth-century English traveler Samuel Purchas (d. 1626), is God's gift to all.

In *Marvelous Possessions: The Wonder of the New World*, critic Stephen Greenblatt has persuasively argued that, according to Purchas, author of *Hakluytus Posthumus, or Purchas His Pilgrims*, it is writing that sets the boundaries between civilization and barbarism. "God hath added herein a further grace, that as Men by the former exceed Beasts," Purchas declares, "so hereby one man may excell another; and amongst Men, some are accounted Civill, and more Sociable and religious, by the Use of letters and of Writing, which others wanting are esteemed Brutish, Savage, Barbarous." In addition to "the Christians' conviction that they possessed an absolute and exclusive religious truth", and the possession of "navigational instruments, ships, warhorses, attack dogs, effective armour, and highly lethal weapons, including gunpowder", Greenblatt observes that it is this very "Literall advantage" that provided Europeans, "with a very few exceptions", with a most powerful feeling of superiority toward "virtually all the people they encountered, even those like the Aztecs who had technological and organizational skills." For Purchas and other Europeans, Greenblatt goes on to say, the possession of writing was equated with the possession of "a past, a history, that those without access to letters necessarily lack."[46] Through the support of some scholars such as Tzvetan Todorov, Greenblatt reveals that "Purchas's notion of the Literall advantage" has survived with considerable vigor in certain academic circles. In his masterful study *The Conquest of America*: *The Question of the Other*—hailed by Greenblatt as not only "thoughtful" and "disturbing" but also as the inspiration behind his *Marvelous Possessions*—Todorov, in the view of Greenblatt, has argued that "the crucial cultural difference between European and American peoples was the presence or absence of writing and that this difference virtually determined the outcome of their encounter."[47] During the older cultural encounter between medieval Arabs and Chinese, "the presence or absence of writing" was not a crucial cultural difference between Muslims and Chinese. Nor was it, as attested by al-Tajir and other medieval Muslim travelers, an "important" let alone "*the* most important element" in the medieval situation of the two "lettered" cultures, as it was the case with the European–American "situation", at least as delineated by Todorov.[48]

In the same connection, despite its brevity, al-Tajir's account of Chinese justice is particularly remarkable. Not only does the Muslim traveler notice with admiration the absence of bureaucracy, but he also speaks with awe of the Chinese *al-dara*: "Every town has a thing called *al-dara*. This is a bell placed near [lit. 'at the head of'] the ruler of the town and is tied to a cord stretching as far as the road for the [benefit] of the common people." If a person is wronged by another person, he/she shakes the cord that is linked to *al-dara*. When doing so, al-Tajir observes, "the bell near the ruler starts ringing. So he [the wronged] is allowed to enter [the palace] to relate personally what the matter is and to explain the wrong done to him."[49] The result of this medieval Chinese "wonder" was the amazing accessibility of the public to the political and judicial hierarchy. In medieval China, it seems, injustice was panoptically controlled and justice was impressively disseminated. This conjures up the modern theory of panopticism. Whereas modern states, as understood by Louis Althusser and Michel Foucault, function through this panoptical controlling of their citizens, the medieval Chinese state, to the surprise of all, used panopticism to repress injustice. Not found even in the most democratic of modern societies, the Chinese *al-dara*, it appears, is a more utopian wor(l)d.

Al-Tajir was also very much interested in Chinese political institutions, for he seems to have been convinced that such a successful government, dealing with its subjects with impressive justice and providing them with numerous economic and social services, must have behind it a very effective political system. This can be inferred from the numerous passages he devotes to the political hierarchy, especially that of the emperor and the regional *muluk* (kings). Among the reasons that lay behind the success of the Chinese political system was the age of the regional governors. "Among them," he says, "no one becomes a ruler unless he is forty years of age, for they say that [at this age] a person becomes mature due to his experiences." Even more interesting are discipline, judicial accountability, discretion, financial transparency, and healthy diets. "The king does not sit [in session] to mete out justice," al-Tajir notes, "unless he eats and drinks beforehand, so that he may not commit an error."[50] These excellent governing qualities of the Chinese, in addition to other natural qualities, made the China visited by al-Tajir, especially when compared to India, not only a thriving but also a pleasant and healthy place to be. "China is more pleasant and beautiful than India. In most parts of India there are no towns, while the Chinese have large fortified cities everywhere. China is healthier, has few diseases and is most pleasant climatically." It is no accident, therefore, that in this (at least in worldly terms) ideal medieval country "one cannot find a blind or one-eyed person there nor anyone suffering from a disease, but these are found in large numbers in India."[51] Perhaps knowing that al-Tajir was describing the China of the Tang dynasty (618–906), hailed by Herbert Gowen in *An Outline History of China* as "the most powerful, and the most economically and culturally developed empire in the world",[52] justifies al-Tajir's fascination.[53]

In this medieval "Chinatopia", socialism was a royal matter. "Wherever there is a rise in prices," al-Tajir observes, "the king releases food [food grains] from his stores and sells it at a rate cheaper than the current prices in the market."[54] Likewise, al-Tajir was impressed by the free health services that the Chinese authorities provided to the poor. "If a person is poor," al-Tajir informs us, "he is given the price of the medicine from the treasury." Even more "modern" is the financial assistance enjoyed by aged persons who receive pensions from the treasury. These pensions are provided from the taxes that aged people used to pay when they were active in the workforce. Indeed, al-Tajir notes with accuracy that although the government does not impose any taxes on lands and other private properties, from the age of 18 to 80 all working men provide the treasury with a percentage proportional to what they earn. When they reach the age of 80, in turn, the government is obliged to pay them back and provide for their living. Behind this modern social pension lies the government's firm belief in justice and equity; as al-Tajir puts it, "They say: we took from him when he was a youth, and we pay him a salary when he is old."[55]

In addition to these taxes, the rich and equitably managed treasury of the Chinese government relies heavily on the revenues of a wondrous herb that the Chinese produce abundantly and transform into China's most popular and most expensive drink. This herb, according al-Tajir, is "leafier than green trefoil and slightly more perfumed, and has a soury taste". In order to transform it into drink, the Chinese "boil water and then sprinkle the leaves over it". This hot drink, which the Chinese take as a cure for many diseases, "is called *al-sakh*".[56] Such is al-Tajir's description of China's universally valued tea. This passage about tea not only makes him the first Muslim traveler to mention tea in his account, but also proves the authenticity of his account of China. This is in stark contrast to Marco Polo, whose omission of tea, among other things, has led many people to question the veracity of the latter's visit to China.

Finally, al-Tajir's description of the Andaman Islands may be the most inviting passage in the entire *Akhbar al-Sin wa-'l-Hind*. This is especially true in relation to this essay's aspiration to revisit some of the essentialist views of a number of postcolonial theorists and their dismissal of traditions and discourses of Otherness in medieval Arabic literature and culture. As we shall see, al-Tajir's description of the island and its inhabitants conjures up *Robinson Crusoe* (1719) and other Western narratives of encounters with non-Europeans, especially during the height of colonialism. The specific passage runs as follows:

> On the other side of these [islands] there are two islands, and between them there is the sea. They are called Andaman. Their inhabitants are cannibals. They are black with curly hair, and have ugly faces and eyes and long legs. Each one had pudenda, that is to say, his penis, nearly a cubit long; and they are naked. They have no canoes, and if they had them, they would have eaten up anyone passing by them. Sometimes it so happens that the boats slow down, and their speed is retarded due to the [strong] wind. The drinking water in the boats gets used up; and so they [sailors] approach these [islands] and refill the water. Hence, sometimes they [the cannibals] capture some of them [the sailors], but most of them escape.[57]

One is stunned not only by al-Tajir's, or probably his editor al-Sirafi's, 'scientific' confirmation of the cannibalistic activities of these *hamaj* (uncivilized/barbarian) islanders, but also by his implicit equation between their barbarism/cannibalism, their presumed *qubh* (ugliness), and their manifest *sawad* (blackness).[58]

Indeed, the islands are there, the 'cannibals/Calibans' are there, the gaze of power and the power of gaze are there, but it is obvious that al-Tajir's report of this human *mirabilia* is rather from his 'innocent' interest in and fascination with the marvelous and the unfamiliar. Evidently, many postcolonial readers may legitimately see in this excerpt a textual proof that betrays not only al-Tajir's Orientalist/colonialist discourse but also a medieval Muslim Orientalism/colonialism. Although none can impose a single interpretation upon literary texts, it seems that al-Tajir, in the quoted passage, is too 'innocent' to be an Orientalist/

colonialist. Perhaps one should direct some of this textual 'innocence' toward the assessment of a number of Westerners who have described the East.

The obvious example is Marco Polo himself. Like al-Tajir and his editor/co-author al-Sirafi, in his description of the Andamans "as cruel cannibals who liked their strangers raw and highly spiced", Polo—or perhaps Rustichello of Pisa, his editor/coauthor,—was keenly interested in the "grandsimes mervoilles et les grant *diversités*" of the East in "innocently" embracing his own culture's "topography of wonder". In contrast to al-Tajir and al-Sirafi's description of the cannibalism of some Eastern/African races, Polo and Rustichello "were more taken by the monstrosity of the mythical dog-headed Cynocephali that were among the most widely discussed and variously described of the exotic human races."[59]

It seems evident, therefore, that *Akhbar al-Sin wa-'l-Hind* illustrates a cultural relativism that foreshadows, for instance, Montaigne's *Essais*. Apart from his repulsion at what he deemed un-Islamic rituals, lack or rather imperfection in matters of cleanliness, un-halal meat, and widespread and legalized heterosexual and homosexual prostitution, al-Tajir finds no reason not to extol many of the cultural, political, economic, and social achievements of those "infidels" whom he met. In general, al-Tajir does not make any use of suffixed formulae such as *la'anahum allah* (may God curse them) or *dammarahum allah* (may God destroy them), a common practice in Muslim writings about *al-rum* (Byzantines) and *al-ifranj* (Franks) during the hostile times of the Crusades. This makes more ideological sense when one remembers the Quranic injunction to Muslims to favor *ahl al-kitab* (the People of the Book) over the *mushrikin* (polytheists) of China and India. "On est surpris, du reste," André Miquel writes, "que rien dans ces voyages n'atteste le sentiment d'une dégradation des choses et des êtres *à* mesure qu'on s'éloigne du centre vivant du monde et de la foi vers les terres mystérieuses de l'infidélité."[60] In many other instances, the 'Orient of the Orient' served as a space of sociopolitical self-criticism and cultural experimentalism.

As briefly mentioned in the introduction, modern postcolonial theories of Orientalism have confined the complex relations between East and West to the latter's colonialist enterprise in the 'Orient.' By doing so, they have somehow forgotten that every Self has its own Other and that every literature has its own alterity. Throughout Islam's classical age of discovery and expansion, evocative of Europe in early modern times, the Orient had its own Orient but not, it seems to me, its own Orientalism in the essentialist Saidian sense. Nowhere is this better exemplified than in the various accounts of India and China, especially during the golden age of the Abbasids. Although none can deny the fact that this interest was in many ways instigated, perpetuated, consolidated, and driven by religious propaganda, territorial expansion, economic interest, or political endorsement, not every Muslim in the age of expansion who wrote about the Orient's own Orient was supremacist, colonialist, or racist. The interest is more related, perhaps, to the centrality of the literary and cultural leitmotif of *al-'ajib/al-gharib* in medieval and early modern Arabic travel literature.

Of course, one could challenge this seemingly innocent Arabic tradition of *al-'ajib/al-gharib* through applying, for instance, Stephen Greenblatt's deconstructive critique of the poetics and politics of wonder in *Marvelous Possessions*.

Greenblatt probes the "cultural poetics" of what has generally been perceived as a mere human emotion (i.e., wonder). This is particularly true of his exploration of the cultural and discursive (in the Foucauldian sense) foundations of wonder, as illustrated by the European encounter with the New World—especially as exemplified by Cortes's encounter, contact, and military clash with the Aztecs. Wonder, Greenblatt argues, was an indispensable stage in the "othering" of the Other, for it subverts and ultimately contains all possible spaces of "sameness" in that very Other. Indeed, it is the discursive response of the "same" that overwhelms the emotions of wonder.[61] By conjuring up his/her "sameness", the intruder, explorer, or traveler sets a boundary between "self" and "Other". Such a "cultural" boundary would certainly construct the possible space for what Mary Louise Pratt has aptly termed as "contact zone".[62] In Greenblatt's view, this "contact zone", however successful in setting a space of cultural exchange, fails in the end to destroy the "red lines" that protect the "self" from the different "Other". Greenblatt goes on to assert that wonder was crucial in the ultimate "dispossessing" of the natives by a possessive/ing Other. The latter comes to the shores, intrudes into native territory, meets the native, and wonders at his/her appearance, habits, speech, and so forth. Through an "imperialist" consciousness and unconsciousness of the "self", the intruder confers his/her "sameness", intrudes into the difference of the native, differs in a Derridean sense, and infers through "descriptions judgments, and actions" his/her Otherness. Fortunately, Greenblatt has somewhat questioned his own essentialism when he exempts figures such as Herodotus, Jean de Léry, Montaigne, and Mandeville from the artful maneuver of the experience of wonder for colonial appropriation and consolidation. These authors, Greenblatt concludes, found in the experience of wonder a vehicle for cultural relativism and understanding.[63]

Perhaps it is no exaggeration to suggest that, had Greenblatt been familiar with the Arab Islamic tradition of wonder in cultural encounters, the list of exemptions would have been longer. Otherwise, one would be likely to concur with Nabil Matar's position, however debatable it may appear to some, on the theoretical ineffectiveness of some Western theorists when applied to the Arabic tradition. "The Arabic travel accounts cannot therefore be approached through the theoretical models," Matar writes, "with which European accounts have been studied by writers as different as Stephen Greenblatt, Edward Said, and Gayatri Spivak. They belong to a tradition that is different not only in its history but epistemology."[64]

In sum, in addition to showing that medieval Muslims were not uninterested in the non-Muslim Other, my main objective in referring to the "Oriental theme" in medieval Arabic *adab al-rihla* (travel writings) is to question, if not challenge, the postcolonial equation of travel literature and the traveler's gaze with dominant discourses of power such as Orientalism and colonialism. Cultural Othering is one way, among many, of constructing self-definition and self-identification. Cultural encounters between different humans in different contexts, however, are too complex a phenomenon to be 'essentialized' in restrictive Western theoretical models, let alone through a set of binary opposites—Self/Other, civilized/barbaric, white/black, West/East, and so forth. Islam's encounter with its own

Orient challenges not only such essentialism but also its own medieval encounter with Europe and the Euro-Christians, a subject that has been neglected in the ongoing and heated debate about relations between Islam and the West. Medieval Muslims were not interested solely in the Far East; through a number of textual and physical journeys, many medieval Muslim writers, geo-cosmographers, travelers, envoys, and captives from the Mashriq and the Maghrib, with their curious pens and inquiring eyes, ventured into different parts of medieval Europe as well and left us with extraordinary accounts of what they saw and experienced.[65]

Notes

1 Zaki Muhammad Hassan, *Al-Rahala al-Muslimun fi'l-'Usur al-Wusta* (Beirut: Dar al- Ra'id al-'Arabi, 1981), p. 3. (Author's translation).
2 Nabil Matar, *In the Lands of the Christians: Arabic Travel Writing in the Seventeenth Century* (New York: Routledge, 2003), pp. xiii–xiv.
3 For the original French essay, see Jacques Le Goff, "L'occident médiéval et l'o*céan Indien: un horizon onirique*", in idem, *Pour un autre Moyen Age: temps, travail et culture en Occident: 18 Essais* (Paris: NRF-Gallimard, 1977).
4 Jacques Le Goff, "The Medieval West and the Indian Ocean: An Oneiric Horizon", in Anthony Padgen (ed.), *Facing Each Other: The World's Perception of Europe and Europe's Perception of the World* (Burlington: Ashgate/Variorum, 2000), pp. 1–21.
5 Ibid., p. 3.
6 Scholars such as De Goje, Blachère, Kratschkovsky, Kimble, Miquel, Achoy, Gibe, Palencia, Reinaud, Bartold, Wussienfeld, and Sarton.
7 Abu Dulaf was a poet and a traveler named by Ibn al-Nadim and other medieval chroniclers as a *jawwala*, or globe-trotter. In spite of the debate over its authenticity, he is thought to be the author of his own account of India. This account was published with a Latin translation in Berlin in 1845 (S. Maqbul Ahmad, *Arabic Classical Accounts of India and China* (Shimla: Indian Institute of Advanced Study, 1989), p. 115).
8 Peter Boxhall, "Arabian Seafarers in the Indian Ocean", *Asian Affairs*, vol. 20, no. 3, (1989), pp. 287–295.
9 As demonstrated by George F. Hourani in his classic *Arab Seafaring in the Indian Ocean in Ancient and Early Medieval Times*, even long before Islam, Arab seafarers and traders were familiar with the Indian Ocean (Princeton, NJ: Princeton University Press, 1995).
10 Iain Macleod Higgins, *Writing East: The "Travels" of Sir John Mandeville* (Philadelphia: University of Pennsylvania Press, 1997), p. 6.
11 Andre Wink, *Al-Hind, The Making of the Indo-Islamic World: Early Medieval India and the Expansion of Islam, 7th–11th Centuries* (Leiden: Brill, 2002), p. 17.
12 S. Maqbul Ahmad, *A History of Arab-Islamic Geography* (Mafraq: Ahl al-Bayt University, 1995), p. 38.
13 Hassan, *Al-Rahala al-Muslimun*, p. 6.
14 Ahmad, *A History*, p. 38.
15 Ibid., p. 38.
16 He was known as al-Turjuman, Arabic and Persian for "translator". Ibn Khordadbeh mentions that his mastery of many languages was the primary reason he was chosen by al-Wathiq for this mission of discovery: *Kitab al-Masalik wa'l-Mamalik* (Baghdad: Maktabat al-Mathna, 1954), p. 163.
17 The literal translation of the Arabic name is the one possessing two horns. The historical identity of *dhu'l-qarnayn* has generated a heated debate among Muslim and non-Muslim scholars alike, some of whom identify him as Alexander the Great. Owing

to the many differences between the Quranic character (who is described as a pure monotheist and a faithful follower of God) and the historical Alexander the Great, many Muslim scholars refuse this identification.

18 Mohsin Malallah, *Adab al-Rihla 'Inda al- 'Arab* (Baghdad: al-Irshad, 1978), p. 31.

19 Hassan, *Al-Rahala al-Muslimun*, p. 15.

20 Malallah, *Adab al-Rihla*, p. 31.

21 See Gabriel Ferrand's *Voyage du marchand arabe Sulayman en Inde et Chine, rédigé en 851 suivi de remarques par Abu Zayd Hasan (vers 916)* (Paris: Classiques de l'Orient, 1922).

22 Ahmad, *A History*, p. 42.

23 In addition to the accounts of al-Mas'udi, al-Biruni, Abu Dulaf, and Ibn Battuta, other major accounts include those of al-Ya'qubi (d. 880), Ibn al-Faqih (d. 902), al-Maqdisi (d. 980), al-Gardizi (d. 1060), al-Marwazi (d. 1125), al-Idrisi (d. 1165), al-Gharnati (d. 1170), al-Hamawi (d. 1229), and al-Qazwini (d. 1283). Gabriel Ferrand counted approximately 39 medieval Muslim reports of India and China, most of which are in Arabic (33), 5 in Persian, and 1 in Turkish.

24 Hassan, *Al-Rahala al-Muslimun*, p. 8.

25 A growing number of mostly Western scholars have maintained that the source of the account is anonymous. This argument has been rejected by a majority of scholars, especially those from the Middle East and India, who cite that medieval Muslim historians regarded al-Tajir not only as the person who recorded the account but as its uncontested author.

26 Ahmad, *Classical Accounts*, p. 33.

27 Ahmad, *Classical Accounts*, p. 33.

28 Muhammad J. Zaki, *Arab Accounts of India During the Fourteenth Century* (Delhi: Idarah-i Adabiyat, 1981), p. 45.

29 Ahmad, *Classical Accounts*, p. 53.

30 Jonathan Clemens, *Marco Polo* (London: Haus Publishing, 2007), p. 33.

31 Tim Mackintosh-Smith, *The Travels of Ibn Battutah* (London: Macmillan, 2002), p. 158.

32 Ahmad, *Classical Accounts*, p. 53.

33 See R. C. Zaehner's classic study *Hindu and Muslim Mysticism* (London: Athlone Press, 1960).

34 Ibid., p. 53.

35 Ibid., p. 54.

36 Ibid., p. 56.

37 In Islamic law, although *al-haydh* (menstruation) is seen as a time of ritual impurity during which women, like men after sexual intercourse, are prohibited from staying in mosques and exempted from some obligatory *'ibadat* (acts of worship)—such as *salat* (prayer) and *sawm* (fasting)—they are not considered, as many think, *najis* (religiously impure) and thus "untouchable" as in Judaism's ritual of *niddah* (Hebrew for separation). In fact, although being *junub* (ritually impure) during menstruation, Muslim women are permitted to engage in their regular lives, such as cooking, touching food and clothes, and so forth. In addition, they stay in their homes and sleep in their regular beds with their husbands. As for marital sex, physical intimacy is allowed, and the couple has a normal sexual life with the exception of *ilaj* (full penetration of the penis into the vagina).

38 Divorce has been recently introduced into Hindu law, as Ahmad, *Classical Accounts* states (p. 77).

39 Clemens, *Marco Polo*, p. 131.

40 Ahmad, *Classical Accounts*, pp. 54–55.

41 Zaki, *Arab Accounts*, p. 47.

42 Clemens, *Marco Polo*, p. 132.

43 Ibid., p. 115.

44 Ahmad, *Classical Accounts*, p. 47.

45 Ibid., p. 52.
46 Stephen Greenblatt, *Marvellous Possessions: The Wonder of the New World* (Chicago: University of Chicago Press, 1991), pp. 9–10.
47 Ibid., p. 11.
48 Tzvetan Todorov, *The Conquest of America: The Question of the Other* (New York: Harper & Row, 1984), p. 160.
49 Ahmad, *Classical Accounts*, p. 49.
50 Ibid., p. 48.
51 Ibid., p. 57.
52 Herbert Gowen, *An Outline History of China* (Safety Harbor: Simon Publications, 2001), p. 111.
53 I am indebted to S. Maqbul Ahmad for this reference.
54 Ahmad, *Classical Accounts*, p. 49.
55 Ibid., p. 52.
56 Ibid., p. 56.
57 Ibid., p. 36.
58 There is a rich body of medieval Arabic literature that deals with Arab Muslim views and perceptions of *al-sud* (blacks) that is yet to be explored and investigated. In addition to the brief, but succinct, reference to this rich corpus by Aziz al-Azmeh in *Al-'Arab wa'l-Barabira* (London: Dar al-Rayes, 1991), the most comprehensive study, in my view, came to light quite recently with the publication of Nadir Khadhim's book *Tamthilat al-Akhar: Surat al-Sud fi'l-Mutakhayyal al-'Arabi al-Wasit* (Beirut: Al-Mu'assasa al-'Arabiyya li'l-Dirasat wa'l- Nashr, 2007). For a Western study, see G. Rotter's PhD dissertation, 'Die Stellung des Negers in der islamisch-arabischen Gesellschaft bis zum XVI: Jahrhundert' (Bonn: Rheinische Friedrich-Wilhelms-Universitat, 1976), and David M. Goldenberg's *The Curse of Ham: Race and Slavery in Early Judaism, Christianity, and Islam* (Princeton, NJ: Princeton University Press, 2003).
59 Clemens, *Marco Polo*, pp. 31–34.
60 André Miquel, *La géographie humaine du monde musulman jusqu'au milieu du 11e siècle* (Paris: Haye, 1975), p. 73.
61 Greenblatt, *Marvellous Possessions*, p. 127.
62 Mary Louise Pratt, *Imperial Eyes: Travel Writing and Transculturation* (London: Routledge, 1992), p. 6.
63 Greenblatt, *Marvellous Possessions*, pp. 128–135.
64 Matar, *In the Lands of the Christians*, p. xxxii.
65 See Nizar F. Hermes, *The [European] Other in Medieval Arabic Literature and Culture, Ninth-Twelfth Century AD* (New York: Palgrave Macmillan, 2012).

Bibliography

Ahmad, S. Maqbul, *Arabic Classical Accounts of India and China* (Shimla: Indian Institute of Advanced Study, 1989).

——, *A History of Arab-Islamic Geography* (Mafraq: Ahl al-Bayt University, 1995).

al-Azmeh, Aziz, *Al-'Arab wa'l-Barabira* (London: Dar al-Rayes, 1991).

Boxhall, Peter, "Arabian Seafarers in the Indian Ocean", *Asian Affairs*, 20, 1989, pp. 287–295.

Clemens, Jonathan, *Marco Polo* (London: Haus Publishing, 2007).

Ferrand, Gabriel, *Voyage du marchand arabe Sulayman en Inde et Chine, rédigé en 851 suivi de remarques par Abu Zayd Hasan (vers 916)* (Paris: Classiques de l'Orient, 1922).

Goldenberg, David M., *The Curse of Ham: Race and Slavery in Early Judaism, Christianity, and Islam* (Princeton, NJ: Princeton University Press, 2003).

Gowen, Herbert, *An Outline History of China* (Safety Harbor: Simon Publications, 2001).
Greenblatt, Stephen, *Marvellous Possessions: The Wonder of the New World* (Chicago: University of Chicago Press, 1991).
Hassan, Zaki Muhammad, *Al-Rahala al-Muslimun fi'l-'Usur al-Wusta* (Beirut: Dar al-Ra'id al-'Arabi, 1981).
Hermes, Nizar F., *The [European] Other in Medieval Arabic Literature and Culture, Ninth-Twelfth Century AD* (New York: Palgrave Macmillan, 2012).
Higgins, Iain Macleod, *Writing East: The "Travels" of Sir John Mandeville* (Philadelphia: University of Pennsylvania Press, 1997).
Hourani, George F., *Arab Seafaring in the Indian Ocean in Ancient and Early Medieval Times* (Princeton, NJ: Princeton University Press, 1995).
Ibn Khordadbeh, *Kitab al-Masalik wa'l-Mamalik* (Baghdad: Maktabat al-Mathna, 1954).
Khadhim, Nadir, *Tamthilat al-Akhar: Surat al-Sud fi'l-Mutakhayyal al-'Arabi al-Wasit* (Beirut: Al-Mu'assasa al-'Arabiyya li'l-Dirasat wa'l- Nashr, 2007).
Le Goff, Jacques, "The Medieval West and the Indian Ocean: An Oneiric Horizon", in Anthony Padgen (ed.), *Facing Each Other: The World's Perception of Europe and Europe's Perception of the World* (Burlington: Ashgate/Variorum, 2000).
——, "L'occident médiéval et l'océan Indien: un horizon onirique", in idem, *Pour un autre Moyen Age: temps, travail et culture en Occident: 18 Essais* (Paris: NRF-Gallimard, 1977).
Mackintosh-Smith, Tim, *The Travels of Ibn Battutah* (London: Macmillan, 2002).
Matar, Nabil, *In the Lands of the Christians: Arabic Travel Writing in the Seventeenth Century* (New York: Routledge, 2003).
Miquel, André, *La géographie humaine du monde musulman jusqu'au milieu du 11e siècle* (Paris: Haye, 1975).
Pratt, Mary Louise, *Imperial Eyes: Travel Writing and Transculturation* (London: Routledge, 1992).
Rotter, G. 'Die Stellung des Negers in der islamisch-arabischen Gesellschaft bis zum XVI: Jahrhundert', PhD dissertation, Bonn: Rheinische Friedrich-Wilhelms-Universitat, 1976.
Todorov, Tzvetan, *The Conquest of America: The Question of the Other* (New York: Harper & Row, 1984).
Wink, Andre, *Al-Hind, The Making of the Indo-Islamic World: Early Medieval India and the Expansion of Islam, 7th–11th Centuries* (Leiden: Brill, 2002).
Zaehner, R. C., *Hindu and Muslim Mysticism* (London: Athlone Press, 1960).
Zaki, Muhammad J., *Arab Accounts of India During the Fourteenth Century* (Delhi: Idarah-i Adabiyat, 1981).

13 Ibn Baṭṭūṭa in wanderland: voyage as text

Was Ibn Baṭṭūṭa an orientalist?

Ian Richard Netton

> The rabbit-hole went straight on like a tunnel for some way, and then dipped suddenly down, so suddenly that Alice had not a moment to think about stopping herself before she found herself falling down what seemed to be a very deep well.[1]

Hugh Haughton notes that "Carroll's heroine, at the heart of these adventures, is very much concerned with questions of meaning."[2] And the same is true of Ibn Baṭṭūṭa (AD 1304–1368/69 or 1377): he seeks meaning, self and God through the medium of a journey. Evoking the words of an old carol, we can say that he wanders to wonder, to explore himself as much as to explore the lands he visits, or claims to visit. He has a need both to impress and to be impressed, and the Arabic tradition of writing about *'ajā'ib* (marvels, miracles, wonders)[3] very much lends itself to fantasy and the description of things fantastic.

The clue to Ibn Baṭṭūṭa's own intentions lies in the full title which he, or his scribe Ibn Juzayy, gave to his *Travelogue* which we call briefly in Arabic his *Riḥla*. This full title was *Tuḥfat al-Nuẓẓār Gharā'ib al-Amṣār wa 'Ajā'ib al-Asfār* and its ponderous Arabic rhymes have been rendered a little more loosely by L.P. Harvey as *For the Curious, a Rare Work Concerning Wondrous Things in Great Cities, and Marvels ('ajā'ib) Encountered on Journeys.*[4]

Haughton goes on: "To read the Alice books is to plunge into a world of narrative distortions ..."[5] And the same *can* be true of Ibn Baṭṭūṭa. For not only does he write sometimes within, and even encapsulate, this genre of 'marvels' (*'ajā'ib*) but he writes always within the "great tradition", to borrow a Leavisite phrase, of *riḥla* as *adab*, travel narrative as literature, literature which is not always pure fact but often pure entertainment, embellished by literary artifice, in other words, *voyage as text.*

The genre of riḥla

The Encyclopaedia of Islam defines *riḥla* as "a journey, voyage, travel; also a travelogue."[6] The article indicates that the root word *raḥala* "was originally associated with camel husbandry" and that "the word *riḥla* thus connoted the act of saddling one or more camels and, by extension, a journey or voyage."[7] A quest for knowledge, underpinned by the injunction in the ḥadīth (important and popular, whatever its true status) became articulated in the phrase *al-riḥla fī ṭalab al-'ilm* ("travel in pursuit of knowledge"); such implicit wanderlust was facilitated by the obligation on every able Muslim once in his or her lifetime to make the pilgrimage to Mecca, one of the five pillars (*arkān*) of the faith. All found literary expression in travel journals, *riḥla* literature, whose finest exponents are considered to be the Moroccan Ibn Baṭṭūṭa and, a few generations before him, the Hispano-Arab Ibn Jubayr (AD 1145–1217).[8] With the latter we have the *ḥajj* (pilgrimage) as a vehicle for guilt: Ibn Jubayr travels between AD 1183 and 1185 and his *Travelogue* (*Riḥla*) became a model for Ibn Baṭṭūṭa and his editor and scribe, Ibn Juzayy.[9] By contrast, Ibn Baṭṭūṭa deploys the *ḥajj* as a vehicle for wanderlust/wonderlust! As I have put it elsewhere, "with the Riḥla of Ibn Baṭṭūṭa we reach the peak in the articulation of a genre which should be perceived much more in terms of a literary art form than a formal geography."[10] It is an art form which relishes the mundanities of an expanding, chaotic world in flux as well as its marvels or *'ajā'ib*, "the believable and the incredible".[11] As such, the geographer or historian who would mine its many felicities, claims and encounters, human and topographical, is obliged to proceed "with extreme caution". Did Ibn Baṭṭūṭa visit China? Did Ibn Baṭṭūṭa visit Bulghār?[12] Did he actually encounter the abdicated Byzantine Emperor Andronicus II? This is voyage as entertainment, voyage as text, and things are not always what they seem or as they are stated in the *Riḥla*.

With Alice in her Wonderland, Ibn Baṭṭūṭa may be forgiven for being accused of thinking "that very few things indeed were really impossible",[13] at least where what we might term "virtual" or imaginary travel was concerned. "'Oh, I've had such a curious dream!' said Alice. And she told her sister, as well as she could remember them, all these strange adventures of hers …"[14] These sentences occur towards the end of Carroll's famous novel. Then we recall that Ibn Baṭṭūṭa dictated his own adventures to an amanuensis, Ibn Juzayy, finishing in AD 1357, reliant in large measure on pure memory for his picaresque tale, having lost his notes.[15]

Was it an embellished memory, padded out with a desire to claim places visited and persons encountered with no reality behind the claim? The role of Ibn Juzayy, the scribe, is also a curious one. Was *he* the literary éminence grise who suggested the incorporation of Ibn Jubayr's accounts of Mecca and Medina, or was that, also, the product of Ibn Baṭṭūṭa's own compulsion to be regarded as the *Raḥḥāla*, Globetrotter, of the Age, an Islamic Marco Polo, to whom he is so often compared?

The Riḥla of Ibn Jubayr

The *Riḥla* of Ibn Jubayr, prototype for so many which followed,[16] is worthy of study in its own right. Here it will be surveyed briefly. As we have already observed, it is the narrative of a *ḥajj* as a vehicle for guilt, a *riḥla* of expiation.[17] For Ibn Jubayr was in the service of the Governor of Granada, Abū Sa'īd 'Uthmān b. 'Abd al-Mu'min, employed as Secretary, and the Governor, in a fit of whimsy mingled with arrogance and power, forces his hapless Secretary to drink wine. A cowed Ibn Jubayr obeys but is at once mortified and guilt-stricken.[18] Ibn Jubayr's translator continues: "The prince was [then] seized with sudden pity, and in remorse had seven times filled the cup with golden dinars and poured them into the bosom of his servant's gown. The good man, who long had cherished the wish to discharge the duty of the pilgrimage to Mecca, at once determined to expiate his godless act by devoting the money to this end."[19]

Thus Ibn Jubayr launches himself on a pilgrimage voyage to the holy cities of Mecca and Medina which lasts from 3 February 1183 to 25 April 1185. It is a voyage which contains its fair share of dangers and mishaps, wonders and paradoxes: "He travelled in 'the Age of the Crusades' yet he is happy to travel on Christian ships. He travels by sea yet it is clear that he hates the sea and, at one point, he actually suffers shipwreck.[20] We get a vivid sense from his *Travelogue* both of the man himself with all his contradictions and delicacy of conscience, and also of contemporary history."[21] In a later age he would be lauded as one whose very piety was the confirmation of what he claimed to have experienced and written.[22] "He travelled for far less a period of time than his fourteenth-century 'successor' in the *riḥla* genre, Ibn Baṭṭūṭa, whose own double-edged 'tribute' was to plagiarise parts of Ibn Jubayr's work quite shamelessly, or at least allow his scribe, Ibn Juzayy, to do so. But by his perspicacity and very humanity, Ibn Jubayr brings the Mediterranean and its environs to life in a way that few travellers before or since have done."[23]

The Riḥla of Ibn Baṭṭūṭa

If Ibn Jubayr's *Riḥla* is the prototype, then Ibn Baṭṭūṭa's is the masterpiece, plagiarism and fantasy notwithstanding. For it exhibits the *ḥajj* as a vehicle par excellence for wanderlust/wonderlust. With Alice, Ibn Baṭṭūṭa wishes to make his readers' "eyes bright and eager with many a strange tale, perhaps even with the dream of Wonderland of long ago."[24] And he suffers severe homesickness,[25] seasickness and shipwreck[26] in pursuit of that dream. He is, fundamentally, a "little" man, a minor legal scholar of the Mālikī *madhhab* (legal school), whose enlarging ego demands more as his journey increases in length and severity and as he himself grows in self-respect and the respect of others.

His lifespan occupied more than two-thirds of the fourteenth Christian century and a large part of that was spent wandering through Asia, Europe and Africa. He brings a sense of time as well as place to each region he visits.[27] At the end of his travels, his scribe, Ibn Juzayy, admiringly observes: "It is obvious to anyone of intelligence that this shaikh is the traveller of the age (*raḥḥāl al-'aṣr*). If anyone were to call him 'the traveller of this (Muslim) community' (*raḥḥāl hādhihi al-milla*) he would not exaggerate."[28] Ibn Baṭṭūṭa has come a long way, emotionally, physically and in terms of prestige, from the shy scholar who sets out from Tangier in AD 1325 aged 22: he has become a judge (*qāḍī*) in both Delhi and the Maldives[29] and he claims to have covered a large part of the known world on his travels. *How much was fact and how much was fantasy?*

Three arenas of fantasy

Andronicus II

> There followed the Knave of Hearts, carrying the King's crown on a crimson velvet cushion; and, last of all this grand procession, came the King and Queen of Hearts.[30]

The most casual reading of Ibn Baṭṭūṭa's *Riḥla* shows that he likes to mix with – and boast of having mixed with – the great and the good of the Age.[31] He is an obsessive collector of people as well as places and events. A minor legal scholar, often unsure of himself – we note his tears as he leaves his native land[32] – he seeks to boost his own ego by such collections and encounters, and boost his career as he collects qāḍīships in the Maldives and Delhi.[33] And not only does he collect such secular honours; he collects spiritual honours too, by affiliating himself to Ṣūfī orders, thus making his mark as pious pilgrim, traveller and Ṣūfī *manqué*.[34] Together with this is his collecting of miraculous events[35] and *'ajā'ib* (wonders) like the sighting of the *rukhkh*,[36] a monstrous bird of Islamic mythology. He hates the sea[37] and regales us at an early stage with the whole of the *Litany of the Sea* (*Ḥizb al-Baḥr*)[38] and his shipwrecks,[39] as an inveterate collector of heroics and to bolster an intrepid traveller's mask for a future readership. Finally, he collects prestige by association; witness his service to the very dangerous Sultan of Delhi, Muḥammad b. Tughluq. It is at this point that we are obliged to reconsider his alleged encounter with the ex-Emperor of Byzantium, Andronicus II.

In John Fowles' early novel, *The Collector*, the heroine, who has been kidnapped and is being held against her will, says to her captor:

> I hate scientists. I hate people who collect things, and classify things and give them names and then forget all about them. That's what people are always doing in art. They call a painter an impressionist or a cubist or something and then they put him in a drawer and don't see him as a living individual painter any more. But I can see they're beautifully arranged.[40]

Of course, Ibn Baṭṭūṭa does not kidnap those whom he encounters, but by meeting, and later recording, those of fame, prestige and, perhaps, wealth, he organises and validates his own life with the charisms of others; he gives that life a kind of extra meaning if, by *riḥla* in Ibn Baṭṭūṭa's extreme form, we intend a solipsistic and prolonged search for identity as well as knowledge and a pilgrim satisfaction. Thus it is that Ibn Baṭṭūṭa "collects" the ex-Emperor Andronicus II in his *Riḥla*[41] in a city which Tim Mackintosh-Smith describes as being "in a state of terminal loucheness".[42]

The encounter is briefly narrated: on arrival in Constantinople, our traveller claims to have encountered two Byzantine Emperors: a reigning one, whom Ibn Baṭṭūṭa, confusing name and designation,[43] calls Takfūr,[44] and whom H.A.R. Gibb identifies as "Andronicus III (*reg.* AD 1328–1341), who was the grandson of his predecessor Andronicus II (abdicated 1328)", as well as Andronicus II himself.[45]

This first encounter is unproblematic. On the fourth day after he arrives in Constantinople, Ibn Baṭṭūṭa is summoned to the Palace, carefully searched on entry and taken into a grand audience hall with a tree-lined water feature. Thence he moves "to a grand pavilion" and encounters a very genial Emperor sitting on his throne (*wa 'l-Sulṭān 'alā sarīrihi*). Ibn Baṭṭūṭa answers all the Emperor's questions to the latter's satisfaction, via a Jewish interpreter. The Emperor showers him with a number of presents including a robe of honour, a horse, and a guide to show him the City of Constantinople.[46]

One would have thought that such a successful interview, culminating in such honour and such presents, with the highest dignitary in the land, the reigning Byzantine Emperor himself, would have been sufficient for any man. But, as we and Mackintosh-Smith have noted,[47] Ibn Bạ ṭṭūṭa is an inveterate collector of people, and he now claims to have met the direct predecessor of Andronicus III, Andronicus II, now abdicated and become a monk.

In a section of the *Riḥla* entitled, in Gibb's translation, "Account of the king Jirgis, who became a Monk" (*Dhikr al-Malik al-Mutarahhab Jirjīs*), Ibn Baṭṭūṭa writes:

> The king invested his son with the kingdom, consecrated himself to the service of God, and built a monastery … outside the city, on the bank [of its river]. I was out one day with the Greek appointed to ride with me when we chanced to meet this king, walking on foot, wearing hair-cloth garments, and with a felt bonnet on his head. He had a long white beard and a fine face, which bore traces of his austerities; before and behind him was a body of monks, and he had a pastoral staff in his hand and a rosary on his neck.[48]

Ibn Baṭṭūṭa's Greek companion promptly dismounts and tells Ibn Baṭṭūṭa to do the same, saying that "this is the king's father".

Ibn Baṭṭūṭa is greeted by this alleged ex-Emperor and the traveller is amazed at the latter's inter-faith civility as they discuss Jerusalem and the Christians who live there. But that inter-faith exchange only goes so far: the monk tells the traveller that anyone who wishes to enter the church "must needs prostrate himself before the great cross", which Ibn Baṭṭūṭa is unwilling to do and so the monk and his entourage enter the church alone, without Ibn Baṭṭūṭa.[49] Ibn Baṭṭūṭa is clearly fascinated by his two encounters, by that with the reigning Emperor and that with the alleged ex-Emperor, and he relishes the stark contrast between the two. But did he actually meet Andronicus II?

H.A.R. Gibb is absolutely adamant that he did not: "By no possible chronology can Ibn Baṭṭūṭa have visited Constantinople before the death of Andronicus II on 12/13 February 1332. [We may remind ourselves that the traveller left Tangiers at the start of his *riḥla* in AD 1325.] Since, moreover, the monastic name of the ex-Emperor was Antonius, it is evident that he either misunderstood or was misled by his guide as to the identity of the monk 'George'."[50]

There is, of course, another very real possibility, and that is that the whole episode is an aspect of Ibn Baṭṭūṭa's collector's instinct whereby he claims to have encountered as many of the great and the good as his imagination can muster. This would then put the encounter with the alleged Andronicus II in the realms of invention and fantasy but would serve to underline the whole idea of voyage as *adab*, voyage as a text whose primary purpose is the entertainment of the reader or listener by means of retailing fantastic stories, true or imaginary, by means, in other words of *'ajā'ib*, wonders. Many other notable scholars of Ibn Baṭṭūṭa, including L.P. Harvey, Charles Beckingham, Ross E. Dunn and Ivan Hrbek share Gibb's profound scepticism about the whole encounter with the alleged ex-Emperor.[51] Hrbek, for example, is quite dogmatic about Ibn Baṭṭūṭa's capacity for invention: "He did not meet an Emperor-monk but with all probability some personage belonging to the high clergy of the Orthodox Church. And our traveler made him the ex-Emperor – of whose monastic life he certainly heard in Constantinople – to add a further item to his collection of personal acquaintances with the sovereigns and to show his readers what an important person he was on his travels."[52]

Ross Dunn is only slightly kinder: "The supposed meeting with the ex-emperor Andronicus II … is only the most egregious of his misunderstandings." Tim Mackintosh-Smith is kindest of all, but then he is an ardent aficionado of the traveller. "Perhaps," he suggests, "*pace* Gibb, the conundrum of IB's chronology *could* be twisted into a solution, like a four-dimensional Rubik's Cube."[53]

Misunderstanding, possible fact, or outright fraud and fantasy? The reader is left to be the ultimate judge!

The Voyage to Bulghār

However, in the notorious episode of the alleged visit to Bulghār, there is far less possibility of acquitting Ibn Baṭṭūṭa of mere misunderstanding. This is much more imaginary voyage as wonderful text! In the succinct words of Stephen Janicsek, "the trip to and from Bulghār which Ibn Baṭṭūṭa claims to have undertaken is the only narrative in the whole record of his wanderings which seems to be, beyond all doubt, a falsification."[54]

> She had plenty of time as she went down to look about her, and to wonder what was going to happen next. First, she tried to look down and make out what she was coming to, *but it was too dark to see anything* ... she looked up, *but it was all dark overhead*: before her was another long passage …[55]

At the beginning of Alice's adventure in Lewis Carroll's famous novel, the feelings of falling, alienation and darkness are profound. In Ibn Baṭṭūṭa's account, the perception of falling is replaced by a motif of haste and speed, but there is a similar sense of alienation and darkness.

So, where was Ibn Baṭṭūṭa's own Wanderland here? Where were Bulghār and the Land of Darkness, and why did he choose to invent a journey to those regions with which to entertain his readers? Tim Mackintosh-Smith provides a neat summary: "Bulghar, originally the capital of the Volga Bulgars, lay near the left bank of the Volga, some seventy miles south of Kazan. IB's account of the journey – a 1,600 mile round trip, impossible in the time stated – is drawn from literary sources and may well be an interpolation by his editor.[56] Geographical texts have also supplied the subsequent information on the Land of Darkness, a semi-legendary region beyond the trans-Ural steppe."[57]

Ibn Baṭṭūṭa takes us in his *Riḥla* on a whirlwind journey more imaginary than actual. He has heard about the City of Bulghār and wishes to see it, being intrigued by the short nights there in one season and short days in another. He claims that Bulghār is ten days' journey from the camp of the Ruler of the Golden Horde, Sultan Muḥammad Üzbak Khān (*reg.* AD 1312–1341), whom he has visited "in the vicinity of al-Māchar (Burgomadzhary)"[58] below the Caucasus. He claims to have been given a guide by the Sultan to bring him there and back, and to have reached the City of Bulghār during Ramaḍān:[59]

> And when we had prayed the sunset prayer we broke our fast; the call to the night prayer was made during our eating of this meal, and by the time that we had prayed that … the dawn broke. So too the daytime becomes as short there in the season of its brevity. I stayed there three days.[60]

Ibn Baṭṭūṭa then tells us that he would like to have gone on to the Land of Darkness (*Arḍ al-Ẓulma*) (i.e. the land beyond "the northern trans-Ural steppes"),[61] a further forty days' journey from Bulghār; and although he gives an account, drawn from literary sources, of this Land, at least he does not try to bluff us into thinking that he goes there as well![62]

Led by Stephen Janicsek, the vast majority of Ibn Baṭṭūṭa scholars hold that his alleged journey to Bulghār was impossible in the time stated and the huge distance to be covered (800 miles × 2 in one month!),[63] and so has to be accounted a fabrication.[64] It is a beautiful fabrication, an intriguing fabrication which fascinates and enchants the reader and is designed to evoke admiration and respect in equal measure; but it is a fabrication nonetheless!

If we then ask why Ibn Baṭṭūṭa did this, Janicsek provides a most plausible explanation: "If we study the whole narrative of [Ibn Baṭṭūṭa's] travels, we see that his principal intention in undertaking them was to visit all the countries of the earth inhabited by Muslims … But when he heard that it was so far away, instead of going to Bulghār in person, he preferred to write or dictate his trip to Bulghār as if he had actually accomplished it."[65]

Ross E. Dunn confirms this: "We must remember, however, that the *Riḥla* was composed as a *literary* (my emphases) survey of the Islamic world in the fourteenth century … If IB did not go to Bulghar, he might nonetheless satisfy his readers' expectations by saying he did."[66]

There are diverse aspects of the *Riḥla*, and the journeys described therein, which are, to say the least, suspect and/or plagiarised but, as Dunn notes,[67] and Janicsek and Hrbek confirm,[68] "The Bulghar trip is the only section of the *Riḥla* whose falsity has been proven beyond almost any doubt."

L.P. Harvey's words are salutary and put Ibn Baṭṭūṭa's, and Ibn Juzayy's, literary techniques and wander/wonderlust aspirations in a modern context: "From a travel book, readers expect and usually get a coherent narrative arranged in an ordered sequence, and they willingly put their trust in the author's truthfulness … We modern readers of Ibn Baṭṭūṭa bring to the book our modern ideas of what a travel book ought to be, and when those expectations are not met exactly, we feel baffled."[69]

Yet, if, with the medieval reader and voyager, we privilege the idea of descriptions of *'ajā'ib*, wonders, over exact truth,[70] then we can more adequately appreciate the authorial traveller's intention in the famous narrative of the journey to the City of Bulghār. This whole concept of voyage as textual narrative of wonders was fully accepted by that most perspicacious of modern commentators on Ibn Baṭṭūṭa, Tim Mackintosh-Smith, as he retraced the footsteps of his hero in his book *Travels with a Tangerine:* "As we reached the mainland at Ras Nus I wrote in my notebook: 'Sea still full of *'ajā'ib*, – even if wonders now = e.g. whale songs.'"[71]

It is that single Arabic word *'ajā'ib* which resonates throughout the *Riḥla*, from its initial articulation in the very title of Ibn Baṭṭūṭa's work, and which provides the real key to, and explanation of, the Bulghār episode.

China: the lure of the exotic other

> "Curiouser and curiouser!" cried Alice.[72]

Could we describe Ibn Baṭṭūṭa as a proto-Orientalist in the actual Saidean sense? Certainly, he was in love with and, indeed, collected, the "exotic".[73] And certainly, the alleged visit to China is another section of his *Riḥla* which has been viewed with considerable suspicion by many Ibn Baṭṭūṭa scholars.[74] As I have put it elsewhere: "While the historian and History of Art scholar may relish the descriptions of Mecca and Medina in the *Riḥla* of Ibn Baṭṭūṭa (partially plagiarised from the earlier *Riḥla* of Ibn Djubayr), they must treat with extreme caution the former's description of his visit to China in view of the controversy over whether he actually visited that area in person."[75]

Ross E. Dunn expresses "uneasy skepticism" about the whole China narrative and believes that "it is the least satisfying and most problematic section of the entire book."[76] Certainly, Tatsuro Yamamoto is in a distinct minority when he writes: "I think there is reason enough to presume that Ibn Baṭūṭa's [*sic*] visit to China was a fact," although he does modify this assessment with reference to Ibn Baṭṭūṭa's account being "interwoven with events that had taken place prior to his visit together with some other inaccurate remarks."[77]

L.P. Harvey's attempt at a solution is ingenious. Noting that "Ibn Battuta's mission to China is the great puzzle and the great mystery of the *Travels*",[78] Harvey surveys the evidence[79] and suggests: "A prudently conservative view might be that he probably reached South China, but got little further than the ports of the China Sea, and that he pieced the rest together from hearsay and the tales of other travellers."[80]

Certainly, an examination of the footnotes in Gibb and Beckingham's Volume IV translation of the *Travels* leads one to a profound scepticism about the entire visit to China: for example, right at the beginning of the China narrative, Ibn Baṭṭūṭa refers to a river called by the Persian words *Āb Ḥayāt*, which Ibn Baṭṭūṭa translates into Arabic as *Mā' al-Ḥayāt* ("The Water of Life").[81] Yet Gibb and Beckingham note in their footnote that "there is, of course, no such river".[82]

Harvey makes the intriguing suggestion (without evidence) that "in the matter of the China embassy, rather than setting out to mislead us, his readers, [Ibn Baṭṭūṭa] may in the first place have been duped and misled himself, have been the victim of a hoax on a grand scale."[83] Does the sadistic ruler of Delhi, Muḥammad b. Tughlug (*reg.* AD 1325–1351), play with our traveller by sending him on a futile and non-existent joke embassy which then, hopelessly but ineluctably, unravels, leaving an assaulted "Ibn Baṭṭūṭa ... in hiding, an isolated fugitive, near naked, and avoiding all human settlements"?[84]

It is interesting, as Gibb and Beckingham observe, that "no reference to this embassy has yet been traced in either the Chinese or the Indian records."[85]

To follow Harvey's hypothesis, does Ibn Baṭṭūṭa, because he was *supposed* to have gone to China, *claim* to have done so but attempt to cover his back "by saying he stayed indoors and did not go out to look at anything",[86] in case he is later asked too many detailed questions about his trip?

As Ibn Baṭṭūṭa himself puts it:

> China, for all its magnificence, did not please me. I was deeply depressed by the prevalence of infidelity and when I left my lodging I saw many offensive things which distressed me so much that I stayed at home and went out only when it was necessary.[87]

Perhaps that was the cause of the numerous errors in the Chinese section of his *Travelogue*, identified by Gibb and Beckingham.[88]

If he did not visit China, and relied on second-hand reports from others, the errors in his narrative highlight a possible fraud; if he did visit China, but secluded himself in the manner he describes, then his deliberate refusal to embrace the manners and customs of the country with his usual curiosity would also account for many of these errors.

But could Harvey's hypothesis be right? Is the whole China narrative a literary charade and forgery, like the notorious deception of the journey to Bulghār? Harvey wisely points out that "we cannot entirely exclude the alternative hypothesis: that Ibn Battuta never went to the Far East at all".[89] In that case, we have in Ibn Baṭṭūṭa, and his scribe Ibn Juzayy, a practised storyteller and a skilful amanuensis who both knew "how to make good use of second-hand data".[90] Such narrative, literary and secretarial skills would account for the accurate[91] funeral rites of the Mongol Qān which he describes in Khān-Bāliq (Beijing), if he did not witness them himself.[92]

Thus we have in the same text grotesque inaccuracies mingled with careful and accurate description. The scholar is left to try to account for such anomalies!

The well-worn, if weak or even invented, ḥadīth attributed to the Prophet Muḥammad, "Seek knowledge even as far as China", would have been familiar to Ibn Baṭṭūṭa.[93] The obligation to entertain the reader would also have weighed heavily with the traveller. His credibility, perhaps in direct consequence, was suspect from an early age. Even his own scribe, Ibn Juzayy, seems to register a slight disclaimer: "I have related all the anecdotes and historical narratives which he related, without applying myself to investigate their truthfulness or to test them …"[94] The great Arab historian and proto-sociologist of the fourteenth century, Ibn Khaldūn (AD 1332–1406), was well aware that many people regarded Ibn Baṭṭūṭa as a liar and did not believe the stories he narrated in his *Riḥla.*[95] Yet Ibn Khaldūn cites the advice of the *wazīr* who suggests that stories about foreign lands should not be dismissed out of hand simply because one has not visited those lands.[96] The issue, then, was – and is – one of incredulity versus plausibility and possibility.

> "I can't believe *that*!" said Alice. "Ca'n't you?" the Queen said in a pitying tone. "Try again: draw a long breath, and shut your eyes." Alice laughed. "There's no use trying," she said: "one *ca'n't* believe impossible things." "I daresay you haven't had much practice," said the Queen. "When I was your age, I always did it for half-an-hour a day. Why, sometimes I've believed as many as six impossible things before breakfast …"[97]

Ibn Baṭṭūṭa's *Riḥla* embraces at least two distinct paradigms. It embraces what I will term the *Voyage as Text* or *'Ajā'ib* Paradigm, whose primary purpose was to entertain the reader, regardless of factual truth. Its arch-components are the enumerations of *wonders*, famous *people* and outlandish *places.* The alleged sighting of the mythical *rukhkh*, the encounter with the retired ex-Emperor Andronicus II and the visits to Bulghār and China, as we have noted, are all examples of these. Ibn Baṭṭūṭa's is an *adab* paradigm in an Islamic world, whose primary driving motor is the pilgrimage impulse, at least as far as travel is concerned. It is an *adab* whose fabric is woven from the multistranded threads of fantasy as well as fact. In this, the ultimate *telos* of Mecca becomes subsumed in the wider *umma,* community, of the author's well-stocked imagination. His *Riḥla* also embraces the secondary, self-chosen Paradigm of *Exile and Return*, whose several elements appear in so much world literature, from Homer's *Odyssey* to Dante's *Divine Comedy.* We have the sadness of his home-leaving, a series of lengthy journeys punctuated by homesickness, shipwreck, assault and persecution, a rise to maturity and prestige whose apotheosis is perhaps his judgeships in Delhi and the Maldives,[98] and the utter joy of a home-coming after so many years away from his native land.[99]

Ibn Baṭṭūṭa lived and travelled in a world in flux, whether the Islamic world of his homeland, Morocco, or the *dār al-ḥarb* (House of War) of the non-Islamic states beyond. He endeavours to make sense of that world, to write a controlled and controlling textual narrative of that world, by focussing on certain *topoi* such as constitute the elements of our paradigms adumbrated above. The frame of these *topoi* is the *riḥla* as *adab.* This *riḥla* genre welds these *topoi* together into a special relationship within and beyond the narrative, and to the narrator, his scribe and their reader. To use Clifford A. Hooker's term, loosely, they may be characterised as *relata.*[100]

In another scholar's words, "the chaotic labyrinth of relations, that forms an individual's outlook on his world, is in a sense simplified, through the foregrounding of these primary relations. All else is background, out of focus and less important."[101]

Thus Ibn Baṭṭūṭa privileges the elements of our two paradigms, in an attempt at making sense of, and controlling at least textually, the milieu in which he exists, and in so doing, he relegates much else to an inferior level of existence and interest, including what we might regard as the vital parameters of reliability and truth. Leaning on Hooker, Qutbuddin invokes the concept of "relational proposition": for example, if entities that relate, such as the sun and the moon, may be characterised as *relata*, then the fact that one is "greater than the other in size and brightness" is the "relational proposition".[102]

But what we have sometimes with Ibn Baṭṭūṭa is what might be termed "relational disjunction": the narrative interest focussed upon the triple *topoi* of wonder, people and places in the first paradigm is often radically disjoined from the actual truth. It is perhaps only in the second, *Exile and Return*, paradigm that we find an equation of narrative and truth, glimpsing the narrator's actual feelings as he either sets out or returns, and establishes *journey and exile*, on the one hand, and *home and return*, on the other, as true sets of *relata*.

Ibn Baṭṭūṭa's text does not stand alone. We have stressed several times that it is part of a specifically Arabic genre of *riḥla* as *belles-lettres*, *adab*, rather than history or geography.[103] But it also has a much broader, and much more powerful, intertextual dimension. Mikhail Bakhtin observed that "any utterance is a link in a very completely organised chain of utterances."[104] Texts may be said to interact with past, present and future texts.[105] This is abundantly evident in the use specifically made by Ibn Baṭṭūṭa, or his scribe, of Ibn Jubayr's text, the latter written over a hundred years before Ibn Baṭṭūṭa was born.[106]

It is more broadly evident in the writings of Marco Polo (AD 1254–1324) "whose *Il Milione*", Harvey reminds us, "antedates [Ibn Baṭṭūṭa's] *Travels* by perhaps two generations",[107] but whose life provides a neat, actual and intertextual overlap with that of Ibn Baṭṭūṭa.

There is also an intertextual, *forward-looking* dimension in which the work of such authors as Ibn Jubayr, Marco Polo and Ibn Baṭṭūṭa anticipate, in one form or another, the travel literature of later authors as diverse as Rudolph Erich Raspe (AD 1736–1794) and Robert Louis Stevenson (AD 1850–1894). Thus, finally, and in pursuit of a 'golden' intertextual thread, it is to the books of Marco Polo, Raspe and Stevenson that we shall briefly turn. We shall bear in mind, also, the two paradigms, *'Ajā'ib* and *Exile and Return*, with their selected *topoi* adumbrated above, of wonders, people and places, on the one hand, and exilic pain and joyous return, on the other. Over all hang the twin spectres of *Truth* and *Reality*.

The travels of Marco Polo

Comparing Marco Polo (AD 1254–1324) and Ibn Baṭṭūṭa, Tim Mackintosh-Smith has observed: "The fascinating yet somehow bloodless adventures of Marco Polo, whose life and route overlapped with those of Ibn Battutah, seem to belong to a past age. The Venetian's death, shortly before Ibn Battutah started travelling, was nicely timed."[108] There may, indeed, be differences in tone between these two key texts, but the intertextual dimension is inescapable. And it is not the same route, to which Mackintosh-Smith refers, nor the alleged final *telos* of China, which alone constitute this dimension. There is the same key fascination with *wonders*, great *persons* and fabulous, exotic *places*, not to mention the pains undergone on exilic embassies and the ultimate joy of the final homecoming. How much was true?

Marco Polo set out on his travels from Venice in AD 1271. And the motif of *wonders* intrudes right from the beginning of his narrative, in the first few lines of the *Prologue*: "Here you will find all the great wonders and curiosities of Greater Armenia and Persia, of the Tartars and of India, and of many other territories."[109] Never endowed with great reticence, Marco Polo claims in this *Prologue* to have "observed more of the peculiarities of this part of the world [the Mongol Empire] than any other man, because he travelled more widely in these outlandish regions than any man who was ever born, and also because he gave his mind more intently to observing them."[110]

We note immediately the strong emphasis on the "outlandish" and the exotic. With the, perhaps natural, hubris of the great traveller puffed up by his own alleged achievements, Marco Polo's text claims that he is the greatest traveller and explorer in the history of mankind, in the same statement stressing the "great wonders" he has seen.[111] His translator, Ronald Latham, in fact agrees with this seemingly immodest self-assessment, noting that "even among the Arab globe-trotters he had no serious competitor till Ibn Batuta [*sic*] two generations later."[112]

The start of Marco Polo's travels in AD 1271 occurs at a particularly dramatic point in papal history: internecine war between two Tartar rulers disrupts a trading expedition undertaken by Marco Polo's father, Niccolò, and his uncle Maffeo. After several adventures they find themselves at the court of the Great Khan himself, Kubilai Khan (*reg.* AD 1260–1294). The brothers talk to him of the Pope, Clement IV (*reg.* AD 1265–1268), and Kubilai decides to send an embassy to the Pope comprising Niccolò, Maffeo and one of his nobles. Reaching Acre in AD 1269, they learn that Pope Clement has died the year before and the See of Peter is vacant. Larner tells us that "the papal interregnum was to be the longest on record, and for the Polos this must have been a time of ever-increasing frustration".[113]

A papal legate advises them to wait until a new pope is elected, so they go to Venice. Here Niccolò learns of the death of his wife, leaving him only a fifteen-year-old son, Marco. They get tired of waiting for a new pope to be elected and so, in AD 1271, set out from Venice, this time with Marco. Pope Gregory X (*reg.* AD 1272–1276) is elected in AD 1272; the Polos visit him and Gregory, in his turn, entrusts the Polos with an embassy back to the Great Khan, who makes the brothers most welcome.[114]

Thus begins one of the most extraordinary sets of travels in the history of mankind, to paraphrase Marco Polo's own initial observations in his *Prologue*.[115] It is a journey, or set of journeys, which will last twenty-four years and straddle the three continents of Asia, Europe and Africa;[116] it will be a "long and uncertain pilgrimage"[117] whose route will provide meat, industry and entertainment for generations of Marco Polo scholars.[118]

And, *pace* John Larner,[119] Marco Polo encounters his full share of *wonders* as well as great *men* and fabulous *places*. Robin Brown summarises very neatly what happens: "This then is the intimate memoir of a teenager who exceeds his wildest dreams by becoming courtier and confidant to the most powerful ruler on earth, the Grand Khan, Kublai [*sic*], and a traveller *extraordinaire*, outrageously rich and famous."[120] The *Travels* have all the exuberance of a wonder-struck teenager as well as the astonished delight of the seasoned traveller. Not for nothing did Jacopo d'Acqui, writing in the fourteenth century, refer to Marco Polo's book as *Liver Milionis de Magnis Mirabilibus Mundi!*[121]

Yet some of the "wonders" Marco Polo describes are simple misapprehensions and should not be viewed as deliberate attempts to mislead. These include interpreting the "Singing Sands", "caused by the action of wind on dunes", as spirit voices;[122] mistaking crocodiles for huge snakes;[123] and espousing a casual belief in unicorns as a result of sighting the Asian rhinoceros.[124] Scholars have remarked upon Marco Polo's interest in exotic flora and fauna[125] and it is hardly surprising, in a pre-scientific age, that some of his sightings of natural "wonders" should have been misinterpreted. However, Ronald Latham notes that "his descriptions of exotic plants, beasts and especially birds are usually far more accurate and recognizable than those to be found in contemporary herbals and bestiaries."[126]

All that said, Marco Polo is not immune from embellishing his account with fabulous and fantastic tales, reported on his own admission at second hand, of giant birds known as gryphons or rocs (Arabic *rukhkh*s), capable of lifting an entire elephant high in the air and then dropping it so that it "is smashed to pulp, whereupon the gryphon bird perches on the carcase and feeds at its ease."[127]

Such exotic wonders serve the textual purpose of exotic embellishment and we recall that Ibn Baṭṭūṭa's *Riḥla* resorts to the same device in *his* reference to an alleged maritime encounter with the mythical *rukhkh*.[128] However, Ibn Baṭṭūṭa hedges his bets slightly and does not indicate in his text that he actually believes what the sailors have seen is really the *rukhkh*: "We did not see it or know its true shape" (*Fa-lam narahu wa la 'arafnā ḥaqīqa ṣūratihi*).[129]

Similar tales to that of the *rukhkh* are interwoven through Marco Polo's narrative with legends such as that of Alamut, which we shall describe in a short while;[130] there is an Ibn Baṭṭūṭa-ish interest in ascetics and miracles,[131] and an entrenched belief in levitating cups:

> These *Bakhshi* contrive by their enchantment and their art that the full cups rise up of their own accord from the floor on which they have been standing and come to the Great Khan without anyone touching them. And this they do in the sight of 10,000 men. *What I have told you is the plain truth without a word of falsehood.*[132]

Again, this bears comparison with the narrative of Ibn Baṭṭūṭa: "He claimed to have seen the juggler climb a rope after one of his apprentices and then, out of sight, dismember the boy and cast the limbs down to his audience."[133] However, Ibn Baṭṭūṭa's dismay and credulity are laid to rest when he is told by "a neighbouring *qāḍī*" that it is all a trick.[134]

Like Ibn Baṭṭūṭa, Marco Polo collects *great personages* and two, in particular, stand out in his narrative: the encounter with the Great Khan, Kubilai Khan, and the description of the myth-enshrouded "Old Man of the Mountains".

The first meeting between Marco Polo and the Khan was poignant, fraught with significance for the future and clearly made an indelible mark upon the young man's memory:

> When the Great Khan saw Marco, who was a young stripling, he asked who he was. "Sire", said Messer Niccolò, "he is my son, and your liege man." "He is heartily welcome", said the Khan.[135]

Bergreen comments: "One can imagine the youth's cheeks tingling with apprehension at the formality and intimacy of the occasion, as well as its significance, for his father had just committed him to the service of Kublai Khan."[136] Bergreen continues: "Winning Kublai Khan's approval marked the decisive moment in young Marco's life … under the Khan's influence Marco began to evolve into the traveller remembered by history. For seventeen years, Marco Polo and Kublai Khan participated in a most unusual partnership as master and servant, teacher and disciple, and even father and son."[137] Thus begins a startling career for the Venetian, while still a very young man, as an ambassador and emissary of one of the greatest rulers on earth, but also as one of the world's greatest travellers.[138]

There are certain analogies to be drawn here, *inter alia* with the employment of Ibn Baṭṭūṭa by the Sultan of Delhi, Muḥammad b. Tughluq, as an ambassador,[139] although, if we are to accept Harvey's thesis, the Great Khan was a considerably more benign patron to *his* ambassador than Ibn Tughluq was to his!

Jonathan Clements tells us that Marco Polo was "an unexpected hit" at the court of Kubilai Khan;[140] and the respect our traveller seems to have inspired in the Khan was reciprocated in fulsome, almost traditionally embarrassing, measure:

> For everyone should know that this Great Khan is the mightiest man, whether in respect of subjects or of territory or of treasure, who is in the world today or who has ever been, from Adam our first parent down to the present moment.[141]

Marco Polo continues his encomium in the same traditional vein: "And I will make it quite clear to you in our book that this is the plain truth, so that everyone will be convinced that he is indeed the greatest lord the world has ever known."[142] Again, there are intertextual echoes here of the way in which Ibn Baṭṭūṭa and his scribe, Ibn Juzayy, will effusively praise the Marīnid Sultan of Morocco, Abū 'Inān Fāris (*reg.* AD 1348–1358), a few generations later in the *Riḥla*.[143]

Of Marco Polo's dealings with Kubilai Khan there is much that is credible and it clearly gives Marco Polo much pleasure to be able to include the great ruler's name in his travelogue. But the traveller's narrative of the Old Man, or Shaykh, of the Mountain clearly belongs to a different, more romantic and rather more brittle category of reporting.[144] He transmits the story "just as I, Messer Marco, have heard it told by many people",[145] and it is fundamentally that of the alleged, and well-known, tale of the mock Paradise devised by the Ismāʿīlī Assassins of Alamut and their rulers.

Marco Polo is certainly aware of the overthrow of Alamut by the Mongols[146] but he does not claim to have visited the actual castle of Alamut in person. His story about the Shaykh of the Mountain is, however, important textually as a romantic embellishment and an addition to his collection of "great personages". As Bergreen puts it: "Marco and his collaborator realised that recounting tales of the Assassins would send a frisson of horror through their audience, and they played up the cult's sinister mystique for all it was worth."[147] With this tale, Marco Polo succeeded in fixing the deeds of the Assassins sect of Ismāʿīlīs "in the Western consciousness, but as he admitted, his account was based on dramatic hearsay rather than personal experience."[148] Robin Brown suggests that this story "has all the hallmarks of a licentious fairy story, good tabloid stuff, at which [his amanuensis] Rustichello [see below] … was an expert."[149] But Brown goes on to corroborate "the truth of Marco Polo's seemingly fantastical tale."[150] And while there certainly was an Ismāʿīlī stronghold at Alamut, modern scholarship has completely discounted as Frankish fabrications the "so-called Assassin legends", including the "paradise legend", mentioned above, later synthesised by Marco Polo and/or his scribe, Rustichello of Pisa.[151]

Daftary stresses that the Persian historian Juwaynī, who died in AD 1283, and "who accompanied the Mongol conqueror to Alamut in 654/1256 and personally inspected that fortress and its renowned library before their destruction by the Mongols, does not report discovering any 'secret garden of paradise' there as claimed in Marco Polo's account".[152]

It is, however, when we move to the third part of our *ʿAjāʾib* paradigm of *Voyage as Text*, the "collection" of exotic *places*, that we encounter most scepticism from scholars down the ages, with most particular reference to Marco Polo's sojourns in China. Once again, we encounter an overlap with the scepticism with which Ibn Baṭṭūṭa's own alleged visit to China has been greeted. Fundamentally, it has been contended "that neither Marco nor his father and uncle ever were in China, the thesis that brands them as liars and charlatans."[153]

A recurring motif in all the scepticism is that Marco Polo never mentions the Great Wall of China.[154] In Marco Polo's defence, other scholars like Robin Brown and Jonathan Clements both note that the Wall only reached its present size and grandeur from about AD 1500 and thus could easily have been missed in its fragmented form by the casual traveler.[155] The seeming lack of proper reference to indigenous religions like Confucianism and Taoism is also raised against Marco Polo, but John Larner feels able to respond adequately to most of these criticisms.[156] He espouses the solution of John W. Haeger,[157] who believes that the descriptions of Northern China reflect personal experience, contrasting with knowledge "of Southern China only through hearsay".[158]

In any case, reflecting on "Marco's knowledge of China" and fitting neatly into our paradigm of *Voyage as Text*, Larner asks whether any of this really matters "for the historian of geography": "One could say … that what was important was not the author but the Book."[159]

Once again we are forced into an interesting comparison with Ibn Baṭṭūṭa: contrasting with Marco Polo, was it *only* South China that Ibn Baṭṭūṭa himself reached?[160]

As with the latter, the journey brings its fair share of pain: as Larner summarises and reminds us, there are all the risks of "shipwreck ... piracy ... brigandage ... extortion ... and wild beasts."[161] Yet it is the actual *Return* which intrigues. With Ibn Baṭṭūṭa in his *Riḥla*, we feel the very joy in his several returns and the final quenching of his homesickness. He is generously and graciously welcomed by his Sultan.[162] Marco Polo has a rather different home-coming. His actual narrative ends with his return to Venice in AD 1295.[163] Homesickness has clearly imbued father, uncle and Marco with a desire to return, as our traveller shows in his *Prologue*, but they have initial problems in obtaining the Khan's permission to depart.[164] What they cannot have imagined, as Giambattista Ramusio shows in his 1553 or 1559 Preface to Marco Polo's *Travels*,[165] was being unrecognised and thus denied entrance to their own Venetian house.[166]

Bergreen comments: "Marco Polo had learned to overcome being a stranger in the Mongol Empire, only to find that he had become a stranger once more, now that he was home."[167]

Several legends have accumulated about the return of the Polos to Venice, one of the most notable being that of the feast at which the Polos first wear fine crimson robes and then their original Mongol dress in which they had arrived and from which a treasure trove of jewels is made to fall, to the utter astonishment of their relatives and friends. Thus it is proved beyond doubt that the Polos are who they say they are.[168] Ramusio, Bergreen suggests, embellished but did not invent this story.[169] There is pain, then, even in the *Return*, but that pain is followed by recognition and joy.

This story of the feast stands on the cusp of reality and fiction. Together with the whole China narrative, and the scepticism which *that* has engendered down the centuries, we come to a consideration of the essence of Marco Polo's *Voyage as Text:* Truth and Reality *versus* Fiction, Faction, Fable, and Narrative as Pure Entertainment.

On his deathbed, in the presence of a priest in AD 1324, Marco Polo insisted that he had not recorded in his book even a half of all the sights he had seen.[170] Yet this solemn asseveration, whose falsity many mediaevals believed might have imperilled the eternal happiness of Marco Polo's soul, has not prevented a host of scholars over the centuries from characterising his *Travels* as "a romance or fable" and "pure fiction."[171] He was regarded as "an entertainer and fabricator", in the Middle Ages.[172] For perhaps the majority, his work read "like a medieval soap opera".[173] Yet Robin Brown suggests that "there is overwhelming evidence from independent and other sources that ... both the main structure of Marco Polo's travels and a surprising amount of the detail are authentic."[174]

And it is clear that, like Gibb's Ibn Baṭṭūṭa, Marco Polo is a *géographe malgré lui*.[175]

Nonetheless, just as the *Riḥla* should not be classified as a formal geography or guidebook, so too we should beware of treating Marco Polo's *Travels* as "a guidebook to China" and prefer to consider the work as "a literary confection, an artful story",[176] in the same way that Ibn Baṭṭūṭa's *Riḥla* is primarily a work of *belles-lettres, adab*.[177]

In all this, a brief consideration should be given to the role of Rustichello da Pisa, Marco Polo's scribe and amanuensis, with whom he was at one time allegedly imprisoned as a prisoner of war of the Genoese (AD 1298–1299).[178] For Rustichello was to Marco Polo what Ibn Juzayy was to Ibn Baṭṭūṭa; and every Marco Polo scholar has tried to hazard a guess at the extent of Rustichello's influence and impact on the text.[179]

Latham goes so far as to observe that "it is likely that without the aid of Rustichello Marco would never have written a best-seller."[180] Was the book written from dictation or compiled from notes?[181] Or both? Bergreen suggests that Marco Polo had access to his notebooks in prison.[182] To what extent may the *Travels* be described as a properly *collaborative* work between Marco Polo and Rustichello?[183] We shall never know absolutely.

Rustichello specialised in the genre of romance,[184] and it shows. Clements observes that "sometimes, Rustichello's contributions stick out a mile",[185] even if they are not starkly flagged in the same way as Ibn Juzayy's interpolations in the *Riḥla* of Ibn Baṭṭūṭa with such phrases as "Ibn Juzayy said" (*Qāla Ibn Juzayy*).[186] Latham draws attention to the "Arthurian" elements inserted into the narrative by Rustichello[187] and surmises that some of the fantastical or fabulous elements in the *Travels* may also have been inserted by Rustichello.[188]

Brown emphasises that "Rustichello certainly gave the book its entrancing quality as a story, and it may owe some of the literally unbelievable details to his literary invention."[189] Yet it was Marco Polo, rather than his eager scribe, who received the nickname as early as AD 1305 of "Il Milione" or "Marco Millione", that is, a teller of millions of tall stories,[190] "a stuffy, millionaire Munchausen",[191] one who tells a million lies,[192] or even, as Roberto Gallo argues and translates, less romantically, one whose nickname is a corruption of "Vilione", the Polos having purchased the Vilione family palace.[193]

Intertextually, we may identify at least three different categories of *Voyage as Text*: those which *interweave fact and fiction* and sometimes produce what we might term "faction" (the *Riḥla* of Ibn Baṭṭūṭa and the *Travels* of Marco Polo are excellent examples of this genre); those which are demonstrably pure fiction (the extraordinary tales of Baron Munchausen [1785] as related by Rudolph Erich Raspe [AD 1736–1794], scientist, librarian and writer, are the supreme example of this category); and, finally, those which claim to be, and demonstrably are, pure fact (the enchanting *Travels with a Donkey in the Cévennes* (1879) is an ideal example of this last category, whose author, Robert Louis Stevenson [AD 1850–1894], died tragically young).

The Munchausen *Tales* exhibit a radical disjunction from reality in many of their pages; while Stevenson's *Travels* are skilfully and sensitively grounded in that reality. Both works, as we shall briefly show, relate intertextually to our two paradigms, on the one hand of *Voyage as Text* with its tripartite aspects of *wonders*, prominent *persons* and exotic *places*; and, on the other, of *Exile and Return* with its dual *topoi* of painful voyage and joyful home-coming. Ultimately, both belong to the literature of the picaresque in much the same way as the works of Marco Polo and Ibn Baṭṭūṭa.[194] It is true that the quirky personality of the latter shines through in the *Riḥla* by contrast with the sometimes bland impersonality of Marco,[195]or the steadfastness and curiosity of Robert Louis Stevenson. But, ultimately, all four works are concerned with wonders, *merveilles*, *'ajā'ib*, in one form or another.[196]

The Surprising Adventures of Baron Munchausen

One Introduction to *The Surprising Adventures of Baron Munchausen* places the work in the category of *Voyages Imaginaires:* three initial *exempla* are identified: Sir Thomas More's *Utopia* (1516), Daniel Defoe's *Robinson Crusoe* (1719) and Jonathan Swift's *Gulliver's Travels* (1726), each representing "the philosophical, the edifying and the satirical type of fictitious travel."[197] A fourth type, "the fantastically mendacious", is then identified and it is to this particular genre that the Munchausen *Adventures* belong.[198]

It was conceived as a work of satire[199] and a contemporary advertisement in the *Critical Review* of December 1785 boasted that, in it, "the marvellous has never been carried to a more whimsical and ludicrous extent".[200] It went through numerous editions,[201] with embellishments from other hands.[202] The adventures narrated about the Baron are a cornucopia of *wonders* which are literally incredible, despite the author's insistence to the contrary in the "Preface to the First Edition".[203] On the very first page the Baron tells how, during a sea voyage, a storm tore up huge trees into the sky to a height of five miles and then, as it ended, dropped them in their original spots where they rooted once more![204]

Travelling in Poland, he ties his horse to what seems to be a tree stump poking through the snow, only to find in the morning that the snow has melted and that his horse is tied to a steeple![205]

Chapter XVIII describes a second trip to the moon.[206] In a *Supplement* to the volume, which is probably not to be ascribed to the original author,[207] the Baron makes a lengthy trip on the back of an eagle, visiting France, Gibraltar, the Americas, Greenland and England.[208] The text is replete with visits to exotic *places* like Mount Etna and exotic "*people*" like the God Vulcan.

The *pains* of travel are never far away: in Mount Etna our traveller finds himself "bruised and burnt in various parts by the red-hot cinders" but "Vulcan himself did me the honour of applying plasters to my wounds, which healed them immediately."[209] Here, in one extraordinary passage, we find exotic *people*, exotic *places* and the *pain* of travel. The text is both "wanderland" and "wonderland"! And all is fantasy!

The *Return* is no less fantastic:

> Having arrived in England once more, the greatest rejoicings were made for my return; the whole city seemed one general blaze of illumination, and the Colossus of Rhodes, hearing of my astonishing feats, came on purpose to England to congratulate me on such unparalleled achievements. But above all other rejoicings on my return, the musical oratorio and song of triumph

were magnificent in the extreme. Gog and Magog were ordered to take the maiden tower of Windsor, and make a tambourine or great drum of it.[210]

Travels with a Donkey in the Cévennes

By extreme contrast, the mental and physical landscape inhabited by Robert Louis Stevenson is a rather more restrained wanderland/wonderland: it is the region of the Cévennes in South-Central France. Beset by poor health which dictates the courses of his wanderlust, he also seeks non-conformity.[211] Less romantic than Samoa, where he settles, and dies on 3 December 1894,[212] the travels in the Cévennes mark "the beginning of the critical phase in his life … Arguably the process of change and self-examination never ended, and what Stevenson embarked on when he trekked with his donkey into the Cévennes continued at least to Samoa, if not to the end of his life."[213]

The actual journey in *Travels with a Donkey* lasts twelve days (22 September–3 October 1878) and Robert Louis Stevenson covers more than 200 kilometres in this time, travelling from Le Monastier-sur-Gazeille in the Haute-Loire to St-Jean-du-Gard.[214] There are *pains* in abundance, ranging from problems with the load on his donkey, Modestine's, back,[215] cut shoulders and aching arms,[216] to outdoors camping in cold, wet clothes.[217] Stevenson was certainly testing himself physically and mentally.[218] Loneliness, too, tests his mental health.[219]

The divagation to the Cistercian monastery of Our Lady of the Snows is an excellent example of an exotic *place* visited, at least for Stevenson.[220] As Christopher Maclachlan puts it: "To one brought up in the Presbyterian Church of Scotland a Trappist monastery may be an exotic curiosity well worth a detour."[221] And the monks whom he encounters, notably "Father Apollinaris", are *exotic beings* who, nonetheless, engender admiration and some soul-searching.[222]

But of *wonders*, perhaps it is the wonders of nature itself which most enchant and intrigue Robert Louis Stevenson. A view may be "both wild and sad",[223] but "the wind among the trees was my lullaby".[224] Again, he observes: "The mists, which had hitherto beset me, were now broken into clouds, and fled swiftly and shone brightly in the sun. I drew a long breath. I was grateful to come, after so long, upon a scene of some attraction for the human heart."[225]

The home-coming, *return* or, better, arrival at the final point in his journey, the town of St-Jean-du-Gard, is a sad one. He sells Modestine, his donkey and constant companion on the journey, with some emotion: "I had lost Modestine. Up to that moment I had thought I hated her; but now she was gone …"[226] However, Robert Louis Stevenson "had bought freedom" by the sale and he was eager "to reach Alais for [his] letters", travelling on by stage-coach.[227]

The diverse travels of Marco Polo, Ibn Baṭṭūṭa, Baron Munchausen and Robert Louis Stevenson are, in many senses, extraordinarily different from each other. As we have shown, however, they are linked by our two paradigms of *Voyage as Text* and *Exile and Return*, though the different elements in each may be differently articulated and move fluidly between the realms of fact, fiction and the fertile imagination. The wonders, the *'ajā'ib*, are indeed diverse.

Ultimately, however, along with such works as Cervantes' *Don Quixote* and the "entirely fictional" *Travels*[228] of Sir John Mandeville (written c. AD 1366),[229] the travels of our four chosen authors in this essay embrace the literature of the picaresque, in which they sometimes encounter, and even work for, diverse rogues, seek and test themselves within a global cockpit where reality may merge with fiction, and actual, projected and imaginary voyages are metamorphosed into, and presented as, pure texts for entertainment rather than present or future navigation. Indeed, they may become literary "rogues" themselves at various times in their treatment of the truth. In other words, they embrace a world where actual truth and reality really do not matter any more and *where text is all!*

So, was Ibn Baṭṭūṭa an Orientalist? Edward Said defined Orientalism as "a style of thought based upon an ontological and epistemological distinction made between 'the Orient' and (most of the time) 'the Occident'."[230] The stark dicholomy, then, is US and THEM or, US *versus* THEM! For Said, there were "a restricted number of typical encapsulations: the journey [of particular interest for our studies of Ibn Baṭṭūṭa], the fable, the stereotype, the polemical confrontation. These are the lens through which the Orient is experienced, and they shape the language, perception, and form of the encounter between East and West."[231] For Said, "the Orient at large, therefore, vacillates between the West's contempt for what is familiar and its shivers of delight in – or fear of – novelty."[232] The key themes in all these quotes from Said are *exoticism* and *difference.*

For Ibn Baṭṭūṭa, the Maghrib was his West; all else was the Orient and there is no doubt that he was lured by what he perceived as the exotic, whether people or places. China and Bulghār, fascinating and, indeed, distasteful as both may have been, exhibit Ibn Baṭṭūṭa as the explorer of the exotic *par excellence.* Said himself speaks of "the entire range of pre-Romantic and Romantic representations of the Orient as exotic locale."[233]

Thus, in the sense that Ibn Baṭṭūṭa demonstrates a powerful affection for, and indeed, seeks after, exotic places, people, *'ajā'ib* and miracles, he may be described as a pre-Saidean Orientalist! But in terms of an Islamic missionary impulse, or Islamic imperialist fervour, Ibn Baṭṭūṭa was never an Orientalist in the sense that Said intended. Fundamentally, he was a "little man", sometimes promoted beyond his coping and capacity, who was the product of a particular environment in the medieval Maghrib, who enjoyed, sought, and was sometimes repelled by, the exotic manifestations of a world both within and beyond Islam which he could never have conceived, had he remained forever in the land of his birth for his entire life.

Notes

1 Lewis Carroll, *Alice's Adventures in Wonderland* AND *Through the Looking Glass and What Alice Found There*, The Centenary Edition, ed. with Introduction and notes by Hugh Haughton (London: Penguin Books, 1998), p. 10.
2 Haughton, "Introduction", in ibid., p. ix.
3 Hans Wehr, *A Dictionary of Modern Written Arabic*, ed. J. Milton Cowan, 2nd printing (Wiesbaden: Otto Harrassowitz/ London: Allen & Unwin, 1966), p. 591 sv

ajība, pl. *'ajā'ib*. Esther Addley observes: "*I wonder as I wander*, an unsettling carol that expresses amazement that Jesus 'was born for to die for poor orn'ry people like you and like I', was overheard in Cherokee country, North Carolina, in the early 20th century and is unknown in earlier forms" ("Faithful or Not", *Guardian*, Wednesday 8 December 2010, p. 33, my italics).

4 L.P. Harvey, *Ibn Battuta*, Makers of Islamic Civilization (London and New York: I.B. Tauris in assoc. with the Oxford Centre for Islamic Studies, 2007), pp. 5, 62.

5 Haughton, "Introduction", in Carroll, *Alice's Adventures*, p. x.

6 See Ian Richard Netton, art. "Riḥla", *Encyclopaedia of Islam*, Second Edition (hereafter referred to as *EI*[2]), Vol. VIII (Leiden: E.J. Brill, 1995), p. 328 (2 cols); repr. in Ian Richard Netton (ed.), *Islamic and Middle Eastern Geographers and Travellers* [hereafter referred to as IMEGT]: *Volume II: The Travels of Ibn Jubayr*, Critical Concepts in Islamic Thought (London and New York: Routledge, 2008), pp. 5–7.

7 Ibid.

8 Ibid.

9 See Paul Starkey, art. "Ibn Jubayr al-Kinani, Muhammad Ibn Ahmad (AD 1145–1217)", in Ian Richard Netton (ed.), *Encyclopedia of Islamic Civilisation and Religion* (London and New York: Routledge, 2008), p. 256.

10 Netton, art. "Rihḷa", p. 328.

11 Ibid.; see Tim Mackintosh-Smith, *Travels with a Tangerine: A Journey in the Footnotes of Ibn Battutah* (London, Basingstoke and Oxford: Pan Macmillan, Picador, 2002), pp. 9, 64.

12 See Netton, art. "Riḥla", p. 328.

13 Carroll, *Alice's Adventures*, p. 13.

14 Ibid., p. 109.

15 Paul Starkey, art. "Ibn Battuta (AD 1304–68/9 or 1377)", in Ian Richard Netton (ed.), *Encyclopedia of Islamic Civilisation and Religion* (London and New York: Routledge, 2008), p. 253; David Waines, *The Odyssey of Ibn Battuta: Uncommon Tales of a Medieval Adventurer* (London and New York: I.B. Tauris, 2010), p. 8; Mackintosh-Smith, *Travels with a Tangerine*, p. 43.

16 See Starkey, art. "Ibn Jubayr", p. 256.

17 Charles Pellat, art. "Ibn Djubayr" *EI*[2], Vol. III, p. 755.

18 Ibid.

19 R.J.C. Broadhurst (trans), *The Travels of Ibn Jubayr* (London: Jonathan Cape, 1952), p. 15 ("Introduction"). For the Arabic text see Ibn Jubayr, *Riḥla* (Beirut: Dār Ṣādir, 1964).

20 See Ian Richard Netton, "Ibn Jubayr: Penitent Pilgrim and Observant Traveller", in Ian Richard Netton, *Seek Knowledge: Thought and Travel in the House of Islam* (Richmond: Curzon Press, 1996), pp. 96–98.

21 Netton (ed.), IMEGT, Vol. II, p. 2.

22 See Broadhurst (trans.), *Travels of Ibn Jubayr*, p. 20.

23 Netton (ed.), IMEGT, Vol. II, p. 3; see Waines, *Odyssey*, pp. 12, 14–15, 18–19, 22.

24 Carroll, *Alice's Adventures*, p. 110.

25 See Ibn Baṭṭūṭa, *Riḥla* (Beirut: Dār Ṣādir, 1964) [hereafter referred to as IB], p. 17; see Waines, *Odyssey*, p. 159.

26 See Michael Mollat, "Ibn Batoutah et la mer", in Ian Richard Netton (ed.), IMEGT: *Volume III: The Travels of Ibn Battuta*, Critical Concepts in Islamic Thought (London and New York: Routledge, 2008), pp. 179–192; see IB, pp. 244, 601.

27 Netton (ed.), IMEGT, Vol. III, p. 1.

28 IB, p. 701; H.A.R. Gibb and C.F. Beckingham (trans. and eds), *The Travels of Ibn Baṭṭūṭa: AD 1325–1354*, [hereafter referred to as *Travels*] (London: The Hakluyt Society, 1994), Volume IV, p. 977.

29 See n.98 below.

30 Carroll, *Alice's Adventures*, p. 70.

31 See Harvey, *Ibn Battuta*, p. 55.

32 IB, p. 17; see also p. 637.

33 See n.98 below.
34 See my article "Myth, Miracle and Magic in the *Riḥla* of Ibn Baṭṭūṭa", repr. in Netton (ed.), IMEGT, Vol. III, pp. 160–168.
35 Ibid.
36 See IB, pp. 646–647; Gibb and Beckingham (trans. and eds), *Travels*, Vol. IV, pp. 911–912; Tim Mackintosh-Smith, *The Travels of Ibn Battutah*, trans. and abridged by Tim Mackintosh-Smith (London: Picador 2002) [hereafter referred to as *Travels*], p. XV; see Waines, *Odyssey*, pp. 192–193.
37 See above, n. 26.
38 See IB, pp. 26–27.
39 See above n. 26.
40 John Fowles, *The Collector*, Vintage Classics (London: Vintage Books, 1998; repr. of Jonathan Cape edn of 1963), p. 55.
41 For a neat and succinct history of the succession from Andronicus II to Andronicus III, see Mackintosh-Smith, *Travels with a Tangerine*, p. 328.
42 Ibid.; see also Waines, *Odyssey*, p. 9.
43 H.A.R. Gibb (trans. and ed.), *The Travels of Ibn Baṭṭūṭa: AD 1325–1354* (Cambridge: Cambridge University Press for the Hakluyt Society, 1962), Volume II, pp. 488 n. 274, 505 n. 323.
44 IB, p. 349.
45 Gibb (trans. and ed.), *Travels*, Volume II, p. 505 n. 323.
46 IB, pp. 349–350; Gibb (trans. and ed.), *Travels*, Vol. II, pp. 505–506.
47 See Mackintosh-Smith, *Travels*, p. xi.
48 Gibb (trans. and ed.), *Travels*, Vol. II, p. 512; IB, p. 354.
49 Gibb (trans. and ed.), *Travels*, Vol. II, pp. 512–513; IB, pp. 354–355; see Harvey, *Ibn Battuta*, pp. 23–24.
50 Gibb (trans. and ed.), *Travels*, Vol. II, p. 512 n. 342.
51 See Harvey, *Ibn Battuta*, pp. 22–24; C.F. Beckingham, cited in ibid., p. 23; Ross E. Dunn, *The Adventures of Ibn Battuta: A Muslim Traveler of the 14th Century* (London and Sydney: Croom Helm, 1986), pp. 171–172 n. 17; Ivan Hrbek, "The Chronology of Ibn Baṭṭūṭa's Travels" [Originally published in *Archiv Orientālni*, Vol. 30 (1962), pp. 409–486], repr. in Netton (ed.), IMEGT, Vol. III, pp. 256–257. See also Mackintosh-Smith, *Travels*, p. 313 n. 65.
52 Hrbek, "Chronology", p. 257.
53 Dunn, *Adventures*, p. 180 n. 17; Mackintosh-Smith, *Travels with a Tangerine*, p. 332.
54 Stephen Janicsek, "Ibn Baṭṭūṭa's Journey to Bulghār: Is it a Fabrication?" [originally published in the *Journal of the Royal Asiatic Society* (1929), pp. 791–800]; repr. in Netton (ed.), IMEGT, Vol. III, pp. 281–288, see p. 287; Waines, *Odyssey*, p. 9.
55 Carroll, *Alice's Adventures*, pp. 10–12 (my emphases).
56 See Harvey, *Ibn Battuta*, pp. 5–7, 62; Gibb (trans. and ed.), *Travels*, Vol. II, p. 491 n. 285.
57 Mackintosh-Smith, *Travels*, p. 312 n.54.
58 Dunn, *Adventures*, p. 167; see Gibb (trans. and ed.), *Travels*, Vol. II, pp. 490–491; IB, p. 338.
59 IB, p. 338; Gibb (trans. and ed.), *Travels*, Vol. II, p. 490.
60 Gibb (trans. and ed.), *Travels*, Vol. II, p. 491; IB, p. 338.
61 Gibb (trans. and ed.), *Travels*, Vol. II, p. 491 n. 286.
62 Ibid., pp. 491–492; IB, pp. 338–339.
63 Gibb (trans. and ed.), *Travels*, Vol. II, p. 491 n. 285.
64 See Janicsek, "Ibn Baṭṭūṭa's Journey to Bulghār" repr. in Nettton (ed.), IMEGT, Vol. III, pp. 281–288; Hrbek, "Chronology", in ibid., pp. 249–250; Dunn, *Adventures*, pp. 179–180 n.12; Charles Beckingham,"In Search of Ibn Battuta", in Netton (ed.), IMEGT, Vol. III, p. 73; Harvey, *Ibn Battuta*, pp. 21–22; Mackintosh-Smith, *Travels*, pp. 126–127, 312 n. 54.
65 See Janicsek, "Ibn Baṭṭūṭa's Journey to Bulghār", p. 287.
66 Dunn, *Adventures*, p. 180 n. 12.

67 Ibid.
68 See Janicsek, "Ibn Baṭṭūṭa's Journey to Bulghār", p. 287; see Hrbek, "Chronology", p. 250.
69 Harvey, *Ibn Battuta*, p. 4.
70 Ibid.
71 Mackintosh-Smith, *Travels with a Tangerine*, p. 258.
72 Carroll, *Alice's Adventures*, p. 16.
73 See Netton, "Myth, Miracle and Magic".
74 IB, pp. 627–646; Gibb and Beckingham (trans. and eds), *Travels*, Vol. IV, pp. 888–910.
75 Netton, art. "Riḥla", p. 328; Hrbek, "Chronology", pp. 253, 194; Mackintosh-Smith, *Travels*, p. 323 n.8, p. XVII; Harvey, *Ibn Battuta*, p. 8.
76 Dunn, *Adventures*, p. 252; see Waines, *Odyssey*, pp. 9, 62, 191–194; see also Tim Mackintosh-Smith, *Landfalls: On the Edge of Islam with Ibn Battutah* (London: John Murray, 2010), p. 174.
77 Tatsuro Yamamoto, "On Ṭawālisī Described by Ibn Baṭūṭa", in Netton (ed.), IMEGT, Vol. III, p. 326.
78 Harvey, *Ibn Battuta*, p. 41.
79 Ibid., pp. 41–51.
80 Ibid., p. 41.
81 IB, p. 627; Gibb and Beckingham (trans. and eds), *Travels*, Vol. IV, p. 888.
82 Ibid., p. 888 n. 2; see also the rubbishing of Ibn Baṭṭūṭa's text with reference to China in ibid., pp. 889 n. 5, 890 n. 8, 891 n. 16, 895 n. 27, 901 n. 45, 906 n. 58, 907 n. 64.
83 Harvey, *Ibn Battuta*, pp. 43, 44–47.
84 Ibid., pp. 44–45; see IB, pp. 531ff.
85 Gibb and Beckingham (trans. and eds), *Travels*, Vol. IV, p. 773 n. 1; Harvey, *Ibn Battuta*, p. 43.
86 Harvey, *Ibn Battuta*, p. 47.
87 Gibb and Beckingham (trans. and eds), *Travels*, Vol. IV, p. 900; IB, p. 638.
88 See above n. 82.
89 Harvey, *Ibn Battuta*, pp. 47–48.
90 Ibid., pp. 48, 50; see Waines, *Odyssey*, p. 23.
91 See Gibb and Beckingham (trans. and eds), *Travels*, Vol. IV, p. 909 n. 71; Harvey, *Ibn Battuta*, p. 50.
92 Harvey, *Ibn Battuta*, pp. 50–51; IB, pp. 644–646.
93 Mackintosh-Smith, *Travels*, p. x.
94 H.A.R. Gibb (trans. and ed.), *The Travels of Ibn Baṭṭūṭa: AD 1325–1354* (hereafter referred to as *Travels*) (Cambridge: Cambridge University Press for the Hakluyt Society, 1958), Volume I, p. 7; IB, p. 13.
95. Mackintosh-Smith, *Travels*, p. xvii [Foreword]; see Ibn Khaldūn, *The Muqaddimah*, trans. and ed. Franz Rosenthal (3 vols, Princeton: Princeton University Press, 1958), Vol. 1, pp. 370–371 cited in Dunn, *Adventures*, p. 316. For the Arabic text, see Ibn Khaldūn, *Muqaddima*, ed. Darwīsh al-Juwaydī, 2nd edn (Beirut: al-Maktaba al-'Aṣriyya, 1996), p. 170.
96 See ibid.; Waines, *Odyssey*, p. 6.
97 Carroll, *Through the Looking-Glass and What Alice Found There*, p. 174.
98 See IB, pp. 512–513, 588.
99 See, e.g., ibid., pp. 657–658.
100 See Clifford A. Hooker, "The Relational Doctrines of Space and Time", *The British Journal for the Philosophy of Science*, Vol. 22:2 (1971), pp. 97–130 esp. p. 129. (I am indebted to Aziz K. Qutbuddin, *Taḥmīd: A Literary Genre?*, Vol. 1, unpublished PhD thesis, University of London (SOAS), 2009, pp. 108 n. 161, 304 for this reference.).
101 Qutbuddin, *Taḥmīd*, p. 108.
102 Ibid.
103 Netton, art. "Riḥla", p. 328.

104 Mikhail Bakhtin, "The Problem of Speech Genres", in Caryl Emerson and Michael Holquist (eds), *Speech Genres and Other Late Essays*, (Austin: University of Texas Press, 1986), p. 69, quoted in Qutbuddin, *Taḥmīd*, p. 256 n. 379.
105 See Qutbuddin, *Taḥmīd*, p. 256.
106 See Netton, art. "Riḥla", p. 328.
107 Harvey, *Ibn Battuta*, p. 41.
108 Mackintosh-Smith, *Travels*, p. viii.
109 Marco Polo, *The Travels of Marco Polo*, trans. Ronald Latham (London: Penguin Books, 1958) [hereafter referred to as MP, *Travels*/Latham], p. 33.
110 Ibid., pp. 41–42.
111 Ibid., p. 33.
112 Ibid., p. 7 ("Introduction").
113 John Larner, *Marco Polo and the Discovery of the World* (New Haven and London: Yale University Press, 1999, 2001), p. 35.
114 MP, *Travels*/Latham, pp. 34–40. See Laurence Bergreen, *Marco Polo: From Venice to Xanadu* (London: Quercus, 2008), pp. 35–36, 41; Marco Polo, *The Travels of Marco Polo [The Venetian]*, ed. Manuel Komroff (New York: Liveright, 2003) [hereafter referred to as MP, *Travels*/Komroff], pp. viii–x; Jonathan Clements, *Marco Polo* (London: Haus Publishing, 2007), pp. 14–17; Robin Brown, *Marco Polo: Journey to the End of the Earth* (Stroud: Sutton Publishing, 2007), pp. 12–13; Larner, *Marco Polo*, esp. pp. 33–41.
115 See MP, *Travels*/Latham, p. 33.
116 Bergreen, *Marco Polo*, p. 315.
117 Ibid., p. 37.
118 Brown, *Marco Polo*, p. 19; compare Hrbek's endeavours with Ibn Baṭṭūṭa in his magisterial article "Chronology", cited above n. 51.
119 Larner, *Marco Polo*, p. 83.
120 Brown, *Marco Polo*, p. 27.
121 MP, *Travels*/Latham, p. 19n, p. 26n ("Introduction").
122 Bergreen, *Marco Polo*, p. 82; MP, *Travels*/Latham, pp. 84–85.
123 Bergreen, *Marco Polo*, pp. 180–181; MP, *Travels*/Latham, pp. 178–179.
124 Bergreen, *Marco Polo*, pp. 189–190, 270; MP, *Travels*/Latham, pp. 188, 253.
125 MP, *Travels*/Komroff, p. xxx ("Introduction"); Jeremy Catto, "Foreword", in Brown, *Marco Polo*, pp. viii–ix.
126 MP, *Travels*/Latham, p. 21 ("Introduction").
127 Ibid., pp. 300–301; see also ibid., p. 24n; Larner, *Marco Polo*, pp. 80–83, esp. p. 81, pp. 98, 107.
128 See IB, pp. 646–647.
129 Ibid; Gibb and Beckingham (trans. and eds), *Travels*, Volume IV, p. 912.
130 MP, *Travels*/Latham, p. 18.
131 See ibid., pp. 109–112; see also Netton, "Myth, Miracle and Magic".
132 MP, *Travels*/Latham, p. 110 (my emphases).
133 Netton, "Myth, Miracle and Magic", p. 163; IB, p. 641.
134 Ibid.
135 MP, *Travels*/Latham, p. 40 ("Prologue").
136 Bergreen, *Marco Polo*, p. 119.
137 Ibid., p. 123.
138 Ibid., pp. 166, 167, 182, 302; MP, *Travels*/Komroff, p. xvii("Introduction").
139 See above n.84; Larner, *Marco Polo*, pp. 182–183.
140 Clements, *Marco Polo*, p. 33.
141 MP, *Travels*/Latham, p. 113.
142 Ibid.
143 See IB, pp. 10–12, 657–664.
144 See MP, *Travels*/Latham, p. 18 ("Introduction").
145 Ibid., pp. 70–73; Bergreen, *Marco Polo*, p. 55.

146 MP, *Travels*/Latham, pp. 72–73; see also, and compare, Mackintosh-Smith, *Travels with a Tangerine*, pp. 175–177.
147 Bergreen, *Marco Polo*, p. 54, see also p. 55.
148 Ibid., p. 55.
149 Brown, *Marco Polo*, p. 4.
150 Ibid., pp. 5–6.
151 See Farhad Daftary, *Ismailis in Medieval Muslim Societies*, Ismaili Heritage Series 12 (London and New York: I.B. Tauris in assoc. with the Institute of Ismaili Studies, London, 2005), pp. 33–35, 162–165.
152 Ibid., p. 34. See also p. 33.
153 Larner, *Marco Polo*, p. 46; Bergreen, *Marco Polo*, p. 360; see Waines, *Odyssey*, p. 5.
154 Larner, *Marco Polo*, p. 59; Brown, *Marco Polo*, pp. 3–4; Clements, *Marco Polo*, p. 54.
155 Clements, *Marco Polo*, p. 54; Brown, *Marco Polo*, p. 4.
156 Larner, *Marco Polo*, p. 59.
157 J.W. Haeger, "Marco Polo in China? Problems with internal evidence", *Bulletin of Sung and Yuan Studies*, Vol. 14 (1978), pp. 22–30 cited in Larner, *Marco Polo*, pp. 65, 203 n. 50.
158 Larner, *Marco Polo*, p. 67.
159 Ibid.
160 See Harvey, *Ibn Battuta*, p. 41.
161 MP, *Travels*/Latham, p. 19 ("Introduction").
162 See IB, p. 657; see Waines, *Odyssey*, p. 195.
163 MP, *Travels*/Latham, pp. 45, 16 ("Introduction").
164 Ibid., p. 42.
165 Ibid., p. 16 ("Introduction").
166 See ibid.; see also Bergreen, *Marco Polo*, pp. 317–320 Clements, *Marco Polo*, pp. 124, 127; MP, *Travels*/Komroff, pp. v–vi.
167 Bergreen, *Marco Polo*, p. 316.
168 MP, *Travels*/Komroff, pp. vi–vii; Bergreen, *Marco Polo*, pp. 319–320; MP, *Travels*/ Latham, p. 16 ("Introduction').
169 Bergreen, *Marco Polo*, p. 320.
170 Larner, *Marco Polo*, p. 45; Brown, *Marco Polo*, p. 3; Clements, *Marco Polo*, p. 138; MP, *Travels*/Komroff, p. xxiv ("Introduction").
171 Larner, *Marco Polo*, pp. 1–2, 105ff, 108ff, 133, 164; Brown, *Marco Polo*, pp. 1–2, 8; MP, *Travels*/Latham, p. 22 ("Introduction").
172 Bergreen, *Marco Polo*, p. 344; MP, *Travels*/Komroff, p. xxiv; Clements, *Marco Polo*, p. 135; Brown, *Marco Polo*, p. vii.
173 Brown, *Marco Polo*, p. 2.
174 Ibid., pp. viii, 3; MP, *Travels*/Komroff, p. xxv.
175 H.A.R. Gibb (trans. and ed.), *Ibn Battuta: Travels in Asia and Africa 1325–1354* (London: Routledge & Kegan Paul, 1929), p. 12; Brown, *Marco Polo*, p. 1; see Larner, *Marco Polo*, pp. 67, 77.
176 Brown, *Marco Polo*, p. viii.
177 Netton, art. "Riḥla", p. 6.
178 MP, *Travels*/Latham, pp. 16–17; Bergreen, *Marco Polo*, p. 8.
179 Larner, *Marco Polo*, pp. 3, 46–58; see also Waines, *Odyssey*, pp. 4–5.
180 MP, *Travels*/Latham, p. 18.
181 Larner, *Marco Polo*, p. 54; Clements, *Marco Polo*, p. 36.
182 Bergreen, *Marco Polo*, pp. 325–326, see also pp. 327–330.
183 Larner, *Marco Polo*, p. 68.
184 Bergreen, *Marco Polo*, p. 325.
185 Clements, *Marco Polo*, pp. 129–130.
186 E.g. IB, pp. 660, 661. Ibn Juzayy, of course, recorded the travels of Ibn Baṭṭūṭa at the precise command of the Marīnid Sultan of Morocco, Abū 'Inān Fāris (*reg.* AD 1348–1358): see ibid., pp. 12–13; see Waines, *Odyssey*, pp. 4–5, 65.

187 MP, *Travels*/Latham, p. 17; Brown, *Marco Polo*, p. 17.
188 MP, *Travels*/Latham, p. 18.
189 Brown, *Marco Polo*, p. VII.
190 Ibid., pp. 3, 17; MP, *Travels*/Latham, p. 19; Bergreen, *Marco Polo*, p. 132; see also Larner, *Marco Polo*, pp. 77–78.
191 Clements, *Marco Polo*, p. 3.
192 Ibid., p. 132.
193 Larner, *Marco Polo*, p. 44.
194 See ibid., p. 183.
195 Ibid.
196 See ibid., p. 182.
197 Rudolph Erich Raspe, *The Surprising Adventures of Baron Munchausen* (n.p.: Dodo Press, n.d.; repr. of 1895 edn.), p. [i] ("Introduction").
198 Ibid.
199 Ibid.
200 Ibid.
201 Ibid., pp. [i–iii].
202 Ibid., pp. [ii, xii, xiv–xv].
203 Ibid., pp. [xvii–xviii].
204 Ibid., p. 1.
205 Ibid., p. 5.
206 Ibid., pp. 44–46.
207 Ibid., pp. [ii–iii, xii].
208 Ibid., pp. 56–61.
209 Ibid., p. 48.
210 Ibid., p. 100.
211 See Robert Louis Stevenson, *Travels with a Donkey in the Cevennes* AND *The Amateur Emigrant*, ed. with Introduction by Christopher Maclachlan (London: Penguin Books, 2004), pp. xiii–xv.
212 Ibid., p. x.
213 Ibid., p. xvi.
214 Ibid., p. xviii.
215 Ibid., pp. 15, 17.
216 Ibid., pp. 18–19.
217 Ibid., pp. 30–31.
218 Ibid., pp. xviii–xix.
219 Ibid., pp. xx, 58.
220 Ibid., pp. 37–47.
221 Ibid., p. xxii ("Introduction").
222 Ibid., pp. xxii–xxiii ("Introduction"), 37–47.
223 Ibid., p. 18.
224 Ibid., p. 31.
225 Ibid., p. 38.
226 Ibid., p. 95, see also p. 96.
227 Ibid., pp. 94–95.
228 Brown, *Marco Polo*, p. vii.
229 See John Mandeville, *The Travels of Sir John Mandeville*, trans. C.W.R.D. Moseley (Harmondsworth: Penguin, 1983); MP, *Travels*/Latham, pp. 24, 368; Bergreen, *Marco Polo*, pp. 344–345, 347; Larner, *Marco Polo*, pp. 130–131, 135. Larner (in ibid., p. 130) notes: "No genuine traces of this man have been found and it is clearly a work constructed in its entirety from earlier sources" ; Waines, *Odyssey*, pp. 12–13; see also Robert Irwin, *For Lust of Knowing: The Orientalists and their Enemies* (London: Penguin Books, Allen Lane, 2006), pp. 50–53.
230 Edward W. Said, *Orientalism: Western Conceptions of the Orient* (London: Penguin, 1995; repr. of Routledge & Kegan Paul edn. of 1978), p. 2.

231 Ibid., p. 58.
232 Ibid., p. 59.
233 Ibid., p. 118.

Bibliography

Addley, Esther, "Faithful or Not", *Guardian*, 8 December 2010.

Bakhtin, Mikhail, "The Problem of Speech Genres", in Caryl Emerson and Michael Holquist (eds), *Speech Genres and Other Late Essays* (Austin: University of Texas Press, 1986).

Beckingham, Charles, "In Search of Ibn Battuta", in Netton (ed.), IMEGT, Vol. III.

Bergreen, Lawrence, *Marco Polo: From Venice to Xanadu* (London: Quercus, 2008).

Broadhurst, R.J.C. (trans.), *The Travels of Ibn Jubayr* (London: Jonathan Cape, 1952).

Brown, Robin, *Marco Polo: Journey to the End of the Earth* (Stroud: Sutton Publishing, 2007).

Carroll, Lewis, *Alice's Adventures in Wonderland* AND *Through the Looking Glass and What Alice Found There*, The Centenary Edition, ed. with Introduction and notes by Hugh Haughton (London: Penguin Books, 1998).

Clements, Jonathan, *Marco Polo* (London: Haus Publishing, 2007).

Daftary, Farhad, *Ismailis in Medieval Muslim Societies*, Ismaili Heritage Series 12 (London and New York: I.B. Tauris in assoc. with the Institute of Ismaili Studies, 2005).

Dunn, Ross E., *The Adventures of Ibn Battuta: A Muslim Traveller of the 14th Century* (London and Sydney: Croom Helm, 1986).

EI^2: *Encyclopaedia of Islam*, ed. H.A.R. Gibb *et al.*, 2nd edn, 12 vols inc. Suppl. (Leiden: E.J. Brill/London: Luzac [for some vols], 1960–2004).

Emerson, Caryl and Michael Holquist (eds), *Speech Genres and Other Late Essays* (Austin: University of Texas Press, 1986).

Fowles, John, *The Collector*, Vintage Classics (London: Vintage Books, 1998; repr. of Jonathan Cape edn of 1963).

Gibb, H.A.R. (trans. and ed.), *Ibn Battuta: Travels in Asia and Africa 1325–1354* (London: Routledge & Kegan Paul, 1929).

Gibb, H.A.R. (trans. and ed.), *The Travels of Ibn Baṭṭūṭa: AD 1325–1354* (Cambridge: Cambridge University Press for the Hakluyt Society, 1958), Vol. I; (1962), Vol. II; with C.F. Beckingham (London: The Hakluyt Society, 1994), Vol. IV.

Haeger, J.W., "Marco Polo in China? Problems with Internal Evidence", *Bulletin of Sung and Yuan Studies*, Vol. 14 (1978), pp. 22–30.

Harvey, L.P., *Ibn Battuta*, Makers of Islamic Civilisation (London and New York: I.B. Tauris, in assoc. with the Oxford Centre for Islamic Studies, 2007).

Hooker, Clifford A., "The Relational Doctrines of Space and Time", *The British Journal for the Philosophy of Science*, Vol. 22:2 (1971), pp. 97–130.

Hrbek, Ivan, "The Chronology of Ibn Baṭṭūṭa's Travels", *Archiv Orientālni*, Vol. 30 (1962), pp. 409–486; repr. in Netton (ed.), IMEGT, Vol. III.

Ibn Baṭṭūṭa, *Riḥla* (Beirut: Dár Ṣádir, 1964).

Ibn Jubayr, *Riḥla* (Beirut: Dár Ṣádir, 1964).

Ibn Khaldūn, *Muqaddima*, ed. Darwīsh al-Juwaydī, 2nd edn (Beirut: al-Maktaba al-ʻAṣriyya, 1996).

Ibn Khaldūn, *The Muqaddimah*, trans. and ed. Franz Rosenthal (3 vols, Princeton: Princeton University Press, 1958).

IMEGT: *Islamic and Middle Eastern Geographers and Travellers*, ed. Ian Richard Netton, Critical Concepts in Islamic Thought (4 vols, London and New York: Routledge, 2008).

Irwin, Robert, *For Lust of Knowing: The Orientalists and their Enemies* (London: Penguin Books, Allen Lane, 2006).

Janicsek, Stephen, "Ibn Baṭṭūṭa's Journey to Bulghár: Is it a Fabrication?", *Journal of the Royal Asiatic Society* (1929), pp. 791–800; repr. in Netton (ed.), IMEGT, Vol. III, pp. 281–288.

Larner, John, *Marco Polo and the Discovery of the World* (New Haven and London: Yale University Press, 1999).

Mackintosh-Smith, Tim, *Landfalls: On the Edge of Islam with Ibn Battuta* (London: John Murray, 2010).

Mackintosh-Smith, Tim (trans.), *The Travels of Ibn Battutah* (London: Picador, 2002).

Mackintosh-Smith, Tim, *Travels with a Tangerine: A Journey in the Footnotes of Ibn Battutah* (London, Basingstoke and Oxford: Pan Macmillan, Picador, 2002).

Mandeville, John, *The Travels of Sir John Mandeville*, trans. C.W.R.D. Moseley (Harmondsworth: Penguin, 1983).

Marco Polo, *The Travels of Marco Polo [The Venetian]*, ed. Manuel Komroff (New York: Liveright, 2003).

Marco Polo, *The Travels of Marco Polo*, trans. Ronald Latham (London: Penguin Books, 1958).

Mollat, Michael, "Ibn Batoutah et la mer", in Ian Richard Netton (ed.), IMEGT: *Volume III: The Travels of Ibn Battuta*, Critical Concepts in Islamic Thought (London and New York: Routledge, 2008).

Netton, Ian Richard (ed.), *Encyclopedia of Islamic Civilisation and Religion* (London and New York: Routledge, 2008).

Netton, Ian Richard (ed.), *Islamic and Middle Eastern Geographers and Travellers: Vol. II: The Travels of Ibn Jubayr*, Critical Concepts in Islamic Thought (London and New York: Routledge, 2008).

Netton, Ian Richard, "Myth, Miracle and Magic in the Riḥla of Ibn Baṭṭūṭa", in Netton (ed.), IMEGT, Vol. III.

Netton, Ian Richard, art. "Riḥla", *EI*[2], Vol. VIII.

Netton, Ian Richard, "Ibn Jubayr: Penitent Pilgrim and Observant Traveller", in Ian Richard Netton, *Seek Knowledge: Thought and Travel in the House of Islam* (Richmond: Curzon Press, 1996).

Netton, Ian Richard, *Seek Knowledge: Thought and Travel in the House of Islam* (Richmond: Curzon Press, 1996).

Pellat, Charles, art. "Ibn Djubayr", *EI*[2], Vol. III.

Qutbuddin, Aziz K., *Taḥmīd: A Literary Genre?*, 2 vols, unpublished PhD thesis, University of London (SOAS), 2009.

Raspe, Rudolph Erich, *The Surprising Adventures of Baron Munchausen* (n.p.: Dodo Press, n.d.; repr. of 1895 edn).

Said, Edward W., *Orientalism: Western Conceptions of the Orient* (London: Penguin, 1995; repr. of Routledge & Kegan Paul edn of 1978).

Starkey, Paul, art. "Ibn Battuta (AD 1304–68/9 or 1377)", in Ian Richard Netton (ed.), *Encyclopedia of Islamic Civilisation and Religion* (London and New York: Routledge, 2008).

Starkey, Paul, art. "Ibn Jubayr al-Kinani, Muhammad Ibn Ahmad (AD 1145–1217)", in Ian Richard Netton (ed.), *Encyclopedia of Islamic Civilisation and Religion* (London and New York: Routledge, 2008).

Stevenson, Robert Louis, *Travels with a Donkey in the Cevennes* AND *The Amateur Emigrant*, ed. with introd. by Christopher Maclachlan (London: Penguin Books, 2004).

Waines, David, *The Odyssey of Ibn Battuta: Uncommon Tales of a Medieval Adventurer* (London and New York: I.B. Tauris, 2010).
Wehr, Hans, *A Dictionary of Modern Written Arabic*, ed. J. Milton Cowan, 2nd printing (Wiesbaden: Otto Harrassowitz/London: Allen & Unwin, 1966).
Yamamoto, Tatsuro, "On Ṭawālisī Described by Ibn Baṭūṭa", in Netton (ed.), IMEGT, Vol. III.

Part V
The Occidental Mirror

14 The Maghreb and the Occident

Towards the construction of an Occidentalist discourse

Zahia Smail Salhi

The idea of this essay takes its start from Said's *Orientalism*,[1] where I found the seeds of Occidentalism, both as a concept and as a natural reaction of the people of the Orient to the host of stereotypes and (mis)representations which were created and propagated by some Orientalists about an Orient they often did not know very well. It is the aim of this essay to ponder the concept of 'Occidentalism' and its multifarious meanings as defined by critics from both the Orient and the Occident, with a special focus on the Maghrebi experience of the East–West encounter which ultimately resulted in the creation of an Occidentalist discourse in the Maghreb.

Introduction

Said defines Orientalism as "a style of thought based upon an ontological and epistemological distinction made between 'the Orient' and 'the Occident'."[2] The literature produced thus has the distinction between East and West as the dividing line between Orientalism and Occidentalism. While in Said's view "Orientalism derives from a particular closeness experienced between Britain and France and the Orient",[3] Occidentalism too derives from this same closeness. He elucidates, "Out of that closeness, whose dynamic is enormously productive even if it always demonstrates the comparatively greater strength of the Occident … comes the large body of texts I call Orientalist."[4] I would add that the same relationship also produced, and continues to do so, a huge amount of text by the 'Orientals' on their encounter with the Occident, which I would like to call Occidentalist literature. This same literature is also called colonial and post-colonial, but what I would specifically call Occidentalist literature is that corpus of works concerned with the portrayal of the Occident and the East–West encounter from the Oriental's perspective. Such encounters may have taken place in the 'Orient/Maghreb' during the colonial period or in the Occident during both the colonial and post-colonial periods.

It is this part of the relationship that Said's *Orientalism* did not engage with. His focus was solely on the hegemonic Western popular and academic discourse of the Orient, providing an analysis of the relationship between European colonialism and the intertwined discursive formations constructing the European experience of the Orient. The corpus of literature and other outputs which the Orientals created in response to these discursive formations did not receive Said's attention, and while he scrutinized the Western portrayals of the Orient as meaning the Middle East, which constitutes Egypt and the Arab and Muslim countries East of Egypt, the Maghreb is totally overlooked in Said's *Orientalism*.

This view is shared by Robert Irwin in his book, *For Lust of Knowing: the Orientalists and their Enemies*, which he wrote as a criticism of Said's *Orientalism*. Irwin argues that Said used the word 'Orientalism' in a very restrictive sense as referring to those who traveled in, studied or wrote about the Arab world, while in reality the term should be extended to include Persia, India, Indonesia and the Far East, as it was by A.J. Arberry in his book on *British Orientalists* in 1943.

Irwin's view is indicative of the existence of many Orientalisms; however, since Said's critique is an Arab's response to Orientalism, to cover other regions outside the Arab world would be beyond his remit. I do, however, agree with Irwin's view concerning Said's exclusion of the Maghreb: "he [Said] excluded consideration of North Africa west of Egypt. I cannot guess why he excluded North Africa."[5]

It is my observation that Said was not the first one to do so. In most studies conducted on the Middle East or the Arab world, be they in humanities or in social sciences, the Maghreb is often overlooked. In literary studies, for example, very few include one or two authors from the Maghreb, and even so they will be approached in a somehow cautionary manner, not totally engaging them in the general study of Arabic literature. This is, indeed, symptomatic of the sidelining of this region, which is not a new fact, but goes back to the golden age of the Islamic civilization, when the region was defined as the 'Maghrib' as a part separate from the 'Mashriq', the mainland Arab and Muslim world.

Defining Occidentalism

Occidentalism is often defined as the counterpart of Orientalism. The word 'counterpart' signifies both the equivalent and the opposite, and in this case these two concepts are often presented as opposites, or as the two opposing poles of the gamut.

As a consequence, 'Orient' is presented as the antonym of 'Occident' and the lexical definition of 'Occidentalism' has been structured as the exact reverse of that of 'Orientalism', as follows: "A quality, mannerism, or custom specific to or characteristic of the Occident" and "Scholarly knowledge of Occidental cultures, languages, and peoples".[6]

While it is widely agreed that these functions are those pursued by Orientalism as an academic discipline, it is strictly not the case with Occidentalism, which, it has to be highlighted, is not an academic discipline per se but merely a way or a style of conceiving and representing the Occident, not in an academically scientific manner but mostly in a literary, artistic or polemical manner. This view is in fact highlighted by Said himself, who asserts, "To speak of scholarly specialization as a geographical 'field' is, in the case of Orientalism, fairly revealing since no one is likely to imagine a field symmetrical to it called Occidentalism."[7]

In his article "Beyond Occidentalism: Towards Post-Imperial Geohistorical Categories", Fernendo Coronil[8] refers to Said's 'Orientalists' as 'Occidentalists'. Coronil insists that this shift does not entail a reversal of focus from Orient to Occident, in other words from 'Other' to 'Self'. He explains that, by directing our attention to the relational nature of representations of human collectivities, it brings into focus their genesis in asymmetrical relations of power, including the power to obscure their genesis in inequality, to undo their historical connections and thus to present as the internal and separate attributes of bounded entities what are in fact the historical outcomes of connected peoples.

Coronil defines Occidentalism not as the reverse of Orientalism but as its condition of possibility, its dark side (as in a mirror). A simple reversal, he insists, would be possible only in the context of symmetrical relations between 'Self' and 'Other', which agrees with Said's view above, although he began by disagreeing with him. The end result of both arguments is that, in the context of equal relations, difference should not be cast as Otherness. Therefore, to speak of Occidentalism as the exact reverse of Orientalism leads to the illusion that both Orient and Occident are equal, which has never been the case. The Orientalist *versus* Occidentalist condition is one of hegemony in which one was and still is the superior 'Self' and the second was and remains the inferior 'Other'.

What Occidentalist representation attempts to do is to challenge Orientalism, especially its mode of representation, in a 'counteracting', 'writing against' manner, which was the main impetus behind the emergence of modern Maghrebi literature under colonial France at the start of the twentieth century. What is important to highlight here is that, in the case of the Maghreb, unlike that of the Middle East, such literature was mainly written in the language of the colonizer, which was mastered by native Maghrebi authors who were educated in colonial French schools.

This situation created 'an elite' within the 'Other' who, as a result of its education, aspired to become the 'Self', but because of the colonial condition this elite was not fully admitted to the rank of the 'Self' nor did it accept its natural condition as the 'Other'. The members of this elite stand on the border between Orient and Occident, as they often reject elements of their own culture and substitute them with elements that mimic the Occident.

The position of such a class, and especially that of the colonized Francophone authors, is indeed very motivating, because in my view they became somehow 'dangerously' suspended between Orient and Occident, Other and Self, without fully belonging to any of these categories. Their education inculcated in them a belief that they belonged to the French civilization, albeit through adoption rather than birth, and that their loyalty and allegiance should perpetually be to their *Mère-Patrie*, which had bestowed on them the bounties of civilization. Yet the ultimate outcome of this condition was the creation of hybrids who could not be accurately classified as either 'Orient' or 'Occident', 'Other' or 'Self', nor could they fully adhere to any of these possible categories.

The ultimate reaction of such authors was to challenge Orientalism as a way of Othering and representing the 'Other', often in a stereotypical manner. The resulting discourse took various forms, including political polemic such as in the work of Ferhat Abbas, *Le Jeune Algérien*,[9] *J'accuse l'Europe*[10] and *La Nuit coloniale*;[11] Critical theory such as Albert Memmi's *The Colonizer and the Colonized*,[12] Abdelkebir Khatibi's *La Mémoire tatouée*[13] and *Amour bilingue*;[14] and Frantz Fanon's *Black Skin, White Masks*[15] and *The Wretched of the Earth*;[16] and works of fiction, which make up the main bulk of the 'Occidentalist' discourse in terms of representations of the Occident.

The consequence of challenging Orientalism, according to Coronil, is the disruption of Occidentalism as an ensemble of representational strategies and practices whose effect is to produce 'Selfhood' as well as 'Otherness'. He explains,

> by Occidentalism I refer to the complex ensemble of representational strategies engaged in the production of conceptions of the world that separates its components into bounded units; 1) disaggregates their relational histories, 2) turns difference into hierarchy, 3) naturalizes these representations; and, therefore, 4) intervenes, however unwittingly, in the reproduction of existing asymmetrical power relations.[17]

In lieu of disruption I will argue that challenging Orientalism is in fact the essence and the foundation of Occidentalism, which aims at all the functions listed by Coronil in the above quotation. Let us take as an example Malek Alloula's book *The Oriental Harem*,[18] which examines a collection of colonial photographs of native Maghrebi women in phantasmagorical poses.

Alloula's work exposes the Orientalist mode of representation by publishing photographs of Maghrebi subjects, especially women, produced by colonial photographers. By doing so, Alloula does not change the situation of representation but merely exposes it and gives it wider circulation. This operation resulted in mixed reactions; while some criticized his method as doing further harm to the subject portrayed, others valued his work as a tool for challenging the Orientalist canon through mere exposure. The resulting mixed feelings are in fact a reaction to the situation of 'Othering' through a prejudiced colonial lens.

Alloula's work does in fact (1) disaggregate the relational histories of colonizer and colonized in order for him to situate his book in its historical context; and as to (2) turning difference into hierarchy, it highlights the difference between 'Self' and 'Other' in terms of hegemonic power relations. The subject of the photographs could not be reversed and, interestingly enough, the collection is made up of photographs of 'Others' *only* and not of 'Self', or of the 'Self' together with the 'Other'. A clear delineation is evident in the colonial representations of the 'Other' as being separate and far removed from the 'Self'. This condition is a result of the intrinsic hegemony of colonizer over colonized and the resulting attitude of possessing and objectifying the colonized.

As to point (3) "naturalizes these representations", the resulting critique of the book testifies to the opposite situation, i.e. the revoking of the exposed truth as a false representation. Alloula challenges the photographs as being true to life and exposes them as being a result of the colonial euphoria and phantasm. He explains that as a result of failure to find the portrayed subjects in reality ('paradise found' which turns into 'paradise lost') the colonial photographers created this illusion and sought to create the conditions of the harem in their studios. Such action was a natural means of covering up the disappointment felt at not finding the promised paradise where women roamed freely and at the disposal of the new colony's settlers, who continued to deceive those back in the metropolis that the lucky few who had escaped to the Orient were indeed enjoying its bounties. One photograph, titled *Moorish Women of Algiers*, which represents two Oriental women sitting next to each other, was posted to acquaintances in the metropolis with the inscription "Anatoly's woman, R[...]'s woman".[19] Alloula elucidates,

> Photography steps in to take the slack and reactivates the phantasm at its lowest level. The postcard does it one better; it becomes the poor man's phantasm: for a few pennies, display racks full of dreams. The postcard is everywhere, covering all the colonial space, immediately available to the tourist, the soldier, the colonist.[20]

The exploitation of the colonial subjects, and in this case native Maghrebi women, rendered them thoroughly objectified and ruthlessly used in order to satisfy the colonialists' appetite for the exotic. In other words they were inhumanely exploited as part of the war booty of the French conquest of Algeria. Marnia Lazreg problematizes this condition in the following terms:

> Through Algerian women, French male writers [in this case male colonial photographers] could satisfy their own desires to penetrate Algerian men's intimate life by having their wives and daughters as spoils of conquest. At the same time, Algerian women gave men the opportunity to fantasize about the female sex in general. For, if one stripped the nineteenth-and twentieth century discourse on Algerian women of its colonial trappings one would uncover French men's own prejudices against women in general. In addition in Algerian women French authors found an inexhaustible subject to quench the public's thirst for what Fromentin called 'the bizarre'.[21]

And consequently, point (4) "intervenes, however unwittingly, in the reproduction of existing asymmetrical power relations". It is a fact that without this situation, in which power relations are asymmetrical, the whole Orientalist and the resulting Occidentalist concepts and discourse would not have come about. Power and conflict are at the foundation of these concepts and have always shaped their nature.

Alloula's work challenges the notion of the Orient as the silent and passive 'Other' that lends itself to control and dominance, and adopts a retaliatory form of Occidentalist discourse. He depicts the Occident by confronting it with its own portrayals of the Orient and bluntly states that his book is intended as a huge postcard returned to the sender and exposes the exotic postcard as the vulgar expression of colonial euphoria.[22]

In his seminal study "Orientalism in Crisis", Anouar Abdel-Malek[23] argues that under colonial rule the Orient and its inhabitants almost automatically become an 'object' of study which is "stamped with otherness – as all that is different whether it be 'subject' or 'object' but of a constitutive otherness, of an essentialist character ... This 'object' of study will be as is customary, passive, non-participating, endowed with a 'historical' subjectivity, above all, non-active, non-autonomous, non-sovereign with regard to itself."[24]

Abdel Malek demonstrates that some Orientalist motivations were purely academic and could be ranked as positive, as highlighted by Youssef As'ad Dagher, who distinguishes eight positive elements in the field of Arabic and Islamic studies as follows: the study of ancient civilization, the collection of Arabic manuscripts in European libraries, the establishment of catalogues of manuscripts, the publication of numerous important works, the lesson of method thus given to Oriental scholars, the organization of Orientalist congresses, the editing of studies – though frequently deficient and erroneous from a linguistic point of view, but precise in method – and finally, this movement has contributed to arousing national consciousness in the different countries of the Orient and to activating the movement of scientific renaissance.[25] In the case of the Maghreb, Orientalist anthropology and philology resulted in many important studies which continue to be used as valuable references in the study of the region.

In his article "Faut-it brûler l'Orientalisme? On French Scholarship of North Africa", Abdelmajid Hannoum[26] argues that French Orientalism, the bulk of knowledge that has been built in the context of colonization, though it has changed through time, continues to operate today in both the discourse of the former colonized and that of the former colonizer. He contends that, for the colonial machine, knowledge is not only a means of control and governance but also contains categories by which imaginaries are shaped and colonial relations and attitudes are perpetuated.[27] He explains that Orientalism condemned itself by becoming the tool of colonialism and demonstrates that, in the Maghreb, French colonialism benefited from the expertise of the Orientalists, to dominate and rule over the region. He highlights the important role played by De Sacy in the occupation of Algeria:

> It was he who was in charge of hiring interpreters, his own students, for the French army. He also determined the most important text for knowledge of North Africa, a book by Ibn Khaldûn, a universal history, whose section on the history of North Africa has become a central text for Orientalists. It was de Sacy's student, William de Slane, who translated it (De Slane, 1852–6). This text, with its colonial categories and objects, still conditions French writing on North Africa.[28]

Furthermore, Hannoum posits that colonialism, as a political enterprise, was a major factor in consolidating the establishment of Orientalism. It is, without a doubt, colonialism that allowed the Orientalists "to build whole Oriental libraries, by helping to acquire, gather, and catalogue Oriental manuscripts, and to organize the study of the Orient in institutions founded and totally devoted to this purpose."[29]

In the same vein, Abdel Malek explains that this vision of academic Orientalism accomplished in the universities and scholarly societies, which he calls 'traditional' Orientalism, was not the dominant vision. He warns that, despite all its good intentions, it could not rid itself of some politico-philosophical concepts and methodological habits that often interfered in and compromised the results of their scientific findings. This leads to the second type of Orientalism, which Abdel Malek qualifies as 'collaborating with colonial powers'. He describes this group in the following terms: "This latter group was formed by an amalgam of university dons, businessmen, military men, colonial officials, missionaries, publicists and adventurers, whose only objective was to gather intelligence information in the area to be occupied, to penetrate the consciousness of the people in order to better assure its enslavement to the European powers."[30]

In the case of the Maghreb, Abdel Malek cites the work of the Arab bureau, where, as Jacques Berque observed, "sustained, nourished at the same time and limited by action, the study of the North African societies has been oriented from the start."[31]

Abdel Malek explains that this phenomenon of generating knowledge about specific nations for the purpose of dominating them was built into the structure of the social sciences in the European countries during the period of imperialist penetration and implantation.

As to the view expressed in his title, "Orientalism in Crisis", Abdel Malek explains that this crisis occurs as a result of the rise of national liberation movements, which brought an end to the age of colonial domination. Orientalist scholars faced a crisis because the territories they studied became liberated and were no longer controlled by their nations. This fact resulted in a change in the relationship between the researchers and their studied subject matter.

This view is also shared by Hannoum, who argues that, because Orientalism made itself a tool of colonialism, the two enterprises would have the same fate, i.e., the end of colonialism would automatically bring about the end of Orientalism. This may be true, though I would argue that the mode of representation established by the colonizers towards the colonized continues to influence the ways in which Orient and Occident view each other at the present. As ever, knowledge is not objective data about objects and subjects, but a form of social relations, a form of power by which and through which domination is assured and guaranteed. According to Foucault,

> Knowledge linked to power, not only assumes the authority of 'the truth', but has the power to make itself true. All knowledge, once applied in the real world, has effects, and in that sense at least, 'becomes true'. Knowledge, once used to regulate the conduct of others, entails constraint, regulation and the disciplining of practice. Thus, there is no power relation without the correlative constitution of a field of knowledge, nor any knowledge that does not presuppose and constitute at the same time, power relations.[32]

Let us not overlook the fact that Western Orientalism was generated in the colonial epoch, and, in the light of Foucault's view, we should ask the tantalizing question as to whether Arabs/Orientals cultivated a field of research specializing in the study of other nations during the time of the expansion of the Islamic Empire. Before doing so, we need to reiterate that the Occidentalist discourse which is the focus of this essay is not the study of Western people and their mannerisms or customs, as in the case of Western anthropology, but rather a matter of writing to (or back to) and about the Occident as a reaction, and not as an enterprise initiated by the 'Orientals' to study the people of the Occident – hence the absence of Occidentalist scholarship, on the one hand, and its irrelevance, on the other.

Furthermore, while Orientalism is a discipline which dates back to the seventeenth century, with the appearance of Barthélemy d'Herbelot's *Bibliothèque orientale* (1697),[33] the Orient – and in this case I mean the Muslim and Arab world – had very little interest in the Occident, or again, in this context, the Christian world. Arabs understood the value of Greek science and philosophy but totally ignored the art, literature and historiography of the Greeks. This should in no way deny Greek influence on Arab thought, the first traces of which appeared in Mesopotamia towards the middle of the eighth century. In his book *How Greek Science Passed to the Arabs*, O'Leary argues that we have very little evidence of philosophical or theological speculation in Syria under the Umayyad dynasty. Such matters seem to have had very little appeal for Arab interests in that period.[34]

This attitude continued to prevail well into Ibn Khaldoun's (1332–1406) time. In his famous *The Muqaddimah*, which stands as the most important history of the pre-modern world, he, in Charles Issawi's words, "paid the price for the selective interest taken by the Arabs in Greek culture."[35] Written in 1377 as an introduction to *Kitāb al-'Ibar* (Book of Advice), *The Muqaddimah* (An Introduction to History) laid the foundations for several fields of knowledge such as sociology, ethnography, economics and philosophy of history. It re-evaluates in an unparalleled manner every manifestation of highly developed civilization and acknowledges that many civilizations preceded the Arab-Islamic civilization and that many civilizations, such as those of the Persians and the Copts, contributed to its making. He asserts that the knowledge that has not reached us is greater than the knowledge that has, and refutes the view, which was popular during his time, that nations of earlier times were better endowed physically and mentally to achieve a high and materially splendid civilization than were contemporary nations. In his opinion, it was merely the decay of political organizations and the power of government that gave his contemporaries the impression that the civilization of their day was inferior to those of the past.

Ibn Khaldoun believes there can be no essential difference between the faculties and achievements of former and contemporary generations, because political and cultural life is moving in never-ending, always repeating circles. He argues that human intellectual power is always constant and capable of producing the highest civilization at any given time.

Ibn Khaldoun speaks of the sciences and civilizations of the Persians, the Chaldeans, the Syrians, the Babylonians, the Copts and the Greeks, yet remarks that the only sciences to have reached the Arabs are those of the Greeks, thanks to the efforts of the Caliph Al-Ma'mūn, who invested large resources to have the works of the Greeks translated, while he remarks with regret that, because of Umar Ibn al-Khattāb's hasty decision, the books of the Persians and all the knowledge they contained were either burnt or dumped in the river.[36]

From *The Muqaddimah* it becomes evident that Ibn Khaldoun's political theories were influenced by Aristotle, whose *Book of Politics* he cites many times.[37] He describes him as "the greatest Greek scientist who enjoyed the greatest prestige and fame. He has been called 'the first teacher'. He became world-famous."[38] Ibn Khaldoun also speaks of Aristotle and his role in improving the methods of logic, and cites his work on logic as being called 'The Text', comprising eight books (volumes), which he describes one by one.

It becomes clear from *The Muqaddimah* that Ibn Khaldoun's knowledge of the cultures and civilizations of other nations was wide and diversified. What I find rather interesting is his way of speaking of all nations and all civilizations in a very objective manner. In other words, there is no friend or foe in knowledge and his book displays no racial or religious bias. He speaks of Muslims, Christians and Jews as different people who belong to different faiths, which was not an obstacle to interaction between them, and spoke of the Muslims as people who desired to learn the sciences of foreign nations. In doing so, they moulded these sciences to their own views and surpassed the scientific achievements of the non-Arabs.

This was obviously happening during the golden age of the Arab-Islamic civilization, when Arabs could, if they had wished to do so, make other nations into subjects of study from their own position of power. Yet, it is difficult to find evidence of this taking place in Islamic history. Ibn Khaldoun and others before him speak of the harmony in which people of all faiths cohabited in Andalusia and the Maghreb and, indeed, in the rest of the Muslim Empire.

This leads us to affirm that the West has never constituted a subject of study for Muslims. Christians and other non-Muslim people lived amongst the Muslims and were given ample opportunity to exercise their faith freely, and often cohabited peacefully with Muslims without prejudice to their faith or beliefs on the part of the people in power, i.e. the Muslims.

As such, while the West/Christian world was largely ignored by Muslim writers and historians, the opposite was not true. Going back to Barthélemy d'Herbelot's *Bibliothèque orientale*, for which Antoine Galland, the first translator of *The Thousand and One Nights* into French, has written the introduction, one finds that the Orient as a concept was formalized in this very book, in which, while it focused on the life of Prophet Mohammed and the history of the 'Saracens' as its main subject, the way these are portrayed established a new manner of viewing the Orient which was adopted by Europeans for many centuries to come.

D'Herbelot's images of Prophet Mohammed as an impostor, founder of a heresy etc. are undoubtedly the basis for many prejudiced views about him which have been and continue to be produced even today in some extremist anti-Muslim media (note the infamous Danish cartoons). Edward Said explains how, through the work of d'Herbelot, "Europe discovered its capacities for encompassing and Orientalizing the Orient."[39]

The image of Islam as a heretic religion is purely a reaction to its being a threat to Christianity, as a result of its expansion into Christian lands and the mass conversion of people of all faiths into Islam. The Islamic expansion, without any doubt, resulted in the fear and the acrimony that were manifested against it by many Christian circles. After all, the Muslim Empire expanded into the lands of other nations and swept away whole civilizations. Irwin argues that "it was natural for Christian thinkers to interpret the unfamiliar and unexpected phenomenon of Islam in terms of what was familiar to them already. Therefore, they tended to present Islam to themselves not as a new religion, but rather as the variant of an old heresy."[40]

The rise of the Ottoman Empire and its wars for domination in the Mediterranean posed a genuine threat to a weakened and vulnerable Christendom. By the 1530s the Western Mediterranean was terror struck at the threat posed by the Ottoman fleets that roamed the sea at will and by the Barbary corsairs of the Maghrebi littoral who controlled the sea traffic and often looted European ships and enslaved those people aboard.[41]

Antoine Galland's translation of *The Thousand and One Nights* (1704–1717) set the seal on the Orient; to the attacks on Islam and its Prophet,[42] *The Nights* added images of a totally imagined and distorted Orient as a land of sensuality, harems, eunuchs which were extremely appealing to Western readers and contributed fundamentally to the establishing of Orientalist art and literature. Such images were often misleading, as their creators often imagined an Orient which had no equivalent in reality; an Orient of extremes which was both violent and lascivious.

In addition to the above sources, one has to take account of Western travelers and soldiers, especially those in Bonaparte's (1769–1821) expedition of Egypt, and their accounts. Though often over-exaggerated and having no place in reality, their reports were trusted sources from which many laymen developed their fascination for and attraction to the Orient. In his book *Sexual Encounters in the Middle East*, Hopwood explains how these sources fed the Western colonial imagination and how the soldiers of the French conquest of the Maghreb based their mental images on the reports of Bonaparte's soldiers in Egypt.[43]

In addition to the soldiers' reports and voyagers' diaries, Napoleon's military expedition included a team of 167 scientists, mathematicians, naturalists, chemists etc. whose work was published in the famous *Description de l'Égypte*. It is believed that the work of this team generated a host of essentialist images which laid the foundations for a long tradition of Orientalism as a way of portraying and studying the 'Other' from a position of power. The same enterprise of studying the locals as subjects of Western anthropology occurred as soon as the French occupation established itself in the Maghreb.

This enterprise has, in effect, never ceased, but has continued to be perpetrated in post-colonial times. What has changed is the awareness brought about by the modern study of Orientalism as a discipline, in the aftermath mostly of the publication of Said's *Orientalism*, but also, and this is important to highlight, of the emergence of anti-colonial and national liberation movements in Africa and

Asia after the Second World War and the victories achieved by these movements in the form of political independence.

Abdel Malek argues that this new political condition is the main factor that plunged the Orientalist profession into a serious crisis, and that it became no longer natural that Westerners should rule the planet and enjoy direct control over Asia and Africa and their inhabitants.

It has to be highlighted that Abdel Malek's critique was published in 1962, well before Said's *Orientalism* appeared in 1978, and that another similar critique bearing the title "English-Speaking Orientalists: a Critique of their Approach to Islam and Arab Nationalism" was published in 1964 by Abdul Latif Tibawi, who was then based at the University of London.

Tibawi was rather perturbed by the way that Islamic topics and the 'Orient' in general were taught at the School of Oriental and African Studies (SOAS). He declared that he did not conceive his critique in any spirit of controversy and that it should not be taken as an apology for any creed, be it religious or national.[44]

Tibawi's critique received a rather harsh evaluation from Irwin, who described it as "a thesaurus of academic abuse" and lists all the "abusive words" used by Tibawi in his attack on the Orientalists and their works.[45] Irwin's defense of the Orientalists through vehement attacks on their enemies, who all happen to be of Arab and Muslim descent, results in a host of direct assaults on individuals including Laroui, Tibawi and Abdel Malek, and a use of demeaning and aggressive discourse which does not benefit the already tense relationship between Orient and Occident in any way.

As explained above, the discourse of those whom Irwin calls "enemies of the Orientalists" is a reaction to decades of stereotyping through a commissioned dominating discourse that accompanied the colonial powers. It was the images of the Orient that made those of the Occident possible, and at the same time as these reciprocal images of Orient and Occident proliferate, it becomes more and more obvious that the problems of Orient and Occident are interconnected and rather common. Furthermore, due to a lack of rapprochement, essentialist images have been fashioned and often propagated. Such images of the 'Other', be they Oriental or Occidental, are never innocent, nor are they free from the hidden agendas that shape them and give them their final form.

This state of affairs ultimately results in each party handling the way they are portrayed with suspicion. This is even more the case in academic fields such as anthropology. The way in which the studied subjects or communities (informants) in Western anthropology react to Western scholars – or even to Arab anthropologists living in the West – who conduct research in the Middle East and the Maghreb is a good example of this suspicion. I would like to refer to a study conducted by Lila Abu-Lughod in Upper Egypt. When she told her host that the results of her field-work in Egypt would be published in English, he argued that it was a pity, as he wanted Egyptians rather than Americans to know its content. He then concluded "Knowledge is power. The Americans and the British know everything. They want to know everything about people, about us. Then, if they come to a country, or come to rule it, they know what people need and they know how to rule.'"[46]

This same view is expressed by academics in their critique of Orientalism, such as in Abdel Malek's study where he explains that the aim of Western anthropology is to penetrate the consciousness of the people in order to better assure their enslavement to the European powers.[47]

Abu-Lughod concludes, "My Bedouin host had brought up an issue about the politics of scholarship that we as Western-oriented scholars have only recently begun to explore seriously."[48] She elucidates that any discussion of anthropological theories about the Arab world must begin with this issue, meaning the politics of representation from a Saidian perspective. James Carrier confirms, "While anthropologists conventionally see themselves as producing, and recently have debated their ability to produce, knowledge of societies and cultures outside the core of the West, Occidentalism is the silent partner of their work and debates."[49]

Carrier argues that Occident and Orient and the distinction between them are all shaped by political circumstance, which affects as well as explains the quality and terms of the encounter between Orient and Occident and makes their relationship so fluid.[50] He begins his book with a short definition of Occidentalism as "stylized images of the West" and concurs that Orientalism as defined by Said has become a generic term for a particular, suspect type of anthropological thought and that the criticism of anthropology as a discipline which concerns itself with the study of other nations draws on Said's *Orientalism*.

This state of affairs puts modern anthropologists in a convoluted situation, as the discipline has been so much tarnished by old-style colonial modes of representation whereby, on the one hand, alien/other societies were seen as static and radically dissimilar from the complex and changing West, and on the other hand, these studies were often informed by sets of preconceived ideas which have invariably influenced anthropologists' enquiries, resulting in a mode of essentializing other nations which Said criticizes in the following terms, "objects are what they are *because* they are what they are, for once, for all time, for ontological reasons that no empirical matter can either dislodge or alter."[51]

I should stress here that having preconceived ideas of the 'Other' prior to the enquiry or encounter with this same 'Other' obstructed the view and inquisitive minds of colonial anthropologists, artists and authors. What exacerbates this situation is the colonial condition, which makes the 'Self' an eternal aggressor (even in post-colonial times) in the view of the 'Other', who then handles the 'Self' with eternal suspicion.

What I am trying to get to at this point is that, in consequence, both parties have developed and embedded a view of the 'Other' which cannot rid itself of essentialism. Both Orient and Occident essentialize the other and this condition can only be altered by changing the existing state of affairs in which Orient and Occident are placed apart with a set of binaries attached to them which, despite the progression of the two poles from colonial to post-colonial conditions, separate these two worlds from each other. Such binaries have indeed seen a temporal evolution of some kind, but in general the essential setting of one pole as the opposite/contrast of the other remains.

One very common case is that of the 'sexualized woman'; in Orientalist imagery the Oriental woman is portrayed as a veiled, submissive victim, while in the

Occidentalist imagery the Western woman is often described as a devalued sex object, victim of sexual exploitation. In her article "Orientalism, Occidentalism and the Control of Women",[52] Laura Nader denounces the political agenda which underlies such representations in both Orient and Occident. While Muslim societies use the portrayals of Western women to contrast themselves as the ones that value women and in which women can be secure, Western societies highlight the victimization of Muslim women in contrast to independent and intellectually advanced Western women, so as to solidify and legitimize patriarchal gender relations in the West. In this, Nader insists, both societies are similar in their essentializing and in simplifying their depictions of women, as well as in maintaining a patriarchal order in terms of gender relations.[53]

Furthermore, the way in which the image of the 'Other' is constructed and depicted often betrays part of the 'Self', for the 'Other' is often imagined as the opposite of the 'Self'. While Nicholas Thomas[54] explains how "the capacities of populations to impose and act upon their constructions of others have been highly variable throughout history",[55] Carrier, who agrees with this view, argues that "Westerners have been more powerful and hence better able than people elsewhere to construct and impose images of alien societies as they see fit."[56] Not only this, but Western power can often shape self-conception. A good example is the way that some societies in the Middle East and the Maghreb replicate Western phantasms and thirst for exotica as part of the tourist industry, which mainly targets Western consumers.

While we have so far argued that Occidentalism is produced by countries in the 'Orient'/East, Carrier speaks of two distinct forms of Occidentalism which are produced in societies in the Occident and elsewhere. While the first type is produced by anthropologists the second is produced by ordinary people. He elucidates,

> Occidentalism within Anthropology touches directly on what has been the discipline's primary task since its inception, studying sets of people outside the core of the West ... this sort of Occidentalism is significant because it points out that this task is more difficult than we may think ... The Western Occidentalisms that Anthropologists absorb are shaped by power relations within the West [and] are doubly infused with socio-political relations. In being the bearers and manipulators of these Occidentalisms, Anthropologists meet nationalists, for both are engaged in the politics of identity ... Many Anthropologists object to the West as they Occidentalize it and do what they can to protect the people they study from its more unsavoury effects.[57]

As to the second form, Carrier describes it as an "Occidentalism outside anthropology" and "ordinary people's Occidentalism", which in his view touches the discipline less directly. This form of Occidentalism relates most directly to the topic of national identity and similar phenomena: "National, ethnic, and racial identities revolve around an opposition between an us and a them, and in many parts of the world those identities reflect in part an assumption or rejection of 'the West' in one or another of its guises."[58]

While Carrier maintains that it would be dangerous to think that these two forms of Occidentalism are so distant from each other, I would argue that what concerns us more directly in this essay is the second form of Occidentalism, while it would be unwise to ignore the first form.

In their book, *Occidentalism: A Short History of Anti-Westernism*, Ian Buruma and Avishai Margalit call Occidentalism "The dehumanizing picture of the West painted by its enemies."[59] This definition is charged with a political slant which, from the beginning of the book, positions the Orient and Occident as enemies. Accordingly, this view reveals that Occidentalism is all about the discourse against the West, produced by its enemies from across the world. The authors insist on Occidentalism's being the dehumanizing picture of the West painted by its enemies and define it as follows:

> The view of the West in Occidentalism is like the worst aspects of its counterpart, Orientalism, which strips its human targets of their humanity. Some Orientalist prejudices made non-Western people seem less than fully adult human beings; they had the minds of children, and could thus be treated as lesser breeds.[60]

They argue that Occidentalism is at least as reductive; its chauvinism merely turns the Orientalist view upside down. They remark, "to diminish an entire society or a civilisation to a mass of soulless, decadent, money-grubbing, rootless, faithless, unfeeling parasites is a form of intellectual destruction",[61] and assert that Occidentalism as a nationalist and nativist resistance to the Occident reproduces responses to forces of modernization that have their roots in Western culture itself, among both utopian radicals and nationalist conservatives who see capitalism, liberalism and secularism as destructive forces.

Buruma and Margalit's views are rather simplistic in the way they position Orient and Occident as born enemies. To reduce Occidentalist literature to a meager discourse of hatred which merely demonizes the Occident is a grave oversight of the bulk of Occidentalist creativity. Their views are indeed easily rendered fallacious by the many diverse portrayals of the Occident by Oriental writers who, while they may not escape generalizations and preconceived views of the Occident, never failed to reflect on the two contrasting facets of the Occident.

Buruma and Margalit's criticisms of various parties betray a Eurocentric stance and the whole study becomes rather speculative, and loaded with words such as 'loathe', 'hate', 'violence', 'enemy'. Their attacks on named individuals we find quite erratic, as in the following example where they deploy a fierce assault on the French humanist Jacques Vergès,

> A prominent supporter of Third World revolutionary causes, Arab terrorists, and other enemies of liberal democracy is the French lawyer Jacques Vergès. He has defended Algerian militants in court … Vergès might have personal motives for his hostility to the West. He was born in Réunion, an old French penal colony in the Indian Ocean, and his mother was Vietnamese, a

> circumstance that blocked his father's ambition to be a French diplomat. But the reason for bringing up this notorious but marginal figure is his eloquent argument against the banality of democracy. Vergès loathes "cosmopolitanism". He hates honor higher than morality and has a taste for violent Action.[62]

To categorize Occidentalism as the discourse of those who 'loathe' liberal democracy betrays Buruma and Margalit's lack of understanding of such a discourse, on the one hand, and their one-dimensional and biased views, on the other. The actions of humanists of the likes of Vergès, Fanon, De Beauvoir, Halimi[63] and many others were in fact in defense of liberal democracy and not the other way around. Vergès' defense of the victims of the French colonial machine and the revolutionary heroes of the Algerian war of independence should in no way be classified as the defense of 'Arab terrorists'.[64]

Contrary to Buruma and Margalit's argument, Occidentalism as a discourse is not anti-Western. We have to clarify that exposing the Orientalist methodology and modes of representation in no way aims to promote anti-Western feelings. Quite the opposite, the aim is to bring awareness to Western audiences that the image created of the Orient is not only wrong but harmful. The objective of such exposure is to change the ways in which the West views its 'Others' and vice versa. After all, most of the authors who produce the Occidentalist discourse are educated in the West, most of them continue to live in the West and have drawn their methods of evaluation and code of ethics of representation from Western understandings.

Telling the West about its failures in terms of essentializing its 'Others', producing sets of misrepresentations about the East, the contradictions inherent in its universal principles of human rights and democracy which exclude those from outside Europe etc. is almost a plea for bridge building, cultural exchange and dialogue, and not the opposite. Furthermore, one should not mistake the fundamentalist discourse of Islamic terrorism, which Jean Baudrillard[65] calls 'Talibanish Occidentalism', as part of the Occidentalist discourse we are pursuing in this essay. Such a discourse does in fact produce radicalist attitudes against both the East and the West and should in no way be taken as a justification for labeling Occidentalism as the discourse of hatred of the Occident.

The Maghreb and the Occident

The impetus on behalf of the people of the Maghreb to present to the world a true image of them and their people, is extraordinary. Without necessarily engaging in a fierce war of words, and in a tacit manner, authors from the Maghreb emerged to tell French authors, "you have told us who you are and we have understood the message, but you do not know us enough in order for you to write about us and tell the world who we are. Therefore, because of this lack of knowledge about us, you have misrepresented us."[66]

This misrepresentation is so damaging that it has generated bad feelings and an assault on people's dignity that has generated responses in the form of a counter-discourse, albeit in an academic or literary manner. One such example is Malek Alloula's *The Colonial Harem*. While Alloula's work is a form of writing back to the Occident, other authors have engaged in 'speaking to' the Occident in an attempt at possible reconciliation and bridging of the gap between Orient and Occident.

In a letter to the French writer Emmanuel Roblès, dated 6 April 1959, Mouloud Feraoun, one of the first Maghrebi authors to have engaged in a literary dialogue with his French counterparts, wrote:

> I think there is an interesting parallel to be drawn between writers of European origin and writers of Muslim origin. It was the talent of the former, Camus, Roblès, etc. that enabled them to open for us a literary horizon previously closed to us. I had never really thought it was possible to put an authentic Kabyle character into a novel before encountering Dr Rieux [*La peste*] and young Smail [*Les Hauteurs de la ville*]. You know what I mean. You were the first to say: As for us, this is what we are. And so a dialogue began between you and us. It never got off the ground. We had to fight.[67]

While acknowledging the influence of French authors on their Maghrebi counterparts in terms of engaging with writing in the genre of the novel, the message also expresses the desire for a dialogue which, in Feraoun's words, never got off the ground. The author also implicitly expresses his view that the native characters in the French authors' works lack authenticity precisely because of this same absence of dialogue between the two communities.

In correspondence with Albert Camus, Feraoun expressed in a more explicit manner his regret that Maghrebi characters either are absent from French colonial literature or, if present, then they are misrepresented. He remarked that French colonial authors, while they identified with the Maghrebi location which they relentlessly claimed as a land returned to the bosom of the Roman Empire, failed to make the local people part of it, except in demeaning roles which portrayed them as the bad, ugly and lazy Arabs whom the civilized new Romans, 'the French', tried but failed to civilize. This aspect of being 'uncivilized' gave the colonial armies authority to colonize these lands and bestow the benefits of civilization on their peoples, and because the latter proved '*uncivilizable*', it became legitimate for the French to remain in these lands and appropriate them.

An important corpus of literature was written by French authors during the early years of colonization to justify France's conquest of the Maghreb, which they sometimes called 'Africa' and at other times 'the Orient'. In the nineteenth century Guy de Maupassant described Algeria as a mysterious 'Oriental' place, yet devoid of any trace of human life. He speaks of an intense desire and a deep nostalgia for the 'ignored' yet alluring desert.[68]

Using a host of Orientalist motifs, Pierre Raynal describes an Algiers which is attractive and repulsive at the same time. While he finds the climate 'excellent' and the land 'admirable', he claims that nothing could equal 'the bizarre ugliness of Algiers', and 'nothing could equal its magnificence either'. On the women of Algiers he writes in a disappointed tone that they 'seem to have fled Africa', reflecting the Orientalists' expectation of finding women everywhere and at hand in the Orient. Another favorite Orientalist motif is that of the Turkish bath, of which he says, "the baths here are part of a woman's life and the most jealous of husbands, in this country of Othellos, cannot prevent his wife from going there". As to Oriental music, which he calls 'Moorish', he describes it as barbaric.[69]

Louis Bertrand's *Le Sang des races*[70] brought an end to the literature of Exoticism produced by the creators of the Orientalist canon in the Maghreb. His position is not that of a traveler discovering bizarre locations and enthralling sites, but that of a crusader recovering a land stolen from the Christian world. In his book he explains how his journey to the Maghreb was actually a journey to rediscover his Latin ancestors. He declares that French intervention in Africa was motivated by the desire to recover a province which had been lost to the Latin world: "French Africa today is the Africa of the Romans, an Africa which is still alive and has never lost its vitality, even during the most troublesome, barbarous times."[71] This Latin theme is used by Bertrand to create a common identity which would bring together the European settlers who came from different parts of Europe to settle in the new colony. Through a set of extreme binaries he glorifies the settlers for their hard work, strength and dexterity and criticizes the locals for being lazy, weak and maladroit, which visibly justifies the appropriation of their land by the hard-working colonials, who will know better how to develop it.

As to the Catholic Church, it regarded the occupation of the Maghreb as a Christian victory over Islam and an act of justice against the barbarians who for many centuries had worked for the erasure of the Christian Creed from Africa. In order to restore things to their original condition, Christian missionaries worked unremittingly, along with the schools, to convert young people to Christianity. In this, conversion was often mixed up with civilization. To civilize also meant to convert, as both institutions, the church and the schools, worked hand in hand to convert, assimilate and civilize.

In his novel *Les Misérables* Victor Hugo contests this tendency to colonize in order to civilize. He speaks of Algeria as a country conquered with more barbarity than civilization,[72] and rightly demonstrates that one cannot civilize and colonize at the same time, especially when colonization is associated with extreme violence. Furthermore, the colonial project impoverished the local populations and deprived them of their source of livelihood. Likewise, the people of the Maghreb rejected this 'civilization' because it came in the wake of colonization, and resisted the French schools for many decades because they signified a means to move their children away from their own culture and religion. Such resistance lasted for many decades and it was only after a century of colonization (in the case of Algeria) that the natives decided to send their children to French schools, as the only route to better employment prospects.

By the 1940s a group of educated natives emerged as a new class of Maghrebi authors and intellectuals whose main endeavor was to invent, alter and create alternative images of their people, while at the same time exploring and discovering French culture, literature and, when possible, the metropolis, the home of the great French humanists, the principles of civilization and the human rights that they were told about at school but did not see in the colony.

Such endeavor characterized the early encounters between the Maghreb and the Occident. Later encounters were shaped by the evolution of the relationship between France and the Maghreb. These authors were aware of the lack of contact between the Maghreb and the Occident, despite the annexation of the Maghreb to France as part of its provinces overseas. They were, however, more particularly perturbed by the position of the French humanists vis-à-vis the idea of colonization and the disdain shown towards the colonized, whether they embraced French culture and civilization or not.

In his novel *Idris*, Aly Al-Hammamy expresses his bitterness about this fact, saying, "Neither Lamartine nor Hugo, nor anyone else for that matter cares about the invasion of the Maghreb or the attack on Islam … Lamartine and Hugo have put themselves in the same bag as Chateaubriand in matters concerning us. Other authors followed them in erecting towers of prejudice."[73]

While El-Hammamy's novel could be described as uncompromising and a totally anti-colonial text which speaks of the tricks of colonialism and unveils the true face of colonial France, which he portrays as a person who displays civilization in one hand and carries a deadly weapon in the other, showing thus the contentious aspect of the Occident, the texts which followed took a more tactful turn in trying to engage in a dialogue with the Occident, in the hope that a peaceful solution could be reached.

These authors tried to differentiate between the colonial Occident and the Occident as the bearer of civilization, human rights and democracy. It has to be added, nonetheless, that the trust of the natives in the Occident almost always ends up in a deep sense of loss and disillusionment. This demonstrates the ambivalence which existed during colonial times and continues to exist today between the Maghreb and the Occident in general and France in particular.

What is Occidentalism?

My answer to this question will be in the form of a set of questions revolving around whether, as in the case of Orientalism as defined by Said, the texts produced by authors from the 'Orient' actually belong to a collective formation which we may call 'Occidentalism', and whether there exists a synthesis between these texts and their authors and this complex collective formation to which they consciously or unconsciously contribute.

In other words, did these authors work towards the construction of a discourse and a way of thinking which we may call Occidentalism? A way of thinking that is charged with feelings of revulsion, anger and disgust in the same way as Orientalism is charged with feelings of domination and superiority towards an Orient which is depicted as barbaric, inferior and flaccid?

Is Occidentalism a rejection of, if not a rebellion against, Orientalism? Have these authors produced their texts as a counter-discourse against Orientalism? If so, are they motivated by a desire to change the negative and stereotypical images produced about them? Or to create an equally damaging set of (mis)representations that would dehumanize the Occident, or at least unmask it for its inhumane deeds during and after colonization whose legacy is seen as the main source of the ills of the present?

And if so, what is the purpose of this endeavor? Is the Orient engaging in a war of words which often justifies, whether in a direct or an indirect manner, the many political wars which exist today between Orient and Occident?

On the other hand, isn't this intellectual dialogue between Orient and Occident an attempt at reconciliation and rapprochement? Isn't distortion in representation often a result of a lack of genuine encounter?

The term 'Occidentalism' is often defined as an inversion of Orientalism, which also entails an inversion of its function; while Orientalism is a mode of representation of the Orient in a stereotypical manner, Occidentalism is also defined as stereotyped and sometimes essentialized views on the Occident.

What is of major importance in this study is the evolution of the relationship between Orient and Occident, how it all began and how it developed. Is it really all about hatred and revulsion? If so, what are the causes which resulted in such feelings and why is it that the Occident was and remains till this date a major attraction to people from the East? How could hatred and revulsion for the Occident make it at the same time a pole of attraction to people from the Orient, in both colonial and post-colonial times? Could one speak of a love–hate relationship? Or of a mission of revenge by the people of the Orient for the deeds of the Occident during the colonial period, and for the host of prejudices and misrepresentations which it propagated about them?

El-Enany insists, "With few exceptions, Arab intellectuals, no matter in which period, have never demonized the European other or regarded him in sub-human terms,"[74] a view which I would support even though the Maghrebi encounter with the Occident differs in many respects from the Middle Eastern encounter on which El-Enany focuses in his book. This is mainly due to the colonial past and the nature of the encounter with the Occident, which has naturally shaped the quality of the resulting discourse.

Therefore, while we may argue that Occidentalism is still an evolving concept, being constantly nourished by the ongoing relationship between the Orient and the Occident, we should also bear in mind that there are many Occidentalisms. It is hoped that it is evident from the above discussion that the term 'Occidentalism' seems to be very amorphous and has a resemblance to phantasm. That is to say, if Orientalism has been the conception of the Orient by Europeans only, Occidentalism is not the conception of the West by the people of the Middle East and the Maghreb only. Indeed, it is the multi-conceptions produced by multi-nations – not only as reactions against Orientalism, but also as the attitudes of at least four continents out of six towards Western civilization and Westernization.

Consequently, by observing the diverse encounters with the Occident through literary discourse, we have reached diverse forms of reactions, which can be classified as follows:

1 hatred of the Occident: Occidentophobia
2 love of the Occident: Occidentophilia
3 ambivalence towards the Occident.

While the colonial period produced texts written in the colony and in the language of the colonizer about the encounter with Western thought and civilization, the post-colonial period offers the reader two categories of texts: the first category comprises texts written in the Maghreb both in French and in Arabic, and the second constitutes texts written in the diaspora and mainly in French and English, as this latter has become, in the last three decades, the language of globalization and has proved to be very popular amongst the Maghrebi diaspora.

The main questions which emanate from the study of this period revolve around issues of Muslim identity and the element of diversity, which should be born in mind when looking at all Muslims as one uniform crowd. Al-Azmeh remarks: "Algerians in Aulney-sur-Bois, Kashmiris in Bradford, Kurds in Kreuzberg all live in similarly diverse conditions. Yet, we are told repeatedly Muslims, Europeans or otherwise, are above all Muslims, and that by this token alone they are distinctive and must be treated as such."[75]

Without doubt, Al-Azmeh's point is directed against a tendency to group all Muslims under one umbrella regardless of their country of origin, colonial past and historical circumstances of migration. In the post-9/11 events the West, and this time I mean Europe and the United States, engaged in a frenzy of forums and symposia around the issue of 'Islam in the West', a concept which takes us back to Orientalism's calling Europe's 'Others' the Orient.

The many literary works written by Maghrebi authors in the post-9/11 period focus on the element of diversity, and instead of one Islam they speak of many Islams, and particularly of 'Maghrebi Islam'. Although Edward Said affirms that, unlike the United States, Europe has become more educated in matters of stereotyping the 'Other', describing migrant communities in the West whose religion is Islam as 'Muslim communities' demonstrates that not much has changed since the colonial period. In fact, the situation as we see it today is that the question of identity which has, for the last two centuries, been the chief dilemma of Europe's subjects has now reached the center itself, i.e. the Occident. Many studies have recently focused on the status of Europe in the post-9/11 events, and who gets to call themselves 'European'.

Conclusion

How have the 9/11 events, together with the global financial crisis, remodeled our understanding of Europe and the West? Also, how does Europe view itself in relation to the rest of the world, and more particularly the Maghreb? Many argue that, while the French–Maghrebi situation was improving by the 1990s, it suffered a huge setback following 9/11. During the 1990s, particularly in major cosmopolitan cities such as London and Paris, the melding of cultures was producing a society in which the creation of an 'Other', though not totally eliminated, was at least minimized. Both active discrimination and the more passive or less perceptible stereotyping have increased dramatically in the years following 9/11, when discrimination has become religion-based, as opposed to racially or ethnically based as it was in the past. As a result, stereotyping can have a pernicious effect on individuals that is as disruptive to the formation of identity and a sense of belonging as direct discrimination can be, precisely because it is subtle and pervasive.

One question to pose is: what do Europe's new and/or continuing internal divisions say about its own differentiated colonial histories? And is it possible for Europe to conceive of itself as a 'post-colonial' space? How is Europe situated within current East–West and North–South cultural debates as shaped by the 9/11 events? And how do all these dilemmas shape the East–West, almost becoming Muslim–Christian relations/encounters? I would like to end this essay with a quote from Khatibi's *Amour Bilingue*. He says:

> And if sometimes the triumphant Occident was singing its Nietzschean loss, what would happen to me and my culture?
>
> [...] To love the Other is to speak of the lost space of memory, and my insurrection which in an earlier time was nothing but a history imposed on me, now perpetuates itself in an acknowledged resemblance, for the Occident is part of me, a part that I can only deny insofar as I resist all the 'Occidents' and all the 'Orients' that oppress and disenchant me.[76]

Notes

1 Rasheed El-Enany, *Arab Representations of the Occident: East–West Encounters in Arabic Fiction* (London and New York: Routledge, 2006), p. 1.
2 Edward Said, *Orientalism* (London: Penguin Books, 2003), p. 2.
3 Ibid., p. 4.
4 Ibid.
5 Robert Irwin, *For Lust of Knowing: The Orientalists and Their Enemies* (London: Penguin Books, 2007), p. 6.
6 www.thefreedictionary.com.
7 Said, *Orientalism*, p. 50.
8 Fernendo Coronil, "Beyond Occidentalism: Towards Post-Imperial Geohistorical Categories", *Cultural Anthropology*, Vol. 11 (1996), pp. 51–87.
9 Ferhat Abbas, *Le Jeune Algérien* (Paris: La Jeune Parque, 1931).
10 Idem., *J'Accuse l'Europe* (Alger: Libération, 1944.)
11 Idem., *La Nuit coloniale* (Paris: Julliard, 1962).
12 Albert Memmi, *The Colonizer and the Colonized* (London: Souvenir Press Ltd, 1974).
13 Abdelkebir Khatibi, *La Mémoire tatouée* (Paris: Denoël, 1971).
14 Idem., *Amour bilingue* (Montpellier: Fata Morgana, 1983).
15 Frantz Fanon, *Black Skin, White Masks*, translated by Charles Lam Markmann (New York: Grove Press, 1967).
16 Idem., *The Wretched of the Earth*, translated by Constance Farrington (New York: Grove Press, 1963).
17 Coronil, "Beyond Occidentalism", p. 57.
18 Malek Alloula, *The Colonial Harem* (Manchester: Manchester University Press, 1986).
19 Ibid., p. 31.
20 Ibid., p. 4.
21 Marnia Lazreg, *The Eloquence of Silence: Algerian Women in Question* (New York: Routledge, 1994), p. 39.
22 Alloula, *The Colonial Harem*, p. 29.

23 Anouar Abdel-Malek, "Orientalism in Crisis", *Diogenes*, Vol. 44, Winter 1963, pp. 104–112.
24 Ibid., pp. 107–108.
25 Ibid., p. 107.
26 Abdelmajid Hannoum, "Faut-it brûler l'Orientalisme? On French Scholarship of North Africa", *Cultural Dynamics*, Vol. 16, 2004, pp. 71–91.
27 Ibid., p. 71.
28 Ibid., p. 76.
29 Ibid., p. 75.
30 Jacques Berque, "Cent vingt-cinq ans de sociologie maghrebine", *Annales*, Vol. XI, No. 3, 1956, pp. 299–321, cited in Abdel-Malek, "Orientalism in Crisis", p. 107.
31 Ibid.
32 Michel Foucault, *Discipline and Punishment* (London: Tavistock, 1977), p. 27.
33 Barthélemy d'Herbelot de Molainville, *Bibliothèque orientale, ou dictionnaire universel contenant tout ce qui regarde la connaissance des peuples de l'Orient*, 4 vols. (The Hague: Quatro, 1777–1799).
34 De Lacy O'Leary, *How Greek Science Passed to the Arabs.* First published in Great Britain in 1949 by Routledge and Kegan Paul Ltd. www.aina.org/books/hgsptta.htm – accessed 13 October 2010.
35 Charles Issawi, *Cross-Cultural Encounters and Conflicts* (New York and Oxford: Oxford University Press, 1998), p. 72.
36 Ibn Khaldun, *The Muqaddimah: An Introduction to History*, trans. Frantz Rosenthal (Princeton and Oxford: Princeton University Press: 2005), p. 39.
37 Ibid., pp. 41, 214.
38 Ibid., p. 373.
39 Said, *Orientalism*, p. 65.
40 Irwin, *For Lust of Knowing*, p. 20.
41 For more details see: Roger Crowley, *Empires of the Sea: The Siege of Malta, the Battle of Lepanto and the Conquest for the Center of the World* (London: Random House, 2008).
42 See William Bedwell, *Mohammedis imposturae*, 1615, and Humphrey Prideaux, *The True Nature of Imposture Fully Displayed in the Life of Mahomet*, 1697.
43 Derek Hopwood, *Sexual Encounters in the Middle East: The British, the French and the Arabs* (Reading: Ithaca Press, 1999).
44 Abdel Latif Tibawi, "English-speaking Orientalists: a Critique of their Approach to Islam and Arab Nationalism", *Islamic Quarterly*, Vol. 8, 1964, pp. 25–45.
45 Irwin, *For Lust of Knowing*, pp. 319–320.
46 Lila Abu-Lughod, "Zones of Theory in the Anthropology of the Arab World," *Annual Review of Anthropology*, Vol. 18, 1989, p. 267.
47 Abdel Malek, "Orientalism in Crisis", p. 108.
48 Abu-Lughod, "Zones of Theory", p. 267.
49 James G. Carrier (ed.), *Occidentalism: Images of the West* (Oxford: Clarendon Press, 2003), p. 1.
50 Ibid., p. 26.
51 Said, *Orientalism*, p. 70.
52 Laura Nader, "Orientalism, Occidentalism and the Control of Women", *Cultural Dynamics*, Vol. 2, 1989, pp. 323–355.
53 Ibid., p. 333.
54 Nicholas Thomas, "Anthropology and Orientalism", *Anthropology Today*, Vol. 7, No. 2, 1991, pp. 4–7.

55 Ibid., p. 7.
56 Carrier, *Occidentalism*, p. 10.
57 Ibid., pp. 12–13.
58 Ibid., p. 12.
59 Ian Buruma and Avishai Margalit, *Occidentalism: A Short History of Anti-Westernism* (London: Atlantic Books, 2004), p. 5.
60 Ibid., p. 10.
61 Ibid., pp. 10–11.
62 Ibid., p. 56.
63 Maitre Gisèle Halimi defended Djamila Boubacha, an Algerian freedom fighter who was arrested and tortured in prison while she was a minor. For more details see: Simone De Beauvoir and Gisèle Halimi, *Djamila Boupacha: The Story of the Torture of a Young Algerian Girl which Shocked Liberal French Opinion*, trans. Peter Green (London: André Deutsch Ltd and George Weidenfeld and Nicolson Ltd, 1962).
64 Maitre Jacques Vergès defended the famous Djamila Bouhired, who, like Boubacha was also a freedom fighter who was arrested and tortured in prison. She later became Vergès' wife.
65 Jean Baudrillard, *The Spirit of Terrorism* (New York-London: Verso, 2002).
66 Mouloud Feraoun, *Lettres à ses amis* (Paris: Le Seuil, 1962), p. 154. (My translation).
67 Ibid.
68 Guy de Maupassant, *Au Soleil* (Paris: Ollendorff, 1902), pp. 5–6.
69 Philipe Lucas and Claude Vatin, *L'Algérie des Antropologues* (Paris: Maspéro, 1982), pp. 96–99.
70 Louis Bertrand, *Le Sang des races* (Paris: Albin Michel, 1899).
71 D.M. Gallup, "The French Image of Algeria: Its Origins, Its Place in Colonial Ideology, Its Effect on Algerian Acculturation", PhD thesis, University of California, 1973), p. 274.
72 Hopwood, *Sexual Encounters*, p. 89.
73 Aly El-Hammamy, *Idris* (Algiers: Entreprise Nationale du Livre, 1988), p. 261.
74 El-Enany, *Arab Representations*, p. 6.
75 Aziz Al-Azmeh and Effie Fokas (eds), *Islam in Europe: Diversity, Identity and Influence* (Cambridge: Cambridge University Press, 2007), p. 208.
76 Khatibi, *Amour bilingue*, pp. 105–106.

Bibliography

Abbas, Ferhat, *Le Jeune Algérien* (Paris: La Jeune Parque, 1931).
Abbas, Ferhat, *J'Accuse l'Europe* (Alger: Libération, 1944).
Abbas, Ferhat, *La Nuit coloniala* (Paris: Julliard, 1962).
Abdel-Malek, Anouar, "Orientalism in Crisis", *Diogenes*, Vol. 44, Winter 1963, pp. 104–112.
Abu-Lughod, Lila, "Zones of Theory in the Anthropology of the Arab World," *Annual Review of Anthropology*, Vol. 18, 1989, pp. 267–306.
Al-Azmeh, Aziz and Effie Fokas (eds), *Islam in Europe: Diversity, Identity and Influence* (Cambridge: Cambridge University Press, 2007).
Alloula, Malek, *The Colonial Harem* (Manchester: Manchester University Press, 1986).
Baudrillard, Jean, *The Spirit of Terrorism* (New York and London: Verso, 2002).
Bedwell, William, *Mohammedis imposturae*, 1615.
Bertrand, Louis, *Le Sang des races* (Paris: Albin Michel, 1899).
Buruma, Ian and Avishai Margalit, *Occidentalism: A Short History of Anti-Westernism* (London: Atlantic Books: 2004).

Carrier, James G. (ed.), *Occidentalism: Images of the West* (Oxford: Clarendon Press, 1995).
Coronil, Fernendo, "Beyond Occidentalism: Towards Post-Imperial Geohistorical Categories", *Cultural Anthropology*, Vol. 11 (1996), pp. 51–87.
Crowley, Roger, *Empires of the Sea: The Siege of Malta, the Battle of Lepanto and the Conquest for the Center of the World* (London: Random House, 2008).
De Beauvoir, Simone and Gisèle Halimi, *Djamila Boupacha: The Story of the Torture of a Young Algerian Girl which Shocked Liberal French Opinion*, trans. Peter Green (London: André Deutsch Ltd and George Weidenfeld and Nicolson Ltd, 1962).
de Maupassant, Guy, *Au Soleil* (Paris: Ollendorff, 1902).
d'Herbelot de Molainville, Barthélemy, *Bibliothèque orientale, ou dictionnaire universel contenant tout ce qui regarde la connaissance des peuples de l'Orient*, 4 vols. (The Hague: Quatro, 1777–1799).
El-Enany, Rasheed, *Arab Representations of the Occident: East–West Encounters in Arabic Fiction* (London and New York: Routledge, 2006).
El-Hammamy, Aly, *Idris* (Algiers: Entreprise Nationale du Livre, 1988).
Fanon, Frantz, *The Wretched of the Earth*, translated by Constance Farrington (New York: Grove Press, 1963).
Fanon, Frantz, *Black Skin, White Masks*, translated by Charles Lam Markmann (New York: Grove Press, 1967).
Feraoun, Mouloud, *Lettres* à *ses amis* (Paris: Le Seuil, 1962).
Foucault, Michel, *Discipline and Punishment* (London: Tavistock, 1977).
Gallup, D.M., "The French Image of Algeria: Its Origins, Its Place in Colonial Ideology, Its Effect on Algerian Acculturation", PhD thesis, University of California, 1973.
Hannoum, Abdelmajid, "Faut-it brûler l'Orientalisme? On French Scholarship of North Africa", *Cultural Dynamics*, Vol. 16, 2004, pp. 71–91.
Hopwood, Derek, *Sexual Encounters in the Middle East: The British, the French and the Arabs* (Reading: Ithaca Press, 1999).
Ibn Khaldun, *The Muqaddimah: An Introduction to History*, trans. Frantz Rosenthal (Princeton and Oxford: Princeton University Press, 2005).
Irwin, Robert, *For Lust of Knowing: The Orientalists and Their Enemies* (London: Penguin Books, 2007).
Issawi, Charles, *Cross-Cultural Encounters and Conflicts* (New York and Oxford: Oxford University Press, 1998).
Khatibi, Abdelkebir, *La Mémoire tatouée* (Paris: Denoël, 1971).
Khatibi, Abdelkebir, *Amour bilingue* (Montpellier: Fata Morgana, 1983).
Lazreg, Marnia, *The Eloquence of Silence: Algerian Women in Question* (New York: Routledge, 1994).
Lucas, Philipe and Claude Vatin, *L'Algérie des Antropologues* (Paris: Maspéro, 1982).
Memmi, Albert, *The Coloniser and the Colonised* (London: Souvenir Press Ltd, 1974).
Mouloud, Feraoun, *Lettres à ses amis* (Paris: Le Seuil, 1969).
Nader, Laura, "Orientalism, Occidentalism and the Control of Women", *Cultural Dynamics* Vol. 2, No. 3, 1989, pp. 323–355.
O'Leary, De Lacy, *How Greek Science Passed to the Arabs.* First published in Great Britain in 1949 by Routledge and Kegan Paul Ltd. www.aina.org/books/hgsptta.htm
Prideaux, Humphrey, *The True Nature of Imposture Fully Displayed in the Life of Mahomet*, 1697.
Said, Edward, *Orientalism* (London: Penguin Books, 2003).

Thomas, Nicholas, "Anthropology and Orientalism", *Anthropology Today*, Vol. 7, No. 2, 1991, pp. 4–7.

Tibawi, Abdel Latif, "English-speaking Orientalists: A Critique of their Approach to Islam and Arab Nationalism", *Islamic Quarterly*, Vol. 8, Nos. 1–4, 1964, pp. 25–45.

Index

Abbasids 208
Abdel Malek, Anouar 259, 260, 261, 265
Abduh, Muhammad 106
absence, Orient as 194
Abu Dulaf 207, 208
Abu Ghraib prison 15, 57
Abu Zayd al-Hasan al-Sirafi 209
Abu-Lughod, Lila 265–6
An Account of the Manners and Customs of the Modern Egyptians (Lane) 9, 99
Account of the Rise and Progress of Mahometanism (Stubbe) 6
action-action dynamic 38–9, 42, 43, 46
Acton, Lord John 10
Adams, Dennis 140, 141, 142figs
Adams, Thomas 4
Adorno, Theodor 142
Afary, J. 43
Afghanistan 75
agency, as Foucauldian concept 36, 38–9
Ahmadinejad, President 48
Ahmed, Leila 9
Aiken, E.J. 169
Algeria 128–44; French invasion 128, 260; French language as official 135; identification 135–6; independence 136
'alien' space 60
Alloula, Malek 129, 258–9, 269
Althusser, Louis 215
Amnesty International 136
Amour Bilingue (Khatibi) 275
Anderson, K.B. 43
Andronicus II 226
Andronicus III 226
Anthropology (Topinard) 132, 133fig
anthropometry 132, 134
anti-Semitism 91, 177
Antonius, George 12
Arab Bureau 104, 261
Arab Interior (Melville) 123
The Arab Awakening:The Story of the Arab Nationalist Movement (Antonius) 12
The Arab Mind (Patai) 57
Arab-Israeli wars (1967) 87
Arafat, Y. 162
Arberry, A.J. 3, 107, 256
architecture 121, 131
Armstrong, Sir William 121
Arnold, T.W. 11
art 117–23
Arts and Crafts movement 120
Aryanism 89–90, 91, 101, 177, 182–3
The Ascension (Doré) 180, 181fig
Ashkenazim 159
Asiatic Short Stories (Gobineau) 92, 94
Asin Palacios, Miguel 102
At Prayer (Deutsch) 123
Auerbach, Erich 59, 63, 68, 72
Auerbach, Jeffrey 119
authoritarianism 8, 10, 14, 43, 136
al-'Azm, Sadik 17
Al-Azmeh, A. 274

Bakhtin, Mikhail 233
Baldick, Julian 102
Balfour, Andrew 65
A Bargain (Weeks) 123
Barthes, Roland 70
Barzun, Jacques 92
Baudrillard, Jean 269
Beckingham, C.F. 230, 231
Bedwell, William 4
Beginnings: Intention and Method (Said) 66, 67, 68
Behdad, Ali 91–2
Ben-Arieh, Y. 165
Berendsen, Everade 101

Bergreen, 236, 238
Berque, Jacques 261
Bertillon, Alphonse 133
Bertrand, Louis 271
Bey, Osman Hamdi 123
Bhau Daji Lad Museum 119
The Bible: access to 189; illustrations 190; orientalization of 176–83; study of 179
Bible Lands: Their Modern Customs and Manners Illustrative of Scripture (Van-Lennep) 190, 191, 192, 196
bibliolatry 187–201; The Bible and the Orient 187–91; Bible lands 191–3; depictions of Arabs 196–201; images 193–6
Bibliothèque orientale (d'Herbelot) 262, 263
Bilad al-Sham 165
binarism, cultural 107, 117–18, 123, 168, 218, 266, 271
A Biography of Disappearance: Algeria 1992 (Amnesty International) 136
Birdwood, George 120
al-Bisṭāmī, Abū Bāyazīd 101
Boissel, Jean 93
Bonaparte, Roland 132, 133, 264
Bond, Alvan 189
Bouvard et Pécuchet (Flaubert) 89
Boxhall, Peter 208
Brennan, Timothy 71
Bright, John 10
Britain: Arts and Crafts 120, 121; assumed superiority 8, 10;attitude to Islam 11, 16; concept of history 4; dominance in Middle East 12;and India 7; and Oriental Studies 67
British Orientalists 256
Brotton, J. 15
Brown, John Porter 101
Brown, Robin 235, 237, 238
Browne, E.G. 11, 101, 104
Buddhism 101, 212
Burges, William 120
Burke, Edmund III 98, 103, 105, 107
Burton, Sir Richard 99, 198
Buruma, Ian 61, 268

Calvin, John 189
Cambodia *see* Khmer
Cambridge, University of 4
Campbell, Donald 99
Campus Watch 73
Carlyle, T. 9
The Carpet Seller (Lewis) 119
Carrier, James 266, 267
Carroll, Lewis 223, 224, 228
Catholicism 4, 166, 167, 168, 171, 271
Celik, Zeynep 140
Challe line 143
Chamberlain, Houston 183
Chebel, Malek 131
Chetrit, Sami Shalom 158
China 209, 212, 215, 216, 237–8
Christianity: conflict, Protestant-Catholic 188; debate over 11; missionaries 165; racial supersessionism 176–83; 'superiority' of 10
civilisation, scale of 8 10, 13, 64
classifications, racial 90, 94, 133–6, 182
Clements, Jonathan 213, 236, 239
Clifford, James 58, 70
Cobbett, William 10
Cobden, Richard 10
Cohn, B.S. 89
Cold War 12, 26n91
The Colonial Harem (Alloula) 129, 269
Colonial and Indian Exhibition (1886) 120
colonialism: 'barbarism' as justification for 6; British, post WW1 12; civilisation, scale of 14; French 270–1; justification for 9–10; stereotyping 7
The Commentator on the Koran (Lewis) 123
Communism 13, 41, 104, 144
Constantinople 177
Constitutional Movement 11
A Coppersmith, Cairo (Wilda) 122
Coppolani, Xavier 103, 104
Coronil, Fernendo 257, 258
Coupland, Reginald 12
Covering Islam (Said) 34, 65
crafts 119–20
Cromer, Lord Evelyn 11, 65, 198
Culture and Imperialism (Said) 63, 64, 65, 69, 117, 160
culture, Arabic, as static 179
'culture of identification' 134
Cuvier, G. 90
Czechoslovakia 41

Dabistān 106
Daftary, Farhad 237
Dammann, Carl 132, 133
Daniel, Norman 12
Dārā Shikūh 107

Darwinism 10
De Atkine, Norell B. 57
De Wandelbourg , A.H. 166–71
decolonialisation12
deconstructionism 59
Deleuze, Gilles 37, 39
Depont, Octave 103, 104
Derrida, Jacques 69
Descartes, René 5
The Descent of the Spirit (Doré) 180, 181fig
Description de L'Egypte 64
despotism 5, 7, 8, 10, 13, 14, 90
Deutsch, Ludwig 123
d'Herbelot de Molainville, Bathélemy 262, 263
Disraeli, Benjamin 181
dissidence 41
Doré, Gustave 180, 181figs
doublure (double) 37, 45, 46
Dow, Alexander 6
Dowson, John 10
Dozy, R. 101
dress, Arabic 177
Duhousset, Emile 132
Dunn, Ross 228, 229, 230

EIC (The East India Company) 6, 7, 101
Eichhorn, Johann Gottfried 179
Elliot, H.M. 10
Elphinstone, Mountstuart 8
Emerson, Ralph Waldo 100
The Encyclopedia of Islamic Civilisation and Religion (ed. Netton) ix
Enkrateia 37
The Enlightenment 7, 16, 66
Ernst, Carl 99, 106
Essay on Pope's Odyssey (Spence) 177
Essay on the Inequality of the Human Races (Gobineau) 87
essentialization 60, 62, 63, 218, 266, 267, 269, 273
ethnography, visual 128–44; identity cards 133–6; identity cards and the disappeared 136–8
Etudes et Souvenirs de l'Orient et ses Missions (De Wandelbourg) 166–71
Eurocentrism 16, 43, 63, 72, 73, 268
exiles, intellectual 161–2
Expansion of England (Seeley) 10

Fabian, Johannes 180
Facing Each other: The World's Perception of Europe and Europe's Perception of the World (Pagden ed.) 207
Femmes Algeriennes 1960 (Garanger) 138
Feraoun, Mouloud 270
Ferguson, Niall 14–15
Finkel, Caroline 13
Flaubert, Gustav 89, 91, 198
For Lust of Knowing: The Orientalists and Their Enemies (Irwin) ix, 256
Foucault, Michel: and agency 41–8; and *Enkrateia* 37; as 'Eurocentric' 43; and Iran 42–8; knowledge and power 261; on power 33–49; power and resistance 36–40; and Said 69, 70; surveillance 134, 215
Foundations of the Nineteenth Century (Chamberlain) 183
France 67, 103, 104, 133–6
Franciscan Custody 166
From Babel to the Dragomans (Lewis) 14
Fromentin, Eugene 122

Gabeau, Charles 135
Galland, Antoine 263
Gallo, Roberto 239
Garanger, Mark 138, 141
Garratt, G.T. 12
The General Historie of the Turkes (Knolle) 5
Gérôme, Jean-Léon 180, 200
Gibb, H.A.R. 12–13, 226, 227, 230, 231
Gibbon, Edward 7
Giddens, Anthony 38
Glasgow International Exhibition 120
Gobineau, Arthur 87, 90–4
Goldziher, Ignaz 103
Gopal, P. 15
Gowen, Herbert 215
Graham, James William 101
Grammar of Ornament (Jones) 121
A Grammar of the Persian Language (Jones) 7
Gramsci, Antonio 59, 69, 71
Great London Exhibition (1851) 119
Greenblatt, Stephen 214, 217, 218
Gulag Archipelago (Solzhenitsyn) 41
Gulistān (Sa'dī) 99

Habermas, Jürgen 38
Haeger, John W. 237
Ḥāfiẓ 101
hajj 224, 225
Hajji Baba (Morier) 92

Hall, Stuart 70, 75
Hannoum, Abdelmajid 260
Hartmann, Richard 101
Harvey, L.P. 229, 230, 233, 236
Haughton, Hugh 223
Hegel, G.W.F. 181–2, 183
Hegelian synthesis 38, 48
Heller, Kevin Jon 39
Hersh, Seymour 57
Het Islamisme (Dozy) 101
Hhareem Life (Lewis) 123
Higher Criticism 191
Hinduism 101, 211–12, 213
The History of British India (Mill) 8
History of the Decline of the Roman Empire (Gibbon) 7
The History of India as told by its own Historians (Dowson) 10
The History of the Saracens (Ockley) 6
Hobson, J.A. 10
The Holocaust 156, 157, 158
Holy Land 165–71, 187–201; The Bible and the Orient 189–91; Bible lands 191–3; images of 193–6; portrayals of Arabs 196–201
Hooker, Clifford A. 232, 233
Hopwood, D. 264
Horten, M. 101
Hourani, Albert 98, 103, 105
Hours with the Mystics (Vaughan) 100
How Greek Science Passed to the Arabs (O'Leary) 262
Hrbek, Ivan 228
Hugo, Victor 271
humanism 70–3, 161
Hume, David 6
Hunter, William 10
hunting 121–2
Huntington, Samuel P. 55

Ibn al-Farīd 99
Ibn Baṭṭūṭa: and *hajj* 224; and Marco Polo 235, 240; and Orientalism 242; *Riḥla* 225–33; on *sati* 211
Ibn Ishaq 'Abd Allah Muhammad 208
Ibn Jubayr 224–5
Ibn Khaldūn 232, 262–3
Ibn Khordadbeh 208
identity photographs 133–40
India 6–8, 10–12, 119, 120, 207–13, 215, 217
'Indian Mutiny' 10
'indigenous photography' 139–40
industrialism 119
Inequality of Human Races (Gobineau) 90, 91, 94
intellectuals 69–70
Intifada 154
The Invention of Tradition (Hobsbawm and Ranger, eds.) 65
Iqbal , Muhammad 106
Iran 42–8, 55
Iraq, invasion of 15, 75, 107, 159
Irwin, Robert 3, 13, 256, 265, ix
Islam: accuracy of detail, Thomson and Van-Lennep 200; as anti-modern 66; empirical approach 7; fanaticism as viewed by West 104; 'fundamentalism' 55, 75; medieval Christian reaction 3, 4; as 'other' 4, 16; plurality of approaches 9; political activism 11; radicalism 55; re-evaluation of 10, 11; as 'static' 14; study of 4, 5, 6; as threat to Christianity 264
'Islamic concepts' 13
The Islamic Faith (Arnold) 11
Islamic Society and the West (Gibb) 13
Israel 75, 153, 154–5
Issawi, Charles 262

Janicsek, Stephen 228, 229
Jardine, L. 15
Jerusalem 165
Jesus, Aryanization of 182–3
Jew, defined as non-Arab 158
Joinet, Louis 143
Joinet principles 143,144
Jones, Owen 121
Jones, Sir William 7, 8, 101, 188
Journey to the Orient (Nerval) 91
Juwaynī 237

Khatibi 275
Khomeini, Ayatollah 43, 45, 46
Khmer (Cambodia) 208
Knolle, Richard 5
Knox, Robert 90
Knysh, Alexander 98, 103, 104, 105, 106
Kremer, Alfred von 101
Krymskii, Agafangel 102
Kubilai Khan 236
Kurtz, Stanley 74

La Photographie judiciaire (Bertillon) 133
The Land and the Book (Thomson) 193, 194–6
Lane, Edward 8, 9, 99

Larner, John 237, 238
Latham, Ronald 235
Latin Patriarchate of Jerusalem 165–6
Laud, William 4
Lazreg, Marnia 259
Le Goff, Jacques 207
Le Sang des Races (Bertrand) 271
learning, oriental 123
Lebanon 154
Leighton, Frederic 120, 123
Levi-Strauss, C. 70
Lewis, Bernard 3, 12, 13, 14, 16, 55, 67
Lewis, J.F. 119, 123
'liberal imperialism' 7, 14
Life of Jesus (Renan) 183
Life of Mahomet (Prideaux) 5
literacy 213–14
'the Literall advantage' 214
A Literary History of Persia (Browne) 11, 101
literary studies 69
Livingstone, D.N. 167
Lowth, Robert 178
Lull, Ramon 99
Luther, Martin 189
Lyotard, Jean Francois 71

Macaulay, T.B. 8
MacGuckin de Slane, William135
Machon Shalem 155
Mackintosh-Smith, Tim 228, 230, 233
Maclachlan, Christopher 241
Macleod Higgins, Iain 208
Maghreb 135, 242, 255–75; modern literature 257; and the Occident 269–72
Maine, Sir Henry 10
Malcolm, Sir John 8, 101, 106
Malek, Abdel 261, 265
Marco Polo 211, 213, 216, 217, 233–40
Margalit, Avishai 61, 268
Margoliouth, David 10
A Market, Cairo (Muller) 122
Marvelous Possessions: The Wonder of the New World (Greenblatt) 214, 217
Marx, Karl 15
Marxism 158
Massignon, Louis 63, 102, 103, 104
Masuzawa, T. 100
Matar, Nabil 14, 207, 218
'materiality' of text 70
Melville, Arthur 123
Melville, Herman 210
Merx, Adalbert 102
Michaelis, Johann David 178, 179
Mill, James 8
Mimesis (Auerbach) 68
Miquel, André 217
Mizrachim 158, 159, 160
Modern Egypt (Cromer) 11
Modern Trends in Islam (Gibb) 13
'Modernisation theory' 13, 14
modernism, literature 68
monotheism 183
Morice line 143
Morier, J.J. 92
Morocco 131
Morris, Benny 157
Morris, William 120
Mughal Empire 6
Muhammad, Prophet 6, 7, 9–10, 12, 21n34, 231
Muir, William 10
Muller, Leopold 123
Munchausen, Baron 239, 240, 241
The Muqaddimah (Ibn Khaldun) 262–3
Museum of Natural History, France 132
The Muslim Discovery of Europe (Lewis) 14
music 123
The Music Lesson (Leighton) 123
mysticism 99, 100

Nader, Laura 267
Nakbah 156, 157
names, standardization and transcription of 134–5
Napoleon I , Emperor 64
nationalism, Arab 12, 73, 159, 161, 265
neo-Zionism 155, 157
Nerval, Gérard de 91–2, 198
The New Science of Giambattista Vico (Vico) 72
Nicholson, R.A. 102
9/11 55

Occidentalism 60–3, 255–75; definition 256–69, 272–4; Maghreb and 269–72
Occidentalism: A Short History of Anti-Westernism (Buruma and Margalit) 268
Ockley, Simon 6
O'Fahey, R.S. 105
O'Leary, De Lacy 262
The Order of Things (Foucault) 36
Oriental Essays: Portraits of Seven Scholars (Arberry) 3
'oriental globalisation' 15
The Oriental Harem (Alloula) 258

Oriental Renaissance 87–9
Oriental Renaissance (Schwab) 87
Orientalism: coinage of term 177; construction of western vision of Islam 16; debate 3; definition, Netton ix; definition, Said 58, 242; French 260; 'latent' 90; origins of 63–4; as 'Other' 257; in post 9/11 context 55, 56; postcolonial studies 217; post-Orientalism 65
orientalist state 158–62
Orientialisme, in visual art 179, 180
Oslo process 153, 155
Osten, Prokesch 92
'Otherness' 17, 59, 266
Ottoman Empire: conquest of Constantinople 177; and European 'modernisation' 16; expansion 5; fall of 12, 13, 99; intensification of conflict with West 11; positive atrributes 5; Western fear of atrocities 5
An Outline History of China (Gowen) 215
Oxford, University of 4, 11, 177
Oxford History of India: from the earliest times to 1911 (Smith) 12

Pagden, Anthony 207
Pahlavi dynasty 43
Pakistan 75
Palestine 34, 55, 153–62, 165
Palestine Liberation Organization *see* PLO
Palmer, Edward Henry 100, 101
pan-Islamism 11
Patai, Raphael 57
paternalism 10, 14, 104, 105
Persia 92–3
The Persian Ṣūfis (Rice) 101
philology, comparative 89, 90, 100
photography 128–44; identity cards 133–6; identity cards and the disappeared 136–8
Pipes, Daniel 73, 74
PLO (Palestine Liberation Organization) 155
Pococke, Edward 5, 6, 177
Poland 41
police, French colonial 134, 135
policy making, British: and knowledge 12, 13
The Politics of Dispossession (Said) 153, 157
Possetto, A. 170
post-colonialism 71, 74, 160
post-modernism 36, 155
post-Orientalism 65–6
post-structuralism 59
post-Zionism 155, 156
pre-industrial activities 121–2
The Preaching of Islam (Arnold) 11
The Present State of the Ottoman Empire (Rycaut) 5
Prideaux, Humphrey 5, 6
Prison Notebooks (Gramsci) 69
Prochaska, David 107
Purchas, Samuel 214

Quatrefages de Bréau, Jean Louis Armand de 132
Question d'Orient 165
The Question of Palestine (Said) 156
Qur'an 6, 103
Qutbuddin, A.K. 233

Rachik, Hassan 135
Radtke, Bernd 105
Ramusio, Giambattista 238
Riḍā, Rashīd 106
Raspe, Rudolph Erich 239
'rationality' 101
The Reformation 5
Regarding the Pain of Other (Sontag) 140
Religions and Philosophies of Central Asia (Gobineau) 90, 92, 94
Renan, Ernest 87, 89–91, 182
representation 58–60
resistance, Foucaudian 35, 38, 41–8, 43
Rice, C. 101
Rise and Fulfilment of the British Rule in India (Garratt) 12
Roads to Victory 142
Roberts, David 122
Robertson, William 6
Robertson Smith, William 179
Romantic Orientalism 90
Romanticism 8
Roy, Oliver 47
Rustichello 217, 237, 239
Ryan, Tim 74
Rycaut, Paul 5

Sacred Poetry (Lowth) 178
Sa'dī 99
Safavids 106
Said, Edward: on *Aida* 117; and 'alien' space 60; as Anglocentric 98; criticism of 67; and cultural coherence 62;

decrease in influence 74; definitions of Orientalism 58; on Europe 274; and Foucaudian ideas re power and knowledge 33–4, 36, 38, 39, 41; on French colonialism 128; generalization 188; humanism 70–3; knowledge as of its time 16–17; on Napoleon 64; and Nationalism 154; on Occidentalism 256; polemics 73–6; and 'power-resistance dialectic' 36; on racism 159; rejection of post-structuralism 71; on Renan 89–90; on representation 59; on Schwab 87, 88, 89; as seminal work ix; on United States 65; universal humanism 161
Sale, George 6
Sand, Shlomo 182
Sanskrit 88, 188, 212
SAVAK 43
Scènes et Types 128–44; identity cards 133–6; identity cards and the disappeared 136–8
Schimmel, Annemarie 99, 100, 101
Schmidt, Leigh Eric 100
Schopenhauer, A. 89, 90
Schultens, Albert 177
Schwab, Raymond 87–9, 90, 93
Scottish Enlightenment 6, 8
"Secular Criticism" (Said) 70
secular historical method 9
secularism 66
Seeley, J.R. 10
Semitic religions 101
Sexual Encounters in the Middle East (Hopwood) 264
Sharia 102, 104, 105
Shaw, Norman 121
Shenhav, Yehuda 158
Shohat, Ellah 158, 160
Slavin, David Henry 129
Smart, Barry 41
Smith, Adam 6
Smith, Annette 91
Smith, David 91
Smith, Margaret 102
Smith, V.A. 12
Snouck Hurgronje, Christiaan 104
Solzhenitsyn, Aleksandr 41
Somalia 104
Sontag, Susan 131, 140
Southern, Richard 12
Soviet Union 41
Speciman Historae Arabum (Pococke) 5
Spence, Joseph 177
Spinoza, B. 5
Spivak, Gayatri 39, 144
Steichen, Edward 142
stereotypes, visual 131–2
Stevenson, Robert Louis 239, 241–2
Stoler, A. 70, 75
Stubbe, Henry 6
Sufism 98–108; academic studies 99–103; as antithesis Islam 107; classical 105; classical texts 102; colonialism 103–5; neo-Sufism 105; poetry 99; and social morality 104, 105; study in Russia 104; translations of stories 99
supersessionism, racial 180–2
The Surprising Adventures of Baron Munchausen 240, 241
Swoboda, Rudolf 120
symbiosis: Christianity and Islam 15

al-Tajir , Sulayman 209, 210–12, 213, 215, 216, 217
taxation 215, 216
Techelt 155
Terpak, Frances 140
Theory and Critique 160
Tholuck, Friedrich August Deofidus 102
Thomas, Nicholas 267
Thompson, Edward 12
Thomson, William 187, 190, 193, 194–7, 198–9, 200
Three Years in Asia (Gobineau) 94
Tibawi, Abdul Latif 265
Title VI programs 74
Todorov, T. 214
Topinard, Paul 132
torture 15, 57
Toynbee, A.J. 13
Transjordan 166, 170
Travels with a Donkey in the Cévennes (Stevenson) 239, 241–2
al-Turjuman 208, 209
Tunisia 131
The Turkish Letter Writer (Wilkie) 122
'Turks', iconography of 177
Two Musicians (Bey) 123

United States 43, 55, 56, 67, 69, 74, 75
Upanishads 101

Valerga, Mgr 166–7, 170–1
Van-Lennep, Henry J. 190, 191, 192–3, 196, 199, 200, 201
Vaughan, Robert Alfred 100
Vaux, Carde 209

Verdi, G. 117–18
Vergès, Jacques 268, 269
Vernet, E.J-H. 122
Veyne, Paule 42, 48
Vico, Giambattista 68, 72
Victoria, Queen 120
Victoria and Albert Museum 119, 121
Vietnam War 87
Volney, Comte de 64
Voyage en Egypte et en Syrie (Volney) 64
Voyages Imaginaires 241

Wahhabi 107
The Walls of Algiers 140–1
Walzer, Michael 38
The 'War on Terror' 75, 101
al-Wathiq 208, 209
Weeks, Emily 118, 119
Weeks, Lord Edwin 123
Wellhausen, Julius 179
Wensinck, Arendt 102
West, representations of 61
'Western mind' 13
Wiener, Martin 121
Wilda, Charles 122
Wilie, David 122
The Will to Knowledge (Foucault) 39, 43
women 258, 266, 267, 270
Wortley Montagu, Lady Mary 5
Wycliffe, John 189

Yamamoto, Tatsuro 230
A Year Among the Persians (Browne) 11

Zaehner, R.C. 101
Zhukovskii, Valentin 102
Zionism 153, 155
Zochrot 157